THE COMPLETE GUIDE TO

ARTICLE WRITING

THE COMPLETE GUIDE TO
ARTICLE WRITING

HOW TO WRITE SUCCESSFUL ARTICLES
FOR ONLINE AND PRINT MARKETS

NAVEED SALEH

WRITER'S DIGEST
BOOKS

WritersDigest.*com*
Cincinnati, Ohio

For more resources for writers, visit www.writersdigest.com.

17 16 15 14 13 5 4 3 2 1

Distributed in Canada by Fraser Direct
100 Armstrong Avenue
Georgetown, Ontario, Canada L7G 5S4
Tel: (905) 877-4411

Distributed in the U.K. and Europe by F&W Media International
Brunel House, Newton Abbot, Devon, TQ12 4PU, England
Tel: (+44) 1626 323200, Fax: (+44) 1626-323319
E-mail: postmaster@davidandcharles.co.uk

Distributed in Australia by Capricorn Link
P.O. Box 704, Windsor, NSW 2756 Australia
Tel: (02) 4577-3555

Edited by Rachel Randall
Cover designed by Claudean Wheeler
Interior designed by Amanda Kleiman
Production coordinated by Debbie Thomas

DEDICATION

For Dad—I miss you.

ACKNOWLEDGMENTS

Many people helped me write this book, and I'm eternally grateful for the help I received. Here is a partial list: my mentor, Dr. Barbara Gastel; my guardian angel, Mrs. Loretta Robichaud; my editor at Writer's Digest Books, Rachel Randall; my mother, Maliheh; my brother, Fareed; and my wife, Georgia. I would also like to mention Dr. David E. Sumner for his selfless participation. Finally, I want to thank my kids, Zain, Zaid, and Zachary, for inspiring me and keeping quiet while I worked.

ABOUT THE AUTHOR

Naveed Saleh is a full-time freelance writer and editor. Naveed attained a bachelor's degree from Cornell University, a medical degree from Wayne State University School of Medicine, and a master's degree in science and technology journalism (with an informal concentration in psychology) from Texas A&M University. He has written numerous features for publications, including *The New Physician*, *Pregnancy Magazine*, the *Johns Hopkins Medicine Medical Letter: Health After 50*, and *Science Editor*. He's also an expert blogger at Psychology Today. Naveed won a 2010 Apex Award for a feature titled "Don't Mess with TCOM." In his spare time, Naveed likes to play golf, design websites, collect pens, paint in oils, walk along the beach, watch movies, listen to music, and spend time with his wife and kids.

TABLE OF CONTENTS

FOREWORD

INTRODUCTION

EPILOGUE

BIBLIOGRAPHY

INDEX

FOREWORD

See one, do one, teach one. Such was the mantra in medical school. And it is a tradition that Naveed Saleh carries forward—with substance, style, and much success—in *The Complete Guide to Article Writing: How to Write Successful Articles for Online and Print Markets*.

I have known Naveed since 2008, when he applied to the science journalism graduate program that I coordinate at Texas A&M University. Like me, Naveed is a medical-school graduate whose greatest interests turned out to be writing and editing. The abilities and commitment that Naveed showed in our program have helped enable him to produce a valuable book.

The Complete Guide to Article Writing makes me proud to know Naveed and to have contributed to his education. The book is extensively researched and draws on popular and scholarly literature and on interviews with leaders in academia and the media. It is timeless and also timely, containing both classic advice on writing and current guidance on working in online media. Abundant examples illustrate points. The prose is crisp, readable, witty in places, and sometimes edgy. There is an extensive bibliography. In short, the book not only tells how to write successful articles but also demonstrates the craft.

See one, do one, teach one. In the years since I first met Naveed Saleh, he has seen much good writing in both classes and on his own. He also has done much good writing for magazines and the Web. And now, through the current book, he is teaching others to do so. I enjoyed this book, learned from it, and will recommend it to students. I recommend it to you as well.

Barbara Gastel

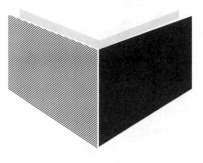

INTRODUCTION

It's hard to write a book about article writing—and more generally journalism—at this juncture in time. You may expect this book to amount to a survey. But how do you survey a field that's in flux? Newspapers are folding, journalists are losing their jobs, and news that once cost money is "freely" available on the Internet.

It's clear that what worked in the past won't work in the future. Old journalism is not only old but dated, too. In order to survive, the journalist of today must understand and champion new media. The Internet, blogs, social media, and smartphone journalism is the vocabulary of our new Lingua Franca. The journalist of today must be just as concerned with learning style and structure as he is with learning to design websites and build a strong Twitter following. Even if you "just want to write articles," you must cultivate various other skills in order to make this dream a reality.

But for those who have the stomach, skills, integrity, and ingenuity, these are wondrous times. The august institutions of yesteryear have been replaced by a frontier mentality typical of the Wild West. There's a need for entrepreneurs and iconoclasts. Ideas that grab the attention of readers and generate digital-ad revenue will breed success.

With this book, I hope to teach you everything I've learned about article writing. Of course, I'll teach you about style, structure, interviewing, narrative, ethics, query letters, platforms, and publication. But I'll also help you understand the history of journalism, its status quo, and its possible future. Anybody who masters the concepts in this book will have a strong understanding of the field. I truly believe this understanding will make you a better writer and help you succeed and see your name in a print or virtual byline.

Please don't skim this book; read it in its entirety, and then use it as a reference.

I want you to know that I consider it a privilege to host you with my words. I strived to ensure that the information in this book is attributable to some great mind. Feel free to regale your friends and classmates with knowledge gathered from this book, and know that it has all been verified. I spent years researching this book and months speaking with experts from national consumer magazines, association magazines, newspapers, universities, and more. I drew on dozens of texts, including the works of Jon Franklin, Roy Peter Clark, William Zinsser, and William E. Blundell. I read many journal articles and studies. I even exploited my own understanding of popular culture, finance, psychology, medicine, and science to make the work more entertaining.

I am also privileged to be a custodian of the more general study of journalism. Journalism is an old profession—even older than prostitution. Early prophets believed they were reporting on God.

I think that most people who write books like this one have spent their lives scaling some professional mountain and preach while perched on the summit. The book becomes an extension of some larger ego. I can't pretend to be so weathered. This realization dawned on me early, and I redoubled my efforts to turn out the best product.

I was originally trained as a science (medical) writer, and, at times, this book tends to evaluate and analyze the craft of article writing with an eye toward science and research. Moreover, I believe that every type of writer can benefit from this scientific purview. It should be noted, however, that some fantastic journalism scholars approach the craft of article writing from a humanities or creative-writing perspective. For completeness, I do my best to introduce the reader to some of this thinking.

With respect to word usage, you'll see words like *writer* and *journalist* or *article* and *story* used interchangeably. (If you're reading this book and interested in becoming a writer of articles, feel free to call yourself a journalist—as I discuss later, there's no license to practice journalism.) In the realm of journalism, many words lack clear-cut operational or functional definitions. Other words such as *source* have broad definitions and can refer to people (interviewees) or written sources. Moreover, the word *coherent* has shades of meaning, too. A coherent explanation can mean a consistent explanation, a clear explanation, or an explanation that offers options. (It can also mean all three.) When writing about the practice of journalism in more theoretical terms, this last meaning is key.

With professional opportunities for budding writers to garner real-world experience dwindling, it's important to acclimate readers to variations in newsroom lingo and jargon. That's why I sometimes refer to documents or ideas in various fashions. For example, although I may write *features*, *features piece*, *feature article,* and so forth, all of these terms refer to one type of story. Developing an ear for the lingo will help anybody, including the freelancer who may never work in a brick-and-mortar setting or the writer of articles who ends up in a newsroom.

Although I do my best to maintain consistency and practice what I preach in terms of style and structure, I acknowledge that this book may suffer occasional lapses—either conscious or unconscious. Please remember that style and structure take a lifetime to learn and are, above all, coherent guides and not dogma. Furthermore, the astute reader will notice that some of my advice on style differs from that of Writer's Digest Books, the publisher of this book, including suggestions on number usage and the use of generic singular pronouns. And this is absolutely fine … publications and individuals have their own preferences!

When I asked my former graduate school advisor and mentor, Dr. Barbara Gastel, what it was like to write a book, she told me that it felt like writing several feature articles. This book felt like writing twenty feature articles, each on its own deadline. (I definitely approached this book with a journalist's mentality.) I spent much time gathering excellent information for this book; it was absolutely necessary to get this information sourced and make sure that it was verified, transparent, and coherent. Fortunately, the world abounds with good information on journalism, style, and writing, and new information and research comes out every day.

I hope the information in this book and input from editors help you find your own voice. And I hope this voice informs and entertains countless others.

Enjoy this book in good health, and feel free to e-mail me with any comments or insights.

Naveed Saleh
writer@naveedsaleh.com
4/8/2013

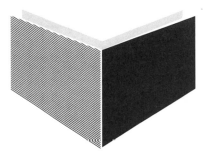

chapter 1

A PRIMER ON STYLE

The skill of any good writer is in large part based on *style*. Style is defined as writing conventions or tenets. Some of these conventions are well accepted, while others are a writer's call. Oftentimes certain style conventions are recommended (or required) by the publication to which a writer is submitting work and can be found in the publication's *style guide*. In my own writing, if a convention makes good sense to me, I'm likely to include it in my writer's arsenal regardless of the style guide it comes from. Developing your own style is particularly important when you're not working with an editor. For example, if you are writing a posting for your own blog, feel free to use your own style.

With style, writers make their writing clear, cohesive, comprehensible, concise, and correct (the five *C*s). Ultimately, all writers can use style to their advantage. Keep in mind that style is different from *voice*. A writer's voice is the distinct fashion in which the writer pieces together words. Although all good writers adhere to conventions of style, each good writer has a distinct voice.

Figure 1.1

THE FIVE CS

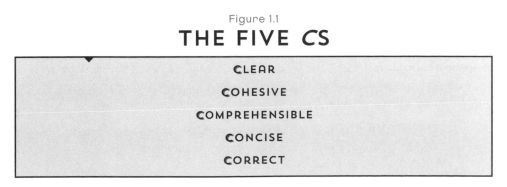

CLEAR

COHESIVE

COMPREHENSIBLE

CONCISE

CORRECT

Aside from the five *C*s, there are other good reasons for a writer to adhere to style. For example, a strong understanding of style enables a writer to write more easily. When starting a piece, I write whatever I feel ("practice write") and then go back and content edit or rewrite whatever I've written with tenets of style in mind. Another example of why style is important involves an international audience. By adhering to certain conventions of writing, English becomes readily understandable to the nonnative English speaker. For example, although few native speakers would have trouble with the expression, "I went to the parking lot quickly," a nonnative English speaker may be confused by the distance between the adverb *quickly* and the verb it modifies: *went*. Consequently, "I quickly went to the parking lot," reads more clearly to the nonnative speaker.

The following are two alphabetized lists of conventions that have guided my own writing. These lists draw on information that spans several style guides and texts. Whenever relevant, I have cited the style guide or text from which I derived this information. If mastered, these lists will equip any writer with a bread-and-butter style that he can adjust to fit most publications' preferred style conventions. The first list is a general list of conventions and pointers and deals with punctuation, grammar, parts of speech, and more. The second list focuses on word usage.

GENERAL POINTERS

ABBREVIATIONS. Many people haphazardly use abbreviations. In most writing, the only abbreviations that can stand alone on first use are the ones we all know: FBI, CIA, and so forth. Otherwise, abbreviations must always be spelled out on first use.

It's best to avoid abbreviations in short pieces of writing: writing that's under two or three pages. In longer pieces, unless the abbreviated term is used on more than three occasions (some pundits suggest five occasions), it's also best to avoid abbreviations.

Remember that it's important to anticipate your reader's needs. Your reader will not want to thumb backward through the text to remember what an abbreviation means. The only way a writer can ensure that the reader understands an abbreviation is if that abbreviation is used several times in close proximity. In fact, with longer works that have multiple abbreviations, it's prudent to include a list of abbreviations in the front or back matter (beginning or end of the text).

When abbreviating professional titles, including MD (medical doctor), DO (doctor of osteopathic medicine), PhD, and so forth, either enclose the abbreviation in commas or don't use commas at all. Additionally, you don't need to use periods with these abbreviations. Of note, the abbreviation *Jr.* doesn't need commas surrounding it either.

> **CORRECT:** Jonas Salk, MD, developed the polio vaccine.
> **CORRECT:** Jonas Salk MD developed the polio vaccine.
> **WRONG:** Jonas Salk, MD developed the polio vaccine.

ACTIVE VERBS. When I was in high school, I had a teacher who would deduct points for using verbs of being (conjugations of *to be*) when writing. Although I prefer to use active verbs when writing, sometimes it's impossible to avoid using verbs of being. But whenever I can, I will switch out verbs of being in favor of active verbs.

> **AWKWARD:** Racing motorcycles is invigorating for me.
> **BETTER:** Racing motorcycles invigorates me.

ACTIVE VOICE. When writing for a general audience (for more on types of audiences, please see Figure 6.2), it's preferable to use the active voice instead of the passive voice. Fortunately, for most writers, it takes effort to construct a sentence in the passive voice.

> **ACTIVE VOICE**: Tim and Bob saw the new *Transformers* movie.
> **PASSIVE VOICE:** The new *Transformers* movie was watched by Tim and Bob.

With the passive voice, the subject and the object are transposed—meaning the object comes before the verb. In the example above, the object *movie* comes before the subject *Tim and Bob*. Additionally, with the passive voice, the past participle (*watched*) is preceded by a conjugation of the verb *to be* (*was*). Finally, the preposition *by* is always implied (*by Tim and Bob*).

When writing for scientific audiences—for example, when writing a research article—it's sometimes acceptable to use the passive voice. Using the passive voice in scientific writing takes the emphasis off the researchers and allows the findings to be depersonalized. In journalism, you'll also find the passive voice used when law enforcement officials act as the subject. (In many cases it's unimportant to identify specific law enforcement individuals who work on behalf of a larger organization.)

> The experiment was performed to test for water quality. **This construction allows the author to shift focus away from the understood subject *we the researchers*.**
>
> The criminal was apprehended in July 2008.

ADVERBS. Oftentimes a writer needlessly uses adverbs. Many adverbs can be omitted from polished prose and replaced with stronger verbs.

> **WORDY:** Joseph walked slowly and aimlessly through the zoo.
> **PREFERRED:** Joseph meandered through the zoo.

ADVERB PLACEMENT. Adverb placement can be tricky. When choosing where to place adverbs in your writing, it's best to identify the verb and place the adverb as close to the verb as possible.

According to *The Chicago Manual of Style*, with intransitive verbs (verbs that don't take an object), the adverb is placed after the verb.

> He prayed quietly.

With transitive verbs (verbs that take an object), it usually makes sense to place the adverb before the verb.

> He secretly took the book.

> He quickly took to knitting. **In this example, *to knitting* is a gerund phrase (and prepositional phrase). A gerund phrase functions like a noun, and *to knitting* is the direct object of the transitive verb *took*.**

Sometimes a verb consists of two parts: the auxiliary verb, or "helper verb," and the principal verb. In such cases, place the adverb in between these two parts.

> He would swiftly take the lead.

The word *only* is a tricky adverb to place. The placement of *only* can alter the meaning of a sentence. It's important to carefully decide where to place *only* in your writing.

> He only took the books that he needed. **Meaning that he took the books and did nothing else.**

> He took only the books that he needed. **Meaning that he took the books that he needed but not the books that he didn't need. Additionally, in this construction, *only* is closer to *books*, the word that it modifies.**

Finally, remember that an adverb can modify a verb, an adjective, another adverb, a clause, a phrase, a preposition, or a sentence. Placement of the adverb depends on what part of speech it's modifying.

> Running quickly will make me lose my breath. **The adverb *quickly* modifies the gerund (noun) *running*.**

> Running will quickly make me lose my breath. **The adverb *quickly* modifies *make*. Note the change in meaning.**

On a final note, when deciding where to place adverbs, it's a good idea to consider these suggestions, but when this advice makes a sentence sound weird—like some affectation—follow your ear.

ANTECEDENTS. Every pronoun should clearly and correctly refer to an antecedent.

> **CLEAR:** He took the book of charts and the box of nails. These items were all that he could carry.

UNCLEAR: He took the book of charts and the box of nails. It was all that he could carry. **Unclear because *it* could refer to the load as a whole or an individual item.**

Of note, demonstrative pronouns including *this*, *that*, *these*, and *those* should often be followed by an antecedent when they refer to an aforementioned noun or nouns and begin a new sentence or are embedded within a new sentence.

WRONG: Lance bought a tablet, folders, mechanical pencils, and notebooks. He needed these for the proposed project.
BETTER: Lance bought a tablet, folders, mechanical pencils, and notebooks. He needed these *items* for the proposed project. **Here *items* is the antecedent.**

ANTILOGIES. Antilogies are words that have two contradictory meanings. For instance, when discussing an estimate, the word *conservatively* can mean purposefully low or purposely high depending on whether you are addressing a lay or scientific audience. Other examples of antilogies include *clip*, *cleve*, *bound*, *probe*, *literally*, *table*, and *dust*. It's best to avoid an antilogy; nevertheless, when using an antilogy, make sure that its intended meaning is clear.

ARTICLES. Words including *the*, *a*, and *an* are articles. Although most people appreciate that *a* is used before a word starting with a consonant and *an* is used before a word starting with a vowel, this understanding can be extended. The word *a* is used before a word starting with a consonant sound, and *an* is used before a word starting with a vowel sound.

A dog, an owl, an hour **(vowel sound)**, a hotel **(consonant sound)**

Oftentimes native English speakers drop articles in their speech and writing. If writing with an international audience in mind—in the age of the Internet, it's best to assume that all audiences are international—consider sticking those articles back into your prose.

OKAY: The Flower Fields of Carlsbad are seeded with Giant Tencolote Ranunculus, a bulb flower with long, straight stems and lush three- to five-inch blooms.
BETTER: The Flower Fields of Carlsbad are seeded with the Giant Tencolote Ranunculus, a bulb flower with long, straight stems and lush three- to five-inch blooms.

According to *The Elements of Style* (affectionately referred to by many as Strunk & White), an important distinction when using articles involves the series. An article can be used with each element in a series or only with the first element of a series (assuming that the other elements of a series take the article, too).

> **WRONG:** He took a bat, ball, and a glove.
> **RIGHT:** He took a bat, ball, and glove.
> **RIGHT:** He took a bat, a ball, and a glove.

ATTRIBUTIVE NOUNS. A client once asked me which expression was more correct: *communicative skills* or *communication skills*. The term *communication skills* is preferred because, in this case, *communication* is an attributive noun that functions as an adjective. Another example includes *surgery* (as opposed to *surgical*) *skills*.

BACK-FORMATIONS. A back-formation is a neologism, or new word derived from another word. With back-formations, the suffix or the ending of the original word is removed and oftentimes replaced. Some traditionalists have problems with back-formations, but I find they often make for colorful writing. Pundits at the *Oxford American Dictionary* agree: "Back-formations are a perfectly respectable way for creating new words in the language."

> *Enthuse* is a back-formation of the word *enthusiasm*.
> *Euthanize* is a back-formation of the word *euthanasia*.
> *Tweet* is a back-formation of the proper noun *Twitter* (the social networking and micro-blogging website).

BALANCE. Strunk & White suggests that the emphatic, stressed, or important parts of the sentence should be placed at the end of the sentence—commonly the position of the predicate. In other words, it's a good idea to weigh down the rear of a sentence with important information. Specifically, the dependent clause is the less important part of a sentence because it logically depends on an independent clause.

> **OKAY:** Paul went to the gym usually on Sunday afternoons.
> **BETTER:** Usually on Sunday afternoons, Paul went to the gym.

You'll find that both print and broadcast news is often delivered with this idea of balance in mind. This balance is also useful when writing for a virtual audience (blog postings or online articles).

BEGINNING A SENTENCE WITH A CONJUNCTION. When done sparingly and for effect, it's okay to begin a sentence with a conjunction such as *and, or,* or *but*.

> **ACCEPTABLE:** We all thought Alfred would win the talent competition. And then Amber took the stage. **Starting the second sentence with the conjunction *and* emphasizes Amber's performance.**

BIAS-FREE LANGUAGE. The *AMA Manual of Style* does an excellent job of recommending how to avoid biased language when writing. I doubt that most writers make a conscious decision to present biased language, whether it be sexist, racist, ageist, or so forth. Nevertheless, it's imperative to vigilantly check for biased language and, when possible, avoid descriptors that stereotype a person or group of people. For a comprehensive explanation on the subject, I encourage you to reference section 11.10 of the *AMA Manual of Style.* Here are some specific recommendations based on the *AMA Manual of Style*:

Age. It's best to refer to older people by listing their specific age. Nevertheless, *older person, elderly person, older adults, aging adults, persons 65 years and older,* and so forth are okay. Make sure to avoid using *elderly* as a noun.

Disability. I'm surprised by how many media outlets use insensitive and patronizing language when referring to people with disabilities. A person should never be referred to as *disabled* rather than *with disability.*

> **WRONG:** Brenda is a paraplegic.
> **RIGHT:** Brenda is a person with paraplegia.
>
> **WRONG:** Larry is a diabetic.
> **RIGHT:** Larry is a person with diabetes.
> **RIGHT:** Larry is a diabetic patient.
>
> **WRONG:** Ralph is crippled.
> **RIGHT:** Ralph is physically disabled.

I was once asked to analyze a newsletter that a well-known physician had written. I was surprised and saddened to find that he had referred to a patient as a "poor quadriplegic." First, he should have specified that the woman was "with quadriplegia." Second, it's demeaning for anyone, especially a physician, to describe a patient as "poor." (In all fairness, I'm sure this physician was trying to be compassionate.)

On a similar note, according to the *AMA Manual of Style,* writers should avoid terms such as *afflicted with, maimed, stricken with,* and *suffering from.*

Fortunately, the editors of the *AP Stylebook* have finally moved away from labeling people with disability. For example, they will no longer refer to people as "schizophrenic" and instead write, "a person who was diagnosed with schizophrenia."

Finally, the words *handicap* and *disability* have different meanings. According to the *Health Writer's Handbook*:

> A disability is a condition that interferes with one or more major life activities, such as walking, hearing, breathing, or learning. In contrast, a handicap is something that is a barrier to a person with a disability. For example, a man whose legs are paralyzed has a disability, not a handicap. However, stairs may be a handicap to him, as may the attitudes of some employers.

Gender. When possible, it's best to refrain from specifying gender. Some words are intrinsically gender specific such as *layman* or *salesman*. Better alternatives include *layperson* and *salesperson*. Furthermore, men and women (human beings) should not be referred to as *male* or *female*. With humans, *male* and *female* are to be used only as adjectives—a point that the *AP Stylebook* makes. The terms *boy, girl,* and *infant* are also acceptable.

When writing in a general sense, generic singular pronouns (nominative pronouns that refer to gender) such as *he* and *she* should be avoided when possible. (Some experts think that generic singular pronouns can *always* be avoided by rewriting the sentence in question.)

> **UNADVISABLE:** A physician should show compassion for his patients.
> **OKAY:** Physicians should show compassion for their patients.
> **BETTER:** A physician should show compassion for the patient.

Immigration status. In a continued push to move away from labeling people and instead focus on a person's action or condition, in April 2013 the editors at the *AP Stylebook* discontinued the use of *illegal immigrant*. From now on people who move to this country illegally will be designated as such. Of note, the general term *illegal immigration* is still acceptable.

> **UNADVISABLE:** Michael is an illegal immigrant.
> **BETTER:** Michael moved to this country illegally.
> **BETTER:** Michael is living in this country illegally.

Furthermore, according to the *AP Stylebook*, people who move to this country illegally should not be referred to as "undocumented" because they may have some form of documentation other than a visa or citizenship records.

Interestingly, although the Associated Press announced its decision to do away with the term *illegal immigrant* in the midst of immigration reform and activism against the stigma of the term, representatives from the organization deny their decision was political.

Race. When referring to race, words including *white, black,* or *African American* (no hyphen in adjectival or noun form)*, Latino, Hispanic,* and *American Indian* are acceptable. When designating race, try to be as specific as possible. For example, *Mexican American* is preferred to *Hispanic*. Don't use *Hispanic* or *Latino* as nouns. It's best to avoid words such as *Caucasian*, which refers to whites originally from the Caucuses, and *Oriental* as well as classifications that use a *non-* prefix (*nonwhite*).

Sexuality. The word *gay* can be used as an adjective describing a homosexual man (*a gay man*) but shouldn't be used as a noun. The term *lesbian* is acceptable for a homosexual woman. Avoid using *homosexual* as a noun. When referring to a same-sex couple or same-sex marriage, use words such as *spouse, companion, partner*, or *life partner*. Avoid the phrase *sexual preference* because it implies that sexual orientation is based on a voluntary decision.

In epidemiology circles, the terms *sex worker* or *commercial sex worker* are preferred to the more derogatory *prostitute*.

CAPITALIZATION. Always capitalize proper nouns that refer to a specific person, place, or thing—for example, the Republican Party, the Constitution, the Bill of Rights, the Nobel Peace Prize, and Michael Jackson. Currently, many editors and writers prefer down style (as opposed to up style), which means that it's best to minimize the use of capital letters. Personally, whenever I'm in doubt, I leave whatever I'm concerned about in lowercase letters.

Company or trade names. There's no need to put a trademark (™), service mark (ˢᴹ), or registered symbol (®) after a company or product name. Simply capitalize the company or trade name—for example, Costco, Microsoft, Twitter, and Facebook.

Disease names and medical specialties. Capitalize only the part of a disease name that contains a proper noun (Cushing's syndrome). Disease names that don't contain a proper noun aren't capitalized (diabetes mellitus). Don't capitalize medical specialties—for example, family medicine, orthopedics, obstetrics and gynecology, cardiology, and pediatrics.

Geographic places. Capitalize geographic places that are proper nouns—for example, American Southwest. Don't capitalize cardinal directions—for example, north, south, and northeast.

> **WRONG:** Harold lives to the West of Canada.
> **RIGHT:** Harold lives to the west of Canada.

Personal titles. When a title directly precedes a name, capitalize both the title and name—for example, President Obama. Don't capitalize a title when it stands alone—for example, "The current president of the United States is Barack Obama."

Prescription drug names and medical specialties. Generic prescription drug names (omeprazole) aren't capitalized. Trade names (Prilosec) are capitalized.

Seasons. According to the *AP Stylebook*, don't capitalize seasons when they stand alone or are used as adjectival modifiers (fall, spring, spring semester, and so forth). Capitalize seasons when they are part of a proper noun (Summer Games).

Some other examples of capitalized words and expressions: Central Standard Time, Internet, World Wide Web, Web, and Ford Explorer. Of note, the Internet, World Wide Web, and Web refer to a specific place and are therefore proper nouns.[1]

CITATIONS. As many would expect, plagiarism is a big deal. Writers from different cultures may not realize how serious plagiarism is. In Western cultures, writing is proprietary,

---

[1] Although *Web* is a proper noun, when paired with another noun, it's common for many writers to write *Web* without a capital letter (*website*, *web address*, or *web design*). When *Web* is used by itself, however, it's probably best to capitalize it. For example, "I searched the Web for deals on a lawn mower."

which means that it's okay to disseminate information as long as it's cited properly. Furthermore, with Google searches and plagiarism programs, it's a sure bet that anybody engaged in plagiarism will likely be caught.

Whenever you use a direct quotation or indirect quotation, you must cite the source. When citing a published work in journalistic style, it's sufficient to mention the publication, author, or title of the work without providing a footnote or endnote.

CLICHÉS: It's best to use few clichés in your writing. Oftentimes a cliché is better expressed in your own words.

> **UNADVISABLE:** Hiring my wife for the job puts me between a rock and a hard place.
>
> **BETTER:** Hiring my wife for the job poses a dilemma for me.

COLONS. Colons can be used to introduce lists, to qualify an independent clause, and in the salutation of a formal letter. When used in a sentence, a colon must be preceded by an independent clause. This clause can end with the words *as follows* or *the following*. When the clause introducing the list is a dependent clause and ends with words such as *for example* or *that is*, don't punctuate the clause with a colon. (In other words, if the list begins with an incomplete sentence that depends on the list for meaning, don't use any punctuation when introducing the list.) Of note, if the clause following the colon is an independent clause, the first word following the colon is capitalized.

> Jeremiah spent all his money on cars: Cars were all he cared about.

COMMAS. Comma use is difficult to understand, and commas are difficult to use properly. It's outside the scope of this book to list every situation that requires a comma. Nevertheless, I'll do my best to hit on some of the main uses of the comma, and for clarity's sake, I'm going to list some of their uses in a table.

USE	EXAMPLE
Two independent clauses joined by a conjunction (*and, or, but*, etc.)	I took the Mercedes for a test drive, and I got in an accident.
Dependent clause preceding an independent clause (e.g., a participle phrase, prepositional phrase, or adverbial phrase)	**Introductory participle phrase:** Holding back his anger, Aaron said nothing. **Introductory prepositional phrase:** On the table by the chair, you will find the check. **Introductory adverbial phrase:** While I was sleeping, my house was robbed.

USE	EXAMPLE
Sentence beginning with an adverb	Unfortunately, our store offers no discounts.
Setting off a nonrestrictive phrase	SpongeBob and Patrick, two close friends, like having a good time.
Series	I like to eat bananas, oranges, and apples. *Note that with some nonscientific or nontechnical writing—for example, general interest journalism or creative writing—there's often no need for a serial (Oxford) comma or comma preceding the final* and *or* or *in a series. More specifically, with some nonscientific writing and nontechnical writing, the meaning of a series is unchanged when the serial comma is omitted. With scientific writing and technical writing, however, it's best to include the serial comma; thus, the serial comma ensures that the meaning of a series remains intact. Similarly, with instructive texts—like this book— it's best to use a serial comma, too. Finally, some people find that the serial comma provides aesthetic appeal.*
To prevent misreading	As recounted by Peter, Samuel did much to help his community.
Two short interdependent clauses	One if by land, two if by sea.
Addresses and dates	Jessica's address is 455 Mercy Street Apartment 103, Phoenix, Arizona 85001. *Note that there's no comma between the street address and apartment number and state and zip code.*
	Ethel was born on March 1, 1946, at 9:00 A.M. *Note that the year is set off by commas.*
	Ethel was born in March 1946. *No comma needed between the month and year.*

USE	EXAMPLE
Salutations	*When writing a salutation, place a comma after a greeting (e.g., hello, greetings, and good day). (We place a comma after such greetings because they are nouns and need to be separated from the proper nouns or nouns that follow.) Furthermore, with formal letters, place a colon after the name of a person or persons to whom the letter is addressed. (With memos and short e-mails, it's acceptable to use a comma instead of a colon.)* Hello, Jennifer: *If the salutation begins with an adjective (e.g., dear or honorable), no comma is placed after this first word. (The adjective modifies the noun or proper noun.)* Dear Jennifer:

Don't use commas with a compound predicate unless the meaning is unclear.

> **WRONG:** Jerry showered, and shaved before he left the house.
> **RIGHT:** Jerry showered and shaved before he left the house.

Never use a comma to join two independent clauses! Doing so results in the dreaded *comma splice.*

> **WRONG:** Jerry showered and shaved before he went to work, Jerry had a bagel and cup of coffee for breakfast.
> **RIGHT:** Jerry showered and shaved before he went to work. Jerry had a bagel and cup of coffee for breakfast.

COMPARATIVE AND SUPERLATIVE FORMS OF ADJECTIVES. As explained in *The Copyeditor's Handbook* by Amy Einsohn, when the base form of an adjective has one or two syllables, the comparative or superlative form of the adjective is one word. Participles that act as adjectives are exceptions.

> Nice, nicer, and nicest
> Shallow, shallower, and shallowest
> Taught, better taught, and best taught. ***Taught* is a participle.**
> Unhappy, unhappier, and unhappiest. **Here, the base form is *happy*, not *unhappy.***
> Damaged, more damaged, and most damaged. **Here, the base form is a participle.**

When the base form of an adjective has three or more syllables, the comparative or superlative forms of the adjective consist of two words.

> Sanitary, more sanitary, most sanitary

COMPOUND WORDS. If you're unsure whether a word is written as two separate words, hyphenated, or compound, look it up in the dictionary. Although everybody knows that *grandfather* is one word, what about the word *online (on-line* or *on line)*?

With increased use, words evolve from separate to hyphenated to compound. *The Chicago Manual of Style* supports a move towards compound words, especially when the word is in widespread use (like *online*). *The Chicago Manual of Style* recommends writing a word as compound "when the closed spellings have become widely accepted, pronunciation and readability are not at stake, and keystrokes can be saved."

The book *Words into Type* offers good guidelines when determining what form a compound word takes. For example, when a verb is followed by an adverb or preposition, the resulting compound verb is written as two words. However, when the resulting expression is used as a noun or adjective, it's either written as one word or hyphenated.

> The police broke up the party.

> Esther and Tom weathered a tough breakup.

CONTRACTIONS. Some traditionalists argue that contractions have no place in formal writing. Personally, I use contractions when I write because it makes my writing sound more fluid. In *The Copyeditor's Handbook*, Amy Einsohn brings up a very good point about the phrase *aren't I*. No matter who you are, this contraction is always preferred to the choppy and pretentious alternative: *am I not*.

COORDINATE ADJECTIVES. Sometimes two or more adjectives are used to describe a noun. When the order of the adjectives is important and the sentence loses meaning if their place is transposed (switched), these adjectives are called coordinate adjectives. Don't use a comma to separate coordinate adjectives.

> I love this red shag carpeting.

Noncoordinate adjectives can be transposed and should be separated by a comma.

> Thanks for buying me these shiny, expensive rubies.

To test whether adjectives are noncoordinate and require a comma, either transpose them or link them by the conjunction *and*. If the meaning is retained and the resulting sentence sounds okay, then these adjectives are noncoordinate.

COPULATIVE VERBS. Copulative verbs are *verbs of being* rather than *active verbs* and include verbs like *be, become, feel, look, seem, smell, sound,* and *taste.* Whereas most verbs are modified by adverbs, copulative verbs are modified by adjectives.

> **WRONG:** These flowers smell nicely.
> **RIGHT:** These flowers smell nice.

CORRELATIVE CONJUNCTIONS. As suggested by Strunk & White, it's important to pair or group certain conjunctions. These include *not only … but also; neither … nor; either … or;* and *first, second, third, fourth. …* Additionally, it's important to maintain parallelism when using these conjunctions.

> **AWKWARD:** This time is not only for remembrance, but we suggest change, too.
> **PREFERRED:** This time is not only for remembrance but also for change.

CUPERTINO EFFECT. Early spell checkers would often replace the word *cooperation* with the word *Cupertino* (the home of Apple computer). The tendency for spell-checkers to make improper suggestions became known as the Cupertino Effect.

Use good judgment when considering suggestions made by a publishing program's spell or grammar checker. Moreover, don't assume that just because a word or phrase wasn't flagged by a spell or grammar check program that it's correct.

DANGLING MODIFIERS. You'll find dangling modifiers in sentences that begin with participle phrases. If a sentence contains a dangling modifier in the form of a participle phrase, it's unclear which word the participle phrase is associated with.

> While walking to the store, the alarm rang on Jeremy's watch. **Confusion: Was Jeremy's *watch* walking to the store?**
> **BETTER:** The alarm on Jeremy's watch rang while Jeremy walked to the store.

> Forced to defer his admission to college, Jeremy's plans were derailed. **Confusion: Who or what was forced to defer admission to college—Jeremy or Jeremy's plans?**
> **BETTER:** Jeremy's plans were derailed after he was forced to defer his admission to college.

DIRECT QUOTATIONS. Writing out direct quotations or quotations that are written verbatim can get complicated. In order to explain how they can be recorded in written text, consider the following examples.

> Dr. Lawrence Adams stated the following distinction to his students: "The difference between causation and correlation is significant. Correlation means that two variables are related whereas causation explains the causality of this relationship."

In this example, the quotation is introduced after a colon, which is acceptable. The use of a colon is correct because the clause preceding the colon is independent.

The following two examples are better constructed and more fluid.

> "The difference between causation and correlation," Dr. Lawrence Adams said to his students, "is significant. Correlation means that two variables are related whereas causation explains the causality of this relationship."

> "The difference between causation and correlation is significant," Dr. Lawrence Adams said to his students. "Correlation means that two variables are related whereas causation explains the causality of this relationship."

Now consider the following examples of shorter quotations.

> "Causation and correlation are different," said Dr. Lawrence Adams to his class.

> Dr. Lawrence Adams said to his class, "Causation and correlation are different." **Capitalize the first word of an independent clause that follows the dependent clause introducing the quotation.**

When introducing a quotation, it's preferable to keep things simple and use the words *said* or *state*. With weightier quotations, *state* is often preferred to *said*.

Ellipses can be used to omit some words in a quotation, especially if this information is extraneous. Consider the following long quotation.

> Hector said: "Take me to the beach, and let's bring Juan, too. I want to swim, build sandcastles, and catch crabs. I also want to sunbathe. And afterwards take me to the ice-cream parlor."

> Hector said: "Take me to the beach … and afterwards take me to the ice-cream parlor."

> Hector said: "Take me to the beach, and let's bring Juan, too. … And afterwards take me to the ice-cream parlor." **Note that a fourth period was included before this set of ellipsis because the first part of this quotation was a complete sentence in the original text.**

When recording quotations from a source, brackets are used to indicate omitted speech that is implied by the speaker. If you're going to include information in brackets, you need to do it in such a way that the original source would likely agree with your inclusion.

> Edna was shocked by the barren landscape. "There are no trees," she said, "no buildings, no people … [it's] lifeless here."

If you want to quote speech within a quotation, use single quotation marks.

Mark said, "I thought it was funny when Jenny said, 'Fuzzy drank my wine.'"

Finally, in most American writing, periods and commas go inside quotation marks whereas semicolons and colons go outside quotation marks. Additionally, if you're using quotation marks and you must choose between two different types of punctuation marks, choose the most important.

WRONG: "Will you go to the movies with me?," asked John.
RIGHT: "Will you go to the movies with me?" asked John.

DOUBLE-NEGATIVE EXPRESSIONS. Double-negative expressions use two (or multiple) self-canceling negative elements in one sentence. Although many people consider double negatives nonstandard and "uneducated," the double-negative expression has a long history—even Chaucer used them! *Fowler's Modern English Usage* suggests that when used sparingly and for effect, simple double-negative expressions are sometimes acceptable.

One strong argument against the use of double negatives is that they make writing less coherent and concise. If you ever find yourself confused by a double-negative expression, simply omit or make positive all negative expressions in order to decipher the meaning.

OKAY: "I am not unopposed to your request." **This could mean that I am not completely opposed to your request and may consider it. If the effect is intended to offer an indefinite meaning, then this expression may be okay.**

CONFUSING: "I ~~infrequently don't~~ like taking long showers. **I struck through the negative elements, which cancel out each other.**
BETTER: "I like taking long showers."

DROPPED VERBS. Dropping a verb from a sentence can confuse the reader. It's best to balance a statement by sticking the dropped verb back in.

UNCLEAR: Dave likes Timothy more than Brandon. **Does Dave like Timothy more than Brandon likes Timothy, or does Dave like Timothy more than he likes Brandon?**
BETTER: Dave likes Timothy more than Brandon likes Timothy.
OR: Dave likes Timothy more than he likes Brandon.

ENDING A SENTENCE WITH A PREPOSITION. Traditionalists tell us to avoid ending sentences with prepositions. Most contemporary writers disagree with this position. Sometimes, if a writer avoids ending a sentence with a preposition, the resulting sentence sounds stuffy.

STUFFY: Do you know in which notebook Dominick wrote?
BETTER: Do you know which notebook Dominick wrote in?

EXCLAMATION POINT. When writing, use exclamation points sparingly.

UNADVISABLE: I made five bucks! **This is no big deal, and there's no need for an exclamation point.**
OKAY: My house is on fire!

ELLIPSES. According to *The Chicago Manual of Style*, ellipses can be used to indicate "faltering or interrupted speech." If you imagine the speaker makes an emotional break in speech or otherwise trails off, use ellipses. When using ellipses, leave a space before and after a set of three single-spaced periods.

> No way ... I mean ... I need permission to take that money.

> I thought about it, and, uh ... I have no idea.

ELLIPTICAL CLAUSES. Elliptical clauses allow certain words to be dropped without compromising the meaning of the sentence. Just be sure that the subject of the sentence is clear.

> **ACCEPTABLE:** Aaron had three dogs, and Sam had one.

> **UNCLEAR:** Though raining, I was dry in my raincoat. **Was I raining, or was it raining outside?**
> **BETTER:** Though it was raining, I was dry in my raincoat.

EVASIVE OR INSECURE LANGUAGE. Many qualifiers cloud the meaning of sentences and make the message weak and less definite. Examples include *somewhat, a lot, perhaps, kind of, really, truly, very, genuinely, quite, seemingly, fairly, eventually, rather,* and *very.* These words can be eliminated from most sentences and phrases.

> **UNCLEAR:** Harold is somewhat tall. **Is Harold tall or of average height?**
> **BETTER:** Harold is tall.

FIGURATIVE LANGUAGE. Before I became a professional writer and before I had read any style guides, I questioned the overuse of metaphors and similes. Apparently I wasn't alone. According to Strunk & White, figurative language should be used sparingly. That being said, a simile or metaphor may provide invaluable insight into an explanation. Above all, make sure not to mix your metaphors.

> **OKAY:** The brain is like the body's computer.

> **WRONG:** Malignant cancer is a wildfire that drowns life. **Mixed metaphor comparing fire to water.**
> **BETTER:** Malignant cancer is a wildfire that immolates life.

FLAT ADVERBS. Not all adverbs have to end in the *-ly* suffix. Many flat, or bare, adverbs can either take an *-ly* suffix or work without the *-ly* suffix in their adjectival form. Some flat adverbs, such as *tight* and *fast,* never take an *-ly.* Flat adverbs sans the *-ly* are often used with the imperative or in colloquial speech.

RIGHT: Drive slow through the school parking lot!
RIGHT: Drive slowly through the school parking lot!

RIGHT: The sun shone bright.
RIGHT: The sun shone brightly.

RIGHT: The police officer wrote me a ticket because I drove too fast.
WRONG: The police officer wrote me a ticket because I drove too fastly.

FORMATTING. Unless otherwise stated, your margins should be aligned to the left (ragged-right configuration). Don't center or justify.

FUSED PARTICIPLES. Famed English lexicographer and philologist H.W. Fowler coined the term *fused participles*, and he hated them. A fused participle consists of a pronoun tacked on to a participle. Nevertheless, fused participles have a legitimate use. Here's an example of a fused participle lifted straight out of Strunk & White.

> Do you mind me correcting Irene? **Here the emphasis is on whether you have a problem with me specifically correcting Irene—maybe you would be okay if somebody else corrected Irene.**

But in a highly similar construction, when *correcting* is preceded by a possessive pronoun, the meaning is different. Consider the following example.

> Do you mind my correcting Irene? **Here the emphasis is on the act of correcting itself.**

GENERIC SINGULAR PRONOUNS. Today fewer editors and readers agree that using a generic *he* is acceptable. After all, women are just as capable as men in every respect. To avoid problems with both editors and your readers, do your best to avoid using *he* and definitely steer clear of strange constructions such as *s/he* and *he or she*. Of note, many publications—including Writer's Digest Books—will alternate the use of *he* and *she* when using generic singular pronouns.

> **UNADVISABLE:** Every student took his notebook.
> **UNADVISABLE:** Every student took their notebook. **Problem with subject-verb agreement.**
> **UNADVISABLE:** A notebook was taken by every student. **This sentence is in the passive voice.**
> **BEST:** Every student takes a notebook.

GERUND OR INFINITIVE. In most cases, whether a verb takes a gerund or infinitive as an object is apparent to any native English speaker, but when in doubt, reference the dictionary or a list.

WRONG: In the morning, I expect having your resignation on my desk.

RIGHT: In the morning, I expect to have your resignation on my desk.

HEADINGS. When splitting up a written work, headings provide an easy and logical way to organize a group of paragraphs with a common theme. Although geared toward a medical audience, Thomas A. Lang's *How to Write, Publish & Present in the Health Sciences* articulates well the distinction between a *descriptive* and *informative heading*. A *descriptive heading* is less informative and simply labels the section whereas an *informative heading* provides more information and does a better job linking the text to the reader. An informative heading sums up the section. When possible, use the informative heading over the descriptive heading.

Victorian architecture **(descriptive heading)**

Aesthetic examples of Victorian architecture **(informative heading)**

A heading can be typed in bold text and subsequent subheadings distinguished by italics. Just be sure to leave adequate spacing both before and after the heading in order to distinguish the heading from surrounding text.

HEADLINES AND TITLES. According to the *AP Stylebook*, only the first word of a headline is capitalized. Proper nouns in headlines are also capitalized.

When capitalizing words in titles, I defer to the *AP Stylebook*'s suggestion that the first word and last word of the title and all principal words be capitalized. Principal words include prepositions that are four or more words in length but exclude articles and shorter prepositions and conjunctions. Don't capitalize articles within a title (unless they are the first or last word). Of note, guidelines in *The Chicago Manual of Style* are more complicated.

There's also sentence style, which is used by the *Los Angeles Times* website. This style calls for the capitalization of only the first letter of a title and any other words that would normally be capitalized in a sentence (proper nouns).

This advice is by no means comprehensive, and I suggest you thumb through style guides to learn more about the capitalization of titles. Keep in mind that whatever style you choose for your own writing, it's important to remain consistent.

HYPERBOLE. Hyperbole is an exaggeration. If you want to write clearly, you must write what you mean without exaggeration—you must minimize hyperbole. For example, think carefully about whether a certain store is the "best" or a certain slice of pie is the "greatest." Use of the word *unique* is a particularly disconcerting example of hyperbole. Although someone or something may be "rare" or "distinctive," it's unlikely that this person or thing is "unique."

HYPHENATION. Hyphenate a compound adjective that precedes a noun unless the first word of the compound is an adverb (ends with *-ly*). Don't hyphenate a compound adjective that follows a noun. Oftentimes there's no need to hyphenate a phrasal verb (verb combined with a preposition, adverb, or both). Furthermore, when different words of a compound noun work as a unit, it's useful to hyphenate all parts of the word.

> Mr. Burns is a first-grade teacher.
> Anna is war weary.
> Henry wrote a thoroughly researched dissertation.
> Chuck threw up all over his date.
> This apron is a one-size-fits-all.

INDENTATION. Many contemporary writers are moving away from indenting the beginning of each paragraph in favor of using block paragraphs.

INDIRECT QUOTATIONS. Should you paraphrase another person's words and place these words into a sentence, it's imperative that you attribute this information. When writing for the public, it may be acceptable to attribute such indirect quotations by merely mentioning the author or work in passing. Consider the following indirect quotation I excerpted from a *Psychology Today* blog posting I wrote titled "The Superhero Within."

> I just finished reading a paper titled "From Student to Superhero: Situational Primes Shape Future Helping." The researchers write that when college students are *primed* or presented with the idea of a superhero, they were more likely to engage in altruistic behavior.

INTENSIFIERS. Intensifiers are qualifiers that add little meaning to the words they modify. Examples include *very, really, pretty, horribly, uniquely,* and *literally.* Consider the following spirited take on intensifiers from Strunk & White: "*Rather, very, little, pretty*—these are the leeches that infest the pond of prose, sucking the blood of words." Suffice it to say, whenever possible, you should expunge mindless intensifiers from your writing.

INTERRUPTERS. When writing a sentence, sometimes some information is nonessential to the intrinsic meaning of the sentence. These interrupters are set off using parentheses, em dashes (long dashes), or commas. Often this information takes the form of a *nonrestrictive clause.*

According to *The Copyeditor's Handbook,* parentheses, commas, and dashes exist on a spectrum of meaning. Parentheses are used for abbreviations, acronyms, ancillary, and trivial information; commas are used to enclose slightly less extraneous information; em dashes or long dashes are used for emphasis. Additionally, em dashes can be used to set off a longer interrupter: an interrupter that contains internal punctuation or a break in syntax.

> The National Security Agency (NSA) employs code breakers.

> John Quincy Adams, son of John and Abigail Adams, was the sixth president of the United States.

> You may take one jacket or the other—not both—to the concert.
>
> I am resolved—in large part, because I've taken an oath to protect this office—to demur.

Of note, if you include an entire sentence in parentheses, place terminal punctuation inside the parentheses.

> Sherry was raised in Flint, Michigan. (She spent the first eighteen years of her life there.)

ITALICS. Except when making headers boldface, whenever a word or idea needs to be emphasized, it's best to use italics. *Never* spell a word in all capital letters or underline it for emphasis! One pet peeve for many professional writers and editors is a preference for some people to choose to boldface text instead of using italics. Unless you're writing an academic textbook, wherein you often find boldface type emphasizing key words, it's best to steer clear of bolded text. (Possible exception: I once edited a newsletter that was meant for an elderly audience. I suggested that the publisher switch out bolded text for text in italics. The publisher disagreed and explained to me that older people with vision problems have trouble reading italics.)

I use italics to distinguish names of books, magazines, journals, newspapers, plays, movies, albums, blogs, and television shows or series that are published or produced separately. I designate titles of songs on an album, television episodes, blog postings, or articles or other works within a publication with quotation marks. For more information, please refer to *The Chicago Manual of Style* or the *AP Stylebook*.

JARGON. Jargon is vocabulary specific to a certain discipline or field. When writing for a general audience, it's advisable to steer clear of jargon and use terms understood by all people. Avoid jargon when writing about politics, sports, crime, business, or medicine.

> **UNCLEAR:** Dolores refused her neb and left the ER AMA. **The word *neb* refers to a nebulizer or breathing treatment often given to people with asthma. The acronym *ER* refers to the emergency room. The acronym *AMA* is medical jargon for "against medical advice."**
>
> **BETTER:** Dolores refused her breathing treatment and left the emergency room against medical advice.

Within the realm of politics, a widespread example of jargon is the word *optics*. The word has come to mean the way an action or issue is perceived by the public. Another example of jargon that's a darling of politicians (and other professionals) is the use of *impact* as a verb.

LISTS. When writing, lists offer logical organization to your work. When there is no sequence to the actions in the list, it's preferable to bullet the list and list entries alphabetically or according to importance, chronology, geography, and so forth. When the actions or entries in a list are sequenced, the list should be numbered.

If the entries in the list are single words or phrases, there's no need to capitalize the first letter unless the first entry is a proper noun. There's also no need to end each entry in a list with a period, but ending each with a comma or semicolon is permissible as long as the last entry ends in a period. When at least one of the entries in a list is a sentence, it's preferable to capitalize the first word of each entry in the list and end each entry with a period—even if some items are individual words or phrases.

When the text introducing a list is a complete sentence, it may end with a colon or period. When this introductory text includes the words *as follows* or *the following*, it's followed by a colon. When the introductory text is a sentence fragment that is completed by the items in the list, it isn't followed by any punctuation at all unless the introductory text ends in "for example" or "that is," in which case you can use a colon or comma to introduce the list.

MEDIAL CAPITALS (CAMELCASE, MIDCAPS, OR INTERCAPS). Some words like PayPal and PowerPoint are spelled with two capital letters. Only use medial capitals if the designated company, institution, group, organization, product, software application, software program, or so forth officially promotes their use. (When in doubt, my advice is to Google an official website and check.) Don't use medial capitals of your own design (doing so would look silly).

MODAL AUXILIARY VERBS. Modal auxiliary verbs are verbs that run a spectrum of meaning. Some modal auxiliary verbs that we're all familiar with include *can* and *may*. The word *can* connotes ability, while *may* connotes permission. If you graduated third grade, you're probably familiar with the distinction.

> Can I go to the bathroom? **Likely response: Of course, you have the ability to go to the bathroom; do you want to use the bathroom?**

> May I go to the bathroom? **Likely response: Yes, you may; here's a hall pass.**

There are other modal auxiliary verbs, too. In addition to *can* and *may*, the ones that I pay particular attention to are *could, would,* and *might*.

The modal auxiliary verbs *could* and *can* are similar. They both denote ability: whether something is possible. The verb *can*, however, is a more forceful and deliberate word and implies immediacy and certainty.

> Can I go to the doctor's office? **Meaning: Do I have the ability to go to the doctor's office right now? For example, do I have immediate access to a car so that I can drive there?**

Could I go to the doctor's office? **Meaning: Do I have the ability to go to the doctor's office either now or sometime in the future?**

Similarly, the modal auxiliary verb *might* differs from *may* in that *might* is less forceful and deliberate than *may*.

Arthur may come to the party. **Meaning: There's a good chance that Arthur will come to the party.**

Arthur might come to the party. **Meaning: There's a small chance that Arthur will come to the party.**

The modal auxiliary verb *would* is conditional.

Would I go to the doctor's office? **Possible response: It depends. ... It's up to you.**

NEEDLESS WORDS. When writing, it's important to think about every word that you use. After much writing, you will reflexively minimize your use of needless words. When I first write a sentence, I write what I intend, no matter how many words it takes. After I've written several sentences or a couple of paragraphs, I scan my work and attempt to identify which subjects, verbs, prepositions, objects, and adverbs are needed to convey meaning. I'll then go ahead and omit any needless words. Reading your work out loud also helps you figure out which words are essential (and whether your writing sounds good).

For instance, whenever I see the word *fact* I try to figure out how to get rid of it. According to Strunk & White, *"The fact that* is an especially debilitating expression. It should be revised out of every sentence in which it occurs." Furthermore, words like *there is, there are, which is, which are,* and *of* are usually needless filler.

WORDY: Despite the fact that Andy gets all the recognition, I still like him. **"Despite the fact that" is wordy and can be replaced by "although."**
BETTER: Although Andy gets all the recognition, I still like him.

WORDY: There are nineteen people who understand this translation.
BETTER: Nineteen people understand this translation.

WORDY: He is the type of person who scares easy.
BETTER: He scares easy.

The following table of needless words and substitute expressions is derived from both Strunk & White and Ian Montagnes' seminal work titled *Editing and Publication: A Training Manual* (offered for free through Google Books).

NEEDLESS EXPRESSION	PREFERRED SUBSTITUTE
as of yet	yet
as to whether	whether
close proximity to	near
despite the fact that	although
during the course of	during
exerts a lethal effect	kills
he is the man who	he
hold a meeting	meet
in attendance at	attend
in a shoddy manner	shoddily
in view of the fact that	because
in the event that	if
in the initial instance	at first
in spite of the fact that	although
is equipped with	has
large number of	many
owing to the fact that	because
regarded as being	regarded
the present book	this book
the question as to whether	whether
the reason why is that	because
there is no doubt that	no doubt (doubtless)
until such time as	until
with a small amount of effort	easily
with reference to	about

Here's a hint about how to use this list until you become more comfortable with it: Search for these expressions using the "Find" function in Microsoft Word to identify them in your writing. This may take some time but will make your writing more concise.

Some expressions are intrinsically redundant and can be replaced by one-word alternatives. Some examples include *armed gunmen (gunmen), totally destroyed (destroyed),* and *completely finished (finished).*

NOMINALIZATIONS. Nominalizations are expressions that rely on nouns to do the work of a verb. Using a verb alternative is more concise.

> **UNADVISABLE:** The team performed an excavation on the tomb. **"The team performed an excavation" is a nominalization. A conjugation of the verb *to excavate* is a more concise alternative.**
>
> **BETTER:** The team excavated the tomb.

NOUN STRINGS. A noun string is a group of nouns that taken together work as an adjective to describe a subject. They are often confusing and found in jargon. Moreover, they make a sentence sound clunky or cumbersome. Noun strings should be rewritten for clarity.

> **UNCLEAR:** The intensive-care-unit physician assistants were helpful.
> **BETTER:** The physician assistants in the intensive care unit were helpful.

> **CLUNKY:** Applicants are subject to a competitive, long, and arduous interview process.
> **BETTER:** Applicants are subject to an interview process that's competitive, long, and arduous.

NUMBERS. Different publications and style guides have their own rules about how to write out numbers—including Writer's Digest Books—and, depending on the type of article that you're writing, it's important to refer to such resources for more details. Of note, my recommendations in this section are not followed in this book because Writer's Digest Books has its own, more literary style conventions.

At the very least, numbers greater than ten should be written using Arabic numerals. In my own writing, I carry over a practice from scientific writing, and I'll write most numbers as Arabic numerals (for example 5, 8, 19, and 1,932). Additionally, as suggested by the *AP Stylebook*, I'll write out million, billion, trillion, and so forth without using zeros or scientific notation. For my own idiosyncratic reasons, I'll usually write out *one* and *two*—for me, at least, doing so seems more aesthetic and clear. When writing for your own purposes, consistency is key: Pick one convention, and stick with it.

Of note, you should never start a sentence with an Arabic numeral unless the number refers to a year.

> **OKAY:** I like 8 of these dresses.
> **OKAY:** I like eight of these dresses.

> **WRONG:** 33 paramedics attended the training session.
> **BETTER:** Thirty-three paramedics attended the training session.

Keep in mind that when dealing with large numbers, you should help your reader visualize how large the number is by using a comparison. Furthermore, sometimes it's unnecessary to burden your reader with exact numbers when rounded-off numbers will suffice.

> **OKAY:** Eighteen thousand people were at the rally.
> **BETTER:** Eighteen thousand people were at the rally—enough to fill a New York Knicks game at Madison Square Garden.

> **UNADVISABLE:** The water level rose 5.63 inches.
> **BETTER:** The water level rose by about 6 inches.

PARAGRAPH. A paragraph is a group of sentences that represents a common idea. Imagine that a sentence is a strawberry, a paragraph is a basket of strawberries, a section (organized under a heading) is a crate of strawberries, and the entire written document is the truck that carries these crates.

Understanding is key to any paragraph's structure. Typically, a paragraph begins with a topic sentence that summarizes the subsequent ideas expressed in the paragraph or begins with a series of sentences that provide supporting evidence for an eventual topic sentence.

The topic sentence is followed by sentences that are thematically linked. Such sentences can be either coordinate or subordinate. Coordinate sentences exist at the same level of specificity as the topic sentence. Subordinate sentences further develop the topic sentences.

Paragraphs that cover similar ideas should be grouped together. For example, if you were writing a detailed article about the appearance of a car, it may be wise to group together paragraphs describing the car's exterior. A separate set of paragraphs could describe the interior.

Sometimes words such as *additionally, furthermore, also, of note, moreover,* and *finally* help a writer transition from one idea to another and make the paragraph more coherent. (For more on transitions, see the sidebar in Chapter 11.)

PARALLELISM. Parallelism refers to the ideal that prose be balanced in structure and syntax. Watch for parallelism in series, lists, and predicates.

> **FAULTY PARALLELISM:** Every morning, Aaron likes drinking an espresso, to take a long walk, and the early-edition newspaper.
> **BETTER:** Every morning, Aaron likes to drink an espresso, take a long walk, and read the early-edition newspaper.

PERFECT TENSE. The perfect and progressive tenses are used to indicate continuing action, and they come in past, present, and future forms.

> **PRESENT-PERFECT TENSE:** Kyle has spent much of his time with his dog. **This sentence means that starting at some point in the past and continuing to the present, Kyle has been in the company of his dog.**
>
> **PRESENT-PROGRESSIVE TENSE:** Kyle has been walking his dog. **This sentence means that Kyle started walking his dog some time ago and continues to walk his dog.**
>
> **INACCURATE:** Kyle has erased his answer. **For most people, erasing an answer takes a few seconds. There's no need for the perfect tense.**
> **BETTER:** Kyle erased his answer.

INACCURATE: Karen has been scratching off the lottery ticket. **For most people, scratching off a lottery ticket takes a few seconds. There's no prolonged process and no need for the progressive tense.**

INACCURATE: He was dropping dead. **For all people, dropping dead is instantaneous; consequently, there's no need for the progressive tense.**
BETTER: He dropped dead.

In addition to implying a process, use of the perfect or progressive tense also connotes immediacy and a sense of action. When used in article writing, they can energize your prose.

OKAY: The House finally passed the gun-law legislation.
LIVELIER: The House has finally passed the gun-law legislation.

POSITIVE FORM. When your writing is framed in positive—as opposed to negative—form, it's surprising how much more forceful your ideas become. The easiest way to frame your writing in positive terms is to consider replacing all expressions that contain the word *not*.

UNCLEAR AND WORDY: He is not honest.
BETTER: He is dishonest.

UNCLEAR AND WORDY: This book is not long.
BETTER: This book is short.

POSSESSIVE. In *The Copyeditor's Handbook*, Amy Einsohn does a good job of explaining the various schools of thought regarding how to form possessive nouns. In his book *The Glamour of Grammar*, Roy Peter Clark wisely advises to "let your ear help govern the possessive apostrophe." In my opinion, the following guidelines are sufficient.

EXAMPLE	POSSESSIVE
common or proper noun ending in a consonant (including *s*)	John's dog, Charles's hobby, mice's cheese, men's razors
exceptions (Biblical names and classical names)	Jesus' Apostles, Moses' teachings or Achilles' heel
plural common or proper noun ending in *s*	Smiths' dog, Jones' home, associations' guidelines
duration of time	one month's furlough, three months' furlough
group possession	Joy and Neda's online venture *Not* Joy's and Neda's online venture

Attributive nouns with plural head nouns can be written without an apostrophe. For example, "Department of Veteran's Affairs" is written "Department of Veterans Affairs." Additionally, you don't need to use an apostrophe when writing plural acronyms, dates, and abbreviations such as GPAs, PDAs, 1940s, and *P*s and *Q*s.

PREFIXES. A prefix such as *anti-, pre-,* or *post-* is combined with the root word to form one word (*pretest* or *postwar*). Sometimes a prefix is linked to the root word using a hyphen. There are several instances in which you should hyphenate prefixes. First, except with the words *cooperate* and *coordinate,* hyphenate if the prefix ends in the same vowel that the root word begins with and if failing to do so would cause confusion (*anti-insurgence, co-opt,* and *pre-election*). Second, and as suggested by the *AP Stylebook,* hyphenate words that denote occupation or status (*co-founder* and *co-worker*). Third, hyphenate when the prefix is attached to a proper noun (noun beginning with a capital letter) or number (*anti-German* or *pre-1929*). Fourth, hyphenate when the prefix is *self-* (*self-interest*). Finally, when the hyphenated word has a different pronunciation and meaning (*un-ionized* as opposed to *unionized*). When in doubt, check the dictionary.

When a prefix begins or ends in a vowel and the root word begins with a consonant, no hyphen is needed (*asexual* or *hydrophilic*).

PREPOSITIONS. Do you bid *on* a house or bid *for* a house? You bid *on* a house. Usually it's apparent which prepositions follow a verb, but when in doubt, check the dictionary. Additionally, *Words into Type* has a good, albeit truncated, list of which prepositions follow which verbs.

PRONOUNS. Pronouns exist in three forms: nominative, objective, and reflexive.

PRONOUN TYPE	EXAMPLES
nominative-case pronouns	*I, you, he, she, who, it, we, they*
objective-case pronouns	*me, you, him, her, whom, it, us, them*
reflexive pronouns	*myself, yourself, himself, herself, ourselves, yourselves, themselves*

Nominative-case pronouns serve as subjects that precede a verb. They can also take the form of a predicate nominative that follows a conjugation of *to be.*

> Marissa and I went to the picnic.

> The loser is he.

Objective-case pronouns are direct objects, indirect objects, or objects of a preposition.

> I like him. **The pronoun *him* is the direct object.**

I made her an omelet. **The pronoun *her* is the indirect object, and *omelet* is the direct object.**

I am mad at him. **The pronoun *him* is the object of a preposition.**

Reflexive pronouns are used when the subject and object are the same. The word *myself* can be edited from a sentence without loss of meaning.

OKAY: Ellen is particularly hard on herself.

WORDY: Ali is happy and I, myself, am happy.
BETTER: Ali and I are happy.

UNADVISABLE: Natalie took Benny and myself to the movies.
BETTER: Natalie took Benny and me to the movies.

Yesterday, I ate forty-three bananas by myself. **A case can be made for use of *myself* in this sentence. Here, *myself* functions as an intensive pronoun that emphasizes an amazing feat—eating forty-three bananas in one day.**

SEMICOLONS. Many people misuse semicolons. There are only two major reasons to use them: when joining two independent clauses that share a similar idea or when separating elements of a series that have internal punctuation.

I am a movie aficionado; I go to the cinema twice a week.

I like working with at-risk youth; consequently, I volunteer at the community center.

I wrote the business office a formal letter; thus, I aired my concerns.

Whenever Joanna goes to the market, she buys a mixed bag of apples, oranges, and lemons; a mixed assortment of muffins, bagels, and croissants; and a bouquet of roses, daisies, and lilies.

SIGNPOSTING. Signposting is when an author tells the reader to refer to certain parts of the text for further information. Too much signposting is bad practice and indicates that the text is poorly organized.

UNADVISABLE: As discussed in paragraphs 14 and 18, hiring practices were closely monitored.

SPACING. I was taught to type on a typewriter. On typewriters, it's customary to leave two spaces after a period or colon and one space after a comma or semicolon. Today, some people suggest that this convention is outdated because it's easier to discern spacing on computer screens; consequently, these people contend that there only needs to be one space after any punctuation mark, including periods and colons. Ultimately, you can space however you want; just make sure you're consistent. (In other words, choose one spacing convention and stick to it.)

SPLIT INFINITIVES. Despite what some traditionalists may insist, it's fine to split infinitives.

> Roy demanded to see the results quickly.

> Roy demanded to quickly see the results. **This split infinitive has a similar meaning, and** *quickly* **is closer to** *see,* **the word it modifies.**

> Roy quickly demanded to see the results. **Note that the meaning of this sentence is different from the first two examples.**

SQUINTING MODIFIER. A squinting modifier is a misplaced adverb that could modify either noun that surrounds it. Fix a squinting modifier by moving the adverb.

> **UNCLEAR:** The convenience store that sells video games occasionally hires new employees. **Does the convenience store occasionally sell video games or occasionally hire new employees?**
> **CLEAR:** The convenience store that sells video games hires new employees occasionally.

SUBJECT-VERB AGREEMENT. Whenever I need to decide whether a verb is singular or plural, I first discount all prepositional phrases and then ask myself whether the *intended* subject is singular or plural. I also remember that *anybody, each, either, every, everybody, everyone, nobody,* and *neither* are usually singular.

> Everyone takes a book. **This sentence means that each individual person takes a book.**

> Each ~~of the politicians~~ has a college degree. **Discount the prepositional phrase "of the politicians," and it's apparent that** *each* **denotes each individual politician and takes a singular verb.**

> Fifty students ~~in line~~ need sandwiches. **Discount the prepositional phrase "in line." This sentence means that fifty students as a group need sandwiches.**

Despite the misconception that the word *none* is derived from *no one*, according to *Fowler's Modern English Usage*, it actually comes from the Old English word *nan*, which means "none" or "not one," and ever since the time of King Alfred, *none* has taken on singular or plural forms depending on context—apparently including information conveyed by surrounding prepositional phrases. In short, the word *none* may take a singular or plural verb.

> None of the teachers understands the problem.

> None of our problems are serious.

In many cases, when two subjects are linked by words such as *and* or *in addition to*, the subject becomes plural and takes a plural verb.

> A rabbit and chipmunks live in my backyard.

When two subjects are linked by *or*, the verb agrees with the second subject. If one subject is singular and one subject is plural, place the plural subject second.

> A rabbit or chipmunks live in the enclosure.

Finally, subject-verb agreement also affects pronoun choice. A singular verb takes a singular pronoun.

> **WRONG:** Each of the male wrestlers took their book.
> **RIGHT:** Each of the male wrestlers took his book.

SUBJUNCTIVE MOOD. Using the subjunctive can get complicated, and in much writing its use is optional. Personally, I worry about the subjunctive in one instance: conditional expressions of uncertainty or desire.

When using the subjunctive, the dependent clause usually begins with *if*. Furthermore, the subjunctive is often constructed using *were* instead of a conjugation of *to be* and is followed by a modal auxiliary verb or helping verb such as *would* or *could*.

> **OKAY:** If I was king, I would seek revenge.
> **BETTER:** If I were king, I would seek revenge. **Because this sentence is a conditional expression, the dependent clause (starting with *if*) should be placed in the subjunctive—in this case *were* is the alternative form of *was*.**
>
> **OKAY:** If I was rich, I would be happy.
> **BETTER:** If I were rich, I would be happy.

TENSE. It's been my experience that people needlessly fret over tenses in their writing. (For more on tense, check out my discussion of the historical past and historical present in Chapter 11.) Mostly, I decide which tense to use based on logic. As Strunk & White advises, when recounting an anecdote or summarizing a series of events in some literary work, make a logical decision and stick to one tense. If you choose the past tense, use the past-perfect and past-progressive tenses to describe continuing actions. If you choose the present tense, use the present-perfect and present-progressive tenses to describe continuing actions.

TIME. To many readers, the most confusing thing about times is whether 12 A.M. is noon or midnight or 12 P.M. is noon or midnight; consequently, it's best to spell out this information.

> I waited for the bus between 12 noon and 2 P.M.
> I was at the party between 12 midnight and 4 A.M.

When specifying time zones, be sure to properly refer to daylight savings time or standard time.

> I will call Walter on January 5, 2012, between 4 P.M. and 6 P.M. EST.

> I will call Walter on July 5, 2012, between 4 P.M. and 6 P.M. EDT. **Note that in July we use daylight savings time (DT).**

UNIVERSITY NAMES. When writing, be sure to write out a university's name in its entirety; failing to do so can lead to confusion. If you're unsure, check the university's website.

> **UNADVISABLE:** Harry was a college student at U of M. **Does this mean the University of Michigan or the University of Minnesota?**
> **BETTER:** Harry was a college student at the University of Michigan.

VERB CHOICE. The process of choosing the right verb is a great opportunity to flex your vocabulary skills. Although many verbs have similar meanings, even the smallest difference can change a sentence's meaning. For example, *walk, meander, saunter,* and *traipse* all refer to different types of walking.

> **OKAY:** The political cartoonist changed President Bush's appearance.
> **BETTER:** The political cartoonist transmogrified President Bush's appearance.

VOCABULARY. Many people believe that "big" words are preferable to "small" ones. This belief is wrong. Never use a "big" word when a "small" or more readily understood word will suffice. If you're interested in looking up slang that's too fresh for a formal dictionary entry, try the crowd-sourced website Urban Dictionary.

If you're unsure what a word means, check for its meaning in a dictionary. A useful online aggregator of dictionary definitions is www.onelook.com.

Dictionaries can be categorized as prescriptive or descriptive. A prescriptive text like *Webster's New World College Dictionary* presents language as it "should" be and is preferred by adherents to the *AP Stylebook*. In other words, most big news organizations like this prescriptive text. A descriptive text like the *Oxford English Dictionary* (OED) catalogs language and presents what "could" be.

It's important to note that no reference text is complete; consequently, on its website, the *AP Stylebook* recommends the following sources.

> First reference for spelling, style, usage, and foreign geographic names: *Webster's New World College Dictionary, Fourth Edition*, Wiley, Hoboken, N.J. Other references for spelling, style, usage, and foreign geographic names: *The American Heritage Dictionary of the English Language, Fourth Edition*, Houghton Mifflin Company, Boston (and) New York *Concise Oxford English Dictionary, Eleventh Edition*, Oxford University Press, *Oxford Webster's Third New International Dictionary of the English Language*, unabridged, Merriam-Webster, Springfield,

Mass. *National Geographic Atlas of the World, 8th Edition*. National Geographic Society, Washington, D.C.

(Because the above quotation exceeds four lines of text, it's imperative to use a *block quote* or quotation with left and right indentations.)

If you plan to use a synonym for a word, check your thesaurus. Sometimes synonyms are useful because they break the monotony of repeating the same word on several occasions. Keep in mind, however, that if you need to repeat the same word because no other word will suffice, that is acceptable.

I've noticed that some "big" words are becoming increasingly popular among writers. Although I try to steer clear of big words, I always look up the big words I come across in my reading, and I list them in my own "hit parade," or vocabulary list.

Understanding the derivation of words can help you better remember the meanings of words. For example, the word *chiasmus* describes the relationship between two clauses where parallel structural elements are inverted or reversed. Consider the following example of chiasmus from *The Gospel of Matthew*: "So the last will be first, and the first will be last." Chiasmus is derived from the Greek word *chi* or *X*. Note that the letter *X* is drawn using inverted structures.

Now consider another derivation that sheds light on an English term borrowed from French. The term *pied-à-terre* means "feet to ground." English speakers have appropriated this expression to mean a second or temporary lodging often intended for travelers or those with their "feet to [the] ground." If a woman lives in Upstate New York but frequently travels to New York City on business, regular lodging in the city—an apartment or condominium that she owns—can be called a *pied-à-terre*.

WEBSITES. Never before has technology affected language as it does today, and web addresses are often included in writing. According to the *AP Stylebook*, when referring to specific web addresses (URLs), start with "http://" followed by the rest of the address. Many writers, however, find that including "http://" before a website is clunky and redundant. Simply referring to a web address by its proper name (BuzzFeed, Mashable, or Twitter) or with the digital prefix "www." is easier and sufficient.

When referring to a website that's a company, refer to it by its official name. Go to the website, and read how the company representatives refer to it. For example, Facebook is referred to as Facebook, not Facebook.com, and Google is referred to as Google, not Google.com.

WHITE SPACE. White space is a writer's friend. For clarity, titles, tables, or lists should be separated by white space.

WORD USAGE

AWHILE OR A WHILE. The word *awhile* is an adverb meaning "for a time." The expression *a while* is used as the object of a preposition and is a noun.

> **WRONG:** I haven't seen you in awhile.
> **RIGHT:** I haven't seen you in a while.
> **RIGHT:** I thought awhile.

AMPERSAND (&). Unless already part of a proper noun, avoid using the ampersand symbol (&) in your prose.

> **WRONG:** I like peanuts & chocolate.
> **RIGHT:** I like peanuts and chocolate.
> **RIGHT:** I like peanut M&Ms.

ABOUT. *About* is an imprecise word. Whenever possible, try to replace *about* with a more specific expression of quantity. Note that sometimes it's okay to use *about* when rounding off numbers.

> **UNADVISABLE:** About twenty years ago, the Berlin Wall fell.
> **OKAY:** In 1989, the Berlin Wall fell.
>
> **OKAY:** About 400,000 people attended the rally—that's the population of Miami!

ACCIDENT. According to the public health community, it's best to avoid the term *accident* when referring to injury. Instead, consider specifying the method of injury.

> **UNADVISABLE:** Clay's hand was amputated after an accident with a chainsaw.
> **BETTER:** Clay's hand was amputated after he was injured by a chainsaw.

ACCORDING TO. Don't use *according to* when referring to speech. Use *according to* only when referring to written material.

> **UNADVISABLE:** According to Tom, "These pills are expired."
> **BETTER:** Tom says, "These pills are expired."
> **BETTER:** According to Tom's letter, he's "doing well."

One hint about the use of *according to*: I've found that when I'm interviewing for articles, some sources like to answer by e-mail. (As discussed in this book at length, whenever possible, it's always best to interview by phone or in person.) Obviously, this practice is different from a verbal interview. Use of *according to* enables the writer to allude to the sometimes frowned on practice of receiving quotations via e-mail without blatantly acknowledging this fact.

AFFECT AND EFFECT. According to the *AMA Manual of Style*, when used as a verb, *affect* means to "have an influence on" and *effect* means "to bring about or to cause." When used as a noun, *affect* means "an immediate expression of emotion" (as opposed to *mood,* which is a sustained state of emotion) and *effect* means "result."

> During his last term in office, Senator Thorn affected our nation's economic recovery. **This sentence means that Senator Thorn had an influence on economic recovery.**
>
> During his last term in office, Senator Thorn effected our nation's economic recovery. **This sentence means that Senator Thorn caused the economic recovery.**

> I wonder what the effects of his treatment were.
> The patient's affect is depressed.

Of note, the term *side effect* is mostly used to refer to secondary consequences of prescription medication. Furthermore, a side effect can be either good or bad whereas an adverse effect is bad. Diseases don't have side effects; they have symptoms.

AFTERWARD AND AFTERWARDS. Although these words are synonymous, according to *Fowler's Modern English Usage,* the use of *afterward* is typical of North American English speakers and *afterwards* is typical of British English speakers.

AGE OR AGED. According to the *AMA Manual of Style,* the adjectival form *aged* is preferable to the noun form *age.*

> **UNADVISABLE:** Hector is a teenage boy.
> **BETTER:** Hector is a teenaged boy.

AGGRAVATE AND IRRITATE. There's some disagreement about the use of *aggravate* and *irritate.* Some texts, including Strunk & White, hold that a person *aggravates* a situation and *irritates* another person and that one person can't *aggravate* another.

What's definite is that in a medical context, according to the *AMA Manual of Style,* these words have different uses. *Aggravate* (or *exacerbate*) is used when an existing condition is made worse. *Irritate* is used when explaining an excessive reaction to a stimulus.

> **RIGHT:** Harry is with diabetes, and this condition was aggravated by poor diet.

> **RIGHT:** Paul's eye was irritated by the foreign body.

ALLUSION AND ILLUSION. An allusion is a reference to something and is often used when indicating a literary device. An illusion is a false image.

ALMOST. According to Strunk & White, *almost* is preferable to *most.*

> **UNADVISABLE:** Most every member of the fan club went to the movie theater for the film's midnight showing.

BETTER: Almost every member of the fan club went to the movie theater for the film's midnight showing.

ALTERNATE AND ALTERNATIVE. *Alternate* means every other item in a series or one of two possibilities. When switching back and forth between items, use *alternate*. *Alternative* means any other option.

The colors alternate between red and green.

Are there any alternatives to this option?

ALTHOUGH AND THOUGH. When used as adverbs, *though* and *although* are synonymous. But when choosing a conjunction, it's best to use *although* because *though* is considered an informal abbreviation.

UNADVISABLE: Though Astor withdrew his donation, he still supported the charity.
BETTER: Although Astor withdrew his donation, he still supported the charity.

OKAY: Much of the wilderness in this area remains undeveloped. The tract in question, though, is scheduled for development.

ALTHOUGH AND WHILE. Many writers assume that *although* and *while* are synonymous. Most of the time they are. Nevertheless, as explained by *Fowler's Modern American Usage* and Strunk & White, *while* has a temporal connotation and should be used with expressions of time. *Although* is used with expressions of contrast. This distinction should be kept in mind in the rare instances when meaning between the two words can be confused.

UNCLEAR: Oscar ran to the store while Francis walked to the store. **This sentence is confusing because of its implied meaning. First, this sentence could mean that Oscar ran to the store at the same time that Francis walked to the store. Alternatively, this sentence could mean that, for whatever reason, Oscar ran to the store and Francis walked—denoting a contrast of two elements. (Maybe Francis is lazier than Oscar.)**
BETTER: Although Oscar ran to the store, Francis decided to walk to the store because he was tired.
BETTER: Because Oscar ran to the store, he arrived before Francis.

AMONG AND BETWEEN. Although there is some debate about this topic, *among* is best used when choosing from more than three options. *Between* is used when choosing from two options.

UNADVISABLE: Darren had to choose among having a cup of coffee or having a cup of tea.

BETTER: Darren had to choose between having a cup of coffee or having a cup of tea.

UNADVISABLE: Darren had to choose between chocolate, vanilla, or strawberry ice cream.
BETTER: Darren had to choose among chocolate, vanilla, or strawberry ice cream.

ANTICIPATE AND EXPECT. Strunk & White makes the distinction that *anticipate* and *expect* are not synonyms. The word *anticipate* connotes that the subject is not only expecting an outcome but preparing for it, too.

UNADVISABLE: I expect that it will rain, and that's why I'm bringing along a raincoat.
BETTER: I anticipate that it will rain, and that's why I'm bringing along a raincoat.

ANYONE AND ANY ONE. When *any* and *one* form one word, the resulting expression *anyone* refers to any person or thing. When *any* is separate from *one*, as in *any one*, the resulting expression refers to one specific person or thing. The same holds true for *somebody*, *everybody*, and *nobody*. You'll find similar explanations in Strunk & White, *Words into Type*, and other texts.

APT. According to the *AMA Manual of Style*, the word *likely* can be used to refer to both people and objects, but *apt* should only be used when referring to people.

INCORRECT: An earthquake is apt to occur near the fault line.
CORRECT: An earthquake is likely to occur near the fault line.

CORRECT: George is likely to disagree.
CORRECT: George is apt to disagree.

ASSUME AND PRESUME. According to the *Merriam-Webster Dictionary*, *assume* and *presume* can both mean to "expect" or "suppose." A person can assume or presume without proof: A person who *assumes* may feel no need for proof, and a person who *presumes* may simply have no proof. Another difference is that the word *presume* can mean to expect or suppose in an overly confident manner.

WRONG: Based on the results, the researchers assumed that the two variables were correlated. **Because the researchers have proof, the researchers didn't "assume" anything.**
WRONG: Based on the results, the researchers presumed that the two variables were correlated. **Again, there's proof; thus, "presume" is the wrong word.**
OKAY: Based on the results, the researchers concluded that the two variables were correlated.

OKAY: Based on the results, the researchers inferred that the two variables were correlated.

ASSURE, ENSURE, AND INSURE. These verbs are different and should be used in different circumstances. One person may *assure* another of something, and by *assuring* this second person, the first person makes the second person confident or calms any anxiety. If a person were to *ensure* something, then that person would be making a guarantee. Finally, in the United States, *insure* is a financial term.

I assure you that nothing bad will happen.

He ensured his cardiovascular health by exercising daily.

I just insured my house with State Farm.

AT AND IN. When referring to a specific place, the preposition *at* will often suffice. When indicating that a person or thing is a part of or inside a place, use the preposition *in*.

His mailing address is at 1500 Baker Street.

The hotel is in Boston.

Tony is a graduate student in Dr. Felix's lab.

ATTAIN AND OBTAIN. Although *attain* and *obtain* have similar meanings, *attain* connotes a sense of accomplishment and *obtain* connotes monetary value.

Fred attained the rank of Eagle Scout. **Fred worked hard to receive this distinction.**

Fred obtained a nightstand. **Fred bought the nightstand.**

BELIEVE AND FEEL. When writing about facts, it's best to avoid using words like *believe* and *feel*. *Believe* connotes a religious sense, and *feel* connotes emotion.

UNADVISABLE: The researchers believe that their findings are statistically significant.
UNADVISABLE: The researchers feel that their findings are statistically significant.
BETTER: The researchers suggest that their findings are statistically significant.

COMPARE TO AND COMPARE WITH. Many writers have trouble with the proper use of these expressions. Use *compare to* when comparing two items, objects, or things that are measured using different units or scales. Use *compare with* when comparing two items, objects, or things that may be measured in similar units.

The glow of her skin can be compared to the moon. **Except in a figurative sense, a person's skin is nothing like the moon.**

Kilograms can be compared with pounds. **Kilograms and pounds are both units of weight.**

COMPLEMENT AND COMPLIMENT. The verb *complement* means "to add to." The verb *compliment* means "to praise." These verbs also have noun forms.

COMPLIANCE AND ADHERENCE. Although these terms are medical, they are creeping into the everyday lexicon. According to the *AMA Manual of Style*, when referring to a prescribed or advised treatment regimen by a physician or other health-care provider, the term *adherence* is preferred to *compliance*. The term *compliance* can be construed as patronizing or judgmental.

COMPRISE. The word *comprise* means "embrace." A larger entity *comprises* smaller elements.

> **WRONG:** Three bedrooms, three bathrooms, a living room, dining room, and kitchen comprise the house. **This statement is incorrect because the smaller elements (bedrooms, bathrooms, and so forth) don't comprise a larger entity (the house).**
> **CORRECT:** The house comprises three bedrooms, three bathrooms, a living room, dining room, and kitchen.

The expression *comprised of* is never correct.

CONNOTE AND DENOTE. Both of these words indicate meaning. *Denote* means the exact or dictionary meaning. *Connote* refers to implied meaning.

CONTINUOUS AND CONTINUAL. I once read a short autobiographical blurb written by a Columbia journalism alumnus who didn't realize the difference between *continuous* and *continual*. *Continuous* refers to an event or occurrence that is uninterrupted. *Continual* refers to an event or occurrence that is repeated.

> In the wake of 9/11, Homeland Security became a ubiquitous and continuous presence.

> Professor Samuel Avery continually encouraged his students to complete the written exercises.

COUNTLESS. *Countless* is an imprecise word and when possible should be replaced with a specific quantity.

> **INCORRECT:** Armando has written countless articles on aerospace engineering.
> **CORRECT:** Armando has written 112 articles on aerospace engineering.

> **OKAY:** There are countless stars in the sky.

DIE OF. People don't die *from* a disease, they die *of* a disease.

INCORRECT: Manuel died from pneumonia.
CORRECT: Manuel died of pneumonia.

Furthermore, especially in scientific contexts, avoid using words like *pass on* or *passed away* as synonyms for the more accurate *die*.

INCORRECT: Dr. Hassan's patient with diabetes passed away.
CORRECT: Dr. Hassan's patient with diabetes died.

Finally, in scientific contexts, it's also best to avoid the word *sacrifice* when *killed* is a better and more accurate alternative.

INCORRECT: The researchers sacrificed six mice.
CORRECT: The researchers killed six mice.

DIFFERENT THAN AND DIFFERENT FROM. Refrain from using *different than,* and instead use *different from.*

INCORRECT: Adam's intentions are different than Samantha's intentions.
CORRECT: Adam's intentions are different from Samantha's intentions.

DUE TO. In this day and age, you will be hard-pressed to find anybody who will object to using *due to* as a substitute for the expression *attributable to*. Years ago, some traditionalists insisted that *due*—an adjective—shouldn't be followed by *to*—a preposition. Instead these purists argued that *due* can only be followed by a noun or pronoun. Although this argument is interesting, it's dated.

Another dated objection deals with the use of *due to* in a prepositional phrase without a verb. For example, "Partially due to his pride, he could admit no wrong."

E.G. This expression is Latin for *exempli gratia*. It means "for example," and when writing, it's best to spell out *for example* rather than use *e.g.* Note that *e.g.* may be used in charts, lists, tables, figures, and so forth.

INCORRECT: I like hip-hop artists (e.g., Kanye West, Kid Cudi, and Lupe Fiasco).
CORRECT: I like hip-hop artists (for example, Kanye West, Kid Cudi, and Lupe Fiasco).

EMIGRATE AND IMMIGRATE. The word *emigrate* means to leave a place or country in order to live in another place or country. The word *immigrate* means to enter a country or place from another country or place. When thinking about the *e* in *emigrate,* remember the *e* in *exit*. (I picked up this mnemonic from Paul Brians' text *Common Errors in English Usage*.)

ENTITLE AND TITLE. When referencing a paper, book, or other piece of writing, use *title,* not *entitle*. Although you will find dictionaries that argue otherwise, *entitle* sounds too stuffy for daily use.

UNADVISABLE: The article in *JAMA* written by Dr. Pietro Manuel Ferraro and colleagues is entitled "History of Kidney Stones and the Risk of Coronary Heart Disease."

CORRECT: The article in *JAMA* written by Dr. Pietro Manuel Ferraro and colleagues is titled "History of Kidney Stones and the Risk of Coronary Heart Disease."

-ESQUE. The suffix *-esque* means "in the style of," and when used sparingly, it can add variety to your writing.

The movie's dark and insidious themes were Kafkaesque.

ETC. This expression is Latin for *et cetera*. It means "and others," "and so forth," or "and more." As with *e.g.*, it's best to spell out one of these terms rather than writing out *etc.* Of note, like *e.g.*, *etc.* may be used in charts, tables, lists, figures, and so forth.

When used, the term *etc.* should never be preceded by *and* because *and etc.* is a redundant expression.

Similarly, when introducing a list that starts with *including, such as,* or *for example,* don't end the list with *and others, and so forth,* or *and more.* Doing so is redundant.

REDUNDANT: I like some of Adam Sandler's movies—for example, *Billy Madison, Happy Gilmore, 50 First Dates*, and so forth.

CORRECT: I like some of Adam Sandler's movies—for example, *Billy Madison, Happy Gilmore*, and *50 First Dates*.

REDUNDANT: I like some of Adam Sandler's movies, including *Billy Madison, Happy Gilmore, 50 First Dates*, and so forth.

CORRECT: I like some of Adam Sandler's movies, including *Billy Madison, Happy Gilmore*, and *50 First Dates*.

EVOKE AND INVOKE. According to *A Dictionary of Modern American Usage* by Bryan A. Garner, *evoke* is derived from a Latin word *evocare* which means "to call forth" whereas *invoke* is derived from the different word *invocare* which means "to call upon."

Don't use the word *evoke* when calling on a higher power or citing an authority.

WRONG: The pastor evoked the name of God on several occasions.
RIGHT: The pastor invoked the name of God on several occasions.

WRONG: I evoke the power of this office to declare you husband and wife.
RIGHT: I invoke the power of this office to declare you husband and wife.

FARTHER AND FURTHER. These words have different meanings. The word *farther* is used for distance. The word *further* is used for time or degree. A tip: The words *farther* and *away* are both spelled with *a*'s. Furthermore, you would ask, "How *far* away are you?" not, "How *fur* away are you?"

WRONG: Joey lives further away from the stadium.
BETTER: Joey lives farther away from the stadium.

WRONG: Aaron is farther along in school than Belinda is.
BETTER: Aaron is further along is school than Belinda is.

FEVER AND TEMPERATURE. *Temperature* and *fever* are not synonyms. A fever is an above-normal body temperature. (Although what constitutes a "normal" human temperature is disputed, it's been popularly defined as 98.6° F.)

WRONG: Katie is sick; she has a temperature.
RIGHT: Katie is sick; she has a fever.

FEWER AND LESS. *Fewer* is used with quantities of nouns that can be counted. *Less* is used with uncountable nouns.

INCORRECT: The express lane at the supermarket is for ten items or less.
CORRECT: The express lane at the supermarket is for ten items or fewer.

CORRECT: Hillary is less impressed with my performance.

FOREIGN LANGUAGES. When writing, don't use words from foreign languages unless you have no other choice. In other words, only if there are no suitable English-language equivalents.

WRONG: I told the cop that I was driving *la limitation de vitesse.*
CORRECT: I told the cop that I was driving the speed limit.

FRAME AND SPIN. When used as synonyms, *frame* and *spin* both connote changing the public's perception of a person, issue, or thing. *Spin*, however, carries a negative connotation and sounds more sinister or corrupt.

GENDER AND SEX. According to the *AMA Manual of Style*:

> Sex is defined as the classification of living things as male or female according to their reproductive organs and functions assigned by chromosomal complement. *Gender* refers to a person's self-representation as man or woman, or how that person is responded to by social institutions on the basis of the person's gender presentation. *Gender* is rooted in biology and shaped in environment and experience.

GREAT BRITAIN AND THE UNITED KINGDOM. If you're British, you come from Great Britain, which is an island made up of England, Scotland, and Wales. The United Kingdom is made up of Great Britain and Northern Ireland. English people come from England.

HISTORIC AND HISTORICAL. These terms have different meanings. *Historical* refers to a period in history whereas *historic* implies importance.

HOPEFULLY. Traditionalists have problems with the word *hopefully* in prose; they claim the word serves as an ambiguous modifier. Today, use of the word *hopefully* probably confuses few readers. However, it's still best to avoid the word in your writing.

> **UNADVISABLE:** Hopefully, I will attend the Super Bowl. **Do I hope to attend the Super Bowl, or do I attend the Super Bowl with hope (perhaps for my favorite team)?**
> **BETTER:** I hope to attend the Super Bowl this year.

HYPOTHESIS AND THEORY. A hypothesis is an explanation for something. The key point, however, is that this explanation can be tested in some way. If you were to guess that if we continue to burn off fossil fuels all the glaciers will melt within the next one thousand years, there's no way to test that. You won't be around in a thousand years, so you're not suggesting a hypothesis. If you were to propose that during the next five years increased consumption of fossil fuels is correlated with ocean warming, you could probably test this hypothesis.

Problems also arise when people start thinking that *hypothesize* and *theorize* are synonymous. In science, a theory has been rigorously tested and is almost fact. The overwhelming scientific consensus favors a theory. For example, nowadays nearly all scientists accept the theory of evolution. Many people, however, use *theorize* to mean proposing an idea or conjecture—a conjecture that is neither theory nor, in some cases, even testable.

> **WRONG:** I theorize that many of the world's glaciers will melt by the year 2150.
> **OKAY:** I predict that many of the world's glaciers will melt by the year 2150.

I.E. This expression is Latin for *id est* and means "that is" or "in effect." As with *e.g.* and *etc.*, it's best to avoid this abbreviation in your prose. Like *e.g.* and *etc.*, *i.e.* may be used in charts, lists, tables, figures, and so forth.

IF AND WHETHER. The word *if* is used with conditional statements, and the word *whether* is used to introduce alternative possibilities.

> **WRONG:** Johnny is unsure if he will come to your party. **Because Johnny may or may not come, the word *whether* should be substituted for the word *if*.**
> **RIGHT:** Johnny is unsure whether he will come to your party.
>
> **OKAY:** If Johnny were to come to your party, he would bring sandwiches. **This sentence is conditional (and subjunctive).**

The term "whether or not" is redundant and *whether* is sufficient.

> **REDUNDANT:** I was unsure whether or not my brother received the package.
> **BETTER:** I was unsure whether my brother received the package.

IMPLY AND INFER. According to *Merriam-Webster*, shortly after World War I, and for the first time in centuries, some people started objecting to the synonymous use of *imply* and *infer*. Consequently, it's best to use *infer* with facts and *imply* with suggestions.

> **UNADVISABLE:** Based on the results, the researchers implied an association between the two variables.
> **BETTER:** Based on the results, the researchers inferred an association between the two variables.

> **UNADVISABLE:** I hope that my absence doesn't infer that I disagree with your plans.
> **BETTER:** I hope that my absence doesn't imply that I disagree with your plans.

INFLAMMABLE. The words *inflammable* and *flammable* are synonyms. Nevertheless, some people contend that the *in-* in *inflammable* means "not" and *inflammable* means "not flammable." This argument is silly. The *in-* in *inflammable* is not a prefix. In fact, *inflammable* is derived from the Latin word *inflammare,* which means "to burn."

INTO AND IN TO. The word *into* is a word that has a singular meaning whether it denotes entry, insertion, introduction, or so forth. The word *into* commonly answers the question, "Where?" The expression *in to* is different from *into*. With *in to*, even though *in* and *to* happen to be close together, they retain different meanings.

> I walked into the meeting.

> Heather came in to check on us.

Of note, *onto* and *on to* are similar to *into* and *in to*.

INTER- AND INTRA-. *Intra-* means "within," and *inter-* means "between." Hint: Think of an *interstate* highway as running between two states.

INTERNATIONAL. The word *international* involves two or more nations. The words *global* or *worldwide* mean throughout the world.

IT'S AND ITS. The contraction *it's* is short for "it is." The word *its* is possessive. Similarly, the contraction *who's* is short for "who is" and the word *whose* is possessive.

> It's very difficult to pass this test.

> The robot lowered its arm.

> Who's at the door?

> Whose tie is this?

JAIL AND PRISON. Although you'll find locked doors in both jails and prisons, they're different types of places and serve different functions. According to the Bureau of Justice Statistics, although prisons and jails differ from state to state, in general, jails are usually short-term holding facilities where inmates are awaiting trial, sentencing, or both. Jails also hold inmates who are sentenced to terms of twelve months or fewer and are typically guilty of misdemeanors. Jails are usually operated by local governments. Prisons, however, hold felons and inmates serving sentences longer than a year. Prisons are administered by a state government or the federal government.

LIE AND LAY. The difference between these two words is the bane of most writers. In their present tenses, *lie* is an intransitive verb that doesn't take a direct or indirect object whereas *lay* is a transitive verb and takes a direct or indirect object.

An easy way to remember the difference between *lie* and *lay* is that *lie* has a long *i* like the verb *recline*. The word *lie* is often followed by the preposition *down*. The verb *lay* has a long *a* like the verb *place*.

> Esther lies down on her pillow-top mattress.

> When in court, Judge Ellington lays down the law.

Here's a table that lists the conjugation of each verb in different tenses:

PRESENT TENSE	PAST TENSE	PAST PARTICIPLE
lie	lay	lain
lay	laid	laid

Of note, the past tense of *lie* is *lay*. (I know how confusing this distinction is.)

> Esther lay down on her pillow-top mattress just before the repairman arrived.

LIKE AND AS. I always associate the overuse of *like* with Valley girls and Valley speak from the early 1980s. Consequently, I am wary of using the word *like* too many times in my writing. Furthermore, some parsers of language take issue with *like* being used as a conjunction. In *The Copyeditor's Handbook*, Amy Einsohn suggests that *like* could be used when comparing nouns, and *as, as if,* or *as though* could be used when comparing two expressions that include verbs.

> Alligators are like crocodiles.
> Alligators appear as if they evolved similarly to crocodiles.

MEDIATION AND MODERATION. These terms are popular among psychologists and have different meanings. If something *mediates* a cause-effect relationship, it has a direct effect.

For example, the amount of money that I have available in my bank account may mediate my ability to purchase a new computer. If something *moderates* a cause-effect relationship, it has an indirect influence. For example, a compelling advertisement may moderate my choice of a computer.

MODEL. The term *model* means many different things in different situations. For example, a mathematical model is different from a climate-change model, medical model, or model airplane. If you find yourself employing this word, you may want to first check its use with an expert.

NAUSEOUS AND NAUSEATED. These terms aren't synonyms. The term *nauseated* is used to describe the feeling of nausea. The term *nauseous* refers to something that induces nausea or something that makes you want to vomit.

> **WRONG:** I feel nauseous.
> **RIGHT:** I feel nauseated.
>
> **RIGHT:** Some people find sailing nauseous.

NORMAL, ABNORMAL, POSITIVE, AND NEGATIVE. It's unclear to characterize a person's health status using these terms. More specifically, the results of a physical examination, diagnostic test, or laboratory test should not be described as *normal, abnormal, positive,* or *negative.* The writer must be specific when referring to such results.

> **UNCLEAR:** Brenda's routine physical examination was normal.
> **CLEAR:** Brenda's physical examination indicated that she was in good health.
>
> **UNCLEAR:** Antoine's HIV test was negative.
> **CLEAR:** Antoine's HIV test was negative for the HIV virus.

ON AND UPON. Many times the word *upon* can be replaced with the word *on.*

> **OKAY:** This story is based upon real events.
> **BETTER:** This story is based on real events.

Note, however, that the expression "once upon a time" is a completely acceptable way to start a fairy tale or bedtime story!

OVER, MORE THAN, AND UNDER. When expressing quantity, it's best to use *more than* rather than *over.*

> **UNCLEAR:** Belinda worked over thirty hours. **Did Belinda work for a period that lasted thirty hours or for more than thirty hours?**
> **CLEAR:** Belinda worked more than thirty hours.
>
> **UNADVISABLE:** All participants in the study were over thirty years old.

BETTER: All participants in the study were more than thirty years old.

Similarly, it's best to avoid using *under* with expressions that specify age, quantity, speed, and so forth.

UNADVISABLE: All participants in the study were under fifty years old.
BETTER: All participants in the study were less than fifty years old.

PART AND PORTION. According to *Garner's Modern American Usage* by Brian A. Garner, these terms have different connotations. *Part* means a "constituent piece of the whole" whereas *portion* means "a share." A portion is literally or figuratively "cut away" from the whole.

Baguio is located in the northern part of the Philippines.

Alice took her portion of the profits.

PARTIALLY AND PARTLY. These words are not always synonymous. According to Strunk & White, *partially* is used when referring to "condition or state." *Partly* is used to distinguish a part from the whole.

Jesse was partially discouraged by his poor test grades.

My basement is partly submerged in water.

PAST AND LAST. Oftentimes *past* and *last* can be used synonymously without confusing the reader. Occasionally, a writer needs to consider whether to use *last* due to its implied meaning.

UNCLEAR: Did you go to Great-Grandpa Joe's last birthday party? **This statement could imply that Great-Grandpa Joe has since died.**
BETTER: Did you go to Great-Grandpa Joe's past birthday party?

PATIENT, PARTICIPANT, SUBJECT, AND CASE. According to the *AMA Manual of Style*, it's best to avoid referring to people as *patients* unless it's apparent they are being treated by a health-care provider.

WRONG: John is a seventy-five-year-old glaucoma patient.
RIGHT: John is seventy-five years old and with glaucoma.

Similarly, a person who is involved in a research study should be referred to as a *participant,* not a *subject.*

UNADVISABLE: There were 103 subjects in the clinical trial.
BETTER: There were 103 participants in the clinical trial.

Finally, never refer to a person with a disease or condition as a *case.*

WRONG: An eighty-five-year-old case with gout.
RIGHT: An eighty-five-year-old man with gout.

PHYSICAL FITNESS, PHYSICAL ACTIVITY, AND EXERCISE. Within the realms of epidemiology, public health, medicine, kinesiology, and sport psychology, the terms *physical fitness, physical activity*, and *exercise* should have very different meanings. The distinction among these terms is useful to the journalist who wants to remain accurate when reporting and is clearly defined in a paper titled "Physical Activity, Exercise, and Physical Fitness: Definitions and Distinctions for Health-Related Research," which was written by Dr. Carl J. Caspersen and colleagues.

Caspersen and colleagues write, "Physical fitness is a set of attributes that are either health- or skill-related. The degree to which people have these attributes can be measured with specific tests." For example, agility, balance, cardiorespiratory endurance, muscular strength, flexibility, coordination, and body composition are components of physical fitness.

"Physical activity is defined as any bodily movement produced by skeletal muscles that results in energy expenditure. The energy expenditure can be measured in kilocalories. Physical activity in daily life can be categorized into occupational, sports, conditioning, household, or other activities." In other words, any physical movement that burns off kilocalories (Calories)2 is considered physical activity, whether it be gardening, changing a tire, baking a cake, typing at a computer, or even sleeping.

"Exercise is physical activity that is planned, structured, repetitive, and purposive in the sense that improvement or maintenance of one or more components of physical fitness is an objective." In other words, exercise is a type of physical activity where the person performing the exercise is intentionally trying to improve or maintain physical fitness. For example, if you were to run on a treadmill or lift weights with the explicit goal of maintaining or improving your physical fitness, you are performing exercise.

Sometimes the difference between physical activity and exercise is subtler. For example, if you're digging holes because you're a gardener by profession or you are walking to the store because your car broke down and you need milk for your toddler, then you are performing physical activity. Because such tasks must be completed, these actions are typically performed as efficiently as possible. But if you're helping a friend dig holes instead of going to the gym to lift weights or you are walking to the store because you want to "slim down," then your acts are purposeful and meant to benefit components of your physical fitness.

PHYSICIAN TERMINOLOGY. When referring to a physician, it's best to use the word *physician,* not *doctor,* so as not to confuse a person with a medical degree (MD) or doctor of osteopathic medicine (DO) with someone who has a PhD, DDS (doctor of dental surgery),

---

2 According to the *AMA Manual of Style*, kilocalories and Calories (with a capital *C*) are synonymous, and each term refers to the "large calorie." The "small calorie" or calorie (with a lowercase *c*) is a fraction of a large calorie; one thousand calories make up a kilocalorie, or Calorie. If you picked up a snack and read on its nutrition label that it has two hundred Calories, it has two hundred kilocalories, not two hundred calories.

or so forth. On a related note, a psychiatrist is a medical doctor with a medical degree. A psychologist with a doctorate has a PhD.

Occasionally, using the word *physician* instead of *doctor* may sound like an affectation. For example, people go to the "doctor's office" for medical treatment.

A physician may be referred to as a *health-care provider, practitioner,* or *clinician* but so may a nurse practitioner, physician assistant, nurse, psychologist, and so forth; consequently, it's best to refer to a physician by specialty.

> **UNCLEAR:** Ben Thomas is a health-care provider.
> **BETTER:** Ben Thomas is a psychiatrist.

PRECISION AND ACCURACY. Although the scientific terms *precision* and *accuracy* both deal with measurements, they have different meanings. The term *accuracy* refers to how close a measured value is to the actual value of whatever's being measured. For example, if a ruler were to measure the length of a shoe to be 12.09 inches, and in actuality the shoe were 12.1 inches, then the ruler would be pretty *accurate.*

The term *precision* refers to the reproducibility of measured results. For example, if a thermometer measures a person's temperature at 100.3° F every time it's used, then it would be *precise.*

Of note, a test or measurement can be precise but inaccurate. The converse can also hold true: A test or measurement may be accurate but imprecise. For example, if a thermometer were to measure 100.3 every time it's used, but a person's actual temperature is 104.0, then the thermometer would be precise but inaccurate.

PREVENTIVE AND PREVENTATIVE. Although these terms are synonymous, *preventive* is preferable.

PRINCIPAL AND PRINCIPLE. When used as an adjective, *principal* means "main" or "most important." When used as a noun, *principal* refers to a position like a high school principal or, in the case of a loan, the more substantial part of the money (as opposed to interest, which should be less substantial). The word *principle* is used as a noun and means a "fundamental belief."

PUT ON AND PLACE ON. According to the *AMA Manual of Style*, people are *prescribed* medication, not *put on* or *placed on* medications.

> **WRONG:** Allison was put on metformin.
> **RIGHT:** Allison was prescribed metformin.

SEXUALLY TRANSMITTED INFECTION AND SEXUALLY TRANSMITTED DISEASE. In medical circles, *sexually transmitted infection* is a better alternative for *sexually transmitted disease.*

SIGNIFICANT. The word *significant* takes on different meanings in different contexts. *Statistical significance* means that research results are accounted for by something other than chance. Scientists hope that the results of their studies are statistically significant. In everyday parlance, *significant* is synonymous with *important* or *meaningful*. When writing about science and research, be careful when using the word *significant*.

> **UNCLEAR:** The results from the most recent study were significant.
> **OKAY:** The results from the most recent study were statistically significant.
> **OKAY:** The results from the most recent study were important.

SINCE. The word *since* can be used in expressions of time (temporal expressions) or expressions of causality. Some people argue that *since* should only be used with expressions of time, but as pointed out by Paul Brians in *Common Errors in English Usage*, ever since the fourteenth century, the word has also meant *because*.

Oftentimes, whether *since* is referring to time or causality is understood and causes few problems for the reader. When it's unclear whether time or causality is referred to in a sentence, restructure the sentence for clarity.

> **UNCLEAR:** Since I subscribed to Netflix, I don't rent DVDs anymore. **Did I stop renting DVDs because I subscribed to Netflix or ever since I subscribed to Netflix?**
> **BETTER:** Ever since I subscribed to Netflix, I don't rent DVDs anymore.
> **BETTER:** Because I subscribed to Netflix, I don't rent DVDs anymore.

SPEAK TO AND SPEAK WITH. The expression *speak to* (or *talk to*) implies that one person is lecturing another. The expression *speak with* (or *talk with*) implies that two people are having a conversation.

SUBSTANCE ABUSE AND SUBSTANCE DEPENDENCE. These psychiatric terms have different meanings and are distinct. According to *Kaplan & Sadock's Synopsis of Psychiatry*, "People cannot meet the diagnosis of substance abuse for a particular substance if they have ever met the criteria for dependence on the same substance."

The term *substance abuse* means use of the drug (alcohol, marijuana, cocaine, and so forth) has interfered with a person's life. For example, if a person exhibits *substance abuse*, they may have had legal troubles or troubles at work, school, or home on account of the drug. A person who exhibits *substance abuse* may have used the drug while driving or operating heavy machinery—the results of which could be hazardous. The term *substance dependence* could mean that a person has increasing needs for the drug, cannot control his or her use of the drug, and suffers withdrawal when off the drug. In 1964, the World Health Organization suggested that the word *addiction* be substituted with the word *dependence*. Furthermore, the noun *addict* is pejorative.

SUGGEST. Although it's best to be concrete and definite in your writing, sometimes words with less force, like *suggest*, are useful. For example, when researchers publish their results in scientific papers, it's normally impossible for them to conclusively prove anything based on one study or even a compilation of studies. Instead their results *suggest* findings; consequently, when reporting on such findings, it's best to write *suggest*.

TOO. When the adverb *too* is used at the end of a sentence, it's a good idea to place a comma before it.

> Coach Ortega was happy that Ella won, too.

THAN AND THEN. These words have very different meanings. The word *than* is used with comparisons. The word *then* is used with time.

> **WRONG:** I am happier then I was before.
> **RIGHT:** I am happier than I was before.

> **WRONG:** Take a right at Main Street, and than go down Cedars Avenue.
> **RIGHT:** Take a right at Main Street, and then go down Cedars Avenue.

THAT AND WHICH. For many writers, understanding the difference between *that* and *which* is a cardinal professional achievement—at least it was for me. My understanding of the difference between *that* and *which* coincided with my transition from novice to professional writer.

That is used with restrictive clauses: The clause following *that* is integral to the meaning of the sentence.

> The beakers that are marked in blue contain deadly chemicals. **This sentence means that only the beakers marked in blue contain poison. (Maybe the beakers marked in green contain orange juice—who knows?)**

> The beakers which are marked in blue contain deadly chemicals. **This sentence means that the beakers contain deadly chemicals and happen to be marked in blue. Maybe some of the beakers marked in green contain deadly chemicals, too.**

When figuring out whether to use *that* or *which*, set off the clause in question with commas and see if the resultant phrase still makes sense.

> The beakers, which are marked in blue, contain deadly chemicals.

Sometimes it sounds awkward to use *that* more than once in a sentence; consequently, in certain circumstances, it's okay to follow *that* with *which*.

> **AWKWARD:** I borrowed the keys to that car that has a broken tail light.

BETTER: I borrowed the key to that car which has a broken tail light.

Of note, *who,* not *that,* should be used with people.

WRONG: He was angry at the men that mugged him.
RIGHT: He was angry at the men who mugged him.

(In 2012, Gotye had a hit pop song titled "Somebody That I Used to Know." The song was ubiquitous and seemed to blast from every car speaker across the United States and the world. It drove me crazy because I would have preferred it be titled "Somebody Who I Used to Know," especially since the title of the song also served as the refrain.)

UNIQUE. Only use the word *unique* when what you're describing is "one of a kind." Otherwise consider using words like *rare* or *distinct.* Never use the expression *most unique* because this phrase is redundant.

WRONG: Ernie's "Honus" Wagner baseball card is most unique. **Although rare and highly collectible, there are several "Honus" Wagner baseball cards in existence.**
RIGHT: Ernie's "Honus" Wagner baseball card is rare.

RIGHT: At 3,106 carats uncut, the Cullinan Diamond is unique because it is the world's largest diamond.

U.S. When used as a synonym for the adjective *American,* the abbreviation *U.S.* is acceptable. Otherwise spell out *United States.*

UNADVISABLE: Paul was born in the U.S.
RIGHT: Paul was born in the United States.
RIGHT: Paul is a U.S. citizen.

VERSUS. The abbreviations *v.* and *vs.* are short for *versus.* The abbreviation *v.* is used with court cases, and *vs.* is used in less formal situations. With everyday writing, the abbreviation *vs.* should be used sparingly—mostly in parenthetical expressions.

OKAY: I had tickets to the Dream Match (Oscar De La Hoya vs. Manny Pacquiao).

UNADVISABLE: Which toilet paper do you prefer, Charmin vs. Angel Soft?
BETTER: Which toilet paper do your prefer, Charmin or Angel Soft?

OKAY: *Roe v. Wade* was a landmark ruling made by the Supreme Court.

WAIVER AND WAVER. According to the *Merriam-Webster Dictionary, waiver* means to relinquish or abandon a privilege, right, or claim whereas *waver* means to teeter or "vacillate irresolutely between choices."

WHOEVER AND WHOMEVER. The word *whomever* is the objective case of the pronoun *whoever*. Of note, when the word is followed by a verb, it's proper to use *whoever* even if the phrase serves as an object.

> I will vote for whomever.
> I will vote for whoever wins the primary.

> I am surprised that whoever stole the money is a law student.
> Whoever took my notebook is in big trouble!

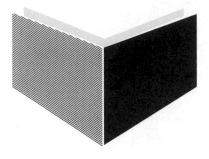

chapter 2

A BRIEF SURVEY OF JOURNALISM: ITS PAST, PRESENT, & FUTURE

Anybody who wants to write articles for newspapers and magazines would probably benefit from understanding the history of these media. This section examines the history, status quo, and possible future of the American newspaper and magazine industry. Although there's considerable thematic overlap between movements in both of these industries, for ease of comprehension, I will separately examine newspapers and magazines.

Before I begin, I want to stress a point: In this book I tout the use of premium encyclopedic sources rather than Wikipedia. Although Wikipedia is freely available and covers a gamut of topics, not all the information on this site is transparent, verifiable, or coherent. As a testament to the power of the "Old Media," I gathered much of the compelling historical information presented in this chapter and others from the *Encyclopaedia Britannica* (a wonderful secondary source to which I have a subscription).

NEWSPAPERS

The beginnings of the American newspaper are deeply tied to the revolutionary efforts of the United States. While America was still under colonial control, the British did their best to suppress the colonists' free speech. For example, in 1690, Benjamin Harris attempted to publish *Publick Occurrences Both Foreign and Domestick*—an attempt which was quickly thwarted by the governor of Massachusetts. Ultimately, this suppression of free speech served to fuel the democratic fervor felt by the founding fathers.

Early colonial editors were interested in both recording the history of the American Revolution for future posterity and supporting the efforts of the revolution. In 1719, Benjamin Franklin's older brother James helped establish the *Boston Gazette*, and the Boston Tea Party was planned in a back room of the newspaper.

The First Amendment guaranteed both freedom of speech and the press. Newspaper editors capitalized on this newfound freedom, and by the early 1800s, many newspapers became homes of political criticism and attack. Eventually, however, the focus of newspapers shifted from bolstering democracy to making money. In the 1800s, newspapers could be grossly divided into two categories: serious publications and commercially successful publications. At this time, newspapers started hiring journalists to create content. Many of these journalists became revered in their own right, and during the Civil War, some journalists who covered and helped prevent the atrocities of war were even more celebrated than the soldiers whom they covered.

Not all newspapers could afford to employ full-time journalists. Consequently, by 1851, Paul Julius Reuter—of Reuters fame—made use of the newly invented telegraph and set up shop in London, where he became a purveyor of information. Meanwhile, around 1846, a conglomerate of New York newspapers pooled their resources and shared content to cover the Mexican-American War. This conglomerate, initially called the New York Associated Press, eventually became the Associated Press. The Associated Press was instrumental in the introduction of syndicated news that was "objective" and reported on the bare facts.

Higher literacy rates, the telegraph, railroad transportation, and later inventions such as the linotype created an environment conducive to the growth of the American newspaper. In 1835, Benjamin H. Day published the first "penny press," *The New York Sun*, which fed the common consumer's hunger for human-interest stories.

Newspapers of this era did much to establish the foundations of modern journalism. In 1835, the *New York Herald* became the first newspaper to establish complete editorial independence from any political party. The *New York Herald* offered varied and entertaining content, including news and commentary packaged in sensationalistic form. In 1841, Horace Greeley established the *New-York Tribune,* which championed Greeley's cause: the abolition of slavery. Meanwhile, in rougher frontier areas, newspapers such as the *Chicago Tribune* presented sensationalistic content to entertain their more adventurous readers. And in the South, newspapers such as *The Atlanta Constitution* rebuilt civic consciousness in the wake of the Civil War. Probably the single most noteworthy event during the era occurred when the editor of *The New York Times* refused and later exposed a five-million-dollar bribe from Tammany Hall politician "Boss" Tweed. By doing so, *The New York Times* helped establish its general and enduring sense of journalistic independence and integrity.

By the 1890s, the prominence of the newspaper editor made way for the reign of the press baron. Press barons often owned many newspapers and cared more about making money through circulation and advertising than reporting "hard" news. Enter the age of yellow journalism.

The term *yellow journalism* specifically refers to the ongoing war for readership and economic dominance that occurred between New York City publishers Joseph Pulitzer and William Randolph Hearst. (Interestingly, the term "yellow" journalism is derived from an employment dispute that occurred between Pulitzer's *New York World* and Hearst's *New York Journal* that involved a cartoon titled "The Yellow Kid." Both newspapers ended up publishing the cartoon.) Both men came up in rough and rugged frontier territories and infused their publications with a dramatic sense of sensationalism. But whereas Pulitzer was idealistic and did his best to maintain editorial independence, expose wrongdoing, and ascribe to some ideals, Hearst would do anything to sell papers. Hearst even went so far as to make up news stories to rile the United States into a war with Spain over Cuba.

Arguably, the era of yellow journalism offered little in the way of social import. Nevertheless, its influence can still be felt in Internet, television, and print sensationalism. For example, in 2013, when the government of Cyprus threatened to confiscate money from citizen bank accounts, the media had a field day and played on people's fears. The sensationalistic media coverage caused people to make a run for the bank and to try to pull their funds. Furthermore, sensationalism changed modern print publication in meaningful ways. For example, the current use of banner headlines, colored comics, and plenty of illustrations is rooted in the practices of yellow journalism.

By the early 1900s, the era of yellow journalism died off and was followed by muckraking, an era of more serious journalism which exposed corruption and social hardship. Lincoln Steffens was an early muckraker whose 1904 book *Shame of Cities* examined corruption in government and instigated reform. During this period, publishers started to worry not only about the commercial success of their papers but also about their social importance. This change can be traced to two main developments. First, powerful publishers such as newspaper magnate Edward Scripps and Adolph S. Ochs of *The New York Times* made great efforts to distance themselves from the "bad" (yellow) journalism of the proceeding era. And second, the practice of journalism became more academic. Schools and societies of journalism started popping up, and along with a formal pedagogy came the sense that a journalist should serve the public interest.

Although objective and detached journalism remained popular throughout the Cold War, by the 1920s it started to become clear to newspaper editors and journalists that straight or objective reporting often meant little to audience members, especially when the paper reported on complex social, economic, and political developments. For example, in the wake of the Great Depression, readers needed help making sense of the New Deal.

Later, with fascism on the rise, readers needed help making sense of what was happening in Germany, Italy, and Japan.

In order to help the public understand what was going on in the world, newspapers started to analyze news, and the practice became known as interpretive journalism. Although there was a subjective element to the practice that required journalists and editors to take stands on issues, such stands were frequently grounded in ideology that most people deemed as democratic and morally correct. At first, newspaper editors and journalists tread lightly into the realm of making judgment calls on the news, but as the years proceeded, experts and scholars felt more comfortable with the practice, especially when reporting on national and international issues. (When reporting on local issues, newspaper journalists and editors were more hesitant to interpret anything—a practice that changed with the rise of civic journalism in the 1990s.)

A win for the practice of interpretive journalism came when the "traditionalists" at the *Journalism Quarterly*, an academic publication, denounced most newspapers of the 1940s for not interpreting and analyzing the news. It should be pointed out, however, that some traditionalists were unconvinced about the value of interpretive journalism and whether its practice crossed the line from interpretation to advocacy. In fact, an article in the *Nieman Reports*, another academic journal, likened the practice to editorial writing.

Despite lingering concerns about the practice of interpretive journalism, by the 1970s, most prominent publications, including the *New York Herald Tribune, Newsweek,* and *The New York Times,* had embraced the practice and used it to report civil-rights issues, the Vietnam War, and Watergate. (In many publications, interpretive journalism came to be labeled "news analysis.") Of note, interpretive journalism flourished when journalists and publishers started seeing the power of the practice to do good, especially when coupled with investigation and research. For example, Philip Meyer, a one-time correspondent with Knight Ridder newspapers, wrote the highly influential *Precision Journalism,* which relied on research and interpretation to expose crime.

By the mid- to late 1900s, the widespread popularity of interpretive reporting was one of two main changes within the realm of journalism and newspaper reporting. The era's other big influence was the New Journalism movement, which was rooted in the form of literary journalism championed by writers of bygone eras, including Stephen Crane, John Reed, John Dos Passos, and James Agee. The advent of New Journalism centered around 1960s counterculture, drugs, sex, and the Vietnam War.

Authors such as Truman Capote, Joan Didion, Norman Mailer, Hunter S. Thompson, and Tom Wolfe started writing nonfiction using narrative and creative-writing elements, including symbols, imagery, mood, and novel structures. In print (and in real life) these authors connected with their characters vicariously and also had unabashed points of view that reflected distinct worldviews.

In a 2001 article titled "'New' Journalism," Scott Sherman writes, "New Journalism hit its stride in the heady period of the 1960s. It was a generational revolt against the stylistic and political restraints of Cold War journalism, a rebellion against the drab, detached writing of the big-city dailies and the machine-like prose of the Luce magazines." Ultimately, the realization that journalism can incorporate storytelling elements influenced the writing of countless journalists. For instance, the influence of New Journalism is well evidenced in Jon Franklin's article "Mrs. Kelly's Monster," which won the inaugural Pulitzer Prize for feature writing in 1979. (You can find a copy of this article on Jon Franklin's personal website.)

The 1990s saw two waves of change in most newsrooms. The first involved structural changes. In a 2000 article titled "Reader Friendly," Carl Sessions Stepp writes, "Papers flattened management, knocked down turf walls, formed teams, and redefined titles."

The second wave of change during the 1990s involved a focus on civic or public journalism. Community issues became central to stories. Sources were members of the community and no longer only "elite" or expert. Divisive issues were either avoided or tackled with a perspective specific to the community. A circumspect sense of community sensitivity pervaded newsrooms and dictated which stories were printed. Decisions were no longer handed down from the highest editorial echelons and were instead made by consensus.

Interestingly, Stepp and others complained that the movement towards civic or public journalism felt forced and that many of the stories lacked interest and zest. Some stories seemed to pander to public interest. Furthermore, Adam Moss, the editor of *The New York Times Magazine*, lamented that new writers of the time lacked ambition and a sense of innovation—they needed to be told what to write.

By the mid-2000s, the Internet changed newsrooms once again. Online newsrooms started to merge with print newsrooms, and news was kicked out twenty-four hours a day. Major newsrooms also started dedicating space to television and multimedia studios. The highly technical aspects of reporting became an opportunity for journalists from Generation X and Generation Y (millennials) to prove their mettle. (Many of these younger journalists are "digital natives," which means they came of age when the Internet was in wide use and grew up using the Internet.) Many newspapers started producing news for the Internet and updating and analyzing the news in print.

Changes in newsrooms coincided with changes in the way news was reported. Self-publishing software made it easy for anybody to report news; consequently, we entered the age of citizen journalism. In 2000, Oh Yeon-ho, a media entrepreneur from South Korea, claimed that "every citizen is a reporter." Yeon-ho helped start the website OhmyNews, a crowd-sourced news site that by 2007 boasted fifty-thousand contributors from one hundred countries.

The rise of citizen journalists has proved appealing in times of turbulence. For example, in 2009, Iranian citizen journalists, who were engaged in protests following the presidential reelection of Mahmoud Ahmadinejad, took to the Internet to report news. Similarly, in 2010 and 2011, citizen journalism played a key role in the Arab Spring and helped unseat Egypt's Hosni Mubarak and Libya's Muammar Gaddafi.

Currently, a notable outgrowth of citizen journalism is "stunt" or "reality" journalism, most notably practiced by VICE Media, a Brooklyn-based company. Representatives from VICE are careful to avoid labeling themselves journalists. Instead they intend to stage newsworthy events in places that other media organizations are unlikely to visit and document the outcomes. VICE has documented civil war (and cannibalism) in Liberia, shopped for bombs in Bulgaria, and in 2013 set up a basketball exhibition game in North Korea featuring Dennis Rodman and attended by Kim-Jong un, the leader of North Korea. Furthermore, VICE has partnered with old media powerhouses including CNN and HBO. Though representatives from VICE don't claim to be journalists, they do disseminate information and to some extent interpret it. For example, after their "basketball diplomacy" stunt, VICE co-founder Shane Smith called for more "dialogue" between the United States and North Korea and claimed that fifty years of attempted diplomacy between the two countries has "failed."

Citizen journalists represent what author Clay Shirky calls the "former audience." These are audience members who transitioned into journalists. For readers, the rise of citizen journalism offers several advantages. News that is disseminated by citizen journalists is available as it happens and reflects the accounts of participants and other interested parties. Citizen journalism also allows the reader insights into news occurring in areas where the news is normally censored. Furthermore, the news and commentary spread by citizens is free. (It should be noted that even though this news is free, it doesn't necessarily mean that it's of poor quality or unverifiable. Many pieces at The Huffington Post, a highly regarded website that provides views on politics and current affairs, come from unpaid writers who are experts in their fields. The Huffington Post has helped facilitate popular citizen journalism campaigns such as OffTheBus.) The appeal of citizen journalism has won many admirers, including Jay Rosen, a prominent media critic who runs the website Pressthink, and Howard Fineman, editorial director at the AOL-Huffington Post Media Group.

Of this new breed of journalist, author Alissa Quart writes, "One need not be elite, expert, or trained; one must simply produce punchy intellectual property that is in conversation with groups of other citizens. Found Media-ites ["Found Media" is a term Quart uses which includes citizen journalists] don't tend to go to editors for approval, but rather to their readers and to their blog community. In many ways, they disdain the old models, particularly newspapers. ..."

Marc Cooper, director of digital news at USC Annenberg, points out that sometimes citizen journalists report news better than their professional counterparts: "Journalism is now a mix of professional and amateur. Sometimes the amateurs are much better than the professionals, and it's true in poker, too. There are professional poker players, and there are amateur poker players, and sometimes the amateurs kick your ass. Journalism is about storytelling. ... There's a lot of natural storytellers out there ... and there's a boatload of journalism students who get master's degrees and still can't tell stories."

In more philosophical terms, journalism has evolved toward the citizen journalist; citizen journalism is an undeniable attractor that inevitably became popular when technology allowed the audience to create and share news. As pointed out in the book *Blog!: How the Newest Media Revolution Is Changing Politics, Business, and Culture*, people have always been interested in expressing themselves and understanding what other citizens have had to say, whether it be in the form of cave drawings, colonial pamphlets, or nineteenth-century journals. Nearly fifty years ago, philosopher Jürgen Habermas envisioned a public sphere where democracy would flourish and people would engage in conversation, argument, and debate.

Historically, access to citizen input has been limited by the media machine, which has allowed only journalists to write for the public, with occasional input from the audience in the form of letters to the editor, reader feedback, or "voice of the reader"-type articles. (The Poynter Institute's EyeTrack studies suggest that such articles are among the most attractive to readers.) Nowadays, however, anybody with a basic understanding of journalism and a smartphone loaded with the necessary apps can produce compelling and engaging news.

Blaming citizen journalism for the downfall of modern journalism is like blaming biology for the evolution of eyesight. Much like citizen journalism, the development of visual organs is an undeniable attractor. Organisms of nearly every species have evolved eyesight independently because processing visual information is an efficient way to access information.

After speaking with dozens of experts and doing much research, I doubt that citizen journalism will undo the work of good professional journalists. Instead I think it will probably complement such work. Just as the development of radio, television, cable, and the Internet hasn't stopped people from reading printed material, news spread by citizen journalists won't take the place of work done by professional journalists. Most likely, people will treat citizen journalism as another taste available to their palates. For example, the next time an uprising occurs somewhere in the developing world, in addition to being able to follow the event on the radio, cable news, the AP wire, or some other professional news organization, people will also be able to read the work of citizen journalists on blogs and social-media sites.

The open spirit of crowd-sourced news and journalism will probably influence the bastions of traditional journalism in positive ways. "And perhaps," writes Alissa Quart, "some of the conventions of traditional newspaper and magazine writing that can make it rigid and bland will fade into the background. Maybe some of the best qualities of the blogs—directness and informality—will positively infect us."

The availability of free news and the rise of citizen journalism have threatened newspaper publishers, editors, and journalists. Nowadays engaging news that's up-to-the-minute is freely available, and this fact, combined with decreasing advertising revenues and decreased trust of conventional media, has put newspapers on high alert.

It's widely recognized that the newspaper business is in trouble. The late 2000s saw excellent general-interest publications, including the *Rocky Mountain News* and the print version of the *Seattle Post-Intelligencer,* go defunct. The Tribune Company, which owns the *Chicago Tribune* and the *Los Angeles Times*, was hocked for $8.2 billion and left in the hands of Sam Zell and Randy Michaels. Not only do these men care little about journalism—Zell half-joked he'd like a "porn" section in newspapers—they also helped bankrupt the company and managed to infuse this venerable institution with an alienating and offensive work atmosphere.

Although newspapers still remain the largest employer in the media sector, with 223,600 employees in March 2012, the ranks of many newspapers are thinning quickly. *Ad Age* estimates that in 2012 newspapers were cutting an average of 1,400 jobs a month. (Internet media is adding four hundred jobs a month and is the second-largest employer in the media sector, with 113,100 people in November 2011.) Even "The Grey Lady" (*The New York Times*) has seen hard times. It cut one hundred jobs in 2009, and that same year advertising revenue was down 30 percent. Overall, the Pew Research Center estimates that the newspaper industry has diminished by 43 percent since 2000.

According to the Alliance for Audited Media, between March 2012 and March 2013, daily circulation for 593 U.S. newspapers that reported results dropped by 0.7 percent. Sunday circulation for 519 newspapers that reported results decreased by 1.4 percent. Newspapers that reported their daily circulation numbers could include digital editions such as "tablet or smartphone apps, PDF replicas, metered or restricted-access websites ("paywalls"), or e-reader editions."

Some journalists and academics are predicting the imminent demise of newspapers. "Newspapers are going to be dead in the next few years because we don't need them," says Cooper. "We now have empowered ordinary people and experts and anybody who can get their hands on a smartphone ... we have empowered them with the ability to publish and bring to us perspectives that we can accept or reject. ... Thank God the monopoly on information has been broken. ... Thank God we have a diversity of content that's not controlled by a small group of priests that gets a stamp of approval from Poynter. ... We don't know yet what the new system or new order is ... but we do know that the old order has been destroyed."

Various experts suggest that in order to survive, most newspapers need to change in several ways. Based on my analysis, here's a composite (and attributable) list of various suggestions:

- Most print newspapers should focus on news analyses rather than breaking news. Breaking news is best left to news organizations with a major online presence.
- Newspapers should stop rehashing national and international news that is ubiquitous to online audiences. Instead they should focus on local news or adopting slants or angles

that focus on how national and international news affects local communities. In other words, they should interpret and analyze issues that relate to their own communities.

- Newspapers could shift away from general-interest topics and expand departments (like home improvement or home decor) that better coincide with the interests of their readers.

It should be noted that many people find this idea preposterous. First—and most obviously—specific-interest journalism is contradictory to the spirit of general-interest journalism ingrained into the purpose of many general-interest publications. And second, according to Peter Funt at *The Wall Street Journal*, general-interest journalism benefits the reader through the "rub-off" effect, and "the disappearance of what could be called the mental rub-off effect is partly to blame for the fact that many Americans are overloaded with information, yet seem to know less than ever about current events. As news packaging shifts from general interest to specific interest, it becomes difficult for mass audiences to rub up against the news—even if accidentally."

- It may also be a good idea for newspapers to stop chasing print readers and focus on online audiences. Of note, it's important for newspapers to realize that online readers differ from print readers in their tastes. For example, at the *Atlanta Journal-Constitution* (and probably most other newspapers), online readers like breaking news, interactivity, and multimedia whereas readers of print like watchdog issues, news analyses, and community news.
- Newspapers would be smart to embrace tablet-friendly editions of their publications. For example, iPads boast attractive interfaces that are user-friendly (they make reading news a "lean-back" experience). Some experts believe that—even if it does so on its own terms—Apple may be able to help the newspaper industry beat back its demise just as it did with the music industry.
- Newspapers and other news organizations should invest more resources into engineering and incorporate "targeted" advertising in their dissemination of news. In other words, lavishing free Twitter feeds on their readers wastes potential revenue.
- Newspapers could stave off their "new" media competition by forming partnerships. After WikiLeaks scooped *The New York Times* with its online posting of the attack on two Reuters employees by American forces in Iraq in April 2010, *The New York Times* apparently learned to respect its nimble, "breaking-news" competitor. In July 2010, *The New York Times* (and *The Guardian* and *Der Speigel*) paired with WikiLeaks to help present thousands of military documents concerning unexplained deaths and questionable tactics employed by the United States in the war in Afghanistan.

By 2012, there were numerous examples of new media working with "old" or legacy media to distribute content and improve (digital) revenue models. Notably, Yahoo signed a content partnership with ABC News, and Facebook created partnerships with *The Wash-*

ington Post, The Wall Street Journal, The Guardian, and others. Nevertheless, according to the Pew Research Center, such efforts are limited, and "the news industry is not much closer to a new revenue model than a year earlier and has lost more ground to rivals in the technology industry."

As we approached the second decade of the new millennium, many of these suggestions bore influence on publishers. More specifically, these suggestions point to digital publication and advertising as an answer to the problems newspapers are facing, and many publishers were eager to seize on digital dissemination as a panacea for their ailments. For example, *The Financial Times, The Wall Street Journal, The New York Times* and *The Washington Post* have developed pay models for digital readers. Additionally, in 2011, *The Guardian,* a leading British newspaper, started a U.S.-based, digital-focused newsroom. Finally, *The Washington Post* has developed some experimental news products, including Trove, a recommendation engine, and a social reader for Facebook. Of note, these companies have also invested heavily in mobile apps, online video, and Kindle Singles, which are works of long form journalism sold through Amazon.

Such efforts to move toward digital dissemination have been met with some success. According to the Alliance for Audited Media, in March 2013 digital editions accounted for 19.3 percent of newspaper daily circulation, an increase from 14.2 percent in March 2012.

It should be mentioned that when it comes to virtual news consumption, legacy media publications aren't the only game in town. Internet start-ups, including Digg, Flipboard, Pocket, and Feedly, have also tried their hands at the dissemination of news on the Internet. They have been experimenting with news aggregation, article recommendation, and bookmarking articles.

Many publishers, however, have realized that this digital bias may not be the answer to decreasing revenues, especially when it comes at the expense of daily print editions. For example, The Daily, a mobile app for the iPad published by Rupert Murdoch's News Corporation, shut down after two years. More significantly, in 2012 *The Times-Picayune* of New Orleans decided to focus on its website NOLA.com and produce a print edition only three days a week. This decision enraged residents of New Orleans and soon backfired. In light of lost advertising revenue, by May 2013 *The Times-Picayune* once again began publishing a daily newspaper.

Regarding this haphazard turn of events, David Carr, a media columnist at *The New York Times,* writes, "The industry tried chasing clicks for a while to win back fleeing advertisers, decided it was a fool's errand, and is now turning to customers for revenue. … Newspapers that have cut their operations beyond usefulness or quit delivering a daily print presence have suffered. The audience has to be earned every day. Newspaper publishing will never return to the 30 percent plus margins it once had, but some people believe there is a business model. Warren E. Buffett thinks that a 10 percent return is reasonable, now that sale prices have sunk."

Another problem with newspapers expanding their digital presence is cost. With declining revenue and circulation, many papers have struggled to pay for digital innovation while producing a daily news product that reflected their publication's fundamental values.

Ultimately, despite all such pontification, there currently exists no clear path for newspapers. We just have to wait and see how (and whether) newspapers find their way out of the financial quagmire that they all seem to be stuck in.

Newspapers Have New Owners

It used to be that many newspapers were large, publicly held companies. But with plummeting circulations and valuations, newspapers are no longer great investment opportunities, and some big newspapers are being sold to private investors. For example, in 1993, daily circulation at *The Washington Post* peaked at 832,332. By March 2013, circulation had dropped to a little more than half at 474,767. Consequently, in August 2013, the cash-strapped *Post* and many of its sister publications were sold to Jeffrey P. Bezos, the founder of Amazon, for $250 million—a price that would have been considered unfathomably low just a few years before. Similarly, in August 2013, The New York Times Company sold its New England Media Group, which includes *The Boston Globe*, for $70 million to a group of local investors—a sliver of the $1.1 billion the Times company bought *The Globe* for in 1993.

Although Bezos is a genius who revolutionized how people consume goods, he has no background in newspapers; thus his possible plans for the newspaper are rife for speculation.

Jenna Wortham and Amy O'Leary from *The New York Times* write, "No baggage—and deep pockets—means room to try new things. Might Mr. Bezos apply tech industry concepts like frictionless payments, e-commerce integration, recommendation engines, data analytics, or improved concepts for mobile reading?"

Wortham and O'Leary go on to write that when it comes to establishing relevance in a digital marketplace, "That is an area where Mr. Bezos might be primed to flex his expertise in analyzing data to find ways to engage a younger audience. In addition, Mr. Bezos's money could come in handy when it comes to adding to the newspaper developers, engineers, designers and others who could radically change the way the organization looks and runs."

If the past is any indication of future success at *The Post*, the culture and commerce of technology from which Bezos emerged has proven engaging and relevant among digital audiences. For example, Facebook, Google, and Twitter have defined online diversion among countless Internet users.

Without a doubt, if newspapers went extinct, they would leave a void. A quick search of any news website such as Newser or Gawker proves just how influential big newspapers are. The news aggregated on these websites comes from publications including *The New York Times*, *The Washington Post*, and *The Wall Street Journal*. Without these big publications, there would be no "free" news. Additionally, some argue that big newspaper publications adhere to principles and standards and that upstart websites have no obligation to adhere to journalism standards celebrated by their legacy-media counterparts. For example, WikiLeaks, which in all fairness is more activism than journalism, has been criticized for indiscriminately dumping anything on the Internet with little concern for the national security of the United States and its allies.

If newspapers were to disappear, the loss would also be felt at the level of civic journalism that focuses on the local news, issues, and concerns of specific communities. According to the Pew Research Center, "The civic implications of the decline in newspapers are also becoming clearer. More evidence emerged that newspapers (whether accessed in print or digitally) are the primary source people turn to for news about government and civic affairs. If these operations continue to shrivel or disappear, it is unclear where, or whether, that information would be reported."

If there has been a silver lining for the news industry, and more specifically newspapers, it's that in 2012 people increasingly immersed themselves in the news—even if by digital means. Thus there's still a hunger for the news, which means that if newspapers and other legacy organizations figure out how to better tap this growing interest, there may be hope. According to the Pew Research Center, "Mobile devices are adding to people's news consumption, strengthening the lure of traditional news brands and providing a boost to long-form journalism. Eight in ten who get news on smartphones or tablets, for instance, get news on conventional computers as well. People are taking advantage, in other words, of having easier access to news throughout the day—in their pocket, on their desks, and in their laps."

Worries about the fate of the printed word on newspaper broadsheet can be extended to the fate of all types of print journalism. Although there's no reason to make the foregone conclusion that audience attention is a zero-sum game and time spent surfing the Internet comes at the direct expense of print media, it's interesting to wonder whether, in the future, all printed media could be replaced by digital media. When I asked technology journalist and Contently co-founder Shane Snow for his opinion on the matter, he offered me a detailed answer that hinted at the future of journalism.

"I don't think that print will completely go away because there's still an appetite for it," says Snow. "Anything that's working in print or online is getting niche or more targeted. … Article writing for general interest is getting tougher and tougher—article writing for 'just the facts ma'am' news. There's this crazy technology that can have a machine write these human readable articles. Some of that is going to be replacing breaking news and crowd-reporting stories and Twitter-breaking news. The writers who are now doing that sort of work are going to shift to interviews in profiles that the robots and the crowd [can't do,] which in the long run is positive. … We can get more interesting insight. … It takes humans doing research and talking to people to distill rather than the crowd coming together or machines analyzing data. I think that's a trend we'll see.

"Feature content and entertainment, the whole lifestyle, sports [and so forth] are going to be fueled by a different economic engine ... in a lot of cases crowd funding ... people buying individual stories or brand sponsorship. I would predict, based on the science that we're seeing, that there will be a lot less crappy content out there on the Web because it won't be economically viable ... because computers and social media can leapfrog the bad stuff and get to the good stuff. There will be more of a market for more thoughtful content in the future."

Figure 2.1

MOVEMENTS IN JOURNALISM

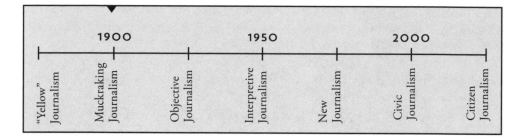

MAGAZINES

Aside from their physical characteristics, magazines have classically differed from newspapers in several ways. Some main differences between newspapers and magazines include tempo, function, and format.

Newspapers are often published daily, and the news carries immediacy. Magazines are printed as periodicals, and to a larger extent, their content is meant to be more evergreen. For example, when you're waiting at the dentist's office, you'll likely be given the choice of reading several magazines, many of which are several months old. Despite their older age, these magazines will appeal to many readers who would hardly notice their age because more than likely a Q&A with Oprah Winfrey will still be interesting a year after it was written.

The history of magazines also differs from the history of newspapers. The first American magazines could be considered "periodicals of amusement," as they printed uplifting and entertaining content. Additionally, in colonial America, the first magazines were pretty expensive and intended for a wealthy audience. Before 1800, around one hundred magazines were published in America, with the first being Andrew Bradford's *American Magazine* and Benjamin Franklin's *General Magazine,* both published in 1741. (Neither magazine lasted long.)

By the 1830s, magazines became less expensive and more affordable to the more general public. (Much like a penny was to be an attractive price for newspaper publishers of the era, a dime was the magic price for many early magazine readers. And because inflation didn't become an issue until the United States was taken off the gold standard in the 1940s, a penny or dime retained much of its same buying power for several decades.) These magazines focused on general amusement, improvement, enlightenment, and family issues.

Dime Novels and Pulp Magazines

By the 1880s, the emergence of "dime novels" and "pulp" magazines made magazines more affordable to mass audiences. These publications were shoddily constructed and took advantage of technological advances, including the creation of paper from wood pulp and improved mechanization of the printing process. Many of the stories in these publications dealt with adventure and science fiction thus capturing the imaginations of young boys. For example, however ersatz, Luis Senarens' *Frank Reade, Jr., and His Steam Wonder* (1884) drew from the work of Jules Verne. In general, the stories contained in such publications were poorly written and reductive. Furthermore, the content was often in poor taste and racist.

Shortly after the Civil War, the magazine business boomed in the United States—in large part due to the general expansion of the United States and favorable postage rates. Magazines of this era included *Harper's*, *McClure's Magazine*, and *Cosmopolitan*.

In the years following the Civil War, women's magazines became increasingly popular. Some of these magazines were staffed by women. For example, *Godey's Lady's Book*, which was first published in Philadelphia in 1830, employed 150 women to tint the fashion plates. *Ladies' Home Journal* was initially edited by Louisa Knapp Curtis, the publisher's wife. *Ladies' Home Journal* distinguished itself from other women's magazines by concentrating on serious issues geared towards its women readers. This foresight was rewarded, and its circulation soon reached a whopping 400,000. Another women's magazine of the era that broke new ground was *Good Housekeeping*, which was published in 1885 and presented a forum for consumer goods of the early twentieth century.

In addition to women's magazines, many literary and scientific magazines rose to prominence in the years following the Civil War. At the time, *literary* was a broad term that encompassed political, literary, and artistic content. Many of these magazines endure to this day, including the magazines eventually known as *Harper's Magazine* and *The Atlantic Monthly*, which from the beginning were of high quality and featured work by the likes of Ralph Waldo Emerson, Henry Wadsworth Longfellow, Oliver Wendell Holmes, and famous British novelists. Additionally, *Scientific American*, *National Geographic Magazine*, and *Popular Science* were all founded before 1900.

Many early magazines prided themselves on their literary value and wouldn't include advertising in their pages. Most notably, *Reader's Digest* proved particularly recalcitrant and resisted the pull of advertising money until 1955. By 1900, it became apparent that advertising meant big money for magazine publishers. For example, Cyrus Curtis, the publisher of *Ladies' Home Journal*, purchased the ailing *Saturday Evening Post* for $1,000 in 1897, and by 1922 this magazine was making $28 million a year. By 1947, 65 percent of magazine content was devoted to advertising.

Advertising had varied influence on the content of magazines. On one hand, early advertising advanced the visual appeal of magazines, made them more colorful, and improved the design. On the other hand, some magazine publishers were forced to grapple with a problem that still persists: editorial independence. For instance, in 1940, *Esquire* lost a piano advertiser after printing an article that recommended the guitar as a form of musical accompaniment. Other magazines such as *The Saturday Evening Post, Time,* and *The New Yorker* were pretty good at constructing a wall between advertising and content and making sure that advertising was "minimally offensive."

Women's magazines proved to be a preferred target for advertisers especially because, at the time, many women were the shoppers for their families. Advertisers were particularly drawn to magazines such as *Better Homes and Gardens*, which was first published in 1922 and printed the first service articles intended for homemakers. Interestingly, many women's magazines of the early to mid-1900s, including *Family Circle* and *Woman's Day,* were so intrinsically tied to advertising that they began as house organs for supermarkets.

One magazine that deserves special mention is *Reader's Digest,* which was founded by DeWitt Wallace in 1922. From the beginning, *Reader's Digest* distinguished itself by providing content that was condensed and derived from articles in other magazines. (With its condensed and derivative content, *Reader's Digest* could be called the Internet of its day.) It wasn't until 1933 that *Reader's Digest* started to publish its own original content, and, in an unusual reversal, would often sell longer pieces to other magazines in return for the rights to publish truncated versions. The editors at *Reader's Digest* were particularly interested in evergreen pieces and hoped their articles would have a shelf life of a year or longer. They demanded that their articles exhibit three cardinal characteristics: applicability, lasting interest, and constructiveness.

Lois Long as Lipstick

Using the *nom de plum* Lipstick, Lois Long electrified the pages of *The New Yorker* with her liberated and prurient prose. Her voice was prescient and could very easily find a welcome home today either in a print publication or on the Internet. In both her writing and life, Long flouted social and sexual mores and epitomized the 1920s flapper. She'd spend long nights drinking and dancing in speakeasies and would make her way into the office of *The New Yorker* in the wee hours of the night ready to write. Her readers loved her writing and so did Harold Ross, the first editor of *The New Yorker* and a prim and proper Midwesterner.

In the last three decades of the twentieth century, concerns about decreasing magazine readership—in particular younger readers—influenced the design and budget of many magazines. Between 1986 and 2002, the number of newsweekly readers aged thirty-five and below dropped from 44 to 28 percent. Moreover, the share of young long-form readers dropped from 39 to 20 percent.

In an article titled "Does Size Matter?" author Michael Scherer does a good job of explaining how magazines evolved during this period.

> No one can deny the visual sea change that has overtaken the magazine industry in the last three decades. Most magazines now resemble movie posters more closely than they do the dry pages of a book. They are filled with color, oversized headlines, graphics, photos, and pull quotes. The gray text page, once a magazine staple, has been all but banished by a new breed of art directors who have gradually made their way up the masthead.

At *Rolling Stone*, once an exemplar of long-form journalism, shorter articles and reviews supplanted longer features. The intention was for the reader to string together articles of interest to create their own narrative rather than depend on the narrative of a long piece. Increased choices in the media marketplace had made the reader more savvy and no longer dependent on singular authors to establish a point of view. Even magazines such as *Playboy* that still touted long-form journalism did their best to insert numerous access points into articles in order to attract readers.

It should be noted that despite what some people have claimed, there was no hard-core evidence that readers had become stressed for time, "attention-deficit," and averse to longer articles. During this time, interest in reading books was still strong, and between 1996 and 2002, the amount of time the average reader spent with all media increased by 45 minutes a day. It's just that with the emergence of the Internet and proliferation of cable television, audience members had more choices and became better informed.

Let's fast-forward to the magazines of today. Much like newspapers, magazines are figuring out how to straddle the divide between "Old Media" and "New Media." Although magazines have fared better than newspapers, they are dealing with many of their own issues. According to the U.S. Bureau of Labor Statistics, the size of the magazine industry fell 29 percent, from 156,212 in March 2002 to 111,126 in March 2012. Furthermore, there was a 13.3 percent drop in the number of establishments publishing periodicals, from a high of 9,232 in 2007 to 8,003 in 2012.

"There is mixed information out there about the state of the magazine industry," says Dr. David E. Sumner, professor of journalism at Ball State University. "Some sources I read say that overall magazine revenue is climbing slowly due to growth in digital ad revenue. Print circulation appears to be holding its own, especially among travel, epicurean, hobby, and leisure interest, and magazines aimed at affluent readers."

According to the Alliance for Audited Media, from the first half of 2012 to the first half of 2013, among the 390 consumer magazines that reported results, paid and verified circulation decreased by about 1 percent, single-copy sales decreased by about 10 percent, and paid subscriptions decreased by 0.1 percent.

In addition to conventional print format, many magazines have decided to take their publications online. (Some, like *Newsweek*, which merged with The Daily Beast, have decided to go exclusively online.) Publications such as *The New Yorker* and *Vogue* have digitized their archives and sold parts of them online. According to the Alliance for Audited Media, from the first half of 2012 to the first half of 2013, the number of digital editions increased from 1.7 percent of total circulation to 3.3 percent or 10.2 million copies.

But how are these magazines faring on the Internet? According to a 2010 study (survey) titled "Magazines and Their Websites" done by the *Columbia Journalism Review,* the answer is not well.

> Although those involved with magazines and websites have varying levels of knowledge and sophistication about their métier, it's fair to say that the proprietors of these sites don't, for the most part, know what one another is doing, that there are generally no accepted standards or practices, that each website is making it up as it goes along, that it is like the wild west out there.

To its credit, the study does a good job of suggesting how to improve the online presence of many magazines. First, magazines should devote staffs to online-only efforts instead of having print journalists shoulder both duties. Second, in light of the fact that the online components of many magazines meet less rigorous fact-checking and copyediting standards, institutional organizations such as the American Society of Magazine Editors, Magazine Publishers of America, and Online Publishers Association should come up with standardized guidelines and codes of conduct. Third, instead of concentrating on "paywalls" or paid online subscriptions, magazine publishers should concentrate on revenue generated from online advertising. Fourth, the content provided on these sites should incorporate more aspects of multimedia. Fifth, instead of relying on editorial decisions, privilege, and whim, online magazine content should be dictated by online traffic. Furthermore, more thought should go into cultivating the website's identity and argot. Simply dumping content from the print magazine onto the website may be a bad idea.

In his book *Here Comes Everybody,* Clay Shirky recounts how the introduction of the printing press in the fifteenth century didn't immediately improve the world. In fact, this revolutionary introduction was followed by years of confusion that wasn't resolved until well into the Renaissance. During these years, printers battled it out with scribes who once held a monopoly on the printed word. Similarly, the Internet is a relatively new invention. To expect that within a few years magazines and newspapers can effectively organize, change, and succeed is chimerical thinking.

Although publishing is no longer governed by economic or managerial concerns, a fact that puts print magazines and newspapers at a competitive disadvantage, print publishers still possess one main advantage. Large print publishers are complex organizations that have much experience disseminating swathes of information on an emergent basis. Such expertise lies outside the purview of most citizen journalists or smaller publication efforts and can serve as a foundation for future efforts.

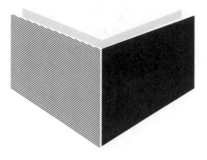

chapter 3

ROLES & RESPONSIBILITIES OF A JOURNALIST

To be a journalist is to be a raconteur … a teller of stories. It's an honorable calling that's remarkably egalitarian. In this day and age, any citizen can be a journalist. If you're reading this book and intend to write for the public, then you are a journalist, too.

In fact, the conception that a journalist belongs to some oligarchy is an arbitrary construct that grew out of scarcity. Before the advent of the Internet, access to publication was a commodity governed by a few gatekeepers who dictated what was newsworthy and codified the practice of journalism. Thanks to the Internet, this dearth of access has disappeared, and the distinction between "journalist" and "amateur" or "citizen" has eroded, too.

Consider the words of Clay Shirky from his book *Here Comes Everybody*.

> What seems like a fixed and abiding category like "journalist" turns out to be tied to an accidental scarcity created by the expense of [the] publishing apparatus. Sometimes this scarcity is decades old (as with photographers) or even centuries old (as with journalists), but that doesn't stop it from being accidental, and when that scarcity gets undone, the seemingly stable categories turn out to be unsupportable. This is not to say that professional journalists and photographers do not exist—no one is likely to mistake Bob Woodward or Annie Liebowitz for an amateur—but it does mean that the primary distinction between the two groups is gone. What once was a chasm has now become a mere slope.

Other journalists echo this sentiment. "Journalism has fortunately never been a licensed profession in the United States," says Marc Cooper, director of digital news at USC Annenberg. "In the U.S., you are a journalist if you have a job. … Journalists have created a number of professional and educational barriers to keep out the unwashed masses … to make sure that if you went to Columbia or Annenberg, and you get your master's degree or you got your job, then you're fine."

Because journalism isn't licensed and anybody with a soapbox—either printed, televised, or virtual—can claim to be a journalist, it's difficult to ascribe some code to all of these journalists. Nevertheless, organizations such as the Society of Professional Journalists, the American Society of News Editors, and the Poynter Institute advocate for certain ethical standards which include truth, accountability, accuracy, impartiality, fairness, and independence. (For a robust list of codes of ethics from various organizations and institutions, check out the Pew Research Center's website, www.journalism.org.) Instead of expounding on such positions, which tend to overlap and can be easily accessed and reviewed online, it's more fruitful to concentrate on specific issues as they pertain to journalists and the practice of journalism.

VERIFICATION

A casual observer of journalism may be tempted to define journalism as *the objective reporting of balanced truth*. Although this answer sounds great, it's inaccurate.

First, "truth" is a slippery subject riddled with semantics. Truth means different things to different people, and scholars can spend all day arguing differences between absolute truth, functional truth, and more. After all, one person's truth can be another person's conspiracy theory. For example, many people purport that the Bush administration extensively manipulated the media in order to start and perpetuate the War on Terror.

Second, journalists don't need to report in a balanced fashion, and doing so may result in false equivalency. If a journalist were always required to be balanced, editors would dedicate precious inches or pixels to discussing the perspective, feelings, and points of view of mass murderers such as Hitler, Idi Amin, Saddam Hussein, Pol Pot, and Joseph Stalin. In more mundane terms, many stories don't need to be balanced because the views of one side are pretty well accepted, and detractors represent a minority or are of inconsequential interest. For example, whereas once upon a time some people debated climate change, currently it's pretty apparent that humans have had a hand in warming the environment. Another example involves waterboarding, which is now indisputably recognized as a form of torture.

Third, like truth, objectivity is elusive and means different things to different people. "Most people," write Bill Kovach and Tom Rosenstiel in *The Elements of Journalism*, "think of objectivity in journalism as an aim, not a method." Although this statement may be true for "most people," it's definitely not true for all people, including Marc Cooper, director of digital journalism at USC Annenberg: "Objectivity is not being neutral. Being neutral means that you're not telling me anything. … 'It might be this or it might be that' … Objectivity is a process; it's not a product. … Objectivity means that you write or you report in good faith so that when you see things and experience things that contradict your pre-conception of something, you don't hide that."

Unlike the terms *truth*, *objectivity*, and *balance*, the terms *verification* and *transparency* mean much more to the practicing journalist. "The key to me is that journalism remains a discipline of verification," writes author and journalism scholar Roy Peter Clark in an e-mail interview. "You go out and find stuff out and check stuff out. You sort through it. Choose the stuff that is the most interesting and important. You share it with audiences for the public good. At the high end, you come to see journalism as a democratic craft."

When writing articles and acting as a journalist, make sure what you write is verified. Make sure to do your research, speak with the right sources, and never deceive or mislead your audience. Unless you're engaged in writing an opinion piece or reporting for some entity such as Fox News, which is much more concerned with the journalism of assertion, then you'll want to make sure that you're doling out as few unfounded inferences as possible. Kovach and Rosenstiel write, "In the end, the discipline of verification is what separates journalism from entertainment, propaganda, fiction, or art."

Fact-checking is the cornerstone of verification. Some publications such as *The New Yorker* employ a seasoned team of fact-checkers who completely deconstruct articles and even speak with sources who weren't interviewed for the story. But even if you have the luxury of a fact-checking team, you should still remain vigilant when reporting facts and attributing information. Fact-checking your own work can be tedious, but the repercussions of sloppy reporting far outweigh the long hours spent checking that your story is factually accurate.

One of the great benefits of the Internet is that bad reporting is quickly weeded out. If you fudge the facts, fabricate, or plagiarize, expect to get caught either with programs such as iThenticate or by the discerning eyes of astute editors and readers. Currently, worries about plagiarism and fabrication are plaguing newsrooms nationwide. Craig Silverman, author of the Poynter-hosted blog Regret the Error, aptly referred to the summer of 2012 as the "Summer of Sin." Transgressors read like a who's who and included Jonah Lehrer, Fareed Zakaria, NPR, *The Boston Globe*, *The Wall Street Journal*, Journatic, and more. Furthermore, reporting on some of the biggest stories of the year was botched, including the Aurora shooting, the anti-Islam video "Innocence of Muslims," and the Supreme Court's ruling on the individual mandate of the Affordable Care Act.

It should be remembered that in the current era of online news, it's hard to undo the damage done by news that's factually incorrect. Even if a news organization were willing to admit sloppy reporting and issue a retraction—which doesn't always happen—the retraction may mean little if the news has already buzzed into every corner of the world. There may be no way to reverse the damage. The individual reporter must carefully weigh the instinctual desire to "scoop" a story with the need for verification.

TRANSPARENCY

Transparency can come in different forms and is accomplished in different ways. For example, if you did your best to find the right sources and experts but still question their knowledge or hoped for more clarity, then inform your audience and mention this in your article. If you feel that one of your sources provided good information but may be biased, then inform your audience and mention this in your article. Another example of transparency involves conflict of interest. For example, if you're writing a restaurant review of an establishment for which you once worked, it's a good idea to—you guessed it—inform your audience and mention this in your article.

According to the Poynter Institute, transparency is defined in the following way: "We do our best to shed light on our own journalistic processes, explaining how and why we make sometimes controversial publishing decisions. We do our best to disclose relevant information that may have influenced or affected our publishing decisions."

Contently is a start-up content provider that delivers work to corporate clients, including companies such as Coca-Cola and publications such as *The Atlantic*. (I should mention that although I've never taken contract work from Contently, I am part of their network of writers.) Michael Howerton, a managing editor for their publication *The Content Strategist* and former editor at *The Wall Street Journal*, stresses the importance of transparency, especially when promoting corporate, publisher, or brand interests.

"Context is everything," says Howerton, "Everything has a context. If you try to fool somebody about context, that's not okay. With transparency, a lot of the ethical gray areas are okay to live in. People are savvy and a lot more savvy than they used to be. People understand that something can be good information and serve a dual (or joint) purpose. People are okay with that duality."

COHERENCE

At a forum sponsored by the Committee for Concerned Journalists, Bill Keller, former executive editor at *The New York Times*, once said, "Whether true objectivity is ever possible—I don't think that's what we're here for. … We strive for coverage that aims as much as possible to present the reader with enough information to make up his or her own mind. That's our fine ideal." Now consider the Scripps motto: "Give light and the people will find their own way." Both sentiments are similar and hint at *coherence*.

In order to provide the reader with options, it becomes the journalist's role to present the news in a coherent fashion. In his book *News Values*, Jack Fuller claims that coherence provides the reader with the full picture; facts out of context mean little. Furthermore, a journalist must use good judgment in order to put the facts in perspective.

Let's consider the case of two competing propositions brought to California voters in the November 2012 elections: Proposition 30 and Proposition 38, both of which aimed to create funding for schools. Proposition 30 was supported by Governor Jerry Brown and relied mostly on raising taxes paid by the rich in order to fund the initiative. In contrast, Proposition 38 was supported by a wealthy lawyer named Molly Munger and intended to fund schools by raising taxes paid by all citizens.

For voters, the propositions were confusing because they both benefited schools. The difference, however, was extremely important, especially to the middle class. With Proposition 30, the middle class would pay little extra to support schools. With Proposition 38, the middle class would pay much more to support schools. Enter the journalist, whose role it is to make the news coherent, make sense of the confusion, and thereby present options to the reader.

Within the greater context of journalism theory, the idea of coherence addresses a fundamental question that most if not all journalists have asked themselves: How does one practice journalism? The answer is that there is no one right way to practice journalism. Moreover, there is no one right way to write. Style, structure, input from experts, and so forth present options. They present coherence.

Let's digress for a bit and consider the general power of coherence. Johannes Kepler, a seventeenth-century German astronomer (and great mind) is arguably most famous for discovering the laws of planetary motion. During his career, he fixated on why the earth orbits the sun at 93 million miles away and thus attributed some special property to the number 93 million. In all reality, however, 93 million was essentially an arbitrary number. By focusing on 93 million, Kepler limited his purview—he limited the options or coherence of a much more universal explanation. A more coherent explanation didn't arise until Isaac Newton discovered the law of universal gravitation several years later—a law that dictated orbits in more encompassing terms.

Inevitably, every journalist or article writer runs into situations that require deep reflection on responsibilities, limits, and boundaries. Bigger questions confound even the simplest stories. When faced with a dilemma, I encourage you to remember the principles of verification, transparency, coherence, and so forth. I did my best to make this section widely relevant and acceptable to nearly every journalist—even those who take issue with terms that lack clear operational or functional definitions such as *social good*, *objectivity*, and *truth*. Read this section, and think about it; I believe that it will help you the next time you question your methods or objectives when writing a story.

AUDIENCE

The journalist's primary responsibility is to write for the audience. The journalist should work hard to provide insight and options to the audience and not pander to the source, editor, publisher, or advertisers. Unfortunately, the days of publishers making 20 to 40 percent margins are long gone, and many struggling newspapers and consumer magazines are under pressure to please their advertisers. In an ideal world, however, these concerns aren't the responsibility of the journalist.

It should be noted that the journalist's privilege to ignore commercial interests and maintain journalistic integrity doesn't mean that a journalist has the privilege to ignore editorial input that may be influenced by advertising interests. Ultimately, the editor has the final call on what goes into the publication, and it's best to let the editor be your guide.

It's also important to mention one caveat. Sometimes the interests of advertisers and audience members are so close that they overlap, and stories promote products either directly or indirectly. This convergence of interest is found with company magazines that serve a public-relations purpose. For example, in the November 2012 issue of *Costco Connection*, a magazine that's sent to all Costco members and serves an explicit public-relations purpose, the cover story titled "Online, and Beyond" describes how Costco has redesigned its consumer website to "make members' shopping experience easier and more efficient."

FALSE EQUIVALENCY

Many reporters and news organizations will try to equate two sides of an issue and report on a contrived middle. This desire for equivalency is particularly evident in political reporting. News organizations often feel that concentrating on a principally Republican or Democratic viewpoint would make them appear to be taking sides. The result is a centrist sense of reporting that many politicians, including Barack Obama, have complained about. A reporter should avoid falling into a trap of "false equivalency."

False Equivalency Can Equal Death

On a particularly concerning note, false equivalency in the media can have deadly repercussions. For example, medical researchers have proven that childhood vaccinations don't cause autism, and the original study published in *Lancet* in 1998 suggesting a causative link has been debunked as fraud (its lead author, Andrew Wakefield, was subsequently stripped of his medical license). Nevertheless, people who support this faulty association (most famously former Playboy Playmate Jenny McCarthy) are still given a platform by the media to spew inaccuracies. Tragically, the resulting false equivalency probably caused a decrease in immunization rates in the United States and Great Britain, which resulted in a U.S. measles outbreak in 2008.

One of the most disheartening examples of false equivalency involved President Barack Obama's status as a natural-born citizen. Throughout his first term in office and election campaign, President Obama had been dogged by the "birther" controversy. A small minority of Americans—most famously Donald Trump—questioned whether Obama was born in Hawaii and postulated that he was instead born in Kenya or Indonesia. Rather than dismissing this notion, which has been confirmed as both baseless and silly, many media organizations provided a soapbox for conspiracy theorists.

SOCIAL GOOD

Many journalists whom I've spoken with or researched believe that part of their job is to advocate for the public or social good, but others are hesitant to associate these terms with their work. Even journalism institutions are hesitant to completely support the idea of social good as some formal responsibility. For example, although the Poynter Institute supports "helpfulness," the help provided chiefly applies to other journalists and less to readers.

One main limitation that discourages some journalists from uttering the words "social good" in the same sentence as "journalist" probably stems from fear of being perceived or labeled an activist. Although these two responsibilities—journalist and activist—aren't mutually exclusive (Julian Assange of WikiLeaks claims to be an activist first and a journalist second), proselytizing change can damage a journalist's reputation and livelihood. More important, most journalists don't feel like activists.

Robert Irion, a science writer who heads up the science communication program at the University of California, Santa Cruz, says, "I haven't viewed myself as writing for the public good but rather as presenting science as a public enterprise … whether or not it's going to be a helpful piece of information or simply a neat thing … it's more a process of informing and revealing."

But even among those journalists who see their work as advocating a social good, what does this "social good" mean? Does it mean advocating for the beautification of a local park or literacy program? In other words, does the sense of social good felt by a journalist, editor, or editorial board necessitate that a story advocate for issues that have no life-and-death consequences?

Social good seems to play a bigger role in civic journalism, where journalists engage the community. But even with civic journalism, research shows that newspaper editors are more interested in creating dialogue than solving community problems.

Some journalists whom I've spoken with believe that it's their role to address injustices that physically and emotionally harm or repress others. But it's harder to figure out whether this advocacy for social good is an objective or a by-product of sensible reporting. Nevertheless, many stories do take a stand against such atrocities as genocide or human-rights violations. On a more local and national level, senseless violence, including mass shootings such as those perpetrated in Aurora, Colorado, or Newton, Massachusetts, are normally decried.

A journalist's sense of social good, especially in light of violent tragedy, may have deep psychological roots. Terror Management Theory postulates that when people are reminded of death, they act to protect themselves against this threat by adhering to cultural worldviews or perspectives. In part, doing so helps a person maintain self-esteem. Most cultures punish murderers and violent criminals; consequently, a journalist who is reporting on such tragedy and is thus reminded of it will likely censure the perpetrator.

Ted Spiker, an associate professor of journalism at the University of Florida and former editor at *Men's Health*, teaches his students to "inform, entertain, and inspire." With certain considerations, the *inspire* part of this mantra correlates well with the idea of social good.

"It certainly depends on the beat that you're covering," says Spiker. "If you're talking about a serious beat, it could be inspired in terms of getting out to vote because of something I [the writer] just learned. In terms of the health writer or health journalist, it could be to make a change in your [the reader's] daily routine or diet that makes you live longer. For a blogger, it might be to inspire somebody to hug their kids a little bit longer instead of flying off the handle for doing something stupid … it's all these little moments. … Maybe a word or two that got somebody to make their own lives better."

ENTERTAINMENT

Every day we're inundated with entertainment, and much of it comes in the form of infotainment. For example, on the website Buzzfeed, you'll find plenty of funny headlines, slideshows featuring cats in silly poses, and so forth. It's hard to characterize such work as journalism; nevertheless, journalism is meant to entertain. In fact, the role of a journalist as entertainer in addition to informer is so important that the core principle of *The New York Times* "is to enhance society by creating, collecting, and distributing high-quality news, information, and entertainment."

I have a pretty loose definition of entertainment," says Spiker. "I think sometimes you say entertainment, and it means fast-paced humor or it's going to make you laugh, but what I really mean by that is being engaged emotionally. Entertainment can be a very sad narrative. It's not entertaining in the classic definition, but it's hitting the emotional aspect of storytelling."

Spiker notes that the need to entertain readers has never been higher than it is now. "We're in an environment where our readers can do whatever they want," says Spiker. "They can click away immediately; they can throw the paper away (if they even get the paper anymore); they can toss the magazine or flip pages. Entertainment has to be a part of it. … If we don't find a way to engage our readers, it doesn't matter what you tell them. … The whole point is: Have you gotten this information and told it in a compelling way? And that is the entertainment part of it."

CONDUCT

In this virtual day and age, any whiff of impropriety can quickly foul a journalist's career. It's best for a journalist to use good judgment and act professional. A good way to learn about professionalism in journalism is to read "The New York Times Company Policy on Ethics in Journalism," which is freely available online.

As a journalist, one easy way to get tripped up by unprofessional conduct is to become too familiar with your sources. When possible, it's best not to accept anything from a source (not even a breath mint!). Some journalists are okay with accepting a free meal or having a drink with a source, but keep in mind that at certain publications like *The New York Times*, such activity is frowned on unless absolutely necessary—even among restaurant reviewers and travel writers who, at other news organizations, are permitted to accept complimentary meals and lodging as a means of access.

Worse than accepting free libations and lodging is accepting money or tangible gifts from a source. It's also best *never* to do business with a source. But in an age where corporate entities are using journalism to brand their products, what happens before a journalist writes for a publication and interviews a new source may be hard to control. If you've ever derived financial remuneration from a potential source, this must be disclosed to your editor and audience as soon as possible. Remember that transparency can mean redemption.

Sometimes a source may be another journalist or editor. If this happens, the waters become more opaque. As a journalist, you may be interviewing an editor one week and writing for that same editor the next. (Or that editor may be writing for you the next week—who knows?) Alternatively, you may be interviewing a journalist at some point and working with that same journalist sometime in the future. Especially in the world of journalism, where turnover at publications and writing ventures can be high, roles are very likely to change. In these cases, it's best to be reasonable and use good judgment. If your intention is to retain your journalistic integrity and remain transparent, then you should be fine.

As briefly mentioned earlier, the one possible exception to accepting free food and lodging occurs when access is an issue. Some reviewers and their respective publications can't afford reviewing food, drink, and services without having them provided gratis and by means of a public-relations firm. Journalists who must accept food and service for free are particularly regimented in their acceptance of free food and services.

"Here's what I say before I take any trip or go to any restaurant," says Roger Morris, an independent writer who specializes in food, wine, and travel. "First of all, I have to know in advance that I'm probably going to like this … sort of know it's worth it. If it's something I didn't respect, I wouldn't go. Second, no one is ever going to see my copy except my editor. I don't promise any stories when they're paying my way to go to these places. Maybe nothing will come out of it, and if something does come out of it they're not going to see it in advance. And they may not agree with everything I'm going to say. No matter how much I like somebody or how good they've been to me, I don't feel like I can compromise my judgment."

Suggestions for the Journalist

- Verify your reporting.
- Remain transparent.
- Write coherent copy.
- Avoid false equivalency.
- Write for your audience.
- Engage and entertain your audience.
- Conduct yourself professionally.

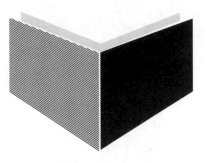

chapter 4

RESEARCH

Good writers spend about 80 percent of their time doing research and 20 percent of their time actually writing. Obviously, doing research is important and has wide-ranging benefits that touch on every aspect of your final product: the article. Good research helps you determine who to interview, what questions to ask, what's important with respect to the issue being explored, and much more.

Margaret Guroff, features editor at *AARP The Magazine,*[1] states, "The key to writing engaging features is doing a ton of research so that you have the details at your fingertips ... so that you really understand your subject and are speaking from a place of authority." Although Guroff is specifically talking about features, her advice holds with all types of stories.

Research resources can be divided into *primary sources, secondary sources,* and *tertiary sources.* In journalism, primary sources can be either written documents or people who you are interviewing. (For more information on human sources, flip to Chapter 5.) Primary sources are unfiltered and haven't been interpreted by a third party. If they've been analyzed at all, the person or group doing the analysis is the person or group who did the research. Examples of primary sources include raw data, statistics, speeches, transcripts from meetings, listservs, newsgroups, questionnaires, first-person accounts, newspaper articles, and some scholarly journal articles published by researchers. Secondary sources are one step displaced from the original data. They analyze, critique, summarize, interpret, and so forth. (In other words, secondary sources normally deal with higher levels of Bloom's Taxonomy. Bloom's Taxonomy is a pedagogy that helps explain how we incorporate and use acquired knowledge. For a more detailed description of Bloom's Taxonomy, see Chapter 8.) Examples include television shows, radio shows, documentaries, books, news analyses,

---

[1] *AARP The Magazine* is the biggest magazine in the United States, with a circulation of nearly 22 million.

and magazine articles. Tertiary sources refer to course syllabi, bibliographies, citations, literature guides, and library catalogs.

When writing an article, it's often a good idea to balance your use of primary and secondary sources. Primary sources such as journal articles provide plenty of good information, especially when writing about science. Secondary sources can help you interpret an issue and explore alternative avenues. It should be noted, however, that secondary sources have their limitations. Most important, you must be careful when directly quoting or re-quoting from a secondary source because with every round of ensuing use, passed-down information risks misinterpretation. In fact, certain publications like *Reader's Digest* and *Men's Health* won't allow their writers to use quotations from secondary sources.

Using information from a secondary source can be compared to playing a game of "telephone." In telephone, one person comes up with a word and whispers this word to another person. This person then whispers the word to another person, who whispers it to the next person down the line, and so on. By the time the word gets to the last person, it is never the same word it was at the beginning of the game. More generally, with each round of transmission, the meaning of information can change.

Sometimes the only way you can get the information that you need is by turning to secondary sources. For example, if you have limited access to a celebrity or important person and you need to put information about this person in your article, referring to a secondary source such as an already-published profile may be prudent. When using information from a secondary source, be sure to cite the publication or source and consider paraphrasing the information instead of directly quoting it. If you have the opportunity, it's always better to gather information from a primary source rather than a secondary one.

RESOURCES

When doing research for an article, there are several places you can turn to for information.

Databases

Databases are great because you can search them using key terms, subject headlines, and search parameters. Plenty of institutions, universities, and public libraries pay for subscriptions to large databases that serve as aggregators for primary- and secondary-source information. If you don't have formal university access to databases, you can usually access many databases by visiting a public, college, or university library.

Figure 4.1
TYPES OF SOURCES

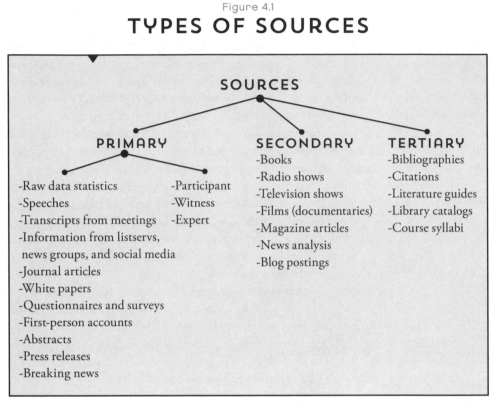

Some popular databases include LexisNexis, which offers access to news, congressional information, and more; Google Scholar, which is a vast searchable database that provides access to tons of scholarly and journal articles; Web of Science, which is a multidisciplinary database that covers science, social science, and more; PubMed, the definitive medical database, which accesses MEDLINE; and (the interdisciplinary) Academic Search Premier, which provides access to 8,500 journals, many of which are full text.

Printed Materials

People sometimes forget that a big library can't be beat when it comes to printed books, journals, magazines, and so forth. However surprising this may sound, there's still much information that exists only in printed form and is not available on the Internet. Libraries have searchable digital catalogs that track down printed resources in the library, and if a library doesn't have the book you need, you can usually get a copy through interlibrary loan. Older newspaper collections are also available on microfilm. In addition to offering access to printed materials, libraries also employ librarians whose job it is to help library patrons. Librarians are founts of knowledge who are happy to spend time with you and help with your research.

One unfortunate limitation of most printed materials is that they are less timely than Internet resources. Because it often takes months or years for most printed materials to be published, the information they contain can become outdated while the manuscript is in development or with the publisher. In contrast, information on a website can be updated in minutes, hours, or days.

Some useful written materials to consider when researching an article include nonfiction works, textbooks, bound dissertations, and even children's books. In fact, a children's book can serve as a valuable introduction to topics that are new to you.

Reference Works

Reference works can be a great way to introduce yourself to a subject and gather basic facts. For example, the *Encyclopaedia Britannica* has an online counterpart that can be accessed for a small fee or for free through the library. Other useful reference works include dictionaries that cover specific topics such as *Dorland's Illustrated Medical Dictionary* and *Stedman's Medical Dictionary*.

If you're interested in learning more about a specific person, you can search the Marquis Who's Who series or the near-monthly magazine *American Biography*. *American Biography* offers lively 2,500-word profiles replete with statistics and bibliographies.

Wikipedia is also a good place to get some ideas about an issue before you start research in earnest. If you were to use any information from Wikipedia, you would need to independently verify it before it goes into your article. Because anybody can access and edit the website, Wikipedia entries can be biased and wrong. Fortunately, many Wikipedia entries are followed by detailed references that will point you toward sources that can be scrutinized more closely.

"As much as I admire the massive accomplishment that Wikipedia has achieved," says Dr. Robert J. Thompson, professor of television and popular culture at Syracuse University, "Wikipedia is not the way to do research. … It's the way to solve bets, but it's not a way to do research."

Websites

Websites provide information on a variety of topics. When deciding whether to use information found on a website, it's important to use good judgment and evaluate the source. *Never assume that information found on a website is correct, and always use information on a website in conjunction with other sources.* Here is a list of questions to consider when vetting a website's authenticity:

- What type of website is it (.edu, .gov, .org, .biz, .net, or .com)? From my own experience, information found on (U.S.) .gov and .edu sources is often more transparent, verifiable, and coherent than information found on other types of websites. Nevertheless, this assertion is soft and in no way means that information found on all .edu and .gov websites is correct. Remember to prudently evaluate and analyze all the information you pull from any type of website!
- Is the website slanted or biased?
- Is the information presented fact, opinion, or both?
- Is the information verifiable using other sources?
- Is the information old or dated?
- Do the hyperlinks on the site function?
- Is the information on the website regularly updated?
- Who authored, maintains, owns, and hosts the website?
- Can the author be contacted by telephone or e-mail or through social media?
- Is the website logical, coherent, and organized? Does the website look professional or amateurish?
- Are there typographical, grammatical, or spelling errors?
- Does the website support a robust internal search function?

Organizations and Institutions

Many universities, institutions, medical centers, corporations, chambers of commerce, associations, advocacy groups, and so forth go to great lengths to provide useful information to the public. Such entities often have public-relations departments that field media requests and are more than happy to send along fact sheets, pamphlets, articles, brochures, annual reports, and more. Remember that you're not inconveniencing these groups by asking for their help. In fact, you're probably helping their cause by focusing on an issue that's important to them.

A quick Google search will likely help you find an organization or institution of interest. Once you find this entity of interest, navigate to its website and search for the information that you need. Other more specific depositories of information include the *Encyclopedia of Associations* and the website GuideStar, which offers background on nonprofits and charities.

Sometimes you must be careful when dealing with materials that originate from an institution or organization because they may represent a specific interest. Press releases often originate from entities with commercial, social, or political interests, so they must be carefully considered before you use any of their information. Even press releases from reputable sources, including PR Newswire and EurekAlert!, which is sponsored by the American Association for the Advancement of Science, must be carefully scrutinized.

That said, press releases can be wonderful resources, and it may behoove you to e-mail the public-relations department at an organization or institution and ask to be put on a recipient list for up-to-date press releases—especially if such press releases represent a "beat" that you report on. For example, the Association of American Medical Colleges routinely sends out press releases to interested parties, including reporters who cover medical education.

Government

In addition to collecting taxes, the U.S. government provides all types of valuable services, including resources for research. If you're interested in primary sources, such as congressional transcripts, visit www.senate.gov or www.house.gov. If you want statistics for a trend piece or other type of article, try visiting www.fedstats.gov.

Various government agencies also make information freely available through education and public-outreach programs, including NASA, National Science Foundation (NSF), National Institutes of Health (NIH), FDA, U.S. Department of Agriculture (USDA), and Federal Aviation Administration (FAA).

Listservs and Newsgroups

Never underestimate the knowledge interested members of the public can provide. This information can be attained from both listservs and newsgroups.

Listservs are electronic newsletters whose audience consists of readers who are interested in a specific topic. You must subscribe to these listservs, and after subscribing, postings are sent to your e-mail account on file. These listservs are fueled by participation from audience members. There are countless listservs in the ether of the Internet. I once subscribed to a particularly active listserv hosted by the American Medical Writers Association, and after a few days, I asked to be pulled off the list because the number of e-mails I received was overwhelming.

Newsgroups are modern-day bulletin boards that anyone can freely access. Like listservs, there are countless newsgroups out there, and many can be accessed through Google Groups.

Google Alerts

You can monitor the Web and receive updated news on a topic in your e-mail inbox through Google Alerts.

Conferences

Conferences can be excellent places to access new stories and emerging research. Conferences allow a journalist to interact with experts in the field and to network with other journalists. For example, every year the American Association for the Advancement of Science hosts an annual meeting that draws thousands of scientists, engineers, students, and journalists from all corners of the planet.

One roadblock that you may encounter while gathering information at a conference is something called an "embargo." Embargoes are placed by prestigious academic journals that plan to publish the research of conference presenters at some future date. Embargoes bar other publications from writing about the research until the publication date has arrived. The vast majority of publications respect embargoes and don't violate them. One unfortunate effect of embargoes is that presenters are often reluctant to discuss their work with journalists present for fear of violating the embargo and losing a chance to be published in a prestigious journal.

Interestingly, the "embargo" concept has extended past scientific research. For example, journalists who evaluate video games for a living often receive advance copies of a video game but are asked not to release their reviews until its release date. Disparaging reviews before a game's release would be bad for sales.

Social Media

In December 2009, *The Seattle Times* engaged in a social-media experiment of sorts. Using Google Wave (which has subsequently shut down) and Twitter to engage the audience, they tracked someone suspected of slaying four police officers.

According to an article in *The Seattle Times*, "Some elements of the Wave included links to police scanner audio, live video, information about road closures, school lockdowns, suspect information, and more. A manhunt map was created inside the Wave and updated by participants. And a map was linked inside the Wave that seattletimes.com then used on the site. It was useful to producers updating the site because they could put information out and get tips back instantly. We then could pass the tips on to the Metro desk and follow along that way. It was like using Twitter with a real-time response and rich content."

This "experiment" hints at the potential for social media to expand a journalist's ability to research and find sources for a story. Sometimes receiving useful information, finding human sources, or even generating story ideas is as easy as requesting help and crowdsourcing concerns and questions. Here are some outlets to consider when using social media to research a story:

- **TWITTER:** When searching Twitter for information, you can either search Twitter itself or search for specific and trending topics on the site whatthetrend.com. There's also TwitterLocal, which follows tweets within local areas.

- **FACEBOOK:** You can engage Facebook users, follow their posts, crowdsource questions, and even search Facebook archives using Google or Bing.
- **REDDIT:** Reddit is an online community where users vote and comment on stories. The most popular stories rise to the top. Reddit or Redditers can develop subReddits (subject forums that follow threads). One very popular Reddit thread is "Ask Me Anything," which has hosted a variety of celebrities, politicians, and so forth. "Ask Me Anything" sessions are essentially crowdsourcing Q&As with Redditers posing the questions. Even President Obama did an "Ask Me Anything" thread.

  Reddit is owned by Condé Nast but operates as a mostly independent entity. The rise of Reddit came at the expense of a very similar website called Digg. Reddit is increasingly being used as a source for breaking news and has aptly been called an "attention aggregator" by Erik Martin, the site's general manager.
- **BLOGS:** Don't limit yourself to mainstream blogs written by major publications—search Google, WordPress, and Blogger, too.
- **MASHABLE:** This website serves as an aggregator for social-media news.
- **ADDICT-O-MATIC:** This search engine searches social-media websites, including Flickr, Twitter, YouTube, FriendFeed, and Google blogs.
- **HARO (HELP A REPORTER OUT):** This website is dedicated to hooking up journalists with expert sources.

Reddit, the Boston Marathon Bombing, and Social Media

In the wake of the Boston Marathon bombings in April 2013, Reddit was thrust into the limelight when Redditers started scanning pictures from the scene in order to identify possible perpetrators. Their theories mushroomed into a virtual witch-hunt for which Reddit subsequently apologized. This crowdsourcing analysis was rife with speculation, and several innocent people were unfairly accused.

Keep in mind that although social-media sites can be used for research and gathering news, they aren't necessarily news sites. The objectives of many social-media sites differ from the objectives of news organizations. Furthermore, social-media users aren't necessarily journalists or citizen journalists.

In an article titled "After Boston, Still Learning," journalist Mónica Guzmán offers some sage advice on how journalists could help social media. "Understand and respect the breadth of platforms where people speak and the voices they speak with. Join them when you can. Most importantly, cultivate a culture of responsibility with everyone who shares information. That's the lesson of the Boston manhunt. It's what this new media world most needs today."

Using social media for research has its limitations. First, you usually have no idea if the information is verifiable or transparent; consequently, you must be discerning. Second, people engaged in social media have no reason to reply to you or answer your questions. There's no social-media etiquette, per se. Third, the world of social media is constantly changing, and there's no guarantee that any social-media site will be up and running next year, next week, or even tomorrow. Some examples of social-media ventures that have folded or are on their last legs include Yahoo!, Buzz, Google Wave, Digg, Myspace, and Friendster. Fourth, jargon can be a big issue when using social media. For example, check out the sidebar below for commonly used Twitter abbreviations and symbols.

Twitter Jargon

- **#** follows a trending topic
- **@** denotes the sender
- **RT:** Retweet
- **DM:** Direct message (When you want to take a conversation private and the person follows you, you can send a direct message to the person.)
- **BR:** Best regards
- **B/C:** Because
- **RR:** Rerun
- **IMHO:** In my honest/humble opinion
- **IRL:** In real life
- **FTF:** Face to face
- **OH:** Overheard
- **FTW:** For the win
- **FTL:** For the loss
- **HT:** Hat tip

On a final note, spending time doing research and immersing yourself in a subject comes with tertiary benefits. For example, sometimes you do so much research for a story that you become a temporary expert or—on the rare occasion—a bona fide expert. The more research you do, the more knowledge you accrue. And remember, knowledge is a journalist's best friend.

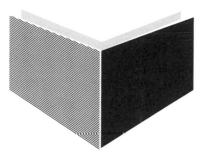

chapter 5

INTERVIEWING

Just like drawing, singing, cooking, and sewing, interviewing is a skill honed by years of experience. No amount of advice can substitute for actual interview experience. When done well, an interview can help make an article great. Although many of today's young journalists fail to appreciate or take interest in interviewing, it is a craft that will endure despite changes in technology and changes in the way information is disseminated. Interviewing a source adds a much-needed personal element to journalism. The following is some advice on interviewing; I've drawn on numerous materials to put together this chapter.

PUBLIC RELATIONS

While doing your research, come up with a list of people or sources to interview. In general, sources to consider interviewing include academics, members of clubs or associations, authors, leaders, professionals, private consultants, and more. If you've identified potential sources, you may either contact them via e-mail followed by a phone call or use a media-relations or public-relations specialist to follow up. Many institutions have press offices whose job it is to field media queries. In addition to setting up an interview, media-relations specialists and press offices can also provide useful information such as press releases and institutional documents that can help with your research.

Dr. George A. Akerlof, an economist who shared the 2001 Nobel Prize, is famous for studying information asymmetry in financial markets. Specifically, Akerlof studied how sellers possess more information about the goods that they sell than the buyers who purchase these goods. This information asymmetry inhibits the equitable functioning of financial markets and can lead to low-quality purchases by the buyer. Consequently, Akerlof suggested that certain instruments and institutions are established in order to minimize the repercussions of asymmetric information. For example, credit scores calculated by credit bureaus help banks evaluate which clients make for good borrowers, and, in this way, keep borrowing affordable. Similarly, with respect to journalism, a sort of information asymmetry also exists. Oftentimes the expert sources whom you interview for a story understand the topic of your article better than you do. Public-relations teams work to aid the reporter and reduce the amount of information asymmetry or imbalance in order to maintain the dissemination of high-quality information.

It should be noted that professionals working in public relations do have their own agenda. According to the *Encyclopaedia Britannica*, "The important elements of public relations are to acquaint the client with the public conceptions of the client and to affect these perceptions by focusing, curtailing, amplifying, or augmenting information about the client as it is conveyed to the publics."

In a 1992 article from the *Columbia Journalism Review* titled "Is the Press Any Match for Powerhouse P.R.?" author Alicia Mundy details the extent that some public-relations firms go to when advocating and defending their clients, including spinning stories and planting op-ed pieces in major newspapers. But the article also promotes the "New Honesty" where public-relations teams are up-front with the story, especially when representing corporate clients. In the years since this article has been published, this sense of honesty seems to have become more pervasive and proselytized by public-relations experts.

In reality, however, there's nothing new about public-relations specialists being truthful. In fact, in 1906, Ivy Lee, a newspaper journalist turned publicity adviser, advocated that his coal-miner clients be forthright when providing the public with information on mining accidents. Ever since then, many of the most successful public-relations campaigns, especially those involving tragedy and disaster, have been distinguished by their honesty. For example, when Tylenol bottles were tampered with in the 1980s, Johnson & Johnson, the makers of Tylenol, were up-front with the public. Their actions instilled good faith in the company that persists to this day.

Public-relations offices can sometimes make it tricky to secure an interview, and they may request that a media-relations specialist be present during the interview. They can also suggest *prepublication review,* or the ability to review quotations before they go to print, which a writer must deny if the publication prohibits the practice. "If it becomes clear that they won't grant the interview unless you accede to the demand … to arrange the conversation for you and listen in … you kind of have to [let public relations arrange the conversation and listen in]," says Robert Irion. "Generally, that's the worst it gets from a PR [perspective]. If they ask to hear or review quotes, you can almost count on them changing quotes."

Remember, it's best not to tell a media-relations specialist or a source the names of others who you're interviewing for your piece. This lapse could be considered a violation of privacy. Just like a physician or lawyer would refrain from divulging information and names of respective patients or clients, the ethical journalist refrains from divulging the names of other sources.

SOURCES

Sources or interviewees fall into three categories: *participant, witness,* and *expert.* The participant has a direct role in the main event or issue underlying a story. The witness is not directly involved in the story but has observed it. The expert isn't directly involved in the story either but can evaluate it on a cerebral level. For example, let's consider Bernard Madoff and his Ponzi scheme, which robbed investors of billions of dollars. Madoff and his investors are participants. All the relatives and friends of the unfortunate investors who lost their money, nest eggs, retirement funds, and so forth are witnesses. The experts may be academics or other financial professionals who can evaluate the situation without having been involved. Each of these sources can provide valuable insight. Of note, the lines between these three categories can blur. For example, if you were doing a piece on kidney transplants and you interview a transplant surgeon who had a kidney transplant herself, she would be both a participant and an expert source.

One advantage of categorizing your sources as participants, witnesses, or experts is that it helps you figure out whether a redundancy exists in who you're interviewing. For example, if you were doing a piece on bank foreclosure in the wake of the subprime mortgage bust and interviewed four people who lost their homes and two friends of people who lost their homes, you would probably have four participants and two witnesses. Where's your expert? You'll probably want to consider adding an expert from the field of banking and an economist so that your readers may better understand the issue.

With respect to journalism, let me always encourage you to err on the side of excess when interviewing, researching, and writing. You can always cut away, but without resources, you can't build more. That being said, when choosing who to interview, keep in mind that you want to interview as many people as you *need to.* If you interview too many people, you will risk redundancy and wasted time, and if you interview too few people (a smaller "sample size") the "power" of your research will decrease.

Figure 5.1

BALANCING POWER AND REDUNDANCY WHEN CHOOSING SOURCES TO INTERVIEW

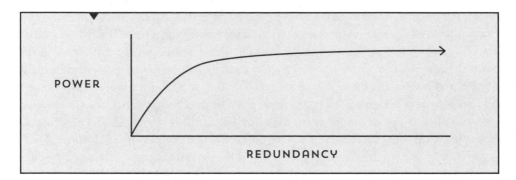

INTERVIEW LOGISTICS

When soliciting an interview, it's best to send a brief introductory e-mail explaining who you are, which publication you're representing, the topic or angle of your piece, and why you want to speak with the source. You can also notify your source that you plan to record the interview for later transcription. If you plan to offer *prepublication review* of direct and indirect quotations, you may want to mention this in the introductory e-mail, too (more on *prepublication review* in a bit). Finally, ask when the source is free to interview and for a preferred telephone number. Don't forget to offer your telephone number, just in case the source would prefer to call you. (Celebrities and other sources who value their privacy may elect to call you instead of divulging their personal contact information. Alternatively, such sources require that you work with a publicist or press office to facilitate the interview.)

Sometimes you'll have difficulty soliciting an interview by e-mail. This difficulty may stem from the fact that your prospective source may mistake your e-mail for spam. You can avoid this problem by making the subject line of your e-mail very specific—something such as "interview for article." Additionally, it may be a good idea to follow up your interview request with a phone call asking the source to interview.

When you set up an interview, give yourself plenty of time to interview the source and factor in some extra time in case the interview runs long. Although your source may be in a rush, you should never hurry through an interview or cut off somebody who's generous enough to share good knowledge with you—especially when the knowledge is useful to your piece. Furthermore, some experts claim that the time of day that you interview a source makes a difference. For example, it may be best to interview a source after work, when a person's guard is down and the person is more open to answering questions. But then again, maybe your source is crabby after work because it was a difficult day. Honestly, the best time to interview a source is at the time the source requests to be interviewed. Do your best to make yourself available at this time.

Occasionally, a source or press office will decline an interview. When this happens and you *need* the interview, you have a couple of options. First, you can have your editor or other third party make a phone call or send along an e-mail on your behalf requesting an interview, thus reinforcing the importance of the interview. (Sometimes a letter from the editor can be the only way into an institution. For example, if you plan to tour a prison and interview prison officials, you'll probably need a letter from your editor in order to do so.) Second, you can tell the media-relations specialist with whom you're communicating that if you don't receive the interview, you must mention in your article that you were refused an interview by the institution or that the institution wouldn't comment on the matter. In order to avoid this consequence and all that it implies and begets—namely, rumor and speculation—press offices may jump into action and facilitate the interview. Sometimes dealing with a press office is like a game, and tactical maneuvering may benefit you.

INTERVIEW TECHNIQUES AND TIPS

In this day and age, most interviews are conducted by phone. The best interviews, however, are done in person because they allow you to observe the environment in which your source lives, relaxes, or works. Observing sources in their own environments—offices, homes, favorite haunts, or so forth—can build on the narrative of your piece, especially if you're writing a profile. If you do have the privilege of sitting down with a source, be sure to take notes on details that your digital voice recorder won't catch, such as source mannerisms, affectations, and place descriptions. You may also want to snap a picture of the setting with your cell phone.

Irion states: "It's very difficult to craft a narrative purely on the basis of telephone interviews. … You can do feature stories by phone, and they're routinely done, but typically they lack the visceral element … multisensory description.

"Observational details can be as simple as how the scientist (source) expresses himself or the way that he walks down the beach when he's explaining coastal erosion to you or the pride that washes across her face when she opens a sample drawer and describes how meaningful it was to discover this particular fossil. [You must create opportunities for] these little moments … to arise naturally in the flow of the interview or conversation, and you can really only do that by being with the person.

"Use notebook moments to jot down what surrounds you in the room or the way they're answering a question or the expression on their face when they come to that transformative moment in the conversation. They don't know what you're writing [in the notebook]. … They assume that you're writing down what they're saying. But for a substantial portion of the interview, you are writing down observational details. ... It can be what's on white-board, it can be the little knickknacks on their shelves, it can be what they're wearing. ..."

Unfortunately, performing an interview in person is often impossible, and you must interview over the phone. After you secure a telephone interview, learn as much about the source and subject as possible—this often requires several hours of research. Additionally, write down a list of potential questions to ask during the interview. Try not to ask questions that can be researched on your own. After all, many sources are busy people, and a journalist shouldn't waste time asking questions with answers that are otherwise readily available.

Whatever you do, resist the temptation to interview via e-mail. When you interview via e-mail, you lose the ability to prioritize and focus on what's important and to ask follow-up questions in an organic manner. Moreover, e-mail interviews are much less memorable than conversations. Asking questions by e-mail is good if you're asking a few questions that are factual or following up with a source after an initial phone interview. Of note, some sources prefer to be interviewed by e-mail. In these cases, you are forced to send along a list of questions and hope for the best.

Your list of questions will guide your interview. I write "guide" because at its best, an interview is a free-flowing conversation between a journalist and a source. It's a conversation that explores ideas. It's important that a journalist never feels compelled to ask questions because they're listed on a piece of paper. If a question no longer seems appropriate or useful during the course of an interview, a good journalist won't waste time drudging it up.

"The most important thing is thorough preparation of the questions," says Dr. David E. Sumner, professor of journalism at Ball State University. "It's very important to know exactly what you want to ask and have the questions all written out before you go into interview. Some people may feel that might restrict your freedom. But it doesn't restrict your freedom at all, because if you have a roadmap in front of you, you can always take a side trip somewhere. [Questions] give some direction and structure to the interview."

Before you begin an interview, first ask, or, if you've already mentioned it in your introductory e-mail, reiterate whether it's okay to tape the interview for later transcription. Although it may be within your right to tape a conversation without a source's consent, for both ethical and legal purposes it's prudent to inform any source that they're about to be recorded. (For more information on the legality of recorded conversations, refer to the media-law section of the *Associated Press Stylebook*.) After you ask to record an interview, make sure to ask the source how they prefer their name spelled—for example, do they use a middle initial—and how they want to be attributed in the article. Sometimes a source will have several positions and titles that may be irrelevant to your story. For example, if you're writing a feature on a physics topic and speak with a top physicist, it may be best to refer to his university position rather than to his title, such as Commander of the Order of the British Empire.

During an interview, don't assume undue familiarity with a source. Address your source as Mr., Mrs., Ms., doctor, or even professor until the source invites you to do otherwise.

When you first start interviewing, explain why you are interviewing the source and how your story relates to them. You may also want to engage in a bit of small talk to put the source at ease. Making brief mention of some commonality between you and the source engenders trust. For instance, maybe you went to the college or university at which the source is faculty. Furthermore, when interviewing, it's important to avoid appearing cynical or threatening. Try to be friendly, interested, and unafraid.

When interviewing a source, try to establish your baseline of knowledge and the gaps that need to be filled in. Because many of the sources with whom you interview are both educated and intelligent, they can often quickly assess your understanding of a topic and may take control of the interview. Relinquishing some control of an interview is prudent because it allows the source to explain what's important to them and allows you to take time to listen and learn. You can perpetuate the interview by carefully listening to what is said and asking insightful follow-up questions. In these situations, you end up using your list of questions as a way to guide the conversation. Be careful, however, not to relinquish too much control and let your source fly off on a tangent. When needed, use your list of questions to politely rope in the source.

One useful way to refocus a source who has digressed is to frame a question in a fashion that acknowledges the tangent but redirects the interview toward your own interests. For example, if you were asking a neurologist about the utility of positron emission tomography and the neurologist starts talking about magnetic resonance imaging (both of which are types of diagnostic imaging used to examine the brain), you may ask this expert to compare positron emission tomography with magnetic resonance imaging and then redirect the interview toward your original line of questioning.

It's also important to make sure the source is speaking to you in terms that your audience will understand. "It's the interviewer's prerogative to dictate not only the flow of the conversation but the level of the responses," says Irion. "If you are finding that your source is consistently talking over your head … and there is no way that the material is going to be usable for a general audience … you really need to rein them in with some gentle nudging. You never want to denigrate your source. You don't want to say 'I don't understand what you're saying' or 'this is too complex.' You say something like 'that's very interesting … and I wish that I had the space to fully explain the processes you're talking about, but I do have to put this in an accessible context for my audience.'"

Keep in mind that during an interview, the first few questions that you ask help verify your intention of securing a serious and informative interview. Ask useful questions that target the source's specific body of work. For instance, when interviewing an academic, consider asking a question that relates to a specific journal article, book chapter, or book that the academic authored. Doing so not only provides clarification but also proves to the source that you've done your homework. Furthermore, don't ask your toughest questions at the beginning of the interview; save tough questions for after you've established some rapport with your source. And when you do ask tough questions, do so in a straightforward and unapologetic manner—ask a tough question once, and don't repeat yourself. Nobody likes to be patronized or fooled into answering a tough question. If a source refuses to answer a tough question—or any question for that matter—that's their prerogative. Don't risk making a source angry and compromising the rest of your interview by belaboring a point.

Holly G. Miller, a veteran reporter and editor at *The Saturday Evening Post*, states that you "have to be sensitive and kind of know when it's right to ask tough questions. Boy, if you get the timing off, the interview can go down the tubes right then, and that's happened to all of us."

The questions that you ask during an interview should be simple to understand and to the point. It's a mistake to ask a question filled with jargon or complicated ideas, especially if you aren't a specialist in the field. Don't make the mistake of trying to impress an interviewer by appearing "smart." On the contrary, revealing that you are unfamiliar with the topic at hand can be a great asset and make for a more productive discussion. If you make a mistake when asking a question, tell the source that you made a mistake and ask the question again. Although being eloquent is nice, getting the right answer is nicer.

Remember that during an interview, silence can be your friend. People need time to think, and it's okay for you to think about the questions you're asking. If you feel the need to fill in gaps with your own rambling, it can distract the source and turn the focus of the interview onto you—something you don't want to do. It's important to wait for your source to answer a question—even if the answer is preceded by a silent pause. Ultimately, giving the source the impression that your speech is pressured undermines your ability to do a good interview. *Remember that a silent gap in conversation is never as long as it seems to be.*

Much like silence, measured enthusiasm can also improve your ability to garner useful quotations. "You don't ever want to sound like you're not interested," says Linda Wang, a senior editor at *Chemical & Engineering News*. "You want to be animated on the phone. Sometimes they'll say something, and I'll be like 'Wow! That's really cool,' and they get energized by that, and they provide me with some really good information. I'm very interested and engaged on the phone."

While interviewing a source, it's important to keep as many questions as possible open ended. *Open-ended questions* encourage a source to answer in a robust and meaningful way. They explore a source's thoughts and knowledge of a subject. They also allow the astute listener to present useful follow-up questions. Typically, open-ended questions begin with words like *why* or *how*. In contrast, *closed-ended questions* cause a source to give less meaningful one-word answers like "yes" or "no." For example, "Do you like Mr. Smith for state senator?" is a much less productive question than, "Why do you like Mr. Smith for state senator?"

One particularly useful open-ended question involves asking a source for "thoughts" on a matter. All you need to do is make a statement or refer to an event or occurrence and ask a source for any thoughts on the matter. By doing so, you will be able to gauge what's most important to the source and, in turn, what may be most important to your story.

Sometimes you can turn a closed-ended question into an open-ended one with great success. For example, if you need to affirm whether a politician supports some new policy change but you suspect that the source may be reticent if directly confronted with a closed-ended question, try asking why the politician supports the policy change. When posed an open-ended question, a source may feel more comfortable giving reasons or clarifying any misunderstanding.

The distinction between open- and closed-ended questions is one that is applicable to interviewing both sources and patients. In fact, physicians—especially primary-care physicians—spend much of their time asking patients questions during history and physical exams, or "H&Ps." Some interview techniques apply to both journalism and medicine, including the avoidance of the double-barreled question (explained below) and questions that lead the source or patient.

A double-barreled question is a question that attempts to do too much. It's a question that is composed of two or more questions. Consider the following double-barreled question: "Do you agree with the candidate's assessment of the issue? If so, why do you agree with the candidate's assessment? If not, why don't you agree with the candidate's assessment?" This question is messy and convoluted and should definitely be broken up.

A leading question is phrased in a way that encourages a source to answer the question in a particular way. It robs your interview of objectivity and inhibits your source from making a spontaneous assessment of the question asked. For example, "Like most Democrats, you probably agree with the Affordable Care Act. Why do you agree with the Affordable Care Act?" is a leading question that not only encourages the source to answer in a certain way but also makes an assumption. Not all declared Democrats agree with the Affordable Care Act (Obamacare).

When interviewing, make sure to avoid a scenario that resembles cross-examination. Your source is a friendly fount of knowledge, not some "perp" on the witness stand. It's not your place to unduly scrutinize every trivial answer and inconsistency. It is your place to gather the information you need from the interview.

Some of the hardest sources to interview are the ones who are quiet by nature or reluctant to speak with you. One useful trick when interviewing sources who are subdued is to ask very specific questions that necessitate an answer. Doing so may break the ice. Sometimes a source or interviewee is quiet because he or she has never been interviewed before. The source may be intimidated by questioning. Put the neophyte source at ease at the beginning of the interview. Clearly advise the source to answer questions as well as possible, and explain that you won't pass judgment or assess their interview skills. Let them know that you're there to better understand the issue.

Another difficult source to interview is the source with an agenda. Imagine the cigarette executive of decades ago who, if interviewed, would do his best to dismiss any notion that cigarette smoking was bad for a person's health. To this executive, it made good sense to push such an agenda. After all, nobody wants to be responsible for the death of millions of smokers. But cigarettes do kill, and no matter how convincing this cigarette executive may be, he is pushing an agenda. It's important the interviewer does enough research and gathers enough knowledge to discern whether an agenda is being forwarded.

Sometimes a source will explain something to you in a fashion that you don't understand. More specifically, an explanation may be filled with jargon and complex concepts. If this happens, ask your source to reiterate the point. If you continue to have trouble, ask your source to explain the concept to you as if you were a high school student. Encourage the source to use analogies to explain the topic. If you still don't understand, try explaining the concept back to your source in words that make sense to you. Then ask your source to correct any misunderstanding.

Another good practice is to ask a source about *power circles* and social networks. *Power circles* is an investigative-journalism term and refers to mapping out authority: Who is important to speak with and why? Furthermore, expert sources can provide insight on well-supported angles for your story. Again, remember that an expert source has spent months, years, or decades dealing with the subject of the story whereas a writer may have spent only a few weeks studying an issue. Social networks refer to the key characters or players with respect to the issue or story that you're trying to report.

Sometimes the structure of the piece you're writing dictates the flow of an interview. For example, if you were interested in constructing a story using a narrative structure with a beginning, middle, and end, then asking questions in chronological order is probably advisable. If you are interested in playing up the narrative in your story and infusing it with details, ask the source to recall specific details. What did the crime scene look like? Was blood spattered everywhere? What was the victim wearing?

Having the source share anecdotes can also provide useful narrative. Remember that anecdotes are more than just stories; they also hint at the psyche of the source and, much like a Biblical parable, Islamic hadith, Aesop's fable, or allegory, have greater meaning. Also, a source may feel more comfortable providing information in anecdotal form.

The most important question during an interview often comes near the end. Don't forget to ask whether you're missing anything important or whether you've misunderstood anything. Sources frequently have a good understanding of what's newsworthy and will explain further if encouraged to do so. Don't stress out if you forget to ask some questions; no interview is perfect, and if you've left a good impression on your source, you can always follow up with another phone call or by e-mail.

Sometimes a journalist must conduct serial interviews with a source during the course of working on the piece. With serial interviews, each interview can serve a purpose—the first being exploratory, the second being more in depth, the third being confirmatory, and so forth.

BAD INTERVIEWS

Occasionally you'll interview a source who, for whatever reason, is irritable or downright nasty. Other times, an interview will deteriorate, especially if a topic is broached that offends a source. I estimate that about 10 percent of my interviews are "bad." But even with a bad interview, it's important for a writer to remain composed. Keep in mind that even good information can come from bad interviews.

If an interview starts to go south, it's good to switch subjects. Refer to your list of questions, and fall back on the base of knowledge you've built up during the research phase. If an interview becomes so bad that you feel it is no longer productive and the source no longer wants to participate, politely thank the source for their time and end the interview. Unless the source is a participant in your story, take solace in the fact that the knowledge possessed by one source is more than likely possessed by another source. In the words of John Brady, author of the classic *The Craft of Interviewing*, "Avoid hard words and harsh feelings." And remember, maybe the person who you're interviewing was irritable because he had a bad day, a bad week, or a bad year.

I once interviewed a communications expert on a piece I wrote which concerned the link between social psychology and clinical medicine. For whatever reason, he was defensive and snippy. Nevertheless, I remained polite, kept my calm, and stuck to my scripted questions. Eventually, I gathered the information I needed and was able to conclude the interview in a cordial manner.

When dealing with a source who, for whatever reason, becomes angry, consider some advice commonly given by marriage counselors. (It may seem weird to compare an interviewer-source interaction to a marriage, but remember that both are dyadic relationships.) Respond to anger slowly and softly and with appropriate silence. Additionally, remain flexible and amicable when faced with resistance because antagonizing a source further with some defensive quip will make the entire interview unsalvageable. By remaining friendly, calm, and collected, you can often redirect the source down a more productive path.

On the very rare occasion, a source may become irate with the line of questioning and threaten to contact your editor and complain. If this happens, keep your cool! Provide the source with your editor's contact information, and cordially end the interview. Again, keep in mind that chances are a more readily agreeable source is willing to interview and provide similar information.

TRANSCRIPTION

After the interview is done, it's a good idea to transcribe it. Some journalists transcribe only parts of an interview based on notes that they've taken during the course of the interview. Other journalists find that transcribing and then rereading the transcriptions helps them better synthesize and progress along Bloom's Taxonomy. I highly suggest that—especially when starting out—you transcribe entire interviews and carefully read through them. It's amazing how much you can learn by transcribing entire interviews. Even veteran journalists such as Holly Miller, who has written more than three thousand articles for every type of publication imaginable, recommend that it's best to transcribe interviews in their entirety.

Different journalists treat transcription differently—some journalists won't change a word, and others are more liberal. With my own work, I normally interview scientists, physicians, researchers, and academics—people who prefer to appear eloquent. Consequently, whenever transcribing an interview, I'll go ahead and check quotations for grammatical errors and glaring lapses in word usage. I'm careful, however, to avoid the temptation to overedit quotations. After all, quotations are supposed to re-create speech. They shouldn't appear as published prose. When transcribing, I'll also omit speech disfluencies. For example, if a source tends to orphan sentences midstream or repeat, "I believe," "I think," "kind of," "you know," "uh," "em," and so forth, I'll expunge this filler from my quoted material. Occasionally, I'll also transpose or switch the order of quotations so they make better sense. *Above all, with whatever changes I make, I'm careful to never change the meaning of the quoted material.* Whenever I tinker with quotations, I'm sure to offer my source prepublication review. Finally, I do my best to respect a person's vernacular or specific speech mannerisms. For example, if a source speaks with a Southern dialect and tends to say "y'all" from time to time, I'll include the occasional "y'all" in my quoted material.

PREPUBLICATION REVIEW

The term *prepublication review* refers to the practice of allowing sources to review and comment on quotations before these quotations go to print. For many reasons, some journalists don't believe in prepublication review—especially if the article is an exposé or investigative piece. Journalists who argue against prepublication review cite many concerns: professionalism, legal repercussions, or fear that a source may move to kill or change a story. Other journalists agree that prepublication review is a good idea.

Prepublication review can assuage a source's fear that he or she may be misrepresented, and, if offered when initially asking for an interview, can lubricate the request. If you do decide to offer prepublication review, make sure the publication you're writing for allows the practice. Some magazines, such as *Science,* allow prepublication review, but others explicitly forbid it. (Because factual accuracy is so important to the readers of many scientific publications, you'll often find editors at such publications more permissive with the practice of prepublication review.)

Whenever I offer prepublication review, I normally do so with an important caveat: I promise only to edit quotations for factual or tonal clarity. For example, if a source were to tell me that the proprietor of a for-profit medical school took a $25-million-dollar loan from his father in order to start the school but he later corrects himself and tells me it was $30 million, I'll change the number. But if a source explains why he is opposed to for-profit education and tries to backtrack and rescind these comments—comments that are important to my piece—I won't budge. Furthermore, should a source attempt to change position on an issue, I'll notify my editor. Remember that if you have something on tape, then you have the right to use it. For more on prepublication review, refer to the *Investigative Reporter's Handbook* published by Investigative Reporters & Editors.

Different journalists practice prepublication review differently. "Everyone has their own way of doing it," says Linda Wang, an associate editor at *Chemical & Engineering News*. "I'll show a draft to my sources and highlight the parts where I quoted them. Some writers will only share the relevant quotes, but I like to share the entire article so they can see their quotes in context. That way, I'm confident that I've gotten the story right."

Personally, when practicing prepublication review, I show my sources their direct and indirect quotations in context. In other words, I sample enough of the surrounding material to ensure the quotations make sense. I also put a deadline on when I would like a response. I don't want the source's input a few days before my own deadline; I want time to work with the feedback. I also like to compartmentalize the process of prepublication review and complete the practice within a circumscribed period of time. Prepublication review almost always changes the fabric of an article, and I like to complete the process before I continue writing. (For similar reasons, I fact-check at the same time, too.)

When considering whether to offer prepublication review, this advice, provided by science writer Robert Irion, may help: "Ultimately, the person who is finally responsible for the accuracy of your article is yourself. The journalist has to do whatever it takes to make sure that what you're publishing under your byline contains no errors. If part of that is sharing portions of text with a [source] ... if there are some complexities involved ... you should do that."

OFF THE RECORD

Popular media has romanticized a source's privilege to go "off the record." In reality, if you don't explicitly offer the ability to go off record, anything you have on tape is quotable, even if a source claims that a comment is "off the record." In principle, if a source has agreed to an interview, the interviewee is accountable for any comments made. Offering your source the ability to go off record creates a possible escape route for the source to avoid important questions.

All that being said, a prudent journalist will judiciously allow a source to go off the record if asked to do so. Such asides should be used for your understanding and not quotation. If somebody slips and tells you something they don't want to see in print or that could hurt them, it may be a good idea to leave it out of your article—especially if what they've told you is not integral to your piece. Remember that a good source can be a lifelong resource, and burning a bridge with the source may inhibit your ability to approach them in the future.

ANONYMITY

With respect to journalism, another topic that's tickled the public's fancy is the idea of source anonymity. Decades ago, anonymity was rarely granted, but after Watergate, source anonymity took on a certain mystique and became more romantic. In the years following the scandal, it seemed that even a gas-station owner could be granted anonymity when commenting on rising gas prices. But the pendulum has swung the other way on this issue. Nowadays, editors and writers must carefully consider whether to offer anonymity. Whenever possible, it's always best to clearly attribute quotations.

One possible reason to consider offering anonymity is if you'll only be able to secure a necessary quotation by concealing the source. Other reasons to offer anonymity may be if the source were acting as a whistle-blower, if the source lacked authorization to comment, or if the source could face serious repercussions for commenting on an issue. For example, in an article titled, "Barely Hanging On," which was published in *Chemical & Engineering News*, sources—who happened to be older, unemployed chemists searching for jobs— were offered anonymity because revealing their identities could compromise their ability to garner employment. Fortunately, the issue of anonymity rarely arises with articles that are not investigative.

EXPERT INTERVIEWING TECHNIQUES

Once you've been interviewing for some time, you may decide to pick up some expert techniques that will help you master the craft and get the most out of your interviews. Here are some expert interview techniques:

- Make occasional small talk, some of it slightly funny or self-deprecating, in order to put the source at ease.
- Use nonverbal communication techniques to put your source at ease. In person, you can open your posturing, lean toward a source, and maintain eye contact. On the phone, you can encourage the source to speak by saying "fantastic," "how interesting," "uh-huh," "um," "yes," "aaah," and even by occasional chuckling.

- Show measured emotion during an interview—empathy, concern, and interest. For example, if a source tells you that a family member recently died, it's good to convey empathy and provide some measure of condolence.
- Provide measured praise, but don't butter up a source. Praise a source only if you truly believe the source deserves praise and your praise won't detract from your source's objectivity; remember that you're a journalist, not a groupie. Alternatively, your source may not appreciate undue flattery that's insincere—few intelligent people like sycophants.

In a weird way, interviews can be cathartic for a source. A good interviewer is an observer who is genuinely interested in the thoughts and feelings of others. This interest can appeal to a source and can cause a source to unload their concerns on the interviewer. If this happens, it's important to remain sympathetic and impartial. Never judge or make fun of the source. In the words of John Brady, "The good interviewer is deeply interested, of course—but he is also disinterested. He is a conduit for the readers."

Interview Checklist

- ☐ Do your research.
- ☐ Clarify source name and attribution (title, position, and so forth).
- ☐ Carefully consider your first question.
- ☐ Let a list of questions guide you.
- ☐ Listen close to answers.
- ☐ Prefer open-ended questions.
- ☐ Avoid leading and double-barreled questions.
- ☐ Use silence to your advantage.
- ☐ When needed, ask for clarification.
- ☐ Keep the source on track.
- ☐ Ask for useful anecdotes and analogies.
- ☐ Keep calm.
- ☐ "Did I miss anything?"
- ☐ Transcribe your interview.
- ☐ If permitted by your publication, consider offering prepublication review.

I'd like to briefly discuss the television show *60 Minutes* and arguably its greatest star, the late Mike Wallace. The show *60 Minutes* is an investigative-news show, and interviews often center around wrongdoing. Many of its segments are contentious, and its correspondents adopt tones that run the gamut from cloying to downright judgmental. Nevertheless, good general interview skills can be gleaned from watching the show and its correspondents in action.

Mike Wallace influenced countless journalists. His temerity, confidence, brazenness, research skills, and force of character were peerless. In a *60 Minutes* segment titled "Saying Farewell to the Extraordinary Mike Wallace," we learn two important lessons that apply to interviewing in general. First, Wallace liked to establish a "chemistry of confidentiality" with his sources. He wanted his sources to realize that he did his research and knew the topic well, allowing his sources to feel comfortable enough to open up and forget the camera. Similarly, when interviewing sources, the article writer hopes to establish a rapport that enables the source to forget the digital recorder and notepad and simply have a conversation. Second, Wallace's interview skills evolved over time, and he eventually came to realize that tough and hard-hitting questions must serve a legitimate and specific purpose: They target truth, accuracy, and understanding.

In conclusion, remember that interviews are a form of research. The information gathered during an interview provides narrative and facts to round out your article. Interviews don't complement your article. Quotations aren't garnish—they're victuals.

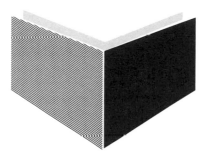

chapter 6

ARTICLES: AN INTRODUCTION

All documents share fundamental characteristics that should be considered before any writing takes place; in other words, every document has a PAST (purpose, audience, scope, and topic). (Medical writer Thomas A. Lang suggested a similar pedagogy; however, I switched out "setting" for "scope.") First, every document has a *purpose* or goal, which should be fulfilled once the document is completed. For example, if you were to write a story on cosmetic surgery that's intended for high school students, the purpose of the cosmetic-surgery story may be to warn high school students about its dangers. Second, every document has an *audience* or intended readership that you must carefully consider when writing the piece. With regard to the cosmetic-surgery piece, because the piece has an audience of high school students, you would best avoid using unexplained medical jargon or technical terms. Third, every document has a *scope* or breadth, and the document's content should be focused to fill this scope. For instance, with the cosmetic-surgery story, the scope of the piece should focus on cosmetic surgery; there's no reason to discuss neurosurgery unless the connection between cosmetic surgery and neurosurgery is clear and thematic. Finally, every piece speaks to some *topic*. Obviously, cosmetic surgery is a medical topic. (Some documents cover various subtopics—for example, the cosmetic-surgery piece could also examine psychology.)

Articles are written differently for different audiences; consequently, it's important that the author carefully considers the audience before any writing begins. With respect to your audience, you must consider the arguments you pose, the vocabulary you use, the allusions you make, the tone you adopt (snarky, cynical, casual, conversational, or academic), the message you present, and even sentence length. An article is tailored for the instruction and enjoyment of the typical member of your audience. For example, after analyzing your audience, you probably wouldn't write an article about gun control in *Highlights*, a magazine intended for children.

Figure 6.1

EVERY ARTICLE HAS A "PAST"

PURPOSE

AUDIENCE

SCOPE

TOPIC

TYPES OF ARTICLES

Most articles or stories written for general and specialized audiences fall into three categories: news, features, and opinion pieces. I've decided to expand this group to include blog postings, which, although similar to other types of articles, have their own distinct considerations.

Figure 6.2

WRITING FOR THE PUBLIC

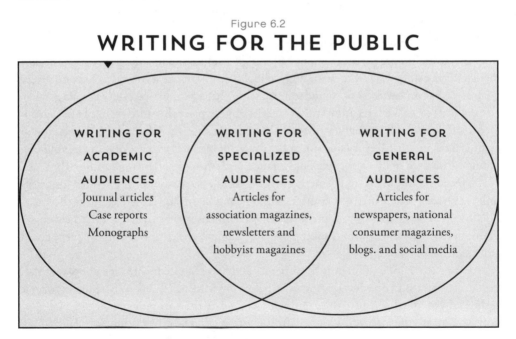

WRITING FOR ACADEMIC AUDIENCES
Journal articles
Case reports
Monographs

WRITING FOR SPECIALIZED AUDIENCES
Articles for association magazines, newsletters and hobbyist magazines

WRITING FOR GENERAL AUDIENCES
Articles for newspapers, national consumer magazines, blogs. and social media

Because characteristics of blog postings, news articles, feature articles, and opinion articles sometimes overlap, they can best be conceptualized on a continuum or spectrum. On one end of the spectrum you have news articles, which focus on facts. In the middle of the spectrum you have feature articles, which principally incorporate opinion (often expert), facts, and narrative or storytelling elements. At the far end of the spectrum, you find opinion pieces and blog postings, which often take the form of columns or commentaries. Blog postings and opinion pieces usually present opinion—either of the publication or the author—as of primary importance and use argument for support.

Figure 6.3

SPECTRUM OF FACT
AND OPINION

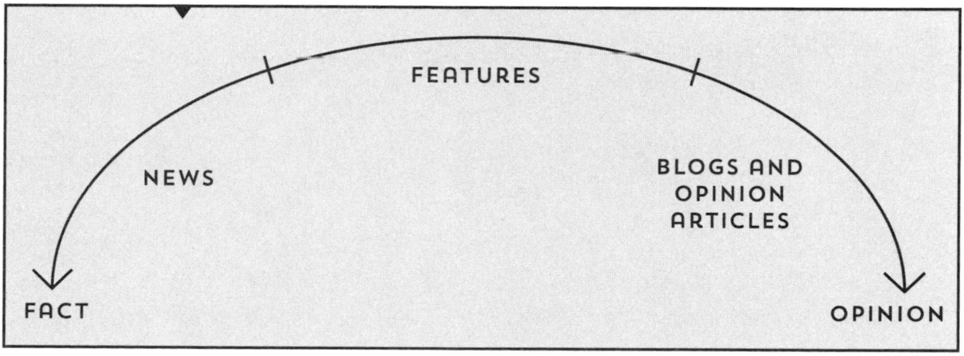

FEATURES

NEWS

BLOGS AND
OPINION
ARTICLES

FACT

OPINION

A Few Words About Feature Articles

Features hold a special place in the hearts and minds of many journalists. They provide a breadth of creativity and form distinct from news and opinion pieces. "I find it to be the most satisfying form of writing there is," says science journalist Robert Irion, "because you can become a temporary expert in this one field or subdiscipline. You get to bring your audience into this realm that they would never otherwise have access to. You are their portal into this other realm that they find fascinating. Through your own words, and through your experiences as a reporter, you're revealing this world to them, and it's a privilege to do that. ... Feature writing is a lifelong pursuit. It's one in which you continue to improve. Your work becomes deeper and richer over time."

Traditionally, feature articles in print format have been associated with magazines, but over time, newspapers have embraced the feature article at the expense of the inverted pyramid. Although feature writing in magazines and newspapers has to a great extent converged, classically, features found in magazines differ from those found in newspapers in several ways. First, whereas features found in magazines are intended to have longer lives and be more "evergreen," features found in newspapers are more likely to analyze issues of the day. Second, magazines will sometimes require that a feature be written with certain structural parameters in mind—an anecdotal lede, tight nut graph, and so forth—whereas newspapers are a bit more free flowing in the structure that their feature writers ascribe to. Third, features found in magazines can be longer, contain more sources, and are more thoroughly fact-checked than newspaper features, which are turned out on stricter deadlines. Finally, features written in newspapers are intended for a general audience whereas magazines often have their own specific audiences.

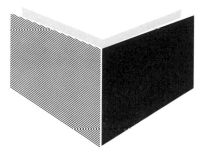

chapter 7

DISSECTING A STORY

This next section examines the different parts that many stories share. Although many of these elements are typical of feature articles, you will find some of them in other types of stories, too.

LEDE (ALSO SPELLED LEAD)

Experts say that if you fail to catch a reader's attention in the first couple of minutes, you'll likely lose them forever. If a casual reader were flipping through a magazine or surfing the Web, the lede or introduction must be compelling enough to catch her attention or she would likely spend time reading somebody else's piece, chatting up a flight attendant, watching television, playing Xbox, walking the dog …

With most features, the lede, or first part of the article, and the conclusion are probably the only parts of a story that truly belong to the writer. They provide an opportunity to showcase a writer's voice. A good lede should be simple, relevant, engaging, and focused. It should also have a good *hook*. A hook is the element of an article that makes it interesting and newsworthy. Ultimately, the lede makes a promise to the reader on which the rest of the story delivers.

Different writers have different preferences about how to begin a story. For example, many writers like to use an anecdote when constructing the lede. Oftentimes good ledes tie back to the greater theme of the piece using narrative or storytelling elements. For many stories, the lede is a four- or five-sentence paragraph. With longer pieces, the lede may span a few paragraphs.

With short features, the lede can be as short as a sentence—for example, a summary sentence; a question; or a witty, irreverent, or insightful comment. Such a lede may be written along with a thematic sentence in a single paragraph (reminiscent of a nut paragraph or "nut graph"—discussed later in this chapter). If you're clever enough, you may be able to create a sentence that serves the purpose of both lede and theme.

Keep in mind that, as with many other style and structure considerations, categorizing different types of ledes is, to some extent, an artificial and arbitrary practice. It may be best for a writer to consider the following options when constructing a lede (but by no means treat these options as dogma).

"I believe that these are models to follow," says Dr. David E. Sumner, a professor of journalism at Ball State University, "but there is some disagreement about how you would interpret them. I like to think of them more as models instead of specific rules, and I think that this is generally true in writing. I believe there are certain principles you have to follow in order to be a good writer, but beyond that, it leads to 30 to 40 percent creativity as well. I tend to be pragmatic as well because I think if you can write and make it interesting and engaging—hey, whatever works."

Types of Ledes

Ledes fall into several categories. The following is an explanation of different types of ledes that work. This explanation is, in part, based on information gathered from various texts, including *Feature & Magazine Writing: Action, Angle and Anecdote* by David Sumner and Holly Miller. For anybody interested in learning more about feature writing, I highly suggest reading the most recent edition (third, at time of printing) of this book.

Summary Lede

The summary lede touches on the five *W*s and one *H* (who, what, where, when, why, and how). News articles often start with a summary lede that introduces an inverted-pyramid structure (see Chapter 12). Summary ledes are useful with complex subjects, too. For example, if you were writing an article on hydraulic fracturing or "fracking," you may want to introduce the process with a summary lede. (Fracking is a process whereby high-pressure fluids are used to break an underground rock layer in order to release petroleum and other types of fuel.)

In a *Newsweek* story titled "What's *That* Doing in My Head?," writer Amanda Schaffer begins with a summary of microchimerism, wherein male cells, usually from a fetus, slip across the placenta and implant in the mother's brain. The rest of the article provides hypotheses on how the cells got there and possible benefits and repercussions.

In case any doubt remained that guys get into girls' heads, for the first time scientists have found male DNA in the human female brain. Researchers at the Fred Hutchinson Cancer Research Center in Seattle examined dozens of women's brains and discovered that the majority of them contained genetic material found only on the Y chromosome.

Quotation Lede

This lede starts off with a quotation. Approach this lede with care. The quotation that you use must be darn good—brief, interesting, and topical. If you like the gist of what a source is saying but it's hard to pull a specific quotation from the speech, then you may want to create an indirect quotation. For example, Gary Busey, an actor just as well known for his work in movies as his time on *Celebrity Rehab with Dr. Drew*, is sometimes unintelligible—he rambles in hilarious fashion. (I often wonder whether this is some sort of affectation, but I digress.) If you were doing a piece that involved him (celebrities who have lost their way?) you may consider paraphrasing whatever relevant gibberish that Busey happened to articulate on the day that you interviewed him.

In a short feature in *AARP The Magazine* titled "Everybody Loves Tony ... and the feeling is mutual," Tony Bennett talks about his early days when he was mentored by Frank Sinatra. The author, Bill Newcott, starts with a quotation lede.

> Tony Bennett remembers as if it were yesterday: "I was playing the Fairmont Hotel in Dallas, and Bob Hope came to see me," he says. "When he was leaving, one of my musicians scooted out and asked him, 'How do you like Tony?'"

Scenario Lede

This lede uses narrative to describe a place. Narrative ledes are good to use when the place that's described is important to the story—almost as if the place is another character in the story. For example, in 2012, James Cameron, of *Titanic* fame, designed and took a vessel to the deepest part of the ocean. Apparently, the landscape was barren, and Cameron described the setting as isolated and desolate—like he was on another planet. If writing a story on this adventure, it may be prudent to construct a lede that describes this barren, deep-sea environment.

In a story published in *The Atlantic* and titled "Swamped!" writer Matt Siegel describes how he visited Tuvalu and was unable to secure interviews with any government officials. Tuvalu is a small country in the South Pacific that may become the first to be swallowed by rising sea levels secondary to climate change. The country received a glut of international attention, and government officials spend almost all of their time in meetings or traveling. In the lede, Siegel sets the scene for an article, which lacks any important interviews, by describing the bureaucratic wasteland.

> On my first morning in Funafuti, the capital of Tuvalu, I left my hotel, walked across the streets to one of the country's few modern buildings, and climbed two flights of stairs to the prime minister's office. The minister was not in, his assistant said, nor was she sure when he would be back. Later today? Could be. Tomorrow? Sure, anything's possible. Still, better to try the foreign minister, she offered; he's just around the corner.

Narrative Lede

A narrative lede could incorporate creative-writing elements, including allegory or figurative language. You may want to consider using a narrative lede when introducing a chronological story. For example, if you were documenting the success of Dr. Augustus A. White III, a black orthopedic surgeon at Harvard and advocate against health-care disparities who broke all types of educational and cultural barriers, you may consider starting a chronological account by describing his roots in the Jim Crow South.

In a 2012 article on Lance Armstrong's doping strategy, writer Juliet Macur uses a narrative lede to introduce the story.

> To start what was deemed a new and better doping strategy, Lance Armstrong and two of his teammates on the United States Postal Service cycling squad flew on a private jet to Valencia, Spain, in June 2000, to have blood extracted. In a hotel room there, two doctors and the team's manager stood by to see their plan unfold, watching the blood of their best riders drip into plastic bags.

Anecdotal Lede

This lede starts off with a story. The story can be provided by a source, the author, a friend, another author, a leader, some professional, or so forth.

In an article from *The New Yorker* titled "Head Start," author Ben McGrath uses an anecdotal lede to introduce a story about Steve Clarkson, a "quarterback guru" who coaches young quarterbacks and charges up to a thousand dollars an hour to do so. Some of his previous clients include Ben Roethlisberger and Matt Leinart. The lede begins the story of David Sills V, who was offered a football scholarship to the University of Southern California when he was thirteen years old.

> When David Sills V was eight, he attended a summer football camp at the University of Delaware, a few minutes from his family's home, in the town of Bear. Sills was a precocious kid, a pee-wee quarterback who actually threw the ball instead of scrambling on instinct. He seemed to see patterns and systems at work amid the chaos of swarming defenders in front of him.

The First-Person Anecdotal Lede

Be careful when using yourself in an anecdotal lede. Some editors and publications prefer that writers avoid interjecting themselves into a feature unless the feature directly relates to the author in some way.

Ted Spiker, an associate professor of journalism at the University of Florida and contributing editor at *Men's Health*, has thought a lot about the first-person anecdotal lede. "The clean answer is to keep yourself out of the lede," says Spiker. "But it's certainly a lot more nuanced than that. … We're in this day and age when there's so much information out there, and you can find out a lot in seconds … so the whole key to writing a good story is not just your writing ability and your tools that you use but [if] you have original content … content that's different, interesting, compelling, and original. … A lot of times, [the reason] why the first-person works is because the situation 'I' just went through is unique because I went through it and you didn't … in a lot of cases that's why it's a decent device. … If it's done right, the first-person lede can work. You have to have that critical ability to say when can I use it, and when should you not and try some other tactic.

"I try to tell my students to use the test: 'Can you cut yourself out of there and still convey that scene?' … In a lot of different settings there is a danger of it being gratuitous or being a very easy device to use. If that's the case, you have to be critical enough of yourself to be able to make that judgment because it can be an easy device, and it can be the easy way out. But I also think that it can be a smart way in. Depending on what you're writing about, your readers may connect with something that's unique, and you can use it as a bridge to get your point across.

"We see the first-person lede in a lot of different settings. I'll use it in weight loss or health. We see that tactic used in celebrity stories … to create dialogue or to create scenes. … I actually think the subtle first person is a pretty nice way to do it. … Maybe you're profiling somebody, and in the middle of the lede, you have a little interaction with that person, and you can introduce yourself softly. It creates a nice little three-dimensional aspect to a story. If you create a tension with the reader that they relate to, and they see that you're vulnerable, they see that you struggled and you're sharing and open about it."

Paradoxical Lede

This lede starts off in a counterintuitive or contradictory fashion. For example, if you were writing a profile on Stanley "Tookie" Williams, you may consider a paradoxical lede that juxtaposes his criminal past with his humanitarian efforts while in prison. (Stanley Williams was a prominent gang leader who co-founded the Crips and was later incarcerated for murder. While on Death Row, he became an influential antigang activist and author.)

Here's the paradoxical lede from an article in *Forbes* aptly titled "Rich Dad, Poor Dad, Bankrupt Dad?"

> Robert Kiyosaki, author of the bestselling Rich Dad, Poor Dad series of financial advice books, is offering his fans yet another lesson in how the rich are different than you and me: They file for bankruptcy not because of ill health or unemployment-related issues, but instead as a strategic business move.

Here's another paradoxical lede from an article titled "Florida's Last Frontier," published in *Cowboys & Indians*.

> In the land of Disney and Daytona, amusement parks and beaches come to mind more than open range and cattle. But Florida, people are surprised to discover, has the longest history of ranching of any state in the country and a legacy of cowboying as long as the peninsula itself.

Shock Lede

Many readers are engaged and entertained by ledes they find shocking. If the story involves some unexpected financial, sexual, or criminal element, you may consider using a shock lede. Let's consider Jack Ryan, who ran for the U.S. Senate in 2004 and was caught up in an alleged sex scandal that involved his then-wife Jeri Ryan, a prominent actress who starred in *Star Trek: Voyager* and was a former Miss Illinois. The story dripped with salacious detail; a good lede for this story may allude to the candidate's alleged dalliances in sex clubs.

In a *Men's Health* story titled "The Dirty Truth about Hospitals," writer Laura Beil starts with a shock lede that questions where a spate of infections after knee surgeries came from. It turns out that the surgical instruments used during the procedures housed crevices that weren't being cleaned properly.

> After the fifth soldier turned up with a post-op knee infection, the staff at Madigan Army Medical Center in Tacoma, Washington, halted all anterior cruciate ligament surgeries. Something was very wrong, but no one could say what. In a little more than three months during 2003, the men had undergone routine reconstruction of ligaments torn when knees had twisted under 100-pound pack loads or ankle ligaments snapped during pickup basketball games. It's usually a safe procedure, and infections are rare (though not unheard of). In four years of repairing ACLs, doctors could recall just one other infection. Now five?

Blind Lede

This type of lede is similar to a shock lede, but instead of shocking with content, it shocks with lack of content; some important detail is left out. For example, every year many people start successful businesses, but few of these businesses are started by small children. Leaving out the detail that a little kid started a multimillion-dollar business and then mentioning it later for effect may make for a good blind lede.

In a *National Review* article titled "What 'Lost' Decade'?" which questions the Pew Research Council's findings that suggest a declining middle class, Scott Winship presents the following blind lede. Note how the lede leaves out important details integral to the story.

> Pop quiz: Which of the following is true? (a) Over the past forty years, the middle class has shrunk; (b) Over the past forty years, the middle class has grown poorer; (c) The middle class just suffered through a "lost decade"; (d) All of the above.
>
> You could be forgiven for answering (d), given the angst-producing state of discourse on the economy, but the truth is that none of these claims about middle-class decline—made most recently by the Pew Research Center (PRC)—are supported by the best evidence. …

Prescriptive Lede

This lede serves as a call to action and instructs the reader to do something. By using pronouns such as *you* and *we*, it connects with the reader. A prescriptive lede may work well with a social issue that affects all of us. For example, in 2012 antibullying efforts became a focus of politicians, educators, and parents alike. Invariably, we've all experienced bullying—as either victims or perpetrators—and have the ability to contribute to antibullying efforts. Consequently, a lede that implores the audience to do all they can to stop bullying may make for a strong opening.

Magazines such as *Men's Health* and *Women's Health* have a history of publishing prescriptive content in the form of service pieces. In a department titled "Know It All," writer Kate White uses a prescriptive lede in a service piece that advises readers of *Women's Health* on confidence.

> Confidence is sexy and exciting. People want to be around someone who has it—to hear what she has to say and learn what she knows. I'm not talking about haughtiness or smugness. Those qualities, I've always found, tend to spring from insecurity and are totally off-putting. Real confidence is both authentic and inviting. And, as your self-assurance grows, you also tend to become gutsier and less afraid of taking risks.

Adopting a prescriptive tone can be tricky. When doing so, it's important to remain authoritative without patronizing or belittling the reader. Ted Spiker recounts how it took him time and experience to master the magazine's prescriptive tone: "It took me two years to really feel comfortable with the tone ... it took a while to find that sweet spot where you weren't talking down to people but you were still goofing a little bit. It was tough."

Opinion Lede

You'll find opinion ledes in editorials. Moreover, in many cases, opinion ledes can be equated to the introduction of an editorial written in essay format.

Here's an opinion lede from an article titled "100 Years in the Making," published in *Medical Economics*. In the article, author Neil McLaughlin argues that the foundation for the Affordable Care Act—a push toward universal health care—is both decades old and bipartisan. He also argues for universal health care.

> That was a rough 100 years.
>
> And the past year of debate on healthcare reform seemed like all 100 wrapped into one. In fact, if you look at the chronology on preceding pages, you will see that what has happened since 2009 in many ways encapsulates the U.S. reform war that has raged since the early 20th century. The intense partisanship and the cries of 'socialized medicine' and the 'death of freedom' are like reruns of a bad soap opera.

Transformative Lede

This lede is of my own design. In some ways, this lede is similar to a summary lede, a paradoxical lede, and a shock lede. In addition to summarizing key points, it also rejects a deeply seated counterintuitive belief. At face value, this rejection can appear both shocking and paradoxical. Before I introduce this lede, I'll first explain what a transformative explanation is.

People are psychologically motivated to protect belief structures and perceptions, especially when such belief structures are ingrained and intuitive. Consequently communication scholars suggest a systematic approach to repudiate such deeply rooted, false perceptions. This systematic approach is called a "transformative explanation."[1]

According to Katherine Rowan, written transformative explanations can be broken down into five steps:

1. "State the lay theory."
2. Explain the lay theory's plausibility.

---

[1] Most of the following information is taken from a blog posting titled "Myths and Pregnancy" that I wrote for *Psychology Today*.

3. Explain the lay theory's shortcomings and inaccuracies.

4. Explain accepted scientific understanding.

5. Reinforce this understanding.

Imagine that you're writing a piece for a pregnancy magazine about having sex while pregnant. According to your anecdotal experiences, you've found that a large percentage of people still erroneously believe that having sex while pregnant will hurt the baby. You want to help people understand that it's okay—and even enjoyable—to have sex while pregnant. The rest of your article fleshes out this angle with facts and narrative. For the lede, you may consider the following transformative one:

> Many people believe that having vaginal intercourse during a normal pregnancy will hurt the baby. These people suppose that an erect penis thrust toward the cervix and uterus can physically harm (poke) the fetus. Additionally, people think that the quivering during an orgasm may crescendo into preterm labor and result in a miscarriage. The baby, however, is protected from the erect penis by both a plug in the cervix and a layer of amniotic fluid, which fills the uterus. Furthermore, although uterine contractions can occur during an orgasm, they're different from the uterine contractions that occur during labor. Because the baby is protected from the outside world—which includes erect penises—sex during pregnancy doesn't hurt the baby. Furthermore, even the biggest, mind-blowing orgasm won't cause preterm delivery.

Botching the Lede

For every example of how to build a good lede, one can probably think of many more examples of how to mess one up. As with the information I presented on how to construct strong ledes, much of the information in the following list is derived from a must-read text titled *Feature & Magazine Writing: Action, Angle and Anecdote*. Here are some tips on avoiding a botched lede:

- Don't burden your reader with too many numbers. For instance, if you were doing a piece on the Appalachian Trail, it may be sufficient to mention how long the trail is in your lede—according to the Appalachian Mountain Club it was 2,168.1 miles in 2001. However interesting, mentioning statistics on elevation, precipitation, and whatever else in the lede will likely turn off your reader.
- Make sure that your lede doesn't read like an entry from an encyclopedia or textbook. You don't want lines and lines of dull facts cluttering your lede. For example, if you were writing an article on controlling blood-sugar levels in the hospitalized patient with diabetes, you would probably want to avoid discussing every class and example of in-

sulin in your lede. If you start mentioning Lantis, NPH, and so forth, you risk putting your reader in a (diabetic) coma.

- Even if you think that you can get away with it, don't make stuff up for a lede. For example, during 9/11 there were probably plenty of freelance journalists living in New York City. After all, the "City" is arguably the worldwide hub of modern publication and has a long history of attracting aspiring writers. Because many freelancers have a bunch of time on their hands, it may be easy for one of them to pretend that they witnessed the destruction of the airplanes hitting the towers. Using media accounts, it may also be easy to fabricate the story. Such a fabrication, however, would not only be an absolute ethical transgression in journalistic terms; it also could be construed as disrespectful to all the people who really did witness the horrible sight—many of whom also lost their lives.

- Don't start a lede with strange words. For example, avoid using onomatopoeia—words that are spelled as they sound, such as *oink, meow,* and *thwack*—in your lede. Furthermore, avoid foreign expressions, especially ones that are tired like *carpe diem.*

- If you have a penchant for thumbing through *Bartlett's Familiar Quotations,* you may be tempted to pull a quotation from some master and stick it in your lede. This passé practice of using an epigraph was once commonplace in personal statements for college and graduate school and should never make the transition to article writing. For example, even if topical, don't start a lede with a quotation from Winston Churchill or Eleanor Roosevelt. Unless either of these figures is mentioned in your article, using a quotation attributed to them is off-topic. You should use the lede to champion your own ideas and your own words, not the words of others.

- Be careful when using humor in your lede, especially if the piece isn't a humor article. Humor is hard to explain because different people find different things funny. If you can gauge that a humorous anecdote is both thematic and would generally be considered funny to your audience, then you may want to use it. Otherwise, my advice is to steer clear. On a related note, stay away from punning, too. Puns are corny; reading a sentence such as "the music teacher changed his tune" will probably make your reader want to flip the page.

- Don't start your lede with a bunch of questions. For example, if you were writing a story about the global financial crises, which began in 2007 and became widely felt in 2008, it's probably a bad idea to question your audience on the subject. Nobody wants to be asked why it happened, whose fault it was, and so forth at the beginning of a piece. More than likely, these questions hint at why the reader is interested in reading your piece. It should be noted, however, that using a few questions in the nut graph following the lede is considered acceptable by many authors and editors.

- Avoid anthropomorphic ledes. Anthropomorphism is the practice of giving human characteristics to an animal. Such narrative is intrinsically inaccurate and belongs in the toolbox of the creative writer. After all, do computers crash because they're vengeful or does a dog feel schadenfreude?

- Imagine that you spent a lifetime studying chemistry, mathematics, and engineering. You then rose to prominence as a leading rocket scientist, patenting a propulsion system for satellites that would keep them in orbit. Now imagine that you started your career in the 1940s and you were a woman—one of the first women—to become a rocket scientist. In your later years, you were honored by the National Inventors Hall of Fame and President Obama. You probably wouldn't expect the lede of your obituary to read like this.

> She made a mean beef stroganoff, followed her husband from job to job, and took eight years off from work to raise three children. "The world's best mom," her son Matthew said.

This lede is taken from a March 30, 2012, obituary for Yvonne Brill, which ran in *The New York Times*. Reader reaction was strong; people complained that presenting Brill as a homemaker first and a rocket scientist second marginalized her accomplishments and appeared sexist. At best, this lede was a failed attempt to be funny.

This example of an insensitive and ignorant lede reflects poor judgment. Had the author (editor, newspaper …) exhibited better judgment, this lede could have been avoided. (In all fairness, it's rare that the *Times* makes mistakes of this magnitude, but when it does, it's interesting for many writers and editors to point out.)

NUT GRAPH (NUT PARAGRAPH)

I've seen the nut paragraph referred to in various ways: "nut graph," "nut," "theme paragraph," and "billboard paragraph." Whatever you decide to call it, the nut graph is a paragraph in a feature article that follows the lede and summarizes the rest of the story. The themes brought up in the nut graph are then expanded on in the body of the feature. The nut graph serves a thematic function, and there are different ways to compose it. Many writers bring up key topics or summary sentences that touch on the five *W*s and one *H*: who, what, where, when, why, and how.

The nut graph serves at least two purposes. First, by using supporting information, it explains why the story is newsworthy and important. Second, it acts as a transition between the lede and the body of the story. Like ledes, nut graphs are found in both newspapers and magazines articles and can be used with trend stories, analytical pieces, breaking news, and more.

Here's a good example of a nut graph. It's from a feature originally published in *Policy Review* titled "Supply, Demand, & Kidney Transplants," written by Dr. Sally Satel, a psychiatrist who received a kidney transplant herself. As the title of the article suggests, the story describes how difficult it is to secure a kidney for transplant. The piece was later re-published in *The Best American Science Writing 2008*.

> Uneasy questions of allocation arise in environments of scarcity. Who will get to stay on the crowded lifeboat, and who will be tossed overboard? This age-old tension between utility to society—the maximum good for the maximum number—and fairness to the individual is notoriously hard to resolve. In the case of the shortage of transplantable kidneys, it is made gratuitously more difficult by a 'transplant community' that resists experimenting with bold ideas to increase the supply.

An interesting way to think about how to write the nut graph can be traced back to the interview process. When interviewing, it's a good idea to be able to summarize your story in a few sentences so your sources will understand where you're coming from. This summary can then be used as the basis for your nut graph.

Another easy way to set up a nut graph is to ask questions that will be answered in subsequent paragraphs. For example, if I were writing an article on a new medical treatment, in the nut graph I may write, "What is the benefit of treatment X? How does treatment X differ from treatment Y?" It should be noted that some editors find this a tired practice.

The length of a nut graph is often directly proportional to the length of the piece—the shorter the piece, the shorter the nut graph. For example, in a feature that only spans a few hundred words, the nut graph may only be a sentence or two. In news articles, which are structured using the inverted pyramid, there's often no need for a nut graph because the introduction provides basic information about the rest of the piece—namely, the five *W*s and one *H*. Furthermore, in features that use a summary lede, there's no need for a nut graph because the lede answers many of the basic questions that a nut graph would.

When the nut graph emerged in the 1970s, many publications felt that the information in the nut graph must be attributed. Predictably, such attributions in the nut graph felt forced, and by the 1990s, even the staid Associated Press allowed the information in the nut graph to be presented without attribution and based on the journalist's knowledge, research, and expertise. Moreover, much of the information within the nut graph will be re-presented in the body of the story with the appropriate attribution.

One word of caution: Make sure the nut graph doesn't serve as a spoiler and discourage audience members from reading the rest of the article. Remember that the nut graph isn't a full-blown summary … just an invitation to the rest of the article.

ANGLE

The angle is the emphasis of the piece; it holds a story together. For example, if a piece concerns weight loss, the angle may focus on surgery and compare the benefits of malabsorptive procedures such as gastric bypass with restrictive procedures such as the laparoscopic adjustable gastric band (LAP-BAND). Research, quotation support from experts, data analysis, and so forth are then used to support this angle. Anecdotes and other narrative elements spice up the facts.

Without an angle, all the writer is left with is the general topic of weight loss. The topic of weight loss is broad and meant for a book or series of seminars. It's not restricted to surgical weight loss and incorporates diet and exercise, too. There's no way a writer could adequately survey all aspects of weight loss with sufficient interest or depth in a 1,000-word article.

If your editor allows you latitude with your piece, you may be able to change your angle while fleshing out your topic. Doing so can be especially helpful when dealing with a topic that's controversial or confusing. After learning more, a writer may decide to adopt an angle that's better supported by research and expert opinion. Of note, when referencing primary sources such as scientific journal articles, a good place to get an idea for the potential angle of a piece may be the discussion section of the article. If you do decide to change the angle, make sure to notify your editor, and be prepared to establish a strong argument for your decision.

Imagine that you were assigned a service piece on weight loss. At first, you establish an angle that focuses on the promising benefit of the new weight-loss drug. But after doing some research, you discover that the drug has numerous intolerable and unpleasant gastrointestinal side effects, including bloating and diarrhea. These side effects make it difficult for people to take the drug. You may instead decide to choose an angle that expounds on the discomfort caused by the weight-loss drug.

In more scientific terms, the angle is analogous to a hypothesis. You will then test this hypothesis through your research, interviews, and so forth.

When interviewing sources for a piece, experts can also provide clues that make for a good angle. For example, while conducting interviews, if a physician tips you off that an established drug has promising off-label uses for weight loss, you may decide to make this observation the new angle of your story. (Off-label uses refer to uses of a drug that are unrecognized by the U.S. Food and Drug Administration.) Quotation support from medical experts and further research may support this new angle.

I once wrote a piece on virtual patients. Virtual patients are computer simulations that mimic clinical interactions. They are teaching tools primarily used by medical students. In my estimation, the topic had never been fully explored in the mainstream media, and after months of research and several interviews, I was able to develop an angle for the piece. My angle examined whether the development of virtual patients should be a public effort—which involves open-source resources—or a private or industry-led effort. This angle was based on the work of several researchers and experts in the field—information that was already extant.

Archetypes

When discovering the angle of a story, it may be useful to consider archetypes. Archetypes are the basic models of storytelling. They are general themes that recur over and over again in the literary canon, in comic books, in graphic novels, in plays, in movies, on television, and more. They also play a prominent role in religion. Archetypes are as old as time. To learn more about archetypes, I suggest reading the work of Joseph Campbell.

- the voyage (Homer's *Odyssey*)
- the brass ring (The Promised Land)
- the resurrection (Jesus Christ)
- dualism of good and evil (God vs. Satan in Abrahamic religions and the creation of the benevolent Spenta Mainyu and the malevolent Angra Mainyu by Ahriman in Zoroastrianism)
- *damnatio ad bestias* or "condemnation to beasts" (Romans threw Christians to animals)
- duplicity and betrayal (Judas Iscariot and Marcus Brutus)
- fall from grace (Milton's *Paradise Lost*)
- gladiators in the Roman Coliseum (Russell Crowe in *Gladiator*)
- steal from the rich and give to the poor (Robin Hood)
- love and loss (the film *The Notebook*)
- star-crossed lovers (Romeo and Juliet)
- the underdog (David and Goliath and the movie *Rudy*)
- tragic hero with hamartia or "tragic flaw" (the hubris of Sophocles' Ajax and Hamlet's irresolution)
- redemption (Hugo's *Les Misérables*)

The story of Rod Blagojevich, a former governor of Illinois, reflects a classic archetype: fall from grace. Blagojevich rose from immigrant working-class roots. He worked his way up the ladder and clinched one of the top political offices in the country before being undone by his own greed. In 2011, Blagojevich was convicted of several conspiracy charges, including those related to his attempt to "sell" Barack Obama's open senate seat. He's currently serving a fourteen-year prison sentence. With respect to recent books and movies, The Hunger Games series is a prime example of archetypes at work. The story, which is set in the distant future, focuses on a pair of teenagers who are pitted against twenty-two other sacrifices in a game to the death. These "Hunger Games" are televised and sponsored. The whole incident is reminiscent of the archetype of gladiators fighting in the Roman Coliseum.

HEADLINE, DECK, AND HEADERS

The distinct organizational elements of a feature consist of a headline, a deck, and headers (subheads). Keep in mind that some of the best articles are divided into portions that are easily consumed by the reader.

Headlines

Headlines introduce stories and can be used to promote the article on the cover, in the table of contents, or in Internet search results. Readers also encounter headlines before the lede, and, as such, headlines play an even more pivotal role in advertising the piece and drawing in readers. Many editors like to come up with headlines on their own, but some turn to the author for advice on headlines. After all, the author of the piece is more intimately associated with the content and can sometimes come up with an excellent headline. Whenever I tender an article manuscript to an editor, in addition to listing my name and the word count at the top of the piece, I also suggest a few headlines. It can be quite satisfying to see that your editor has accepted your suggested headline.

Researchers at the Poynter Institute tried to define and test good headlines. Although their studies didn't yield statistically significant results, their parameters are intriguing. For example, researchers looked for headlines that spoke directly to the reader; used onomatopoeia or other forms of word play; used *I, we,* or *they;* had a conversational tone; asked questions; or surprised the reader.

An article on the Poynter Institute website titled "10 Questions to Help you Write Better Headlines" by Matt Thompson does a pretty good job of explaining how to come up with a good headline. Information applicable to creating headlines can also be found in Ian Montagnes' timeless tome *Editing and Publication: A Training Manual.* (A PDF version of this book is offered for free by the International Rice Research Institute.) Here's a list of pointers derived in part from these two sources:

- The headline should be concise, crisp, accurate, and relevant. Use active verbs and proper nouns when possible.
- The headline should refer back to key words or key concepts in the article's text. In fact, keeping such key words in mind can help you come up with a headline.
- The headline should explain the issue and hit on its significance.
- The headline should use different wording from that found in the rest of the article. Don't repeat the headline word for word in your lede.
- The reader should be able to understand what the article is about after reading the headline.
- The language used in the headline should be easy to understand—you don't want your reader to have to whip out a dictionary before he even begins reading a piece. Avoid jargon in your headline!

- The headline can take the form of a question or informative phrase.
- As advised by Thompson, evaluate whether the headline will benefit from these words: "*top, why, how, will, new, secret, future, your, best, worst*." Also consider whether the headline could benefit from the use of numbers.
- The headline can incorporate elements of wordplay, alliteration, assonance, and so forth. A good headline will often grab the reader's attention in a smart, witty, or irreverent way.
- A headline is normally right branching, with the subject and verb placed first.

Here's an example of a headline I came up with which incorporates some of the aforementioned advice. If I were going to write a piece about how diet soft drinks filled with artificial sweeteners cause weight gain, the headline may be "Diet Drinks Fatten Your Booty." I like this headline because it sums up the message, uses an active verb (*fatten*), is a bit irreverent (*booty* means *buttocks*), uses alliteration, and is counterintuitive.

It's important to mention that headlines for print and online media should be written differently. Online headlines show up *without context* in RSS feeds, in database or search-engine results, and on news-aggregator sites such as Google and Yahoo!; consequently, they should be specific and use proper nouns and searchable key terms. Because print headlines can be paired with images and have context within the print publication, they can be punchier and more playful.

A source told me about the following headline, which appeared in a 2000 issue of *The Sun*, a British tabloid: "Super Caly go ballistic, Celtics are atrocious." When written devoid of context, the headline makes little sense. But when accompanied by a picture and plastered on the printed pages of a regional publication whose audience members are familiar with the soccer teams Inverness Caledonian Thistle and the much mightier Celtic organization, the headline is genius. A headline for the corresponding online story may read, "Inverness Caledonian Thistle Beat Celtic," which is less catchy but more searchable.

Deck

A deck is another line of text that appears below the headline and further expounds on the article's content. The deck adds to the headline and helps the reader decide whether to read the article. In the case of the diet-soda story, the deck may be "Research suggests diet soft drinks can cause weight gain."

Scientific American is a mainstream consumer magazine that does a good job with its headlines, decks, and headers. Anybody who has read a few pieces from this magazine can attest to how complicated its topics can be. Apparently, the editors realize that their articles are mentally taxing and do their best to keep them well organized. For example, in an article titled "Eyes Open, Brain Shut" by Steven Laureys, the deck does a good job of hinting at the content of the article: "New brain imaging techniques are giving researchers a better understanding of patients in the vegetative state." The article deals with the difficulty in diagnosing people in comas and vegetative states.

Headers

Headers (also known as subheads) subdivide the text of the story and establish clarity. Headers mark and thematically introduce each ensuing section. They should also flow with the headline, deck, lede, nut graph, and conclusion. When constructing headers, it's a good idea to keep each header in parallel form. Here's a brief list of possible headers for the diet-soda piece. (By the way, research shows that diet soda may be associated with diabetes mellitus, too.)[2]

- Diet-soda industry
- What's in diet soda?
- Nutritional information on diet soda
- Ingredients in diet soda
- Diet soda and disease
- Diet soda and weight gain
- Diet soda and diabetes
- Diet-soda alternatives
- Nutritionist's take on diet soda

Now for a real-world example: Here are the headers for the aforementioned article "Eyes Open, Brain Shut" from *Scientific American*. Each header is thematic with respect to the section of the article it introduces.

- A Difficult Diagnosis: *This header refers to the difficulty in distinguishing a vegetative state from a minimally conscious state.*
- A Consciousness Region?: *This header refers to scientists' attempts to use functional neuroimaging to measure brain metabolism which, in turn, suggests conscious thought.*
- Tennis in the Brain: *This header alludes to how a young woman in a vegetative state is asked to imagine playing tennis. Amazingly, brain scans registered that she was imagining playing tennis.*

Sidebar

A sidebar contains extra information that's pertinent to the story but isn't placed in the actual text of the story. For example, I once wrote a story about how an osteopathic medical school was planning on opening an allopathic counterpart. (Osteopathic and allopathic

---

[2] To learn more, please read a blog posting that I wrote for *Psychology Today* titled "Diet Soda Double Whammy."

physicians represent different medical pedagogies.) The story was controversial, and only one other medical school in the country had both types of medical schools operating on the same campus: Michigan State University. Although I referred to the allopathic and osteopathic coexistence at Michigan State University in the text of the article, I described this unique academic environment in more detail in the sidebar.

Editors like sidebars because they offer another point of entry for the reader. In other words, a reader may take interest in the sidebar and then decide to read the whole piece. Sidebars also offer visual relief from lines and lines of text.

Obviously the subject of a sidebar depends on the content of your piece. Remember that a sidebar's content should complement the piece. Here are some ideas for possible sidebars:

- Anecdotes
- Audio or video content: With online features, it may be a good idea to provide audio and video content as a sidebar. As when linking to audio or video content in a blog posting, make sure to summarize what's important about such content.
- Examples
- Glossaries
- Interesting or practical lists (Unless chronology is important, it's best to bullet a list.)
- Miniprofiles
- Quizzes, surveys, and games: Be careful with quizzes and surveys. The best quizzes and surveys take much work to create. For example, the questions asked in surveys must be clear, concise, and valid or purposeful. Furthermore, when creating surveys, it's important to consider the order of the questions and whether the language used is leading, redundant, or biased. For more information about survey design, I suggest referencing *Mass Media Research* by Roger D. Wimmer and Joseph R. Dominick.
- References used in the article: Unlike scholarly articles, journalists need not formally cite references used to create the piece. Nevertheless, if you feel that your readers may want to further explore the references you used, you may want to list them in a sidebar.
- Summaries
- Supplemental information: Telephone numbers, physical addresses, e-mail addresses, and websites
- Time lines
- Tips

Graphs, Flowcharts, Diagrams, and Tables

Sometimes graphs, flowcharts, diagrams, and tables can help a reader visually interpret the information presented in an article. For example, *USA Today*, America's third largest newspaper (behind *The Wall Street Journal* and *The New York Times* respectively) is well known for offering up appealing statistics and other information in the forms of graphs, diagrams, and so forth. (Technically, such offerings can be labeled alternative story forms.) These *USA Today* "Snapshots" complement the publication's news offerings.

If you're going to use a graph, consider the following. First, make sure the graph is clear, easy to interpret, and doesn't contain too much clutter. Space out the units on the x- and y-axes and make sure the baseline in any line or bar graph is zero. Furthermore, when rendering a line graph, don't use more than five lines on any one graph. Finally, don't make bar and pie graphs three-dimensional—doing so confuses the reader.

Information that appears in figures, graphs, diagrams, flowcharts, and tables should be labeled with an informative title and complement the information in the text of the article without repeating it. For example, unless a statistic serves a specific purpose, resist the temptation to repeat it in the text of your article. If you're writing an article that deals with Mega Millions lottery winners from Georgia and you decide to include a table listing the number of winners by state during the past ten years, there's probably no need to rehash much of this information in your article.

When possible, avoid specifically mentioning a graph or flowchart in the text of your article. The reader should be able to appreciate the added content without being pointed to it. Nevertheless, if you do need to refer the reader to one of these elements, do so in an unobtrusive manner. Embed references to accompanying elements in the prose of your piece rather than devoting an entire sentence to it. In other words, make any references cohesive. Ultimately, you don't want your article reading like a journal piece.

> **UNADVISABLE:** "See Table 1 for more information."
>
> **BETTER:** "For those interested in comparing the number of lottery winners by state, take a look at the table accompanying this article."

CONCLUSION

When readers sit with your piece, they're forming a relationship with it—even if it's a short relationship. If they have read it to the end, then they're willing to see this relationship through and expect some closure. Consequently, the good writer will continue to deliver quality writing all the way to the end of the piece.

You may conclude your article by expanding the perspective of the piece, looking toward the future, revisiting the introduction, or inserting a relevant quotation.

Expanding the Perspective

Throughout the article, the writer establishes a way of thinking about some topic. In the conclusion, the writer may decide to bring home the point by explaining what it means to the reader. When expanding on the perspective of a piece, make sure that the idea you introduce would appeal to any reasonable person—for example, an unbiased expert—with knowledge of the subject.

A feature in *The Economist* titled "Looking for a Google" provides perspective in the conclusion. In part, this short article deals with the difficulties of setting up large and successful companies in developing countries. The ending provides perspective by means of a possible solution: learning about the management of big business from abroad.

> Learning from abroad, though, makes a big difference. In 1979, Desh, a Bangladeshi garments firm, sent 130 of its staff for an eight-month course at a South Korean textile plant. At the time, Bangladesh had no textile exports and no modern industry. When the trainees got back, almost all of them set up their own firms. Today Bangladesh has 3.6m textile workers, 80% of them women, generating $13 billion of exports a year ...

Looking Toward the Future

If you've done enough research and interviewed enough people, you may be able to predict how the issue will unfold. Much like when your conclusion expands on the perspective of the piece, when you look toward the future, your predictions should be reasonable and appeal to anybody with good judgment, such as an unbiased expert in the field.

In an article published in *High Times Medical Marijuana* titled "The Emerald City Goes Green," the conclusion discusses the future of medical marijuana in Seattle. (As its title may suggest, *High Times* is a magazine that serves an audience of marijuana aficionados, growers, and so forth. It advocates for the legalization of medical marijuana.)

> And so, while the state of medical cannabis in Seattle depends on many factors—and no one can say for certain what the next few years will hold—with patients and collectives working together, the future is looking bright green.

Revisiting the Introduction

One popular way of ending the article is to revisit the beginning. This approach especially works well when the lede is an anecdote. For example, in the piece "Head Start," which focuses on "quarterback guru" Steve Clarkson, the ending returns to David Sills V, the quarterback protégé readers met in the introduction. The piece ends with a bunch of kids who are under Clarkson's tutelage, asking how Sills, who is now fifteen years old, garnered a scholarship when aged thirteen.

> "I don't know," Sills said, sounding a little bashful, and then glanced over at Clarkson, awaiting further instruction.

Of note, in addition to revisiting the introduction, the conclusion also ends with a quotation.

Ending with a Quotation

As with any other quotation that you use in your piece, keep in mind that if you choose to end your piece with a quotation, it must be credible and preferably precise, too. Additionally, the quotation could express an emotion or opinion that is better expressed in somebody else's words. Finally, the quotation should provide a sense of closure.

In addition to starting with a quotation, in the *AARP The Magazine* article "Everybody Loves Tony … and the feeling is mutual," author Bill Newcott also ends with a quotation. The story starts by explaining that during the early years of his career, Tony Bennett was mentored by Frank Sinatra. Bennett then talks about how he had recently collaborated with and mentored younger artists, including Sheryl Crow, Queen Latifah, and Mariah Carey. The feature provides closure in Bennett's own words. Bennett says, "For me, it felt like graduation."

Keep in mind that there are different ways to end a piece, and as with most aspects of article writing, there is no absolute "right" way to proceed. As long as the ending is engaging and it works, you should feel comfortable with it.

BAILOUT POINT AND GOLD COINS

Sara Quinn, director of The EyeTrack Studies at the Poynter Institute, which examine both newspaper and online reading habits, explains the bailout point and suggests that a writer entice the reader with "visual gold coins."

"I wanted to find out … the average amount of time spent reading the first story that somebody came across, and it was about 1.5 minutes or 98.3 seconds—that was the average. And then I [wanted to see] if there's a common point where a person would commit to or stop reading the story altogether, and it was 78.3 seconds. I started to think of that as the 'bailout point,' the point at which somebody thinks, 'Maybe there's something better that I haven't looked at yet,' or they're just not ready to commit to the story.

"At that point, it's important to think about adding a little gold coin to keep people reading. … Something that's pretty substantial, that gets people to realize that there's more to the story. It's just craftsmanship—even of the design .… It might be a quote from someone who hasn't appeared yet in the story. … It might be a small graphic or something that might give more pertinent information. … Maybe it's another informative link … maybe it's something that's fairly transparent and says, 'You're not going to believe what you see at the end of this story.' … "Maybe the real benefit would be to give readers a summary of what they read so they have a level of satisfaction … just two or three key points, so even if they do stop reading there, they come away from that experience feeling satisfied with clarity.

"We can extrapolate and look at print reading. If you turn the page and it's just a galley of type and the design doesn't support it, [in this case] the subheads are very important … or [you can add] a nice visual element that keeps people reading so there's kind of a design or editing point."

Quinn goes on to suggest that gold coins be placed throughout a story. In the case of online stories, these gold coins may be placed every couple of screens. "It's important [that for] every couple of screens, something compels somebody to read … but [it shouldn't be] overdone. … You don't want to muck up a story."

It should be noted that Quinn bases this recommendation to use "gold coins" on the most recent EyeTrack studies, which tested readers using tablets in a controlled environment.

It's admirable that Quinn and Poynter are considering rewarding the reader with some type of "gold coin." It should be noted, however, that the reward system has neuroscientific underpinnings that warrant further examination. The reward system is mediated by dopamine, and its effects are prevalent in a variety of "reward"-triggering activities, including the use of illicit drugs, gambling, and even video gaming.

In order to sufficiently trip the reward system into kicking out "feel-good" dopamine, the gold coin must be appealing enough to the reader. Simply representing information from an article in novel, visual, or textual forms may not provide sufficient impetus to continue reading. Rewards may need to be more significant and may take the form of monetary, social, or virtual payment.

To help illustrate this point, let's consider an online publication that runs long features. In order to attract readers—and thereby generate revenue from targeted online advertising—the publication may consider posing challenging questions to the audience at specific intervals that punctuate reading. These questions require the reader to pay close attention and appreciate each article thoroughly, thus reinforcing interest in the publication (even if by means of cognitive dissonance). In return for answering these questions, the reader could be paid with some type of gold coin. These gold coins serve as feedback that perpetuates the dopamine-reward system and could slowly accrete to some system of material rewards—starting, with say, a special-edition T-shirt—or unlock special content or invitations to exclusive online chat sessions with a celebrity, politician, scientist, or so forth. Alternatively, the payment could take the form of a virtual point system that appeals to reader ego and promotes the reader to some level of expertise.

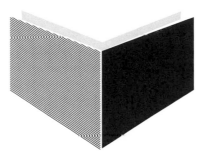

chapter 8

TYPES OF FEATURES

PROFILES AND OBITUARIES

Writing profiles can be a useful professional skill. Oftentimes a publication or company will pay money for profiles on important people (or people whom they suggest are important). Inspiration for possible profile subjects can come from various places, including the Internet, media sources, and personal acquaintances. Publications that routinely purchase profiles include consumer, trade, alumni, and hobbyist magazines. A profile can also be used as a sidebar in a long piece.

As with any feature, it's important to research the subject of your profile thoroughly before you start interviewing. Resumes, Curriculum Vitaes (CVs), publications, news releases, and previous profiles and articles on the person are all good sources of information. Many times, if you diligently study your subject, your subject will appreciate that you took the time to do so.

Begin by researching the subject of your profile on the Internet. A Google search can turn up previous profiles and professional descriptions put out by organizations and companies. It's important to search social-media sites, including LinkedIn and Facebook, for additional information. If the person whom you are profiling is famous enough, a formal literature search is a good idea and includes searches of the Marquis Who's Who series and *Current Biography Magazine*. For physicians and medical researchers, a good place to search is PubMed.

Especially with profile pieces, sitting with a source or subject of the piece in lieu of conducting an interview over the phone is always preferable. When doing a profile piece, it's beneficial to understand the source in his or her own environment—on his or her turf. Furthermore, for longer profile pieces, it's a good idea to interview your source in a couple of different settings with which he or she is familiar. When you're interviewing a source in an office, home, or favorite haunt, pay close attention to the surroundings because these details make for a good narrative. (Take a snapshot on your cell phone for future reference.)

When writing a profile, it's preferable to keep the piece positive. Work-related activities, community service, volunteer work, and hobbies are good topics to explore. Others include professional starts, childhood dreams, setbacks, memorable criticisms, and challenges. You'll also want to flesh out details and anecdotes to create images that will grab the reader's attention.

Many good profiles include input from people who are close to the person being profiled, whether they are co-workers, family members, or friends. Because the overwhelming majority of profiles are positive, it's a good idea to ask your subject for the names and numbers or e-mail addresses of other people who could be interviewed for the profile. For example, a source would likely suggest a trusted co-worker rather than a disgruntled former employee.

Most good profiles involve a judicious mix of a person's professional life, pastimes, social life, and family life. You can also use allegory or figurative elements to compare a person's professional life with personal details. For example, I once interviewed a medical student who lost his hand in a motor-vehicle accident. This disability made getting through medical school difficult. (As you can probably imagine, it's useful to have two hands while dissecting a body in anatomy lab or performing a physical exam on a patient.) I then compared his journey through medical school to running a marathon—one of his favorite pastimes. The comparison made for a strong narrative.

Profiles can be structured in various ways. Here's a short summary of each approach:

- Classic structure: 1) lede; 2) subject's notable achievements, distinguishing accomplishments, and so forth; 3) subject's history or background; and 4) conclusion
- Compartmentalization of different aspects of the subject's life
- Chronology of the subject's life using flashbacks
- Parallel episodes in a person's life: for example, three different successes, one personal, one professional, and one charitable
- Exploring a thesis: for example, exploring Lady Gaga and her shock value
- Question and answer (Q&A)

Remember that when writing a profile, you don't want to overeditorialize and glorify your subject. If you do include detailed complimentary information, it's best to attribute this information to somebody who is close to the subject—for example, a co-worker who admires the subject. Finally, consider incorporating a sidebar to expound on or discuss tangential information about your subject.

When writing a profile, it's a good idea to take an angle that hasn't been used before. Some favorite angles that can yield novel approaches include juxtaposition and contrast. For example, Margaret Guroff at *AARP The Magazine* wrote a feature titled "Stronger Together," which examined the lives of television journalist Meredith Vieira and her husband Richard M. Cohen, a prominent writer. In part, the piece contrasts Vieira and Cohen's ostensibly exciting professional lives with the very real difficulties of raising a family and dealing with Cohen's chronic disease.

It should be mentioned that the "VIP" or celebrity profile presents its own challenges. It's often difficult to secure much time with a famous person; consequently, the writer often relies on other sources to gather information for the article. With especially famous people, it may be hard to develop a new angle. For example, most people know that Tom Cruise is a prominent scientologist, and writing about his current religious beliefs may be tired. It may be more interesting to write about his early seminary education.

"Usually, with a celebrity profile," says Guroff, "you're lucky if you get an hour or two. You have to be sure that you've done enough research so that during that hour you can ask them questions that they won't have answered a million times."

Obituaries

Obituaries are similar to profiles, with one glaring exception: The subject is dead. When writing an obituary, the news of how the subject died is presented before the writer delves into a profile. The writer then references secondary sources for factual and quotation support. The writer may also interview people who knew the deceased.

The main challenge of writing an obituary is to present the subject with vitality—to bring the subject to life—and not simply create a laundry list of accomplishments, achievements, and awards.

"If they're done well, profiles and obituaries are very similar," says Dr. Tom Linden, the director of the Medical and Science Journalism program at the University of North Carolina at Chapel Hill. "An obituary should make the deceased person come to life. If an obituary is simply a recitation of the person's various achievements, and we have nothing of the person's voice or get a feeling of who the person was, then I don't think it's been a successful obituary."

SERVICE PIECES

Good service pieces are both entertaining and informative. They are directly aimed at the reader and dispense information meant to improve the reader's life, whether dealing with health, recreation, finance, or occupation.

I once wrote a service piece on cell phones and cancer risk. (Although the topic is debatable, limited evidence suggests that the electromagnetic waves emitted by cell phones may be associated with the development of glioma, a type of brain cancer.) The service value of the piece dealt with how audience members could minimize their risk of developing cancer if, in fact, cell phones did increase the risk. (Researchers advised readers to use hands-free headsets, text, and minimize talk time.)

When choosing the topic of a service piece, it's best to stick with subject matter that you understand. Because service pieces require directed research and in-depth knowledge, it's likely that a writer who doesn't understand the subject will write a substandard piece. For example, if you were to write an article about rock-climbing equipment and you're a couch potato, you're probably outside of your element. When writing service pieces, it's a good idea to focus on products that are new and that examine considerations such as cost. Time-saving tips also make for engaging copy.

When writing service pieces on products, it's best that your angle focuses on the decision-making process rather than specific products. For example, if you were going to write a piece on digital cameras, your angle (forgive the pun) may focus on whether megapixels affect picture quality. (Many people debate whether increased megapixels actually increase picture quality. They argue that a five-megapixel camera produces pictures just as clear as a twelve-megapixel camera.)

With service pieces, it's important to use the second-person point of view (*you* and *your*). For example, I wrote a cell-phone piece and in the nut graph I wrote, "Is it wise to set aside your cell phone in favor of your landline?" The *you* refers to the reader. Similarly, the lede and body of a service piece should relate to the reader, too.

It's also important to write with authority. If you've done your research properly, making strong statements and recommendations should come naturally. Try to keep your service piece well organized with appropriate headers. It's a good idea to consider using sidebars as well. Possible sidebars include reference boxes, Q&As, and lists (dos and don'ts and advantages and disadvantages). For example, if you were to write a service piece on digital cameras, you may want to include a sidebar that lists the most popular types of digital cameras.

For examples of service pieces, pick up any issue of *Men's Health*. A typical issue devotes almost its entire budget to service pieces—many deal with sex, diet, grooming, and so forth. These service pieces are instructive and entertaining. Of note, this magazine adopts a snarky and prescriptive tone that distinguishes it from some of its competitors.

How-To Pieces

How-to pieces are a subset of service articles. People can write how-to articles on nearly any topic—from building a hutch for a rabbit to baking muffins. When choosing a subject, however, keep safety and legality in mind. (You don't want to instruct your audience on how to program an Internet virus or "dine and dash.")

How-to articles commonly consist of the following parts:

- lede or engaging introduction with transition
- materials
- steps, tips, and suggestions
- illustrations, diagrams, or photos
- a kicker or powerful closing

Materials used are listed at the beginning of the piece, and step-by-step instructions should be written in parallel structure—they should use similar patterns of words and sentences. Instructions should be written with authority and can use words such as *then, when, now,* and *next.* The instructions must be clear and reproducible—you should never write a how-to piece on a process that you haven't tried yourself. It's a good idea to include trouble-shooting tips that anticipate when the reader may make a mistake. Whenever possible, include illustrations, diagrams, or photos in your how-to article so your reader can visualize the process. Make sure the illustrations are accompanied by captions that clearly explain them. Unlike most other sidebars, captions in how-to articles should reiterate information from the article. Additionally, when writing a how-to piece, delineate information as simply as possible. Finally, use quotations sparingly, write in the second person (using words like *you* and *your*), and write in an authoritative tone.

Nobody does how-to pieces quite like *Maxim*, a men's magazine that devotes a whole irreverent department to these entertaining features. For example, in the November 2012 issue, there are five how-to pieces: "How to Walk Away from a Big Explosion," "How to Rock a Famous Mustache," "How to Work Out Like a Sumo Wrestler," "How to Check-mate Like a Champ," and "How to Turkey, Day 2."

TRAVEL PIECES

Travel Pieces: Service

Good travel pieces are hard to write; they need to balance entertainment, service, and information. Although writing a travel piece may seem romantic—jetting off to some foreign place to cover a new and exciting topic—travel pieces are labor intensive and require much thought. They also require the writer to maintain a fresh perspective while keeping an eye on mundane concerns such as room rates, transportation options, and restaurant menus. But if you are able to write a good travel piece, plenty of potential markets are hungry for them, including in-flight magazines, travel magazines, newspapers, and women's magazines.

Travel pieces usually cover one of four service topics: tourists, traveler's experiences, portraits of a place, or specific and unique attractions. When writing a travel piece, it's important to take a novel angle that still captures the essence of the place you're writing about. For example, if you were to write about Seaport Village, a popular shopping and dining spot on the San Diego Bay, you should avoid writing about the variety of restaurants or shops per se. Doing so would be boring and redundant—a quick Internet search will reveal that many others have written this story. Instead consider a different angle and evaluate Seaport Village from a distinct vantage point. Maybe you could profile the buskers (street performers) who work the boardwalk. Whatever you do, don't make your travel piece too broad and cumbersome. As with any feature, it's impossible for a writer to cover everything well, and tough choices must be made about what to include in the travel piece.

When writing a travel piece, get a good feel for the place that you're writing about. Talk to the locals, walk the streets, take public transportations, visit the markets and shops, go to the museums, eat at the local restaurants, or attend religious or cultural ceremonies—do whatever you need to do to get a legitimate taste of an environment's ambience. Think about visiting places at different times of day. Oftentimes locals can give you a distinct perspective of the place that you're visiting. They can even teach you a few new words that may be useful when writing about a place—think of words like *irie* in Jamaica, *salamat po* in Tagalog, or *mahalo* in Hawaiian. Furthermore, it's important to secure good reference materials: maps, travel guides, and sightseeing brochures—many of which can be picked up at the local library or chamber of commerce. (Some useful online resources for travel writers include www.travelwriters.com, the World Chamber of Commerce, and the U.S. Travel Association.)

As many of us can appreciate, good memories of a foreign place may be fleeting. Consequently, it's important to organize your notes and thoughts before you leave the place you're writing about. Have a good idea for how your story will read before you leave. Take pictures and notes regarding images to remind yourself why they're important.

When writing a travel piece, try to keep everything as impartial as possible. Although some travel pieces are sponsored by destinations, a travel piece shouldn't be a promotional piece luring tourists to a destination. If it were, the travel piece would be advertising or public-relations work. Consequently, the travel writer must remain vigilant and retain conscious objectivity.

When writing a travel piece for a publication, the writer is often responsible for taking her own pictures, so it helps to buy a high-quality camera and know how to use it.

Travel Pieces: First-Person Narratives

Travel pieces can also take the form of first-person experiential narratives. In addition to his work as an actor, Andrew McCarthy is a travel writer and editor-at-large for *National Geographic*. He specializes in first-person narrative and has good advice on the subgenre.

"I'm trying to write stories that are personal and revealing in an effort to create identification with the reader. And if we create identification, then there's a feeling of connection. And if we have a feeling of connection, there's a feeling of investment. And once they're invested … we can take them anywhere.

"I don't give a shit about service pieces. I'm much more interested in attraction rather than promotion. I'm trying to create a world that you can enter. … [The belief that travel changed my life and it can change yours] is behind every travel story that I do.

"If you write it well enough, the 'I' disappears and the reader becomes the 'I.' That's what you're after … to make it universal. In order to become universal, it has to start out personal. Otherwise, I'm just talking in theory about something, and who gives a fuck? I'm not some authority on something. All I have to speak from is my experience, and if I lay down my experience … then I've got you. You've suddenly committed to me as a reader. You want the reader to nod their head. Once they nod their head, you're good."

When writing travel pieces, McCarthy adheres to a nut-graph structure: introducing a compelling anecdote in the lede and typically setting up some objective in the nut graph. For example, in the feature "In Search of the Black Pearl," McCarthy opens with a scene in which he jumps into a Tahitian lagoon in order to harvest a black pearl. In the nut graph, we learn the pearl is a present for his mother. The body of the feature prioritizes anecdotes about his trip to Tahiti and eventually brings us back to the initial anecdote with McCarthy plucking a black pearl from the sea.

By McCarthy's own admission, constructing a fluid narrative sometimes requires some cajoling. Events need to be transposed, and sources occasionally need to be asked leading questions in order to elicit a story. But McCarthy is careful never to take too heavy a hand with quotations.

"If you need to massage a quote to make it fit with the point that you're trying to make," says McCarthy, "the point that you're trying to make is wrong. But I have reordered things … to make a narrative work. I feel fine about that … having it build in a different way."

REVIEWS

Reviews fall into two broad categories: *book reviews* and *reviews of the arts*, which include film, television, theater, music, performing arts, paintings, food, restaurants, and wine. To some extent, this distinction is arbitrary—after all, a book can be considered art. Nevertheless, most books share enough characteristics that make them different from plays, films, paintings, and so forth. For example, a book on anatomy and a book on physiology are more similar to each other than either is to a Picasso or a Broadway play.

Reviews of the Arts

Nobody would argue that the writing of critics influences public perception. If you read a bad review of a film that you were considering plunking down fifteen dollars to see, you may wait until it comes out on DVD, streams on Netflix, or runs on cable, or you may choose not to see it at all. In fact, reviews are so influential that some prominent reviewers themselves become celebrities and influential figures. For example, many Americans know well the late film reviewers Gene Siskel and Roger Ebert and their catchphrase, "Two thumbs up."

Most reviews consist of five parts:

- Lede or engaging opening that draws your reader into the review
- Identification of whatever you're reviewing
- Summary (not synopsis) of what you're reviewing
- Opinion supported by argument
- A kicker or powerful closing

As with any feature, when writing a review, it's important to start off with a strong lede. The opening must also give a sense of opinion. Word choice and presentation can set the tone for the rest of the piece. "I'm always thinking about that first grab-you paragraph and grab-you sentence," says veteran film critic Joe Leydon, who writes for *Variety* and other publications.

When writing a review, it's important that the author properly identifies the piece being reviewed, preferably in both the introduction and conclusion. It's also important to provide enough information so that interested audience members know where they can check out the production. Obviously a major Hollywood film is easily viewed at a local movie theater, and thus mentioning the location is a moot point. But with a locally produced play that's only playing on specific dates at a specific theater, it's prudent to mention such information.

As with opinion pieces, a good review makes arguments that are supported by examples. "A good review is an argument. [You] state your case, and you buttress your case with examples," says Leydon. "It's not enough to say this is good, bad, or indifferent. You have to make the case." In other words, you must develop your opinion once you've expressed it. For example, writing that *The Shining* was a scary movie means much less to the reader than writing that in the movie, Jack Nicholson's descent into madness is scary—and then explaining why.

When reviewing, writers sometimes make the mistake of writing a synopsis rather than a summary. A synopsis is a chronological list of events. For example, a reviewer writing a synopsis of *The Shining* may first describe how Jack Nicholson's character and his family arrive at a hotel where he will serve as the winter caretaker (one of the movie's first scenes) and may continue by describing every significant scene until the end (where Nicholson's character dies). Readers don't want to read about every scene in a movie. What they want is to get a gist of the overall piece; they want a summary. A summary of *The Shining* would describe how a writer and his family take winter residence in a spooky hotel as lone caretakers. During the course of their stay, the writer descends into madness and tries to kill his family.

Sometimes it's unnecessary to write a robust summary, especially when the audience is more than likely familiar with the piece that you're reviewing. For example, if you were reviewing a recent adaptation of *Romeo and Juliet*, it's less important to expound on the basic premise of the original Shakespeare play: two star-crossed lovers. Rather it's more important to describe how the most recent adaptation differs from other adaptations.

Some people may find the prospect of reviewing a particular wine, play, or restaurant intimidating, especially if they feel they lack expertise in the subject. In a telephone interview, Roger Morris, an independent writer who specializes in wine, food, and travel, assured me that such expertise can come in various forms.

"I think that reviewers need to be experts in the fields that they review," says Morris. "Experience is very helpful, but there are all sorts of degrees of expert. ... Some people who have a lot of experience bring something to the table. ... There are also a lot people who may not have as much experience but have good observational powers, or they have good ways of thinking about things or looking at trends ... [they have] a lot of power to bring to the table."

As with any document, when writing a review, you must consider your audience. "You try to write a review or write observations according to the publication," says Morris. "For a publication like the *Daily Mail*, the readers are not as much experts as readers of *Wine Enthusiast* or *Sommelier Journal*. It's not a matter of dumbing down or smarting up ... it's more a matter of trying to figure out how much shorthand [jargon you can use]. You can use more shorthand with someone who knows the background. You don't have to explain everything to them. With someone who doesn't have as much background, you need not get in as much detail or explain the detail."

By default, when writing for a general audience, it may be good to write a review in a conversational tone. "I learned a long time ago," says Leydon, "when you're reviewing, a conversational tone is very effective. Hands down, the best film critic in America in that regard is Roger Ebert. It's like he's sitting across from you at a table in a diner and he's telling you what he thought of the movie he just saw. That is very engaging, but it's also very illuminating." (At the time of this interview, Roger Ebert was still alive.)

When Morris reviews wines—or anything, for that matter—he considers his subjects in context. "In literary criticism," says Morris, "there was a school called the New Criticism, which believed that you took everything without a context. [This] meant that if you were tasting wines, you would taste them blind. You wouldn't know who [produced the wines,] and [you would] describe them. ... The other school ... and this is the one I belong to ... believes that with context you get more out of something. When you're tasting [a wine] ... when you know the context within which you're tasting it ... if you're tasting a 2012 Bordeaux, it helps me to know who the producer is because I may know the history of the producer ... as opposed to tasting it totally blind."

Leydon also considers context when he reviews. "You need to have some knowledge about film history to catch all the references that contemporary filmmakers are making within film," says Leydon. "I'm not saying that you need to see every spaghetti western ever made before you try to review Quentin Tarantino's *Django Unchained*, but it would probably behoove you to have some familiarity with a few of the spaghetti westerns—if only the original *Django*—before you try to write about his film."

In addition to considering context, Morris is careful to consider differing tastes when reviewing: "There are differences in taste, and almost nothing is absolute. Let's say you take the Cakebread wines in Napa Valley. Most people who spend a lot of time writing about wine or thinking about wine would say Cakebread is a very good producer, but you would have a number of people who are also very good in their opinions who would say they're highly overrated. The same is [true for] film, and the same is true with everything else.

"I'm willing to defend my reasons for thinking [a wine is good], but I also recognize why other experienced people may not like this wine. … I try not to be didactic. … I try not to be 100 percent one way. I like to say what I like and why I like it, but even if I don't particularly care for something, I will explain the kind of people or palate that might like this wine. [Just] because I don't like it doesn't mean it's poorly made. … One man's virtue is another man's flaw. I only count it as a flaw if the winemaker can't control something, and sometimes you don't even know that without talking to them."

Like Morris, film reviewer Joe Leydon is careful when writing charged statements that may polarize his audience. "Just as one scene that 'jumps the shark' can take you out of the movie," says Leydon, "one sentence can take me out of a review. [I think that] this person doesn't speak the same language I do … this person doesn't feel the same way I do … they got it wrong here."

Sampling Bias

In science, sampling bias occurs when a researcher fails to select a random sample representative of an entire population. For example, if a researcher were trying to estimate the average height of the American man by sampling NBA players, the results would be way off—NBA players are really tall! When reviewing a product or service, smart reviewers will do their best to obtain a random sampling.

"In most cases, instead of reviewing a meal or a bottle of wine, I would rather [review] the general output of a restaurant or winery over time," says Morris. "That's how I approach it, and many food critics do the same thing … [and] go back several times to a restaurant. … You have a certain responsibility to the reader. If they like you, they're going to go along with your recommendation or at least take it into account."

It's particularly important to consider sampling bias when reviewing products or services that change over time, such as food and wine. Finished products such as books and movies don't—for the most part—change over time. "When I wrote about films," says Morris, "I was much younger and probably less thoughtful. If I were writing film reviews now—or a book review even—I would be less kind, less friendly, because it's out there. It's for everybody to see. It's not going to change. … There's not going to be such a thing as 'You hit us on a bad evening,' or, 'That was a bad vintage.' It's out there. … It's a finished work. … It's open to everybody. If I was doing film criticism now, I would be much tougher than I would be for wine and food writing."

But even when reviewing movies, the notion of sampling bias may be relevant—especially for first-time directors. "I may be tempted to give a first-time filmmaker more of a pass than I would be tempted to give a pass to an off work from somebody who I know is capable of better," says Leydon.

Unfortunately, some writers who review the arts are unnecessarily mean. (If interested in learning more about how negative some critics are, I suggest the documentary *Heckler* starring Jamie Kennedy.) When reviewing the arts, keep in mind that those involved in the film, play, or concert probably tried to do their best. There's no reason to be ruthlessly disparaging. For example, I once was invited to review a film by Sony Pictures, and I ended up writing a review where I criticized an actress's smile (she had several snaggleteeth). In retrospect, I thought I was being funny, but I just ended up being mean. The review was okay and some people liked it, but to this day, I feel bad for unnecessarily commenting on the actress's teeth.

When reviewing the arts, there are at least three good reasons to refrain from being unduly critical. The first reason has to do with preserving the livelihood of others. A bad review could not only hurt the restaurant, winery, and so forth but also affect employees who depend on the sale of such products and services to put bread on their own tables.

Morris states, "When you're writing about wineries and food, some organizations are so large that your opinion doesn't really make any difference. But sometimes with someone small or someone new, before I become too cynical or before I make some smartass remark—which I [often] like to do—[I remember] that I've got someone's livelihood in my hands. The reader comes first before the winery or restaurant that I'm reviewing, but … rather than be too snarky or sarcastic about something, I try to explain what I have a problem with. [I try] not to make it so that I'm some Attila the Hun."

The second reason to refrain from being unduly critical is to avoid making a fool out of yourself and eroding your credibility as a reviewer. "It's very easy if you're writing a lot," says Morris, "to make a statement and think it's correct … [even if] you haven't checked thoroughly. Or you're on deadline, and you say something stupid."

The third reason many reviewers try to refrain from doling out negative reviews is because many established critics are generous people who want to celebrate the art they review. Although they may delight their audience members by writing a scathing review, the prospect of doing so is antithetical to why they started reviewing in the first place.

"Everybody remembers the bad reviews more than your good reviews," says Leydon. "They remember your pans more than your raves. … I'm talking about your audience—your readership. … There's this myth that critics … prefer to write pans rather than raves. That's not true. … I'm not masochistic. … I want every film to be good at the very least, and I'm hoping for greatness. If I can discover a great filmmaker, that's a thrill."

A great—or rather pretty despicable—example of a reviewer going overboard is Pete Wells' review of "Guy's American Kitchen & Bar," which was published in *The New York Times*. The restaurant's proprietor is Guy Fieri, the flamboyant host of the television show *Diners, Drive-Ins and Dives*. In the article, Wells uses a series of questions to disparage nearly everything about the restaurant. For example, Wells writes, "Hey, did you try that blue drink, the one that glows like nuclear waste? The watermelon margarita? Any idea why it tastes like some combination of radiator fluid and formaldehyde?"

Ultimately, there's a prevailing opinion among many reviewers that unless some product or service is worthy of a review, it's best not reviewed. Trashing a restaurant, winery, off-off-Broadway show, or whatever else probably won't entertain anybody and will end up squandering readers' attention.

"Mostly people aren't interested in things that you *hate*," says Morris. "In most cases, people want your opinion on things they're going to *like*. If I go to a place and there's nothing I'm going to like, then basically I wouldn't write about it."

On a final note, technology has made reviews instantly available in a variety of formats. Rovi Corporation stockpiles reviews on albums, movies, and television shows and makes them available in the form of metadata, which can be licensed out to other technology companies such as Pandora, an Internet radio service.

Press Kits

Press kits make for wonderful secondary sources when reviewing a movie. The typical press kit can contain historical information regarding events in the film; a short and long synopsis; notes on production, design, and locations; profiles of the actors, producers, directors, and other crew; and photos for use in publication. If a publicist or public-relations specialist is contacting you to review a film, she will likely send you access to the press kit. Otherwise, you can sometimes find press kits online, or you can contact the public-relations firm or divisions associated with the production company or movie studio. Finally, if you're representing a publication or have a publicity contact at the movie studio, you can request access to portions of websites that are password protected and devoted to members of the press.

Grading Reviews

Much to the chagrin of reviewers, in addition to being reviewed, many readers desire that artistic endeavors be graded, too. Many critics argue that letter and number grades encourage readers to skip reading the reviews. Furthermore, gradations lack nuance—for example, even bad films have good moments.

"A sizable segment of people who read reviews want to see stars or letter grades, and that's it," laments Leydon. "And you [the reviewer] better make it pretty clear. It can't be something that waits until the end. This is something that you have to offer [up front]."

Blogging Reviews

Blogs have provided great opportunities for new reviewers to go online and make their opinions known. Once upon a time, budding reviewers often had no place to celebrate their love of the arts. Nowadays, in minutes, anybody can set up a WordPress blog and preach to a little corner of the Internet.

"I like the fact that blogs are giving access to a wide variety of people," says Morris. "Back when I was writing in the '80s and '90s, it was almost impossible to get a job writing about food or wine because there were usually two newspapers in your community and both of them already had a critic. … I spent a lot of my time writing for newspapers and a lot of time not writing because I didn't have a place to write for. … I like the democracy of blogs because they give everybody a chance to write something—even people who should never be writing anything. But … some people come up and start blogs and just do marvelous jobs."

Suspending Disbelief

Most high school English students are taught to suspend their disbelief when reading a book or watching a movie. This formative lesson may incline the neophyte reviewer to refrain from questioning a movie, play, or book's plausibility. Many critics, however, will target disbelief especially when they dislike a movie. "Lapses in logic [or] stretches of implausibility are only noticeable or irritating if you're not into the movie," says Leydon. Questioning such lapses or stretches is "part of your ammunition if you want to say that the movie is bad."

For example, Leydon didn't like the movie *Jersey Girl*; consequently, he questioned the rather odd coincidence that Ben Affleck's character would have the most important job interview of his life at the same moment that his daughter's play was showing. But when faced with the even more preposterous premise that adult conjoined twins Greg Kinnear and Matt Damon moved to Hollywood and hit it big, Leydon was much more forgiving. Leydon—and many other critics—like the film for the good faith and "generosity of spirit" it engendered in audience members.

Book Reviews

Book reviews play several valuable roles. First, a book review can expose a reader to a work they haven't heard of. Second, a book review can evaluate a book's contribution to a field, discipline, or genre. Third, for many people who may otherwise have little time to read an entire book, the book review can serve as a valuable summary of its important points.

For many new writers, book reviews are a great way to not only score a byline or publication credit but also gain experience working with an editor. (For many reasons, any professional writer must learn how to work with an editor; working with an editor improves a writer's understanding of style and helps a writer anticipate the needs of future editors and publications.) There are plenty of places to publish book reviews, including association publications such as *Science Books & Films* (SB&F), which is published by the American Association for the Advancement of Science (AAAS).

Before you decide to write a book review, figure out if you're a good fit for the review. If you're a nurse with a limited understanding of physics and astronomy, you may want to steer clear of reviewing a book on cosmology. Furthermore, if possible, you may want to consider pulling in another reviewer with a different area of expertise to help you review a book. For example, if you're an astronomer and you decide to review a book on astrophysics, consider asking a physicist colleague to help you out.

As with any type of review, a book review includes opinion (most book reviews are two-thirds summary and one-third opinion). If possible, include an opinion of the book at the beginning. When arguing an opinion of a book, it's best to balance this opinion. Every book, no matter how great or terrible, has both positive and negative points. A review that is unbalanced reads as insincere. Aside from opinion, which is supported by examples, a book review should include specific facts about the book itself and can also include background information or a historical perspective.

Here's a list of different topics to consider when writing a book review:

- Purpose of the book and whether the book fills this purpose
- Context of the book (scientific, popular, cultural, or otherwise)
- Scope of the book
- Audience for the book
- Layout and organization of the book (graphic design, images, photos, index, glossary, and more)
- Relevance (scientific, cultural, or otherwise)
- Comparison with other works
- Accuracy
- Points stressed
- Social significance
- Author's background
- Scientific, moral, spiritual, or philosophical views that are described
- How character, plot, and setting reflect the theme
- Style concerns: grammar, punctuation, syntax, word usage, and more
- Flow, coherence, and unity

When structuring a book review, evaluate other book reviews that have appeared in the publication you're writing for. Previous pieces offer guidance on what's worked before and what may work for your book review. Another approach that works well, especially when reviewing scientific texts, is following the outline of scientific papers: the IMRAD structure. The IMRAD construction consists of an *Introduction*, *Methods*, *Results*, and *Discussion*.

The introduction may include an engaging lede and background information. The methods section is particularly important to delineate when reviewing a reference book like a dictionary or encyclopedia, which may be impossible to read in its entirety. A results section could include a summary of the work. The discussion section may expound on your opinion of the book.

After writing a book review, it's helpful to discuss the review with other people—especially experts. For example, if you're reviewing a book on preventive health, consider consulting a family-medicine physician at an academic research center. Consider whether the book review does a good job of surveying the work in a fair and balanced way. Keep in mind that writing a book is a difficult undertaking, and, despite possible shortcomings, nearly every work has some merit.

As when reviewing the arts, unless compelled by assignment, there's no reason to trash a book during a review. Books are of paramount importance in the spreading of knowledge and information. When you review a book, make sure that the book you're reviewing makes a valuable contribution to the world. Don't waste your time reviewing a book just so you can criticize it. Instead, review a book with the intention of helping others.

HUMOR

Unlike a stand-up comic, a humor writer can't rely on voice modulation, hand gestures, facial expressions, or even Carrot-Topesque props. A comic will also tirelessly refine an act onstage, but a humor writer doesn't have the luxury of trial runs. Nevertheless, if you have a flair (and the stomach) for writing humorous copy, then by all means try it; humor is a wonderful gift.

Whether humor writing can be taught is a very meta-journalistic, existential-type question. "I don't think you can teach others to be funny," says Pulitzer Prize-winning humor columnist Dave Barry. "You either are or you're not funny. But most people have a reasonably good sense of humor. … I do think you can teach people to be better at being funny."

Barry offers some useful tips to the budding humorist: "With writing, there are things that you can do right and wrong. It's useless to try to analyze humor too much, and you certainly can't reduce it to rules. But there are mistakes that people make when writing humor that can be avoided. One of the biggest mistakes that people make in attempting to write humor is beating a joke to death … take one idea and offer endless variations on it. You get the joke the first time … then it gets tedious … then [the writer] obliterates the joke. Leave the funny part last. Surprise the reader with the joke, and get on to something else."

Writing well and understanding style can also help the humor writer create compelling and funny prose. "I learned grammar thoroughly," says Barry, "and I found that to be incredibly useful and still do. To be able to know the absolute most precise way of writing something using English grammar … it's all about precision. There's always a difference between one word and another word. There are lots of different ways to say something … and if you're trying to be funny, it helps to know all these other ways I can present this idea—[how] I can word this. I can try different ways and see which is the funniest." Barry goes on to say that for the humor writer to simply write down a joke and think it's good without reworking it may keep the joke from being great.

A humor writer should be careful to realize that a fine line exists between being humorous and being offensive. From a psychology perspective, the porous relationship between humor and insult makes sense. "If you write humor," says Barry, "you have to be much more aware of the fact that you don't see your audience. You don't know who your audience is. If you are going to write for a newspaper or any broad Internet audience, you should be aware that you could write something that is deeply offensive and very funny. But if it is deeply offensive and the audience is not on your side, you'll probably pay a price for that."

Even if a humor writer were successful at creating funny copy that is deeply offensive, Barry cautions that such humor may no longer appeal to a general audience: "If you're going to write humor for a living and you're going to go for far, far, super-edgy rape humor, you're probably going to have a smaller audience and you're going to have people who are unhappy with you."

As with "super-edgy rape humor," a humor writer may want to be discerning when using scatological humor (poop jokes). "My feeling on scatological humor," says Barry, "is it works best if it's a little bit of surprise. I like it. … I think it has its place. … I think it can be really funny. I don't think it should be the heart of the humor. You can use it to emphasize the joke. If you were talking about something really sophisticated and it was suddenly in the bathroom, that could be funny. But [if you use it as] a crutch … maybe that isn't such a great thing."

If you're unsure whether what you've written is funny, show it to somebody. "If I have a question," says Barry, "I show it to my wife who has a good sense of humor and is levelheaded. And if she doesn't get it, she doesn't get it, and that's a useful thing to [know]. I think everybody should show things to my wife—just kidding—but it's good to let somebody look at it—and not somebody like your mom, who will say everything is great. Eventually, you reach a point that you don't need a sounding board, but in the beginning you do."

Without a doubt, writing humor is challenging. "The hardest part," says Barry, "is thinking up the jokes. I usually don't have much of a topic … much of a message. Humor writing is painfully hard. If you write an article about how to defrost your freezer, you've done a little work and you know what the steps are. If you're writing humor, you have absolutely no idea what you're going to say about it. The whole point is to say something new that people haven't seen—including you."

Just as with other types of writing, humor writing requires a large investment of time. "Time is the thing," says Barry. "It takes a lot of time; it's painful; it rarely just flows out. One of the main reasons that so few people make it as humor writers is because they want it to be easier and more fun to do. And it is fun, but it's not easy. You develop it over years … the sense of, 'If I stick with it, it will come. If I rework the sentence enough times, I will get the best wording for it. And if I think about this while I'm driving or running, another joke or part of the joke will occur to me.' It's a slow accretion of parts of humor that slowly build up into the finished piece that makes it work."

Topicality is a big issue among humor writers. Humor writers need to be aware of popular culture and keep in mind that a joke that's funny today may be dated tomorrow. However influential, the musings of Ambrose Bierce, S.J. Perelman, and the Algonquin Round Table are probably less funny today than when they were written decades ago.

Some of the hottest humor articles today are published by *The Onion*, a satirical news publication that dubs itself "America's Finest News Source." To their credit, writers and editors at *The Onion* do such a good job at parody and satire that every few months they manage to punk some politician, organization, or foreign government. For example, in 2012, *The People's Daily*—the mouthpiece for the Chinese Communist Party—was duped into reporting that the pudgy North Korean ruler Kim Jong-un was named the "Sexiest Man Alive for 2012."

Barry sees the future of humor writing moving toward the Web: "Much more of it is going to be on the Internet … Twitter … [and will be] shorter, quicker, and more interactive than it used to be. … Newspaper humor writing, not so much … the heyday for that is over. It's changed so much; I don't see how humorists are going to go that direction and have much luck with it."

Although not everybody is cut out to be a humor writer, sprinkling some humor into your writing can be a remarkable asset. Barry says that humor is "the best single tool that a writer can have in his arsenal. … It's always welcome. People love humor—especially if [your topic is] something boring or predictable. If it's funny, people like that. People should use humor whenever they can—assuming it's appropriate."

SHORTS

When I write about shorts, I'm referring to ultrashort features, which range in length from 250 to 400 words. A reader will normally find these pieces in magazine departments (sections) or newsletters.

Because these pieces are short, the lede can often be reduced to one sentence. The momentum of this sentence should carry the reader through the rest of the piece.

I once wrote a short about how many primary-care physicians (pediatricians, internists, family-medicine physicians, and so forth) end up facing financial hardship in their first years of practice. My lede and nut graph were short and sweet: "Researchers at Dartmouth used economic modeling to figure out that, with expenses exceeding earnings, primary-care physicians, unlike specialists, can end up taking a financial hit in their first three to five years of practice."

When writing shorts, it's especially important to prioritize which information should go into a piece and which information should be left out. As is often the case, if an editor were to allot only a few hundred words for a piece, there's little room for fluff or filler. For example, when writing about how primary-care physicians take a financial hit, I alluded to how they make less than specialists but I never made specific reference to average salaries. If I were to discuss actual numbers, there wouldn't be enough room to cover more important issues, including quoted material from experts responding to these findings.

Just because shorts are shorter doesn't mean you should research any less. Proceed with your regular routine: Do good research, interview the right sources, and be sure to verify facts. It's particularly important to pick potent quotations when writing a short. As with any feature article, you may end up discarding plenty of great quotations, but the sting will be particularly biting in a short feature.

Writing shorts is a great way to introduce yourself to a publication and editors. If you are able to prove your mettle by writing a strong short—which is no easy feat—you will likely impress an editor and be invited to pitch for more substantial stories.

TREND PIECES

A *trend* is a quantifiable increase or decrease in some social, economic, scientific, or popular phenomenon. With respect to science and medicine, a trend can describe the increasing prevalence or total number of people being affected by a disease. For instance, in light of rising obesity rates, more young children are developing type 2 diabetes, a disease that at one time was thought to affect only adults. The increasing prevalence of type 2 diabetes among children is frightening because diabetes is an insidious disease that can cause blindness, heart problems, kidney disease, and more. Another example of a disturbing trend is the rise in unemployment rates ever since the financial crises of 2007. In September 2012, the unemployment rate was 7.8 percent, up from 4.4 percent in May 2007. With respect to a trend in the realm of popular culture, it's hip to own an iPhone, which explains why the market cap of Apple has broken five hundred billion dollars.

In a *Wall Street Journal* article titled "How Do You Spell Hipster? It Could Be B-I-N-G-O," author Julie Jargon writes about how bingo (along with euchre, bowling, and knitting) is enjoying a resurgence among twenty- and thirty-year-olds. Furthermore, bingo has taken on several new iterations, including the global Underground Rebel Bingo Club and "cosmic bingo," which is played under black light. Apparently, this trend has supporters among celebrities, too. Billy Corgan of the band Smashing Pumpkins hosts a monthly bingo night at Madame ZuZu's, a teahouse he owns near Chicago. The event has local celebrities drawing numbers.

Trends often originate as individual observations and anecdotes before they're tracked and become quantifiable phenomenas. An editor may notice a trend and then assign a piece based on this observation. Dr. David E. Sumner, a professor of journalism at Ball State

University, says, "I think all trends start out anecdotally, and then they start to show up as numbers and statistics, particularly in the area of popular culture."

The publication *Ad Age* is a good place to find information on trends. In fact, Ipsos, a leading marketing-research company, paired with *Ad Age* to produce stories on consumer trends, attitudes, and behaviors. According to Ipsos and others, some major American year-end trends in 2012 included continued disappointment in the economy and national politics; an increasing number of Americans attaining college degrees and giving to charities; and a decrease in consumer debt, cancer, teen pregnancy, smokers, drinking and driving, trash generated, and law-enforcement deaths.

Another great place to find out about trends—especially trends in real time—is the website Reddit. At Reddit, users vote and the most popular stories rise to the top.

Remember that simply presenting trends as numbers does little for your audience. It's important to attach a face to the trends—create anecdotes that tell trends as stories. For example, if a writer decided to write a piece on the increasing prevalence of type 2 diabetes in children, it may be a good idea to profile a child with the disease and include this narrative in the piece.

THOUGHT PIECES

Journalists often report on issues that have two sides. Sometimes these opposing sides merely disagree over what could be viewed as trivial or humorous matters—fans from opposing sports teams often disagree with each other with little consequence. (Granted, a riot occasionally crops up after a heated soccer game, and some University of Alabama fans can be quite motley.)

Sometimes, however, the disagreements people or groups of people have are more serious and can be categorized as controversy or even conflict. Nobody would trivialize the emotion and conviction that underlies issues such as gun rights and abortion laws. As we all know, when serious conflict is involved, destruction can ensue, with serious repercussions; wars are waged, and lives may be lost. Fortunately, most reporters are empathetic to tragedy and have the good sense to refrain from exploiting the sadness of others. Nevertheless, if approached gingerly and with good judgment, disagreement, conflict, and controversy can make for engaging copy.

It should be noted that although the investigative piece is similar to the thought piece, it's a different type of article. Investigative pieces are inherently different from thought pieces because they are usually news pieces that explore explicit wrongdoing. Journalists who write investigative pieces reference primary sources and do original data analysis. Furthermore, investigative journalists don't offer their sources prepublication review. In fact, sources in investigative pieces are often unwilling to speak with journalists at all.

Research

I've broadly characterized any feature that deals with opposing viewpoints as a thought piece because they require a lot of thought and work. In order to truly understand any issue with two sides, much research is required. A good reporter will read through primary and secondary sources, such as the *CQ Researcher*, speak with experts, interview people on both sides of the issues, and more. In most cases, a good reporter will adopt a viewpoint that is impartial and choose to speak with educated sources who are also impartial in order to help flesh out the issue.

Bloom's Taxonomy

When dealing with a thought piece, one useful pedagogy to consider is Bloom's Taxonomy. This pedagogy is useful because it helps us understand how we incorporate and use acquired knowledge. Lower levels of Bloom's Taxonomy deal with memorizing knowledge and regurgitating it without truly understanding the concepts. For example, you may be able to teach a four-year-old girl to memorize a Shakespearean sonnet, but whether she's able to analyze it is unlikely. But if you have the requisite critical-thinking skills, you can not only recall the information but also integrate it and apply it. When writing a thought piece, it's important to ascend the Bloom's "pyramid" and synthesize and evaluate the information.

Angle

When entrepreneurs try to solicit funding from venture-capital firms, they draw up a business proposal. Invariably, however, these business proposals change as plans further develop because more information presents itself and complications arise. Similarly, the predicted angle for a thought piece is likely to change as you dig deeper into an issue. Unless you have a deep understanding of the issues that you're tackling and the major players in your potential piece, your angle will evolve with your piece.

When you initially query for a thought piece, you may be able to predict or hypothesize about an angle, but it's always important to inform your editor that this angle may change. If the angle does change, you'll want to keep your editor informed and send e-mails with any new developments. Of note, some publications have little toleration for changing an angle midstream, and you must be aware of this reality before you commence work. For example, at *AARP The Magazine*, the editors expect a piece to come in as promised. When pitching a publication such as this, it's best to make sure that you do plenty of research before you submit a query letter.

Figure 8.1

BLOOM'S TAXONOMY

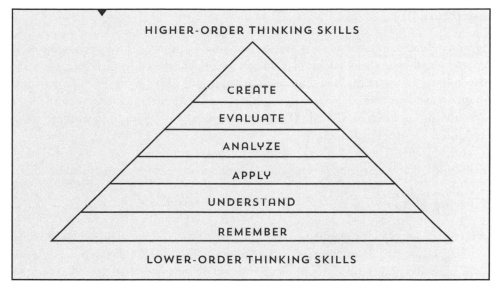

HIGHER-ORDER THINKING SKILLS

CREATE

EVALUATE

ANALYZE

APPLY

UNDERSTAND

REMEMBER

LOWER-ORDER THINKING SKILLS

Angles with thought pieces are complicated because they involve several factors. You must consider who's affected, how they're affected, and how serious the issue is (are people merely miffed, or are they losing their lives?). Additionally, you must consider how long the central development that motivates your piece will last. A baseball team's loss in a play-off game may last only a few hours, and in no time fans will forget it and begin looking forward to the next game. But what about all the tension in the Middle East? We're likely to see change and fallout from the Arab Spring for several years to come, and there's nothing ephemeral about that.

When putting together a thought piece, you also must consider what motivates the participants and understand their mentality. In *The Art and Craft of Feature Writing*, William Blundell notes that concerns about money seem to have an effect on many issues. As many of us can imagine, finances are the lowest common denominator in many situations. For example, during the 2012 presidential debates, the mainstream media had a field day with Big Bird and his threatened extinction. More specifically, when Mitt Romney proposed a cut in funding to the Public Broadcasting Service, fans of Big Bird and his Muppet brethren called foul. (It should be noted that Mitt Romney doesn't have a personal issue with Big Bird, but rather the United States has a several-trillion-dollar debt, and Romney figured the money to pay off some of the debt needed to come from somewhere. Whether it should come at the expense of shuttering Sesame Street is a point of debate.)

Although money is of primary concern when considering different sides of a story, other factors affect peoples' reasoning, too. These factors include social, political, or psychological concerns, or some combination, as was the case with the Montana Freemen, who tried to claim their own autonomy and eventually surrendered to the FBI in 1996.

Structure

It's often difficult to ascribe to any specific structure when you write a thought piece. Of course, you'll have a lede, nut graph, and conclusion, but the body of the piece varies; it depends on the research you've done and the issues at hand. Many times, it's a good idea to group concepts thematically and group direct and indirect quotations by speaker, but even this practice may be difficult. (Maybe you need the quotations to play off each other and thereby resemble a dialogue.)

Organization is key in a thought piece. When possible, using headers is a good idea. Establishing multiple entry points through the use of sidebars and figures may also be wise.

Getting Help

A thought piece typically requires the help and participation of several people. When interviewing, it's okay to tell your sources that you're confused and ask for their input. Fortunately, most sources are helpful and hope that the subject is properly covered. Keep lines of communication open, and drop a source an e-mail when you stumble on something that you don't understand. Be careful, however, not to let your source unduly influence your piece. Remember that it's your piece, and it's your duty to present the whole story without bias.

Prepublication review can be especially helpful when writing a thought piece (see Chapter 5 for more on prepublication review). Sometimes issues dealt with in a thought piece are so complicated that it helps to bring quotations back to your source for review and clarification.

When writing scientific articles, scientists may turn to their peers for help. The best journals are peer reviewed, which means that a group of the authors' peers review the article and make recommendations and suggestions before the piece is ready for publication. Journalists writing for publications don't engage in a peer-review process; nevertheless, the principles of peer review may be useful when writing a thought piece. If you're writing a story and feel that you could use an extra pair of eyes to review it, find an impartial expert to help you along. For example, if you were a professional journalist who usually writes about general-interest topics and you were commissioned to write a piece on a controversial new cancer treatment, you may consider asking an oncologist with no commitment to your piece to review it and provide input. When the piece is ready to go to print, as a courtesy, you can ask your editor to credit this independent reviewer at the end of your article.

One frustrating difficulty when writing a thought piece deals with conflicting information. Specifically, the factual information that a source provides may conflict with published (peer-reviewed) research or the accounts of other sources.

"A peer-reviewed journal is much more accurate," says Sumner. "You can't always believe everything people tell you in an interview, which is why you need more than one source to interview ... [and] why you need to do the background research. ... If an interview conflicts with peer-reviewed research, I would correct it or I would not use it."

On a final note, what tends to unify thought pieces is length—many are long. Although the consumption of long-form journalism is becoming increasingly popular via digital means—if interested, check out the websites Longform, Longreads, and MATTER—many of these articles are still best appreciated in print.

"I think it's more challenging to retain a reader's attention screen by screen rather than page by page," says science journalist Robert Irion. "That may change as the digital natives—the folks who have been using digital media since childhood—grow up and start craving more substantive things online. ... Right now the most defining—the most influential—long-form narrative that we see is in print."

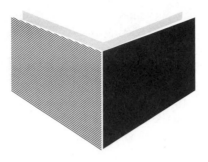

chapter 9

FEATURES: STRUCTURE & CRAFT

How should a person look?

Obviously there's no right answer to this question. Other than sharing some common anatomical parts, all people look different. Some of us are short, tall, skinny, overweight, white, black, and so forth. We look as we look.

Similarly, the structure of an article—most typically a feature article—has no predetermined appearance. It takes on a shape that reflects its purpose, scope, audience, angle, publication, and more. After spending hours, months, or even years researching a piece, the article will reveal its shape to the writer. When this occurs, your relationship with the article is about to be consummated.

"The best stories," writes Chip Scanlan of the Poynter Institute, "often create their own shape; writers consider their material, determine what they want the story to say, and then decide on the best way to say it."

So why do we spend time characterizing the structure of an article? To be fair, many journalists and academics don't spend much time discussing structure, believing that any preordained structure forced on a story will appear contrived. "I just write a story, and based on whatever comes out, I recognize the structure," says Dr. David E. Sumner, professor of journalism at Ball State University. "Structures tend to be fluid and very nonscientific. I tend not to emphasize rigid structures, except the chronological narrative."

I've decided to discuss structure first because I find it interesting, and, more important, the characteristics intrinsic to certain pedagogies of structure may direct you when considering what to concentrate on once your article starts to take shape. For example, if the shape of your article starts to look like the diamond structure—with the specific becoming more general, then the general becoming more specific—you may want to consciously conform to this structure.

Of note, some publications choose that their articles adhere to a certain structure. Typically, this structure is some variant of the nut-graph structure with an anecdotal lede, nut graph, and so forth. In these cases, a writer has less latitude when planning out a story. Furthermore, many award-winning stories have a novel structure that incorporates expert elements of storytelling, including nuanced flashbacks and fractured structures, two things that lie outside the scope of this text.

NARRATIVE STRUCTURE

The narrative structure is probably the best appreciated of all structures used to write a feature article. It is written in a straightforward fashion, with a beginning, middle, and end.

Sara Quinn, a faculty member at the Poynter Institute, says of the narrative structure, "You're led along and don't know how it will end. In a lot of ways, that's like a movie because it's emotional, it has a lot of detail, and it makes you really feel something."

Features written in the narrative structure are often told chronologically. Telling a story in chronological fashion has proven highly successful for many writers. Between 1979 and 2003, nineteen of twenty-five Pulitzer Prize-winning features used narrative (chronology) as either a main structure or combined with some other structure. (If you haven't done so already, I *highly* suggest that you link to www.pulitzer.org to read some Pulitzer Prize-winning articles.)

Some stories are naturally suited for a narrative structure because they have a clear beginning, middle, and end. Let's consider the story of the "Beltway Sniper" who in 2002 terrorized the residents of Washington, D.C., Virginia, and Maryland.

> **BEGINNING:** In October 2002, an unidentified sniper—soon labeled the "Beltway Sniper"—started assassinating unsuspecting victims in Washington D.C., Virginia, and Maryland.

> **MIDDLE:** Citizens of the Washington D.C. area started panicking, and the senseless shootings caught the attention of the nation and the world. Law enforcement spent a few tense weeks tracking down the killer or killers.

> **END:** On October 24, 2002, John Allen Muhammad and his young accomplice, Lee Boyd Malvo, were finally caught. Muhammad was tried and executed by lethal injection. Malvo is serving consecutive life sentences with no possibility of parole.

Obviously, there's much more to the story of the "Beltway Sniper," but the unfolding events make for a good narrative structure. There's a linear and clear-cut complication (a sniper or sniper team is on the loose) and a resolution (the perpetrators are caught).

NUT-GRAPH STRUCTURE

Stories that use the nut-graph structure are also referred to as news or analytical features. This structure was developed at *The Wall Street Journal* and is widely used at this and other publications. This structure's hallmarks include anecdotal leads that hook the reader's attention, followed by alternating sections that amplify the story's thesis and provide balance with evidence that presents a counterthesis. But its chief hallmark is the use of a context section, the "nut graph" in newsroom lingo.

With the nut-graph structure, a writer starts with an anecdotal lede that hooks the reader's attention. The nut graph then presents a thesis. The body paragraphs expound on and support this thesis as well as expounding on and supporting any countertheses.

In a 2012 *Los Angeles Times* article titled "Dengue, Where Is Thy Sting?", journalist Vincent Bevins uses the nut-graph structure to describe the release of genetically engineered mosquitoes to combat dengue fever. Bevins starts with an anecdote about researchers in Brazil releasing mosquitoes outside a family's grocery store. The nut graph explains how the Brazilian government officials are releasing genetically engineered mosquitoes to kill off dengue-spreading mosquitoes.

> The small, sun-scorched neighborhood of Itaberaba in this city in Bahia state is the leading testing ground for a controversial effort to combat dengue fever, the harrowing disease that kills 22,000 people a year worldwide. Scientists backed by the state government are releasing millions of the engineered mosquitoes into the wild with the goal of exterminating the species here—and, perhaps eventually, the entire country or world.

The body of the piece further explains dengue fever—a disease that causes symptoms ranging from flu-like to deadly hemorrhagic fever—and how biologists have engineered male mosquitoes to transfer deadly mutations to their offspring that will kill them off before they mature. The body also introduces the countertheses that some biologists and environmental groups oppose introducing mutated mosquitoes into the wild.

The nut-graph structure is very useful when reporting trends. First, an anecdotal lede illustrates the trend. Second, the nut graph explains the trend and introduces the countertrend. Third, body paragraphs explore and expound on the trend and countertrend.

Chip Scanlan used the nut-graph structure in a 1994 newspaper article titled "Too Young to Diet?" The lede in Scanlan's story introduces Sarah, a ten-year-old dieter. The nut graph explains the dangers posed by childhood dieting, including the risk of developing eating disorders. It also explains how the countertrend, an obesity epidemic in children, has contributed to the dieting trend. The rest of the story examines both issues using facts and narrative.

ORGANIC STRUCTURE: IMAGES, FOCI, AND MORE

Jon Franklin, who won the first-ever Pulitzer Prize for feature writing with "Mrs. Kelly's Monster," has thought *a lot* about this structure. In his book, *Writing for Story*, he draws comparisons between writing features and writing fictional short stories. He also compares feature writing to filmmaking.

According to Franklin's *organic* structure, the fundamental narrative "molecule" of the feature article is the *image*; images are the smallest bits of a story. A set of images forms a *focus*, a larger chunk of copy that "focuses" on an action. Foci are linked together by transitions to form larger foci. These larger foci represent changes in time, mood, subject, and character.

Franklin also uses levels to characterize structure. First, there's the *polish level* that deals with grammar, punctuation, imagery, and style. Second, there's the *structural level*, which deals with the different foci and how they interconnect. Third, there's the *outline level*, which is the most significant and deals with the interplay of characters and action.

Franklin notes that in a story, the first major focus is normally the *complication*, the second major focus is the (three-part) *development*, and the third major focus is the *resolution*. During development, the complication, including its past and present, is explored. The writer will also examine how the complication is being tackled and whether there has been a process of trial and error when tackling the complication. (More complicated narrative structures, such as flashbacks, often find a place in the development focus.)

SIX-PART GUIDE

William E. Blundell, author of *The Art and Craft of Feature Writing*, suggests a structural approach that has won many fans among professional journalists, including science writer Robert Irion. Irion teaches a method of writing features that's inspired by Blundell's work.

Here's a breakdown of the six parts, which highlight questions that the writer may consider when addressing each part. Of note, not all stories consist of all six parts, and not all six parts need to be focused on equally.

1. **HISTORY.** What is the historical significance of an event or issue? Does the past have any bearing on the status quo?

2. **SCOPE.** How widespread is the event or issue? How intense is the development? Does it have a local, national, or international scope? If possible, the writer should try to quantify the scope with numbers and facts.

3. **REASON.** Is the issue or event due to economic, social, political, or psychological reasons, or some combination? Why is it occurring now?

4. **IMPACT.** Who is most helped or hurt by the event or issue? How do they react?

5. **COUNTERMOVES.** Who will be upset by the issue or event? Who will move to oppose the issue or event? How will the issue be opposed?

6. **FUTURE.** How will the development affect the future? How do expert sources feel about the development?

"When I'm teaching magazine journalism," says Irion, "I typically teach a rather standard story structure. It's a canonical research narrative structure that any editor is happy to receive because ... most readers will be able to make the most sense out of the story through this chronological retelling.

"You have your opening section, which has to be very grabby and make the reader want to invest the rest of their time in reading the entire piece—the first 400 to 500 words are so important in that respect.

"But then you want to ... set up the context for the reader by describing what's come before. This history section is something that you can re-create through your own research and by asking the scientists their views about the most important work that's come before ...

"And then you move to ... an essential explanatory [section] in which you're probably going to be relating some on-scene details. ...

"Finally, you move on to implications. ... What does this all mean? ... Why is it important to society or to our knowledge of nature or the universe? What are some of the possible impacts and public policy [implications]? And, possibly, a 'what's next' section. ... What are the some of the main unanswered questions?"

THE HIGH-FIVES FORMULA

The high-fives formula consists of five parts:

1. **THE NEWS.** What's happening? The five *W*s and one *H*.
2. **THE CONTEXT.** Does this issue or trend have a history? Explain the background.
3. **THE SCOPE.** Is a local issue part of a trend or national story?
4. **THE EDGE.** Where is this issue leading? What's going to happen?
5. **THE IMPACT.** Why is this issue newsworthy? Who cares and why?

Many features embrace elements of the high-fives formula.

THE WALL STREET JOURNAL FORMULA

This structure proceeds from specific details to general ideas. It starts with a lede and nut graph, which are supported in the body of the article. Explanations also appear in the body. The conclusion ties back to the introduction.

SECTIONS STRUCTURE

This structure is reminiscent of several short features or book chapters linked together—each with a lede, body, and conclusion (kicker). The sections must flow well and engage the reader. Each new section begins with a list that summarizes key points.

FUNCTIONAL STRUCTURE

When examining an institution or organization with discrete and separate functions, a writer can divide the story into parts describing these functions. For example, if you were examining the Educational Commission for Foreign Medical Graduates, an organization that certifies international medical graduates, you may divide a story to reflect three main functions of this organization: accreditation, acculturation (of international medical physicians), and philanthropic measures.

DIAMOND STRUCTURE

The diamond structure starts out with an anecdotal lede that illustrates what the issue or story is about. From the anecdote, the story then broadens to describe the issue. In the conclusion, the writer returns to the initial anecdote. This structure is figuratively described as a diamond because its scope goes from specific (narrow) to general (wide) and back to specific (narrow). Diamond-shaped features also have nut graphs. The diamond structure can be used to write a feature article, and it is commonly used in broadcast news and newspapers.

Figure 9.1

DIAMOND STRUCTURE

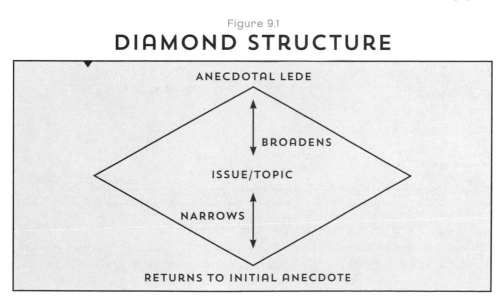

ANECDOTAL LEDE

BROADENS

ISSUE/TOPIC

NARROWS

RETURNS TO INITIAL ANECDOTE

In the wake of the global financial crises, which began in 2007, many people lost their jobs. Unemployment became a big issue. Anecdotes about people unable to pay their bills and care for their kids were rampant. If you were to create a story about unemployment, you might consider a diamond structure that started and ended with a specific anecdote examining one person or family's struggle with unemployment. In the middle of the article, you could then examine unemployment issues in a broader context, including economic, social, and political concerns. The conclusion could return to and expand on the original anecdote that examined an individual's or family's struggle with unemployment, thus narrowing and completing the diamond structure.

HOURGLASS STRUCTURE

The term "hourglass structure" was coined in 1983 by Roy Peter Clark. It is a hybrid between the inverted pyramid structure and the expanding narrative. Although best suited for dramatic stories, it can be used to cover crime, government stories, economic issues, and more.

Figure 9.2
HOURGLASS STRUCTURE

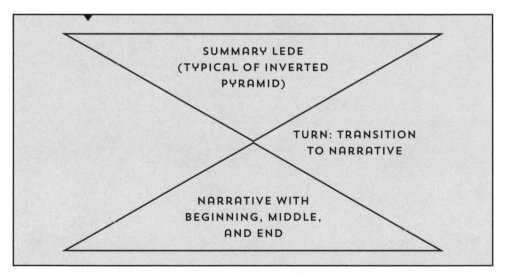

A story shaped with the hourglass structure in mind begins as any typical news story does: with a summary lede followed by a few paragraphs of detail in order of descending significance. The details deal with the most important aspects of the story: the five *W*s and one *H*. In the middle of the piece, there's a distinct "turn" or transition to narrative. This short turn shifts the focus by directly attributing the following narrative to an eyewitness, law-enforcement official, expert, character, victim, or so forth. The last part of the hourglass consists of a narrative with a distinct beginning, middle, and end.

The nice thing about the hourglass structure is that it caters to different types of readers. The beginning part, which resembles the inverted pyramid, appeals to the time-strapped reader who just wants the news. The expanding narrative appeals to the reader who wants to luxuriate in the details of the story.

FIVE-BOXES APPROACH

The five-boxes structure was conceived by Pulitzer Prize winner Rick Bragg. Elements of this approach are apparent in his writing.

Here are the five boxes:

1. The lede presents an image or detail that hooks the reader's attention.
2. A nut graph summarizes the story.
3. A new image or detail (second lede) that introduces the rest of the facts and narrative is presented.
4. Ancillary information is presented. This information is of secondary importance.
5. The "kicker" ends with an image, comment, quotation, or so forth.

In his 1995 *New York Times* feature "Where Alabama Inmates Fade Into Old Age," Bragg uses elements of the five-boxes approach to present the story. In the first box, Bragg introduces Grant Cooper, a convict and one-time murderer who is now with disability from a stroke and with dementia. The second box, or nut graph, presents the theme of the story: aging convicts serving life terms who need special and safe accommodations. The third box starts with the bucolic image of an Alabama prison that houses older prisoners with disability. After this new image is introduced, we learn more about how the entire prison population is graying and how they will need special medical care and facilities. The fourth box presents ancillary information about how these prisoners are no longer a risk to society and pitiful images of prisoners with a low quality of life. The kicker ends with the following quotation about how most of the prisoners die all but forgotten:

> There will be nothing on the outside for him. Warden Berry said that when an inmate reached a certain point, it might be more humane to keep him in prison. Wives die, children stop coming to see him.
>
> "We bury most of them ourselves, on state land," he said. The undertaking and embalming class at nearby Jefferson State University prepares the bodies for burial for free, for the experience.
>
> "They make 'em up real nice," the warden said.

Figure 9.3
FIVE-BOXES APPROACH

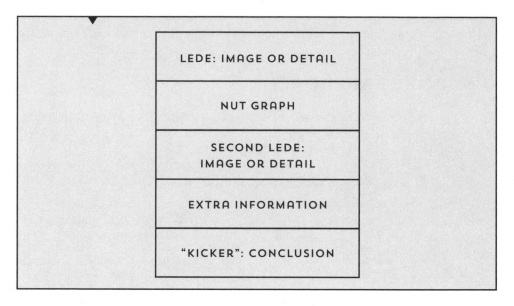

LEDE: IMAGE OR DETAIL

NUT GRAPH

SECOND LEDE:
IMAGE OR DETAIL

EXTRA INFORMATION

"KICKER": CONCLUSION

CRAFTING A FEATURE

The actual crafting of a feature piece is difficult for any writer. Whereas news pieces and opinion articles sometimes follow clear-cut formats—the inverted pyramid and essay respectively—feature articles can take various forms. This diversity of structure makes features particularly hard to construct, especially for a beginning writer. Different writers have their own idiosyncratic methods for constructing a feature piece, which make articulation of such methods even more difficult. Nevertheless, some general tips and approaches may prove useful.

Many writers like to stay organized when writing a feature story. They will pull relevant quotations from their sources and list them in one set of notes, and pull facts, figures, theoretical concepts, and so forth and list them in a second set of notes. By doing so, it becomes easy to refer back to this information as needed. Once all of their quotations and facts are organized, some writers begin a feature in a chronological fashion. They will write the lede, nut graph, body, and conclusion in that order. While writing each section of the story, the writer will consider narrative and structural elements, including images, background, details, conflict, resolution, and impact.

Crafting a story in systematic fashion can be challenging—especially for the new writer. Irion suggests a different method—one he used earlier in his career—which may be useful for those new to the field. It involves mapping out relevant quotations first and filling in details later.

"I'll write down a few to several to a bunch of quotes that I like and that I can see a pretty clear path toward using … somewhere in the piece," says Irion. "I look at those quotes, and as I'm doing that, the architecture of the story begins to take shape in my mind, and I begin to see where I want to use certain sources. There's probably going to be one or two sources who appear throughout the piece and several subsidiary sources who might just pop in once or twice. It will identify for me which are the most impactful, trenchant quotes from those sources, and those will actually be the starting point of my narrative. … Once I've got those down, something interesting happens. … If you're writing a 3,000-word piece, pick the best quotes from those sources and type them in … you realize that you have 300 to 400 words already there … you already have a starting point."

Personally, once I'm pretty deep into the construction of a feature article and a deadline is rapidly approaching, I find that writing out of context is much easier than immediately finding a place for any new addition. In the final hours of the writing process, I take time to plug these additions into place.

On a final note, when crafting a feature, I'm careful to keep all of my writing. It may feel gratifying to delete large portions of text that you no longer feel are necessary, but avoid such temptation! Nothing is more frustrating than later needing something that's already been deleted. Instead of deleting this text, relegate it to a separate document, a boneyard of sorts, for your future reference.

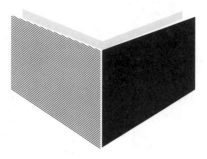

chapter 10

FACT

Every article should contain facts. The key to using facts is to carefully choose which facts you use and refrain from using too many of them. If you use too many facts, you will bore, confuse, or intimidate your readers and risk losing them forever. In most cases, your readers are in no way obligated to read your work; therefore, you should always strive to make your articles interesting and enjoyable.

If you were writing a profile on somebody and among his many pastimes he enjoys competitive feats of endurance, including Ironman Triathlons, marathons, and hiking, it would probably be silly to regurgitate too many facts with regard to any one of these pastimes. For example, if he told you that he hiked the Appalachian Trail as a teenager, it may be sufficient to mention that the Trail is about 2,180 miles long and spans fourteen states. Few readers want to know more (that there are more than 250 three-sided shelters along the trail, that there are 550 miles of trail in Virginia, or that you may encounter skunk cabbage among the flora). And if somebody were interested in learning more about the Appalachian Trail, it's not your responsibility to teach them; they can seek out this information on their own.

UNFAMILIAR TERMS

Sometimes important facts are introduced with new terms or jargon that are specific to a certain field. Whenever you use a new vocabulary word to introduce a fact, define it.

For example, say you were writing an article on diabetes and decided to write the following sentences.

> According to the CDC, in 2010, the prevalence of diagnosed diabetes was 6 percent of the United States population or 18.8 million people.

Without a doubt, "18.8 million" is a lot of people, but a casual reader may be unsure of exactly what this statistic means. She may also be unfamiliar with the term *prevalence*, an epidemiology term that refers to the total number of cases of a disease diagnosed within a given period of time. Or worse, a casual reader may confuse an unfamiliar term for another—in this case mistaking *prevalence* for *incidence*. (The term *incidence* refers to the number of new cases diagnosed within a period of time. For example, "In 2010, the incidence of diagnosed diabetes was 1.9 million people or 0.61 percent of the U.S. population.") The preceding sentence would be best rewritten as follows.

> According to the CDC, in 2010, the prevalence, or total number of Americans diagnosed with diabetes, was 8.3 percent of the U.S. population or 18.8 million people.

Finally, if, for whatever reason, you were going to mention prevalence once again in a different part of your article, it would be good to redefine it in case your reader has forgotten its meaning. Of note, if you mention prevalence several times and in close proximity, there's no need to continually redefine it.

PUTTING FACTS INTO PERSPECTIVE

Readers like perspective, and, when possible, it's a good idea to cite facts in terms that they can appreciate. For example, putting a number or statistic in perspective can help your reader relate to the gravity of your message.

Let's once again consider diabetes. In 2010, 18.8 million Americans were diagnosed with the disease. But how many people is 18.8 million people? This number of people is about the population of Florida. If you want to impress your reader with the sheer number of people affected by diabetes, it may be wise to compare it with the population of Florida.

> According to the CDC, in 2010 the prevalence, or total number of Americans diagnosed with diabetes, was 8.3 percent of the U.S. population or 18.8 million people. This number is roughly equal to the population of Florida.

Facts that involve money always seem to pique reader interest. When discussing money, it may also be a good idea to put the numbers into perspective. Consider the following example:

> According to the CDC, in 2007, the total cost of diabetes within the United States was $218 billion. This amount represents more than three times Bill Gates' 2011 net worth.

Everybody knows that Bill Gates is the richest man in the world. Presenting the cost of diabetes in terms of his wealth attaches meaning to the figure "$218 billion."

CHOOSING FACTS

The facts you choose to present in your article must serve a purpose. Oftentimes you're presented with several facts and must choose the ones that will make the most sense to your reader. Facts often take the form of statistics, which are expressed as numbers and can support arguments or assertions. Although statistics can be manipulated in a variety of ways, they make for good factual support.

Let's consider that you're doing a piece on poverty in the United States and need factual support. You can surf on over to FedStats (www.fedstats.gov) looking for income statistics and choose to be redirected to the website for the United States Census Bureau. (The United States Census Bureau keeps tight tabs on income and poverty levels.)

When writing an article on poverty, it's probably best to concern yourself with statistics that reinforce the purpose of your article: poverty. For example, in 2011, the number of families living in poverty (*poverty* is defined by the government as a family of four making less than $23,021 per year) was 9.5 million, which means that approximately 25 million people are living in poverty. To put this number in perspective, the population of Texas is about 25 million people.

A statistic such as the median household income, which is $50,054 per year, will be less useful to your readers, and it may confuse them to present a number that doesn't sound "poor."

Please note that although I briefly present statistics, a full examination of the topic and how it relates to journalism is well outside the scope of this book. If you are interested in learning more about statistics, I suggest that you read *News & Numbers* by Victor Cohn and Lewis Cope.

FACT-CHECKING

Alarmingly, in light of shrinking magazine and newspaper staff sizes and profit margins, many publications can no longer invest financially in rigorous fact-checking services. In other words, gone are the days when fact-checkers were routinely on staff. Thus, it becomes the writer's responsibility to make sure the facts are correct and assure the editor that the tendered article is factually sound. To this end, it's good to include a brief *source list* at the end of each article that cites primary sources, secondary sources, website addresses, times and dates of interviews, and names and contact information for interviewed sources. Although the source list need not be as rigorous as a bibliography or endnote entry, if need be it should contain enough information for the editor to access the sources easily.

A few stately publications such as *The New Yorker*, *Smithsonian*, and *National Geographic* still invest in fact-checkers. These publications often require the author to thoroughly annotate the article and embed sources of information within a draft of the article. This process can be time-consuming and tedious. Science writer Robert Irion, who has written for both *National Geographic* and *Smithsonian*, points out that an annotated version of a 2,000-word article can easily exceed 5,000 words.

"There are publications that employ fact-checkers ..." says Irion. "The journalist is responsible for preparing a fully annotated manuscript which will give—either embedded within the text or in footnote style—a complete description of where every factual statement came from. ... Whether it came from the original scientific literature, a paper, or a website ... or from an interview on a given date ... all of this needs to be annotated ... and the fact-checker takes it from there. You provide the source list, phone numbers, and e-mail addresses, and that staff person will check all the factual statements in your story. Ideally this is the best way to do it because it removes this potential minefield of source review from the equation because the magazine itself is handling it. ... But in this era of budgetary cuts, some of the fact-checkers are falling to the wayside. ... Ultimately, you have to make sure—by whatever means necessary—that your text is fully accurate before it's published."

One final, pithy piece of advice: Assumption and presumption are the enemies of diligent fact-checking. Just because you think you *know* something doesn't mean you're correct. Every good writer is a bit obsessive when it comes to facts. Check everything!

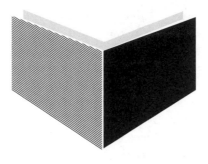

chapter 11

NARRATIVE

No article, whether it be news, feature, or opinion, can consist only of facts. If an article were all facts, it would be boring and would hardly entertain your audience—you don't want the reader to be more interested in reading the periodic table than she is in reading your work. All articles incorporate some narrative or storytelling elements. In fact, it's often easy to attain narrative from the simplest primary sources; for generations, journalists have evoked narrative from documents as mundane as police reports.

Consider the following description of narrative taken from an article titled "Skip the Salad, Pass the Meat" by Robert L. Bryant Jr. and published in the *Columbia Journalism Review*: "Narrative, in this sense, is the red meat of journalism, the sinew of facts interlocked, the relentless march of cause and effect, of progression from A to B to C, of how things happen."

In an e-mail interview, Roy Peter Clark, senior scholar at the Poynter Institute, explained to me how he sees narrative in broad terms. "For me," writes Clark, "the key distinction is between reports and story. The purpose of reports is to transfer information. But the purpose of stories is to transfer experience. A narrative—with its scenes and dialogue—transports the reader to another time and place. It doesn't just point you there; it puts you there."

All articles have some elements of storytelling or narrative. Even news articles that are generated by newspapers and wire services, like the Associated Press (AP), have narrative elements. For example, the AP will construct fifteen to twenty optional ledes per week for big and breaking news stories. These types of ledes were once only intended for "P.M." (after-work) readers but are now typical of stories disseminated at any time. Such narrative ledes are more engaging, provide context, and make for an easier point of entry. Because the reader is likely familiar with the headline because it has been broadcast via radio, Internet, or cable news, using narrative, perspective, and imagery may provide a novel way to attract the reader.

Consider the following two ledes the AP constructed in the wake of Terri Schiavo's death. Terri Schiavo was a woman in a persistent vegetative state that lasted fifteen years. After a long court battle between her husband and parents, her feeding tube was removed in 2005.

Here's the "traditional" or newsy lede that the AP would typically run:

> With her husband and parents feuding to the bitter end and beyond, Terri Schiavo died Thursday, thirteen days after her feeding tube was removed in a wrenching right-to-die dispute that engulfed the courts, Capitol Hill, and the White House and divided the country.

Here's the more narrative "alternative" lede:

> She died cradled by her husband, a beloved stuffed tabby under her arm, a bouquet of lilies and roses at her bedside after her brother was expelled from her room. In death, as in life, no peace surrounded Terri Schiavo.

Especially with newspapers, the use of narrative elements is becoming increasingly popular in both news and feature articles. Consider the following observation made in an article titled "I'll Be Brief" written by Carl Sessions Stepp in the *American Journalism Review*:

> Readership worries definitely are helping drive the trend toward daily storytelling. Research by Northwestern University's closely watched Readership Institute has found "strong evidence that an increase in the amount of feature-style stories has wide-ranging benefits." A more narrative approach to both news and features, the institute said, can raise reader interest, especially among women, in topics from politics to sports to science. "Newspapers that run more feature-style stories are seen as more honest, fun, neighborly, intelligent, 'in the know' and more in touch with the values of readers," it said.

Some may think there's little room for narrative in newspaper pieces, which are short and tightly budgeted. This argument, however, is unfounded. Jack Hart, a long-time editor at *The Oregonian* and a Pulitzer Prize winner, teaches writers that shorter narratives, while working within a shorter time span and using fewer characters and scenes, must be just as dramatic as longer pieces. Furthermore, Hart argues that three well-constructed details are all that is needed to establish a scene for the readers.

ADVICE ON CONSTRUCTING NARRATIVE

It takes a lifetime to figure out how to incorporate narrative elements into article writing. A good place to start learning more about narrative is by reading the work of creative or literary nonfiction writers. I highly suggest picking up a copy of Truman Capote's *In Cold Blood* and reading through a few issues of *Harper's* or *The New Yorker*.

Personally, my understanding of narrative has been heavily influenced by Roy Peter Clark. Many of the teachings presented here are inspired by his book *Writing Tools*. I highly recommend reading this book and internalizing its accessible content.

Character Development

Characters are central to any narrative, and characters need to be developed.

When developing characters for your story, here are some details to consider:

- Character's physical description, including clothes, hygiene, mannerisms, and appearance
- Character's surrounding environment, structure, and community
- Relationship and conflict among characters in your story
- Character's unprovoked actions and reactions to others
- What the character says, thinks, advises, condones, believes, or preaches
- Character's family members, friends, co-workers, employers, employees, acquaintances, and associates
- Character's avocation, hobbies, activities, and religion
- Character's pet peeves, vices, moral transgressions, or criminal past
- Character's habits, quotidian activities, and daily schedule

Keep in mind that when developing a character, it's always best to show rather than tell; in other words, use details rather than adjectives to flesh out your characters.

In an article from *Details* titled "The Overheated, Oversexed Cult of Bikram Choudhury," writer Clancy Martin does an excellent job of developing Bikram Choudhury's character. Choudhury is the über-rich, prurient, flamboyant, and excessive founder of Bikram Yoga, a type of yoga that involves extreme heat.

> Choudhury has other quirks too. He says he eats a single meal a day (chicken or beef, no fruit or vegetables), drinks only water and Coke, and needs only two hours of sleep a night. Then there are the stories about him having sex with his students. When I ask him about this, he doesn't deny it—he claims they blackmail him: "Only when they give me no choice! If they say to me, 'Boss, you must fuck me or I will kill myself,' then I do it! Think if I don't! The karma!"

This story did such a good job of exposing Choudhury that it haunted him two years after it was written. In 2013, Choudhury was accused of sexual harassment by a female student.

Setting up a Scene

Although narrative existed long before cinematography, it's sometimes helpful to make references to camera work when discussing narrative.

Setting up a scene or setting is important. Just as a filmmaker uses a variety of shots, from close up to long, in order to capture a scene, a writer can use descriptive language to do the same. Whether you want to examine blood spatter at the crime scene more closely or pan out and describe the verdant and peaceful neighborhood in which the violent crime took place is your decision and can make for good narrative.

When setting up a scene, keep in mind that you want to do your best to help your readers visualize what you're talking about. Consider your five senses: sight, smell, touch, sound, and taste. Notice important details that may otherwise have been overlooked. If you're on-site and thus immersed in a scene, take a mental (and digital) snapshot of your surroundings. Consider the time and place. Is it so hot that you want to take your sweatshirt off, or is it so cold that you want to huddle underneath a dozen comforters? Think about the scene you want to write for several hours or even several days.

Consider this lede from an article titled "Is Facebook Making Us Lonely?" which was published in *The Atlantic*:

> Yvette Vickers, a former *Playboy* playmate and B-movie star, best known for her role in *Attack of the 50 Foot Woman*, would have been 83 last August, but nobody knows exactly how old she was when she died. According to the Los Angeles coroner's report, she lay dead for the better part of a year before a neighbor and fellow actress, a woman named Susan Savage, noticed cobwebs and yellowing letters in her mailbox, reached through a broken window to unlock the door, and pushed her way through the piles of junk mail and mounds of clothing ...

This lede does a great job of setting up a gruesome and depressing scene—a mummified body in an unkempt apartment. Notice how the author provides descriptions that are like close ups ("cobwebs ... in the mailbox") and descriptions that consider the entire setting ("piles of junk mail and mounds of clothing"). Anybody reading this lede can imagine how sad it must be: a one-time starlet left dead for months in a filthy apartment.

When doing research for a story, it's important that you're proactive and seek out details that will engage the reader. As Margaret Guroff, features editor at *AARP The Magazine* advises, "When you're describing anything, you want to have details to pick from so that what you choose is something that moves the story."

When setting up a scene, you may also want to consider the "reality effect." This term was coined by Roland Barthes in the 1960s and refers to a description that alone is meaningless, but taken in context of the entire piece it provides a sense of reality. For example, describing an overturned Tiffany lamp at a crime scene may mean little by itself but provides a "real-world" sensibility for an article. Keep in mind, however, that the "reality effect" should be used sparingly. As with all other aspects of article writing, words are precious when constructing narrative.

Surprise

In *Writing to Deadline: The Journalist at Work,* author Donald Murray suggests the journalist ask: "What surprised me when I was reporting the story?" He also recommends to "look for what isn't there as much as what is, hear the unsaid as well as the said, imagine what might be."

Surprise can come in the form of cliffhangers or plot twists and can be foreshadowed. The smart writer uses surprise to propel the reader toward the end. The tension of surprise can build like a rollercoaster inching its way up to an initial apex.

Surprise in storytelling is just as appealing as surprise in visual media. Think about all the television series that dangle the carrot of surprise in our faces. In the season six finale of the Showtime series *Dexter*, serial killer Dexter Morgan is caught with one of his victims by his sister, a lieutenant in the homicide division. At the season five midpoint of *Breaking Bad*, Walter White, the once-sedate chemistry teacher turned meth kingpin, is discovered by his brother-in-law, a DEA agent. And then there's the megahit series *Lost,* which eventually tired its viewers with cliffhanger after cliffhanger.

In "The Case of the Vanishing Blonde," published in *Vanity Fair*, author Mark Bowden uses surprise to explain how a young Ukrainian woman was taken from her hotel room and raped. In this real-life story, private detective Ken Brennan agonizes over how it happened.

> Unless this crime had been pulled off by a team of magicians, the victim had to have come down in the elevator to the lobby and left through the front door. The answer was not obvious, but it had to be somewhere in the video record ...

Through some astute detective work—and after several paragraphs of text—Brennan finally figures out how the perpetrator, a large man with glasses, committed the crime. He smuggled the woman out of the hotel in a suitcase. Of note, the man's involvement was foreshadowed earlier in the story.

The Ladder of Abstraction

While infusing your story with narrative flair, think about the Ladder of Abstraction (popularized by S.I. Hayakawa in 1939). At the bottom of the ladder are concrete or specific images, and at the top of the ladder are general issues, topics, or sentiments that are universally appreciated. For example, if you gave your girlfriend or boyfriend roses for Valentine's Day, you are dealing with both the bottom and top of the ladder: The roses are a concrete image that symbolizes the love and admiration that you feel for your lover.

In the Nimruz province of Afghanistan, which borders both Iran and Pakistan, there's little water. Some of the water the residents of this province receive comes from Iran through the Lashkari Canal. In a *New York Times Magazine* article, Luke Mogelson uses the Ladder of Abstraction to compare the perceived width of the pipe providing water with Afghani sentiment for Iranians. The width of the pipe is a concrete image at the bottom of the ladder, and Afghani sentiment for Iranians is at the top of the ladder.

"I found," writes Mogelson, "that you could gauge people's general attitude toward Iran by how big they said the pipe was: An especially embittered official would swear its diameter measured no more than a couple of inches, whereas a frequenter of Iranian medical facilities, say, might call it a four-inch pipe."

We find another example of the Ladder of Abstraction in a *New York Times* article titled "True Blue Stands Out in an Earthy Crowd" by Natalie Angier. According to the article, scientists have taken a greater interest in complexities of the color blue and its appearances in the natural world. In the piece, the author writes about blue at the lowest rung of the Ladder of Abstraction—specific animals and fruits that, in some way or another, exhibit the color blue. She then moves up the Ladder of Abstraction to discuss how blue is associated with creativity, calmness, depression, and so forth.

Just as a ladder is most stable at the bottom, where it rests on the ground, and the top, where it abuts a wall, the Ladder of Abstraction is best understood at either the bottom or top. The middle of the ladder—which is neither fully specific nor fully abstract—can get quite confusing. A good writer will mind this middle part and work especially hard to explain it. For a writer with the ability and patience, the payoff for covering the middle of the ladder can be great. For example, *New York Times* writer David Kocieniewski won a Pulitzer Prize in 2012 for his series of articles "that penetrated a legal thicket to explain how the nation's wealthiest citizens and corporations often exploited loopholes and avoided taxes."

Much of what we write about is at the middle of the Ladder of Abstraction: business, science, art, politics, sports, and so forth. When you write, it's helpful to keep the Ladder of Abstraction in mind. More specifically, learn when to provide examples and explain things in a greater context. Also, make sure to transition into examples and general thinking. Don't be too abrupt with your writing.

Figure 11.1

THE LADDER OF ABSTRACTION

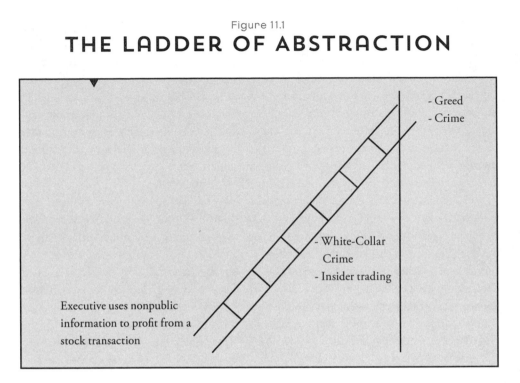

- Greed
- Crime

- White-Collar Crime
- Insider trading

Executive uses nonpublic information to profit from a stock transaction

Juxtaposition

The juxtaposition or contrast of two seemingly disparate objects or ideas can make for great copy. It tickles the reader's fancy and makes your narrative shine.

Most people would think that suicide bombers in Afghanistan and elsewhere would care little about their own safety, but as Mogelson points out, these people are often cowardly when fired on—a strange juxtaposition.

> … these men, who are planning to blow themselves up, always become frightened when you open fire on them. As soon as the shooting starts, the suicider runs and hides. He doesn't want to be shot. He is here to die, but he is scared of bullets. It's strange.

Backstory

Sometimes the best way to explain one of the key characters in your story is to provide a backstory or short description of the character's past. Backstory is similar to a profile but focuses only on the aspects of a character that are important to the story. A few lines of backstory can help readers understand the person who they're reading about and her intentions and capabilities.

In a story titled "What Happens in Brooklyn Moves to Vegas," we meet Tony Hsieh, an entrepreneur who founded the online shoe company Zappos.com. Hsieh now wants to relocate all 1,200 employees of his company to downtown Las Vegas and attract other businesses to the area—a sort of gentrification project. He wants to build a new city that's community focused, replete with random and "serendipitous" interactions among its citizens. It's a novel idea, but will it work? The article's author, Jon Kelly, uses Hsieh's backstory to help the reader understand that if anybody can successfully complete this lofty project, it's Hsieh.

> Though Amazon bought Zappos in 2009 for $1.2 billion, Hsieh still runs the company, and he has endeavored to keep alive its zany corporate culture. This includes a workplace where everyone sits in the same open space and employees switch desks every few months in order to get to know one another better.

From this backstory, we understand that because Hsieh has already built a billion-dollar company based on a corporate culture that he hopes to mirror in his new city, he has a good chance at succeeding.

Figurative Elements

Well-chosen analogies, metaphors, and similes can strengthen arguments and add narrative flair. Consider the following simile. (A simile uses *like* or *as* to compare two things.) It concerns the color blue and is taken from *The New York Times* article "True Blue Stands Out in an Earthy Crowd."

> Another group working in the central Congo basin announced the discovery of a new species of monkey, a rare event in mammalogy. Rarer still is the noteworthiest trait of the monkey, called the lesula: a patch of brilliant blue skin on the male's buttocks and scrotal area that stands out from the surrounding fur like neon underpants.

A reader who isn't a biologist may have trouble conceptualizing a blue lesula, but thanks to this wonderful simile written by author Natalie Angier, we can imagine that the blue lesula looks like a pair of neon blue underpants. (Personally, I imagine a thong reminiscent of something Sacha Baron Cohen's character Borat may wear.)

Later on, we learn that blue in nature exists in two forms: pigment and figment. Pigment is chemical color, and figment is structural color. Obviously, this concept is difficult to appreciate without further explanation, so Angier uses a metaphor that takes the form of an analogy to explain what figment or structural color is.

> Structural blues are essentially built of soap membranes trapped at just the right orientation and thickness to forever glint blue.

An astute reader may question the difference between a metaphor and an analogy. A metaphor uses a conjugation of the verb *to be* in order to compare two things. For example, "the moon is a giant white saucer" is a metaphor. Metaphors are often used by poets and aren't necessarily bound by logic. Analogies, though, are bound by logic and express relationships.

Metaphors and similes can both be analogies—in fact the best ones often are. Consider the following simile and analogy, which explains why looking at objects in the night sky is difficult. It's taken from Robert Irion's article "Homing In On Black Holes" from the *Smithsonian*. For ease of understanding, I display the simile in context.

> The blur of Earth's atmosphere has plagued telescope users since Galileo's first studies of Jupiter and Saturn four hundred years ago. Looking at a star through air is like looking at a penny on the bottom of a swimming pool. Air currents make the starlight jitter back and forth.

If you want to use an analogy to explain a concept in your piece but are unsure of the proper one to choose, consider asking a source for an apt analogy. Scientists and other professionals are often asked to explain their work in terms that the general public can understand; thus they've often managed to test the effectiveness of several analogies and have found the best ones.

Irion has some useful advice on metaphors and figurative elements: "A metaphor for a general audience only works if you can come up with something that can be easily visualized or that they can relate to something from their everyday experience. Places in stories where I try to look for tangible and effective metaphors are in explanatory sections when I'm trying to explain how something works, how some scientific process unfolds ... or something that's remote from our everyday experience. ...

"Always ask the person who you're interviewing if they have ever come up with useful comparisons when they speak with a public audience or friends and colleagues because often the researchers—especially if they have some experience with giving interviews with reporters—will have a way of putting things that can be very useful to helping you develop your own appropriate metaphor. What that kind of question does is help activate a different part of the scientific brain, and [the interviewee will] begin to talk about things more accessibly, even if they don't come up with that useful comparison that you can adapt. Maybe they will help you get started in the right direction with some comparison, and then you, as the journalist, can refine the metaphor and make it appropriate or more technically accurate.

"Coming up with metaphors is a challenge; you have to think about it, and you have to ask for help. Sometimes [you can talk] about the story with your peers and try to get some suggestions for a fresh metaphor that will bring that section of your story alive for readers. It's hard and it's something that you have to play around with, and this is where your editor can be your best ally. You try a metaphor—even if it's a little strained initially—and then your editor can say, 'You're going in the right direction, but let's see if we can make this a little more accessible or a more common experience.' You work together to find something that works."

Trope

An effective but subtle example of metaphor use involves the trope. A trope uses a single verb in a figurative or metaphorical sense. Often this verb choice gets to the meaning of the sentence in a circuitous or roundabout way. For example, when people "harvest" financial benefit, the verb *harvest* evokes images of farmers harvesting their crops.

Names

Using specific names of people, animals, objects, and so forth in your article can provide for excellent narrative. A name can be distinct, symbolic, and telling. In some cases, once you hear a name, you can ascertain what that name signifies. For example, the Terminator, famously played by Arnold Schwarzenegger, probably doesn't go around picking daisies, and if he does, he surely doesn't do so onscreen.

Imagine you just went to a New Year's party that was played by all your favorite hip-hop and rap artists. Simply telling your friend, "A bunch of great musicians rocked the house!" means little. But telling your friend that "Busta Rhymes, Kid Cudi, Mos Def, Lupe Fiasco, Dr. Dre, Snoop Dogg (Snoop Lion?), Jay-Z, Ghostface Killah, and the rest of the Wu-Tang Clan rocked the house!" means more. (I realize that getting all of these guys in one place is nearly impossible. Their styles differ, the cost would be outrageous, and there may be residual hard feelings from some East Coast-West Coast beef.)

Roy Peter Clark is a master at capitalizing on the value of names. When Joe Paterno was involved in the sex-abuse scandal at Penn State, the news deeply affected football fans everywhere, including Clark. In an opinion article titled "Joe Paterno and the stained soul of Penn State," Clark elegizes the once great Paterno, who had fallen from grace.

> An author could not invent a better name: Joe Paterno. St. Joe, father of a holy family of student athletes. JoePa. Papa Joe. Pater, as in Latin for father. Eternal paternal Paterno.
>
> Our father, who art in trouble, hollow be thy name.

In a more humorous take on the value of names (and name-calling), consider this example of video-game developer Jonathan Blow laying into the social network game FarmVille. It's taken from an *Atlantic* article titled "The Most Dangerous Gamer."

> In one talk, Blow managed to compare FarmVille's developers to muggers, alco-holic-enablers, Bernie Madoff, and brain-colonizing ant parasites.

In addition to demonstrating Blow's sentiments with choice names, the author of the piece also used alliteration—repetition of *b*s and *l*s—to add more narrative zing.

Wordplay

Smart writers can further bolster the storytelling appeal of their work by playing with the words they choose. There's a mechanical quality to words that can be leveraged when writing. Examples of wordplay include alliteration, assonance, and repetition.

Alliteration is the repetition of certain syllables such as *s, t, l, b,* and so forth. Consider the following example of alliteration used to describe video-game developer Jonathan Blow. In this example, the letter *s* is alliterated.

> Blow's rigorous personal codes reached their peak severity when he was a child. Authentic spiritual self-reliance became his fixation, escapism and superstition his greatest enemies.

Another example of wordplay is repetition. The mere repetition of key words can engage the reader, evoke emotion, and spark the imagination. Great orators such as Franklin D. Roosevelt, Abraham Lincoln, and Martin Luther King Jr. used repetition for effect. For example, consider a quotation of King's that plays on the word "drum major." As pointed out by Roy Peter Clark in a CNN Opinion piece, drum majors hold a special station in African American culture. (To learn more, watch *Drumline* starring Nick Cannon.)

> Yes, if you want to say that I was a drum major, say that I was a drum major for justice. Say that I was a drum major for peace. I was a drum major for righteousness. And all the other shallow things will not matter.

An inaccurate and contentious paraphrase of the quotation was inscribed on King's memorial in Washington, DC: "I was a drum major for justice, peace and righteousness." The paraphrased quotation gave the very false impression that King was claiming to be a drum major and, as pointed out by famed poet Maya Angelou, unjustly made King sound like "an arrogant twit." Angelou told *The Washington Post*, "He had no arrogance at all. He had a humility that comes from deep inside. The 'if' clause that is left out is salient. Leaving it out changes the meaning completely." Subsequently, plans were made to remove the inscription.

In an opinion article titled "A neighborly gesture is a reminder of the kindness hiding inside of us," Pulitzer Prize-winning columnist and commentator Connie Schultz uses repetition of the word "tomorrow" to reinforce mutual acts of kindness that she shares with her next-door neighbors.

Tomorrow, I vowed as I stepped out the front door to retrieve our newspapers.

Tomorrow I will be the one who races to the end of the driveway to pick up the papers.

Tomorrow I will deliver our neighbors' newspapers next to their garage door, right where they like them.

Short Sentences and Paragraphs

Much like an eighteen-foot king cobra, a long sentence is difficult to control. But a short sentence, a garter snake of a sentence, can pack a venomous punch. Similarly, short paragraphs can be used for effect—as is the case with paragraphs found in news pieces that adhere to the inverted-pyramid structure.

A good example of the power of short sentences embedded in short paragraphs is aptly demonstrated in a piece by ABC news writer Jonathan Karl. In his article titled "A Romney-Biden Administration? It Could Happen," Karl explains how a seemingly impossible occurrence, a split executive office, could transpire should there be an even split in electoral votes during the 2012 presidential campaign.

> It sounds crazy. It would be crazy. But it is possible that this election could result in a President Romney and a Vice President Biden.
>
> Let me explain.
>
> If there is a tie in the electoral college (and, as I explain below, there could be), it will be up to the newly elected House of Representatives to elect a President and the newly elected Senate to elect the Vice President.

In another opinion piece for CNN News titled "Stephen Colbert's Got Sway," Roy Peter Clark reflects on the satire of faux-conservative political personality Stephen Colbert. He closes this opinion piece with the following.

> When I was the age of Colbert's legion of fans, I turned to the novels of Orwell, Huxley, and Burgess to sharpen my skepticism toward the language of those in power. Such fiction is likely to wane in influence in an era when so many read less and care less.
>
> In its place is something quite different but, in its own way, quite good: comedy and satire shining a disinfecting light on the language of scoundrels. Turn on the telly. Pass the popcorn.

You'll notice that the last two sentences are short in order to convey a simple message: Let's not lament the inevitable outmoding of yesterday's great cynics, satirists, and skeptics; instead, sit back and enjoy *The Colbert Report*.

An experienced writer can also use sentence fragments in lieu of short sentences, which have a subject and verb. Such fragments are used for emphasis, inventory, shock, intensity, and informality.

Consider the following:

> I just heard that Jonathan fell down several flights of stairs and sustained great injury. Can you imagine? Both arms, his pelvis, his right leg, and his coccyx. Poor kid!

Finally, some writers like to punctuate a series of long sentences with a short sentence, thus providing some relief for the reader—kind of like an oscillating fan blasting the reader with a current of cool air.

Longer Sentences

I debated whether to advise the reader on the use of longer sentences: I mulled it over for days, weighed the pros and cons, and e-mailed Roy Peter Clark for advice on the matter. (You'll notice that this sentence is long and reflects this agonizing decision.) Roy Peter Clark advised me to instruct the reader on the use of short, medium, and long sentences.

When using longer sentences as narrative fodder to convey emotions such as monotony, longing, pain, frustration, confusion, angst, and so forth, make sure you avoid runons. Even with longer sentences, however complex, one interrelated idea must be conveyed. Be sure to place the principal subject and verb close to each other (thus forming a right-branching sentence).

In the following example, the subject *my son* is separated from the verb *misbehaves* by a long nonrestrictive clause. Consequently, the meaning is muddled.

> My son—who takes the car keys without permission, stays up all night partying, steals money from my wallet, vandalizes street signs, and skips school regularly—misbehaves.

The sentence would read better with the subject and verb in closer proximity.

> My son misbehaves; he takes the car keys without permission, stays up all night partying, steals money from my wallet, vandalizes street signs, and skips school regularly.

Tense

When writing narrative, many writers prefer to write in the *historical past* and occasionally shift to the *historical present tense* for effect. Consider the following.

> I had the perfect Sunday morning. My kids brought me breakfast in bed: freshly squeezed juice, crunchy turkey bacon, and fluffy blueberry pancakes. After breakfast, I took the dog for an invigorating walk through the neighborhood. After the walk, I took a long, hot shower. I couldn't help but marvel that life is good.

This bit of narrative recounts an enjoyable experience and is written in the historical past. The only time I shift to the present is when I declare that "life is good." This shift to the present tense emphatically underscores an enduring sentiment.

Sometimes relying on the historical present works, too. The historical present uses the present tense to describe past events and can energize and invigorate a story. Consider the following.

> Sunday morning is perfect. My kids bring me breakfast in bed: freshly squeezed juice, crunchy turkey bacon, and fluffy blueberry pancakes. After breakfast, I take the dog for an invigorating walk through the neighborhood. After the walk, I take a long hot shower. I can't help but marvel that life is good.

Note that, for effect, headlines are often written in historical present: "President Obama goes to Asia."

Allusions to Traditional and Popular Media

When I was in my late twenties, I lived in an apartment next door to a fifty-something-year-old gentleman who loved music. But he didn't love only the music from his youth (early 1960s?); he loved music from every generation. I'd be just as likely to hear Frank Sinatra or Miles Davis blaring from his stereo speakers as I would Biggie Smalls or Mike Jones.

My brother, who lived in the apartment directly above me, seemed fixated on the idea that this older guy could enjoy modern hip-hop and rap. Several years later, as a professional writer, I came to admire this guy for being able to keep abreast of emerging artists and still appreciate greats from musical generations past. The ability to stay current with respect to popular culture is integral for a journalist or writer. Allusions to popular culture can help you connect with your readers.

Unfortunately, some people consider allusions to popular culture and new media lowbrow. This mischaracterization of popular media as less weighty than traditional media is likely a result of bias. According to media theorist Marshall McLuhan, "The student of media soon comes to expect the new media of any period ... to be classed as 'pseudo' by those who acquired the patterns of earlier media, whatever they may happen to be."

For those who question the value of popular media, it should be pointed out that, as argued by author Steven Johnson, popular media is both engaging and complex. In his book *Everything Bad Is Good for You*, Johnson writes the following.

> For decades, we've worked under the assumption that mass culture follows a steadily declining path towards lowest-common-denominator standards, presumably because the "masses" want dumb, simple pleasures and big media companies want to give what they want. But in fact, the culture is getting more intellectually demanding, not less."

Johnson argues that popular media such as television and video games is actually making people smarter. (Johnson's argument lacks solid scientific proof, but his hypothesis is interesting.) Furthermore, television narratives are becoming complex and entertaining enough to rival any book. Many smart people spend their time not only reading books but also watching television shows such as *Breaking Bad* and playing video games such as *World of Warcraft*. In fact, Dr. Robert J. Thompson, the founding director of the Bleier Center for Television and Popular Culture at Syracuse University, claims that we are in the midst of the Second Golden Age of Television. Today, television shows are more cerebral, cinematic, and literary than ever before.

Granted, some allusions are tired, and a writer should resist such low-hanging fruit. It's passé to refer to Arnold Schwarzenegger as the "Governator" or to "super-size" anything—most of all your waistline. And at this point, it's probably safe to say that most people revile anything having to do with "Gangnam Style." But some allusions are fresh and entertaining.

A source tipped me off to the following headline on news and gossip website Gawker. It does a cute job of emulating a current popular-culture phenomenon: the text message.

> OMG Did Taylor Swift Cheat on Conor Kennedy with His Cousin? Text Me Back When U Get This

For anybody who may have missed it (and for anybody who cares), in the summer of 2012, Conor Kennedy, a high school student and Robert F. Kennedy's grandson (John F. Kennedy's grand-nephew), was dating music star Taylor Swift. Taylor Swift was also linked to Patrick Schwarzenegger, Conor's cousin—hence the headline.

In a short article from *The New York Times Magazine* titled "Is There Mood Lighting, Too?" writer Hope Reeves notes that some cow farmers are building dual-chamber waterbeds for their cows to sleep on. Aside from being more comfortable, the waterbeds are cheaper than replenishing a supply of sawdust and help the cows produce higher-quality milk. The author jokes about how "romantic" it is for two cows to sleep on a waterbed and makes a cultural allusion to the classic-rock band the Eagles.

> They are charging more for their higher-quality milk and saving about $6,000 a year in sawdust piles—the cow's previous sleeping platform. Imagine what might happen if all-night Eagles songs were added to the mix.

Sometimes the astute writer will simply realize when the subject of their article is making a popular-culture reference, as is this case with an Associated Press news piece titled "Obama accuses Romney of suffering from 'Romnesia.'"

> Obama, a broad grin on his face, borrowed heavily from the style of comedian Jeff Foxworthy, known for his "you might be a redneck" standup routines. The comedy offered the president a warm-up of sorts before Monday's final presidential debate in Boca Raton, Fla.
>
> "If you say you'll protect a woman's right to choose, but you stand up at a primary debate and said that you'd be 'delighted' to sign a law outlawing that right to choose in all cases, man, you've definitely got Romnesia," he said.

Allusions can be made to either traditional media—most commonly, Greek mythology, Shakespeare, or the Bible—or to popular media. A good writer will have a broad enough knowledge of traditional media and popular media and be able to make allusions to both.

States Robert J. Thompson, "If you have a writer who is writing with a broad knowledge of American culture and a broad knowledge of world literature and a broad knowledge of the big three—the Bible, Greek mythology, and Shakespeare—you can work in that stuff in a way that makes sense. If you're simply trying to do it to sound smart, it nearly always falls on its face.

"You can sprinkle an article with high-brow references, and if you write them well, they don't have to be lost on people who aren't well read on those kinds of things, and the same is true of popular references as well. You don't have to actually know this stuff to understand a reference in an article. … It all boils down to whether it is written well. Readers don't have to have seen a single episode of *Here Comes Honey Boo Boo* to understand a reference to Honey Boo Boo because they've heard about it. They don't have to have seen a production of *Hamlet* to understand 'good night, sweet prince' or 'to be or not to be.'

"In many cases, references to high culture tend to flatter an audience because they think they've gotten it even if they don't know intimately at all what its context was. We see people slinging around classic canonized literary stuff all the time, and the reference is understood even though the person may never have read the novel or seen the play."

Roy Peter Clark writes, "I like writers who have both Old School and New School sensibilities. Who can refer to Lady Gaga and Thomas Aquinas in the same paragraph. It does not concern me if my readers do not recognize a particular allusion. I will explain it to them or make it clear from context."

Many writers who create work for the public do their best to follow the popular media. For many—including me—it provides the perfect justification for spending four hours a day watching television and movies. "It's part of the business," says veteran journalist Holly G. Miller. "You have to know what's going on; you have to know what people care about; you have to see what movies people are going to."

A writer, however, should keep in mind that beginning with the advent of cable television, popular culture has become increasingly fragmented.

"If you make a reference to a really good quote in *Breaking Bad* or *Mad Men*," says Thompson, "you're going to get a few people from the two million people who watch those shows who are going to get that reference in great depth and with great energy. But you are going to get a lot of people who aren't going to catch it because—as good as those shows are and as much as they've been rewarded—a lot of popular culture is relatively fragmented. We are not in the era of *I Love Lucy* and *The Ed Sullivan Show* where everybody was watching the same thing at the same time. Our best popular culture is watched by 1 percent of the population … we have 300 million plus people in the country, and three million is a pretty big hit on a cable show."

Besides watching television shows such as *The Simpsons* or *Family Guy*, a writer can gather information about the current state of popular culture by following several social media and online resources, including those at the Pew Research Center's website www.journalism.org. On this site, you will find indices tracking new media, talk shows, and campaign and news coverage. Additionally, websites such as Reddit and YouTube generate lists of news and video that reflect the current cultural zeitgeist.

Nonstandard English

Many good writers choose to spice up their prose with colloquialisms often derived from music, television, Internet slang, viral memes, and so forth. When used in moderation, words such as *swag, bling, playa, baller, blowin' up, tebowing*, and so forth can be refreshing to the reader.

Margaret Guroff, features editor at *AARP The Magazine*, invites writers to use new words in their stories. "English is a living language. It's always changing. The question is whether it's the right word."

Interestingly, and probably much to the chagrin of conservative grammarians, many examples of today's slang are nouns that are used as verbs. For example, you can *google* the price of a television and then *text* the price to a friend.

One, Two, Three, and More

The number of elements you cite can have a dramatic effect on your narrative.
Consider the following.

> I am happy.

Okay, so I'm happy. The statement is absolute and probably explains all that anybody needs to know about me right now. Maybe I just finished eating Thanksgiving dinner with my family, and we just plopped ourselves in front of the boob tube to watch the Detroit Lions play the Chicago Bears.

> I am happy and excited.

So I'm not only happy, but I'm also excited. My happiness has crossed over from mere contentment to something more—something that complements my happiness. Maybe I'm both happy and excited because my favorite football team, the Detroit Lions, scored a touchdown during the Thanksgiving Classic.

> I am happy, excited, and optimistic.

This sentence has an inclusive quality to it—as if these three adjectives comprise my current state. It's like a closed set in mathematics; it has boundaries. This list of elements completely explains a situation. Taken together, these elements can imply hope. For example, maybe in the final seconds of the game, the Lions scored a touchdown and nailed the field goal, putting them seven points in front of the evil Bears; in other words, it looks like the Lions will win.

> I am happy, excited, elated, optimistic, contented, cheerful, overjoyed ...

This sentence is similar to an open set in mathematics with no boundaries to the number of elements that can be tacked on. You can string more adjectives similar to the word *happy* onto this sentence, and they probably describe my emotional state. Maybe the Lions won, and after the game was done, I checked my Mega Millions ticket and found I had just won $135 million.

A lot of Internet writing is short and to the point. Paying attention to the number of elements you include in a story can make your Internet writing more concise. Many professional writers realize this fact and carefully choose the number of elements they use when writing articles or blog postings.

In 2012, Yoselyn Ortega, a nanny in New York City, fatally stabbed two young children under her care and then injured herself. It was a terrible and unexpected tragedy. Shortly after the stabbing, in a blog posting titled "The Kids Aren't Safe With Me," Lori Leibovich, a lifestyle editor with The Huffington Post, wrote about her own close call with a nanny who had a "psychotic break."

The lede starts with one simple concept (and the gist of the entire piece): By the nanny's own admission, the kids weren't safe with her.

> "The kids aren't safe with me."
>
> The voice on the other end of the phone was strangely calm and matter-of-fact. It was my nanny (whom I'll call Liane), and she was home with my two young children.

Later, Leibovich offers a bit of backstory to express how great she thought the nanny was when she hired her. In one sentence she includes two elements to explain how the nanny instantly appealed to her young son. During their first encounter, the nanny not only played Legos with the boy but also explained mythology. These two elements complement each other; the nanny would engage the boy in two ways, with physical toys and fantastic ideas.

> She got on the floor with my son and helped him construct Lego castles and introduced him to mythology.

In another explanation of the nanny's backstory, Leibovich uses three elements to expound on just how great she and her husband thought this nanny was before they hired her.

> Once we met Liane, we knew we'd hire her. Her references confirmed what we thought: Liane was loving and smart and fun.

This statement includes three elements that reinforce our understanding that on the surface the nanny is everything a potential employer would desire: She's loving, smart, and fun. What else could anyone want from a nanny? Apparently, she's the total package.

As Roy Peter Clark explains in his book *Writing Tools*, including four or more elements in a sentence helps it break through "escape velocity." It takes a sentence to excess and intentionally overloads your reader.

A while back, I was assigned an article that involved fruit diversity. After doing some research, I was amazed at how many varieties of fruit there actually are—even seemingly mundane fruits such as apples and oranges came in many varieties. I found that other journalists who write about fruit were equally intrigued by the variety and sometimes use lists that include several elements or examples to impress on readers just how many varieties of fruits there are.

In this travel feature from the *Milwaukee Journal Sentinel* titled "Pick your own pumpkins, and apples, too," writer Brian E. Clark impresses the reader with the vast number of apple varieties that grow on one single commercial orchard. The interesting names of the apples contribute more narrative flair.

> Flannery said his orchard produces more than thirty varieties of apples, ranging from the old traditionals, including Macintosh, Cortland, Johnson, yellow and red delicious, as well as newer types such as Honeycrisp, Gala, Fuji, Snowsweet, and Cameo, which is Flannery's favorite.

One final note about the use of elements—specifically as it relates to the use of two elements: As was the case with the examples above, two elements can complement each other or be compared with each other in terms of similarity. But two elements can also contrast each other.

Several years after the 9/11 tragedy, plans for a Muslim cultural center to be built near Ground Zero came to light. Several groups who felt that a mosque built near Ground Zero would be disrespectful seriously opposed this plan. In a CNN online opinion piece titled "Beware loaded language in Islamic center debate," Roy Peter Clark cleverly used the controversy as an example to warn others of loaded language. In doing so, he contrasted two similar elements—Islamophobia and Islamofascism—to make a point. In other words, he uses "vs." with irony.

> And on the other, a new word has been coined to describe such expressions: "Islamophobia." Meanwhile, the right focuses on the dangers posed by fanatics they call "Islamofascists."
>
> Islamophobia vs. Islamofascism. Not much wiggle room for moderate debate there.

Staying on Track

One mistake that many writers make is trying to squeeze too many ideas into their stories. With the possible exception of resulting gastrointestinal distress, the practice is similar to overloading yourself at the $9.99 Chinese buffet—seven plates will make anybody sick! Normally, a good editor will realize that a writer has gone off track and rope him in with heavy editing.

Most good stories have one goal or purpose, and the angle of the story helps the writer achieve this goal. From the beginning, a writer transitions toward an ending that is always in sight. If a reader becomes lost and the promise of this ending is obfuscated, then the writer has failed.

"At its heart," says Michael Howerton, managing editor at Contently and former editor at *The Wall Street Journal*, "every story is about one thing. Every story has one guiding principle … one idea behind it that is its engine. … When the story is about more than one thing, it becomes incoherent."

I once wrote a thought feature about international medical graduates for an association magazine. International medical graduates are physicians who went to medical school in another country and come to the United States in order to do their residency training. The vast majority of these physicians end up practicing medicine in the United States and never return to their own countries. This phenomenon results in what experts have named "brain drain." Brain drain refers to the unintended consequence of another country sending its physicians to the United States for training: a dearth of physicians in their own health-care system.

The training of international medical graduates is governed by an organization called the Educational Commission for Foreign Medical Graduates. In addition to evaluating and licensing these physicians, this commission also provides tools to help these physicians acculturate, including online tutorials and mentoring services. Even though the angle of my piece involved examining international medical graduates with an eye toward brain drain, while writing the story, I became infatuated with these acculturation services. I ended up trying to do too much with my article and unduly focused on issues that were outside the scope of my feature. After cutting hundreds of words out of my first drafts, my editor reminded me to stay on track and deal with brain drain, the issue at hand.

In order to keep a story on track, you may want to prioritize the story's social network. In other words, the participants, witnesses, and experts should be pared down to the most relevant. You don't want your work to read like *Dream of the Red Chamber*—a Chinese masterpiece that requires a genealogy in order to understand it. Keep in mind that when considering which characters to include in your work, you walk a fine line between truth and understanding. Strive to take the fewest literary privileges as possible with the intention of remaining as verifiable or factually accurate as possible.

As a somewhat cautionary tale, consider Ben Affleck's movie *Argo*. Although an excellent movie, it downplayed Canadian involvement in the freeing of six American hostages in the wake of the 1979 Iran Hostage Crisis. Consequently, some have labeled the movie revisionist.

Another useful construct to consider when keeping a story on track is the complication-resolution model. Pulitzer Prize-winning author Jon Franklin touts the complication-resolution model in his book *Writing for Story*. According to this model, every story has a complication, which can be a conflict or issue the story's characters are dealing with. This complication causes tension as the characters in the story try to resolve it. Once the complication is solved or passes, there's resolution.

Many—if not all—the stories that grip the world's attention follow a pattern of complication, tension, and resolution. To illustrate, consider the story six-year-old Elián González, whose mother attempted to bring him by boat to the United States from Cuba in 1999. González's mother drowned, but little Elián was rescued. He was entrusted to the care of relatives in Miami who wanted to keep him in the United States. Meanwhile, Elián's father wanted the boy to return to Cuba. After a protracted legal battle, little Elián was returned to his father.

In Elián's story, the complication was whether he would stay in the United States. The tension was all the legal wrangling that occurred and its accompanying overtones of the strained U.S.-Cuban relationship (a leitmotif that perched higher on the Ladder of Abstraction). This complication resulted in tension with characters on both sides of the issue that were fighting to keep Elián. The resolution was Elián's eventual return to Cuba.

Transitions and Topic Sentences

From a technical perspective, the proper use of transitions and topic sentences help the writer stay on track and keep the narrative flowing.

Transitions link sentences together. Here are some typical transitions used to link sentences together. These transitions are often found at the beginnings of sentences and are adverbs that end up modifying the sentences they precede.

- accordingly
- additionally
- but
- despite
- finally
- first, second, third, fourth … (not one, two, three … or firstly, secondly, thirdly …)
- for example
- for instance
- furthermore
- in other words
- in the meantime
- in the past
- moreover
- next
- of note
- so
- this

In addition to using such specific words as transitions, the subject of a sentence may be repeated or implied in order to establish flow. Relevant quotations can also serve as transitions.

Finally, topic sentences introduce the information in a paragraph and help transition from one paragraph to another. A topic sentence is usually found at the beginning of each paragraph.

Pit Stops: Anecdotes and the Fourth Wall

Imagine you're living in Los Angeles and your friends invite you to come with them on a weekend trip to Las Vegas. You excitedly fill your backpack with the essentials and pile into the backseat of a car packed with your friends. You can't wait to get to the Strip, chow down at the buffets, see a show, and maybe play the five-dollar blackjack tables.

Unless you get stuck in Friday traffic, the drive between LA and Vegas takes about four hours. But few people drive straight through to Vegas, especially on a road trip with buddies. You'll likely make a pit stop to gas up, use the facilities, or grab a gyro at the Mad Greek in Baker, California. (Baker is home to the "World's Largest Thermometer.") These diversions are part of the fun.

An article is like a road trip to Vegas. It's a journey that starts somewhere (Los Angeles) and ends somewhere (Las Vegas). Along the way, there are pit stops, such as restroom breaks and junk-food runs. In articles, these pit stops can take the form of anecdotes.

When written well, anecdotes allow the reader a vicarious, visceral, and emotional experience. Anecdotes are little stories with their own beginnings, middles and ends. For the most part, anecdotes are short, placed strategically, and reflect the theme, scope, and angle of the article.

While doing research, a smart writer will keep tabs on striking anecdotes. "While I'm researching a piece and I'm talking about it with my friends and family," says Margaret Guroff, "I'll make a note of which stories I'm telling them because these are the ones that stand out and these are the ones that are most reflective of what I want to tell the reader about the subject."

Anecdotes may allow the writer to retreat from analyses and fact and encamp behind the *fourth wall*. In theater and film, the fourth wall is the imaginary wall that separates the play from the audience. Sometimes a character will break through this wall and address the audience directly. For example, in the 1970s television show *Three's Company*, character actor Norman Fell, who played the landlord Mr. Roper, would sometimes turn to the camera and smile after he made fun of his wife. Fell's brilliant facial expressions broke the fourth wall, and we, the audience, knew that he was sharing the joke with us. For a more recent example of a character breaking the fourth wall, check out Kevin Spacey's performance in the political thriller *House of Cards*.

In addition to parodying and satirizing nearly every other imaginable literary device, from time to time, the characters on *The Simpsons* break the fourth wall and address the audience. Homer Simpson even broke through the fourth wall in *The Simpsons Movie* when he chastised the audience for being suckers and paying to see characters in a movie theater that they could have watched on television for free.

In a *Best Life* feature article titled "The New Age of Fatherhood," author Jennifer Wolff Perrine skillfully uses anecdotes to illustrate the practice of wealthy single men paying huge sums of money for surrogate mothers to have their children. The anecdotes all involve highly successful professionals, including investors and financial advisors, who, for a variety of reasons, were single but still wanted a baby. These anecdotes are interspersed between the ethical, legal, and financial analysis of the issue. Incidentally, the piece also makes good use of the Ladder of Abstraction with specific anecdotes at the bottom of the ladder and the ethical, legal, and financial concerns higher up.

Quotations and Dialogue

Well-chosen quotations can also contribute to the narrative of an article. Quotations make articles interesting and shouldn't regurgitate facts, definitions, or statistics. Such information is better described in the author's own words.

Many seasoned writers and reporters develop a feel for a useful quotation, especially when the quotation espouses the right sentiment. While interviewing or researching, they'll stumble across something that's best said by another person. Although there's no foolproof method for coming up with great quotations, these useful guidelines should help you choose when a quotation should go into your article:

- It introduces an engaging voice other than the writer's.
- It introduces emotion or opinion.
- It explains something about a subject or issue in a witty, cynical, humorous, irreverent, interesting, pithy, or insightful way.
- It provides perspectives of, or insights into, a character or situation.
- It introduces or foreshadows future events.

Keep in mind that choosing quotations to use in an article is a great responsibility that carries consequences. Holly G. Miller, an editor at *The Saturday Evening Post* and also a publications consultant, says, "As a writer, you have an incredible power to manipulate just by the quotes you pull out of an interview. ... It's a tightrope that you walk."

Miller cautions against sticking too many quotations into your story. "You don't want to be quoting a bunch of clones," says Miller. "So if they all pretty much say the same thing, you need only one person to say it."

Although it's better to err on the side of too many interviews rather than too few, interviewing too many people poses its own risks. "When you talk to a lot of people," says Miller, "the temptation is to make sure they are all included in the article. [Remember] that you're not writing for the people who you're interviewing; you're writing for the reader. If somebody said stuff that really has no depth or didn't add anything to the conversation, you have to leave them out."

Although seldom used when writing articles, dialogue can be a useful tool. Dialogue is a discussion between two characters. Unlike quotations, which are heard and recorded, dialogue is usually overheard or meticulously reconstructed through interviews with both speakers and witness accounts. According to Roy Peter Clark, "While quotes provide information or explanation, dialogue thickens the plot. The quote may be heard, but dialogue is overheard. The writer who uses dialogue transports us to a place and time where we get to experience the events described in the story."

In "The Case of the Vanishing Blonde," Michael Lee Jones, a suspect in a rape case, is questioned by Detective Allen Foote. The dialogue between Foote and Jones does more to develop the narrative than any description in the author's own words possibly could. It also hints at the detective's anger and frustration over this unsolved case.

> "Look, I've got a girl who was raped that week. Did you have anything to do with it?"
> "No, of course not!" said Jones, appropriately shocked by the question. "No way."

"You didn't beat the shit out of this girl and leave her for dead in a field down there?"

"Oh, no. No."

In conclusion, narrative is the lifeblood of any article; it's what distinguishes a list of facts from an entertaining and engaging story. But just as with conventions of style, conventions of narrative take time to learn. No writer can craft a stylistically sound and narrative-rich story on the first go-around. Through the polishing and revision process, a piece can be imbued with narrative elements and the words can be changed into crisp, publishable, and alluring prose. Just as a painter layers watercolor, the writer layers effort and continues to tinker with a piece until it reads well. In part, this polishing process is what distinguishes journalism from science.

"Good narrative writing has a rhythm that unfolds, and the prose helps to shape the reader's experience as they are sitting back and reading it," says science writer Robert Irion. "The structure of paragraphs, the length of sentences, the emphasis within a sentence … all of this is important. It doesn't necessarily happen on draft one. First drafts … are the most painful part of this whole process. Often what you're doing initially is getting a bunch of stuff down so that you're no longer staring at the blank screen."

Ted Spiker, an associate professor of journalism at the University of Florida and former editor at *Men's Health,* echoes this sentiment. "The thing I hate most about writing," says Spiker, "is the first draft because I just hate getting it all down there. But when I feel like the draft is 80 percent there, that's my favorite time. It's like I have the foundation. Now it's time for interior decorating … let's dress this thing up. But it's a fine line. … You want to be careful not to overdecorate because oftentimes tightening up and slimming down are the best parts of revision, but they are the places where you can muscle up your verbs, experiment with sentence structure, and turn a good story into a great one."

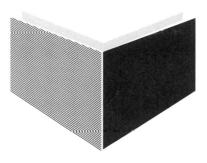

chapter 12

NEWS ARTICLES

The uninitiated may assume that reporting facts without the fluffy extras may be easy (and unromantic). But the truth is that writing news pieces can be a devilishly difficult skill to master. Beginning journalism students struggle with the inverted pyramid because, in addition to brevity, reporting in the inverted-pyramid structure requires analysis and evaluation—higher levels of Bloom's Taxonomy (see Chapter 8). Consequently, it will probably come as no surprise that reporting news has been a breeding ground for many famous writers.

Years ago, most beginning journalists got their start reporting at the local newspaper. These journalists became experts at using the inverted pyramid and reporting news. Nowadays, with newspapers downsizing and media becoming increasingly fragmented, it's feasible that many journalists never receive in-depth exposure to news reporting. Nevertheless, every journalist or writer of articles would benefit from understanding this discipline.

After communicating with many experts and doing much research, I've been able to conceptualize news articles as existing in several forms. The options I present are by no means inclusive.

THE INVERTED PYRAMID

The inverted pyramid is a funny structure. It's a structure that many journalists spend a good part of their lives mastering and the rest of their lives questioning. No matter what its detractors claim, however, the inverted pyramid continues to have an enduring significance in the realms of news reporting and journalism in general.

"I think the inverted pyramid is an extremely useful device that serves a lot of stories well," says Michael Howerton, a former editor at *The Wall Street Journal*. "There was a time when [journalists] thought that you had to move away from the pyramid because it's such a limited version of storytelling and we have to be more magazine style, we have to be more feature style, we have to be more emotional with our writing. And I think that's great, and I agree with all of those things. But the problem is that if you're reading a newspaper and you have every story written in a magazine style, it's too exhausting for the reader. Some stories are very well suited for the inverted pyramid. The inverted pyramid is great for writing strong, quick, and efficient prose."

Although many people believe the inverted pyramid arose from necessity—early telegraph transmissions were costly and required prioritization of the news transmitted—more likely the inverted pyramid faded into existence at about the time of President Lincoln's assassination. The inverted pyramid became more popular during the Progressive Era (1880 to 1910) and the rise of the Associated Press, which distributed fact-weighted news intended for all audiences. (As argued by author and thinker Steven Johnson, many of man's greatest inventions and discoveries slowly materialize—few are, in fact, groundbreaking.) Furthermore, the development of the inverted pyramid and its summary news lede were likely moderated by the advance of science and higher education. Before the inverted pyramid became popular, news stories were often written in dandified prose that read more like fairy tales than modern news. The most important information was saved for last, and that was okay because it took several weeks for news to travel—nobody was in a rush for facts.

The inverted pyramid starts with a summary lede that addresses the five *W*s and one *H*: who, what, where, when, why, and how. This information is normally introduced by an enticing detail or engaging sentence or two. The paragraphs following this lede paragraph present extra information in descending order of importance and from general to specific. Such "extra" information may describe relevance, impact, background, response, consequences, repercussions, and quoted material.

Even though stories written using the inverted pyramid are direct in their presentation of facts, they must still be relevant and engaging to the reader. Tom Linden says that the reader has "to know fairly quickly what [she is] going to get out of the story… the added value of the story."

The sentences and paragraphs in a piece written in the inverted-pyramid style are typically concise. Sentences are often weighted at the end with nonessential elements preceding essential elements. Additionally, quotations are often broken into paragraphs. As with feature writing, grouping the quotations and input from experts is useful with a news piece written using the inverted pyramid.

On March 18, 2013, a story ran that exemplifies the chain of "breaking-news" reporting mediated by the inverted pyramid. At 5:43 A.M., the *Chicago Tribune* and the *South Bend Tribune* published a story titled "2 Killed, 3 Hurt When Small Jet Crashes into South Bend homes." Here is the summary lede of the story, which, after a sentence of narrative, efficiently answers many of the five *W*s and one *H*.

> Frank Sojka was standing in his bedroom when the house shuddered and the ceiling of the living room collapsed in a loud crash.
>
> A small private jet had gone down short of the airport in South Bend, Ind. Sunday afternoon and plowed through three homes, killing two people on the plane and injuring three other people.

The rest of the article contains witness accounts of the disaster.

Later that day, as more information emerged, one of the dead was confirmed to be Steve Davis, a star quarterback at the University of Oklahoma in the 1970s. Shortly after noon that day, in an article written using the inverted pyramid and titled "Ex-Oklahoma QB Killed in Plane Crash in Indiana," the Associated Press covered the story, including the death of Steve Davis—an intriguing and sad detail:

> Steve Davis, Oklahoma's starting quarterback when it won back-to-back national championships in the 1970s, was one of two people killed when a small aircraft smashed into three homes in northern Indiana, officials said Monday.

In this case, we appreciate another summary lede, with the five *W*s and one *H* answered fairly quickly. The rest of the article examines both Davis and details of the crash, which leaked enough fuel that hundreds were forced to evacuate their homes.

In the above examples, the focus of the story shifted from a small plane crash to the death of a one-time American icon; consequently, the "relevance" of the story changed. Undeterred by this dramatic shift in the story, journalists quickly repackaged it, using the inverted pyramid as an algorithm to quickly disseminate the new angle.

The Internet may make a good home for articles either written in—or inspired by— the inverted pyramid. When using the inverted pyramid, Internet readers can quickly probe a piece.

Some view the inverted pyramid—a structure that's remained unchanged for almost two hundred years—and the Internet as unlikely bedfellows. "In the professional world, people who are more skeptical of the Web tend to be more traditional and therefore more married to the inverted pyramid," states Marc Cooper, director of digital news at USC Annenberg. "The concept that underlies the inverted pyramid is not only a great way to tell a story but a great way to think. … It's going to tell people what's most important first … grab them with a lede and back it up. … In that sense the concept of the inverted pyramid is not only a valuable way to write news but a valuable way to express yourself.

"The more structural details and the more rigid formulaic details of the inverted pyramid are being eroded by the Web, and I don't think there's anything wrong with that because the important part of the pyramid is the concept. The Web tends to be more conversational than traditional newspaper and more two-way. A lot of the rigidity that's in the inverted pyramid sort of clashes with the culture of the Web."

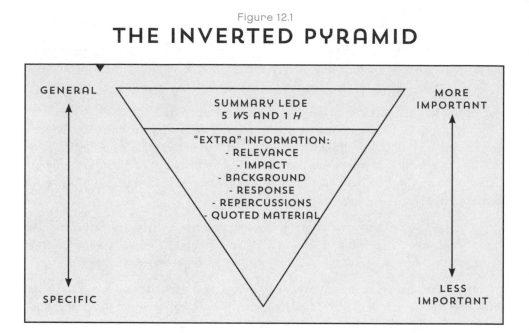

Figure 12.1
THE INVERTED PYRAMID

GENERAL

MORE IMPORTANT

SUMMARY LEDE
5 *WS* AND 1 *H*

"EXTRA" INFORMATION:
- RELEVANCE
- IMPACT
- BACKGROUND
- RESPONSE
- REPERCUSSIONS
- QUOTED MATERIAL

SPECIFIC

LESS IMPORTANT

LiveScience, a publisher of scientific news that is sold to news-aggregator websites like Yahoo! and AOL, often writes its news in the inverted-pyramid style. Moreover, news organizations such as Fox and CNN have incorporated blogs into their online offerings, and news in their blog postings is often presented using the inverted pyramid.

Even though the inverted pyramid has endured for centuries and continues to endure in the digital age, as with any other structure, it's impossible to predict its future. In an e-mail interview, journalism scholar Roy Peter Clark writes, "We all act as if the forms of journalism expression have existed forever. Not true. They are created at particular times in history. Their creation is influenced by the marketplace, by social norms, and by technologies. The inverted pyramid was not created by slaves in ancient Egypt. It is connected to cultural circumstances such as the Civil War, the invention of the telegraph, and the creation of the wire services. Even though we think Shakespeare was one of the greatest writers of English, no one is writing verse plays anymore. So even great forms of writing become exhausted, leaving room for new forms."

ALTERNATIVE STORY FORMS

In recent years, academics and journalists have been particularly interested in presenting news in alternative story forms. Alternative story forms present printed news in a fashion other than straight prose. Although alternative story forms come in various iterations, they share some common traits. First, they tell their own story. Second, studies show that alternative story forms tend to grab readers' attention and are particularly good at helping facts stick in readers' minds. Third, they are drastically underused in print and online. The EyeTrack studies at Poynter found that in a sample of 16,976 print text elements only 4 percent were alternative story forms.

"Alternative story forms," says Sara Quinn, the faculty member at the Poynter Institute who directs the EyeTrack research, "are really good at bite-size digestible things. … Maybe [they are] more scientific-type stories [or] fact-laden stories with clear geographic references. Things that you're going to show side by side [like] putting two candidates up for a mayor's race. You don't want to write around numbers."

Alternative story forms come in, well, many forms:

- Charticle: combinations of text, images, illustrations, graphs, and charts
- Dos and don'ts
- Expert input
- Explainer photo
- Glossary: defines jargon or key terms
- How-to
- Infographic: a visual depiction of information or data
- Instant expert: a guide to an issue, person, place, or thing
- Interest piece: an illustration of reader interest in an event or issue
- Key players
- Key statistics: odds, risks, rates, and so forth
- Lists
- Mini-profiles
- Panel
- Photo story: story told using photos (like a picture book)
- Pros and cons
- Question and answer (Q&A)
- Story so far: If the story is still breaking, this form may be useful to explain events leading up to the status quo.
- Time lines

A full description of every type of alternative story form is outside the scope of this book. I would, however, like to focus on one particularly powerful alternative story form: the Q&A (Question and Answer).

Q&As are reader specific. They frame a story in terms of what readers may ask. They also have multiple points of entry. A reader should be able to understand the article simply by scanning the Q&A and starting at any question. Q&As are probably most closely associated with interviews, but they can also be used with science and medicine.

"The difference between Q&As and more typical narrative profiles is that Q&As require a more dedicated concentration on reading," says Dr. David E. Sumner, professor of journalism at Ball State University. "The reader wants to read all that information. You're not doing any work for the reader. You're just putting the direct quotes out there. It's not something that generally attracts a casual readership who are just scanning through a magazine. The reader has to be somebody who is interested either in that subject or the person who is being interviewed."

Sumner also points out that the subject of the Q&A has to meet certain qualifications. "The Q&A has more points of entry. It works with people who you're interviewing who are more educated and more literate ... a person who won't require a lot of polishing or editing to put their quotes out there."

Despite their low-maintenance appearance, Q&As can be deceptively difficult to facilitate and write. "There are some people who think it's lazy writing," says Joe Leydon, a film critic for *Variety*. "But Q&As can be quite difficult. You have to make every response self-contained. ... If you get somebody who goes off track and wants to tell you a long story ... you get nervous."

Figure 12.2

ALTERNATIVE STORY FORM (CHARTICLE)

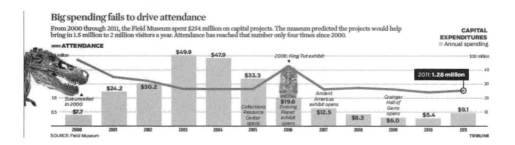

INTERACTIVE DESIGN

With all the budget cuts hitting newsrooms, it's sad that some skimping and scrounging comes at the expense of graphic artists and web-design teams. Some of the most dynamic and exciting types of news come out of interactive news collaboratives that involve the work of journalists, graphic designers, programmers, and more. As with any interactive media, interactive design engages the reader and elicits an interaction. Interactive design is driven by data that the readers have input or plugged in.

In 2008, *The New York Times* put out an interactive news piece titled "Pogue-o-matic," which is hosted David Pogue, a technology columnist for the *Times*. The "Pogue-o-Matic" snarkily evaluated cameras, camcorders, smartphones, and televisions for the 2009 holiday season, required the user to click the answers to questions, and used video and pop-up screens to display options. (For more on the snarky or playfully irreverent voice, refer to the sidebar in Chapter 16.)

In 2012, *The New York Times* put out another interesting interactive design piece that focuses on a mixed-race demographic shift currently occurring in America. The piece is titled "Mixed America's Family Trees," and audience members are encouraged to submit their own family trees. In one example, the family tree of actor Lou Diamond Phillips can be clicked on, and you can hear him narrate his mixed-race heritage. Of note, Phillips is Filipino, English, Irish, Spanish, and more. (Even though he's probably most famous for playing Mexican and American Indian roles, by his own admission in the audio clip, he's about $1/32$ or $1/64$ Cherokee.)

Much like any good example of online interactive media, usability is of principal importance when designing an interactive design piece. It's important to avoid overburdening the reader with too many options.

In a Q&A published in the *Times*, graphics director Steve Duenes writes, "Readers don't want to spend a lot of time figuring out how something works. Even when there's a lot of data, the interface should be designed so that the content is easily accessible. Often that means doing some fairly simple things, like limiting the number of menu options or making the descriptive language very clear."

As with any document, the interactive design piece should serve a purpose and engage the reader. It should take the reader closer to the subject. Finally, because it's difficult and costly to produce interactive pieces, reusability is important to publications, and templates can serve a useful purpose.

A good example of a simple and reusable interactive design titled "Crime in Chicago" can be found on the *Chicago Tribune*'s website. By typing in or clicking on a specific area, the reader can access statistics on property crimes, as well as violent and quality-of-life crimes. As you can probably imagine, this example of interactive design can be paired with a variety of stories.

Although not exactly news, you'll find examples of interactive design in magazines, too. For example, in the January 2013 issue of *Wired*, there's an interactive piece titled "Speaking Bad" that enables tablet users to pair quotations with a corresponding antihero. For example, Tyler Durden, the main character in the movie *Fight Club*, memorably uttered, "It's only after we've lost everything that we're free to do anything."

Keep in mind that a smart writer is always aware of when interactive design will benefit a story. If your editor is amenable to telling stories using digital tools, feel free to make suggestions.

INVESTIGATIVE NEWS

In 2011, I met for lunch with the editor of *The San Diego Union-Tribune* (now called *U-T San Diego*). I was interested in possibly doing some investigative work for the paper—the paper has a remarkable investigative team that won a 2006 Pulitzer Prize for exposing the bribes taken by Congressional Representative Randy "Duke" Cunningham. The editor asked me how comfortable I was with statistics and using statistics programs because a statistician-type job was the only job he could offer me. I told him I had taken a graduate course in statistics and had some familiarity with SPSS Statistics, a statistical software package, but I was no expert. After lunch, we never spoke again. It was at that point that I truly appreciated how different investigative journalism was from the rest of journalism. Proficiency with statistics, however, is only one characteristic that distinguishes the practice of investigative reporting.

Economic concerns are cutting into investigative reporting efforts nationwide. Additionally, some experts contend that the spirit of investigative journalism has been diluted with weekly news shows like *60 Minutes* and local news teams pursuing investigations with dubious social merit—such as personal injury and personal financial concerns. Nevertheless, exciting investigative reporting is still being done. For example, in 2010, ProPublica, a nonprofit newsroom that publishes investigative stories in the public interest, became the first online publication to win a Pulitzer Prize. It then won another Pulitzer in 2011. ProPublica routinely partners with big news organizations when doing investigative work, including *The New York Times*, *The Washington Post*, the *Los Angeles Times,* and *60 Minutes.*

To be sure, investigative reporting has a long and storied history in the United States, dating all the way back to the revolutionary presses and, later, partisan presses. Classically, investigative pieces have been the purview of newspapers, but investigative journalism is also found in books, on websites (ProPublica), and in magazines (*Mother Jones*). Such reporting played a large role in shaping the United States.

By the turn of the century, early investigative reporters called muckrakers had made their mark and helped bring about social change. In the 1960s, science writer and editor Rachel Carson published her landmark work *Silent Spring,* which exposed the effects of pesticides on the environment. In the 1970s, a whole generation of journalists were inspired to enter the profession when *Washington Post* investigative reporters Bob Woodward and Carl Bernstein blew the top off the Watergate scandal.

According to *The Elements of Journalism*, investigative reporting comes in three flavors:

- "Original investigative reporting," wherein reporters uncover new information. Classically, the press has pushed public institutions to investigate and reform through original investigative reporting.
- "Interpretive investigative reporting," which involves the tireless pursuit and analysis of already existing information to shed light on revelations of greater social import
- "Reporting on investigation," which typically involves leaks in information from official investigations

Several characteristics are common to many types of investigative reporting. First, investigative reporters aim to uncover wrongdoing. Second, investigative reporters spend much time sifting through documents and data to make sense of this wrongdoing. Analysis of such data can get complicated and involves the use of statistics and a scientific method to prove hypotheses. Third, investigative reporters often have to deal with a different breed of source, including whistleblowers and "current" and "former" members. Investigative reporters are deeply concerned with the character and motivation of their sources, too. Fourth, sources—especially those at the center of any wrongdoing—are often reluctant to go on record, which poses an entirely different set of obstacles to the investigative reporter. Fifth, investigative reporting practices can be contentious. These practices include the use of anonymous sources, paid sources, ambush interviews, covert reporting, and more.

Although I've touched on investigative stories as a type of news article, a full analysis of this type of reporting is outside the scope of this text. For more information on this topic, I suggest reading *The Investigative Reporter's Handbook* and visiting the Investigative Reporters & Editors website, specifically perusing the IRE Resource Center.

TWITTER

In 2006, Evan Williams and Biz Stone, formerly of Google, launched Twitter. (Williams had also created Blogger, the popular blogging software.) Twitter was written in the programming language Ruby, and its interface allows open adaptation and integration with other online services. In March 2007, Twitter made its public debut at the South by Southwest music festival and soon became a force to be reckoned with. The number of Twitterers or Twitter users has increased by more than 1300 percent in 2009, and by 2011, users were sending a cyclopean one billion tweets a week!

Twitter is a free SMS (short message service) with a social-networking component. Many texts (known as tweets) are sent by a hegemony of self-obsessed Twitterati (Twitter users who attract thousands or millions of users). A 2009 study published by the *Harvard Business Review* suggested that the top 10 percent of Tweeters accounted for more than 90 percent of all tweets. Interestingly, this study also shows that unlike other social-media sites, which are often driven by women users, Twitter appeals to nearly as many men as women.

In 2009, the Oxford University Press Dictionary Team found that the second most common word used on Twitter was "I" compared with its place as the tenth most common word in general English text. Other very popular first words also hinted at egocentrism among Tweeters and included *watching, trying, listening, reading,* and *eating.* (For those of you who are interested, the word *fuck* is much more prevalent in Twitterese than in written English—so much for Twitterquette.)

Even though Twitter is often used by celebrities who have a propensity for showing off their tanlines and self-destructive congressmen tweeting pictures of themselves in their skivvies, the medium has shown incredible promise as a vehicle for disseminating news—especially breaking news. On January 15, 2009, citizen journalist Janis Krums broke the news of US Airways flight 1549 landing on the Hudson and uploaded a picture snapped from her camera onto Twitpic.com. Much like the popular press was used to fuel American democracy in the Revolutionary era, Twitter and other social-media sites have been used to herald democratic and political movements both within the United States and across the world. For example, Twitter was integral during 2009 uprisings in Moldova and during Iran's attempted velvet revolution that same year. Additionally, during his 2012 election campaign, President Barack Obama was a political trailblazer with his savvy use of Twitter and other social-media sites, including Reddit, Spotify, Instagram, Pinterest, and Tumblr. (Sadly, Obama's popular 2008 Facebook campaign was orphaned somewhere near the beginning of his 2012 campaign preparations.) Obama's fondness for Twitter in particular dates to the 2008 election, when he famously amassed twenty times as many Twitter followers as Senator John McCain.

"For its users," write the editors at the *Columbia Journalism Review,* "Twitter has become a lens to just about any news event you can think of—revolutions, volcanic eruptions, State of the Unions—providing an addictive mix of quips, on the scene reports, and recommended links."

What's the best way to use the 140-character count allotted for each tweet? I asked Roy Peter Clark this question, and he suggests using this medium in serial-narrative form—a structure he probably understands better than any other living writer. If the who's, what's, where's, when's, why's, how's, and details could be read in reverse order—so as to make a story out of a Twitter feed—the news being disseminated would make more sense. This advice suggests that narrative transitions may be important when constructing a Twitter feed to report news.

"I enjoy writing on Twitter," writes Clark, "and I try to write as well as I can in short forms. I never dump stuff. I am always crafting and revising. There is a serious problem with Twitter as a news-delivery system: It works if you are experiencing it in real time. If you come to the party late, you may have missed the most dramatic or newsworthy tweet. I wish I could turn the sequence upside down, which then feels more like a serial narrative."

When using Twitter to disseminate news, let hyperlinks and multimedia do some of the work of fact. It may be a good idea to link to other websites (using a service such as bitly or TinyURL to shorten the URL), pictures, and videos. You can also use a hash tag to indicate a Trending Topic and thus beef up your tweets.

Andy Carvin, the senior strategist at NPR, does an excellent job of running his Twitter feed. "Carvin," writes Craig Silverman for the *Columbia Journalism Review*, "sends hundreds of tweets a day that, taken together, paint a real-time picture of events, opinions, controversies, and rumors related to events in the Middle East."

Carvin selectively retweets breaking news but also uses crowdsourcing to learn more and verify information. He also engages other Tweeters to provide supporting information such as photos. In order to instill a sense of verification and transparency in his feed, Carvin will often introduce retweets with questions such as, "Anyone else reporting this yet?" or, "How unusual is this?" He'll also use phrases such as "not confirmed."

According to the *Columbia Journalism Review*, Carvin runs into a number of interesting problems when crowdsourcing his Twitter feeds. First, the citizen reporters he often relies on misuse words like "*breaking*," "*urgent*," and "*confirmed*," which are often spelled out in capital letters. Second, the tweets that he reposts often lack needed links to pictures and videos, which he will then request. Third, transparency is an issue, and it's impossible to figure out whether the source of the original tweet is unbiased. For example, an insurgent in some Arab Springs warzone could be sending out tweets as propaganda.

Transparency seems to be a big problem for all journalists who use Twitter. In the case of some politicians, celebrities, and other well-known people, it's impossible to tell whether a media-relations team, digital staffer, intern, or assistant is behind the tweet. For example, in November 2012, Michael Oren, then Israeli ambassador to the United States, quickly deleted a tweet posted from his account that said Israel was "willing to sit down with" the terrorist group Hamas "if they [Hamas] just stop shooting at us." He then blamed the tweet on a staffer.

Not everyone thinks that judging the verification and transparency of tweets is necessary. Marc Cooper, director of the digital news at USC Annenberg, believes that readers have enough common sense to discern the quality of tweets: "I am much more comfortable with ordinary people using their judgment and whatever resource they have to determine what narratives or what sources they're going to trust rather than have a third party put their stamp of approval on it. ... I think it's a red herring. If certain things are not verifiable or trustworthy, then it implies that there are things that *are* verifiable and trustworthy. ... It has an antidemocratic tinge to it because it implies that there was a time that you could rely on the media to give you this rock-solid information. If you go back to the pre-Web or pre-social media ... you will see that the media was highly unreliable and highly biased and highly parochial. There was some great information, and there was a lot of bad information ... a lot of unwitting propaganda. ... There was a political consensus that permeated the media so you got a certain unrealistic or fragmentary view of the world. In 1955, you could read *The Washington Post* or *New York Times* all day and really be wrong."

Many journalists put much thought into their tweets and draw on their training and experience to craft them. "The skills I would use for a long feature are very similar to the skills I would use in writing a tweet," says Ted Spiker. "I try to spend some time thinking about the rhythm of a tweet and the placement of the words to get the maximum rhythm and voice to the tweet. Which is exactly the way I would edit a long-form story."

One potential problem when reporting news through any social-media outlet, including Twitter, is that the media's existence is dependent on the financial realities and corporate decisions made by the companies who own these sites. Greed for advertising revenue undid websites like MySpace and Digg, and although valuations for sites like Twitter and Facebook are astronomically high, these entities don't generate huge profits. Nevertheless, Twitter continues to show promise as a disseminator of news.

Many journalists, editors, and academics have recognized that the delivery and consumption of breaking news may best be done by digital means. For the time being, at least, news analysis may be best relegated to print journalism. For example, if a shooting were to occur in a city square somewhere in the world, the story could break on a Twitter or blog feed and be further analyzed the next day in the local newspaper.

"The digital form of communication has overridden everything," says Cooper. "The bias of digital is to be very fast and to be very common and shared. ... Not only blogs but also social media, digital communication, and nontraditional forms of journalism have eclipsed traditional journalism at least in breaking news. When it comes to things that are more refined or analytical, you'll need more time and room to digest that. ... Whether you have news that's breaking very quickly ... whether it's a fire or whether it's the overthrow of a government in Egypt ... you're probably going to do better in the initial period by following a Twitter feed than following articles on the CNN blog or AP Wire."

Current research suggests that readers are equally likely to turn to both traditional (newspaper) and nontraditional (online) mediums for their news. But even as the means by which news is disseminated continues to evolve, actual news reporting will always endure. Before we can analyze and reflect, we must first grapple with the gravity of facts. When the space shuttle *Challenger* exploded, when terrorists targeted the Twin Towers, and when Hurricane Katrina wiped out the levees in New Orleans, news reports preceded analysis. In times of exigency, we will always retreat to news in its most basic form, whether it's disseminated by a newspaper, blog, or Twitter feed.

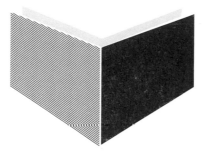

chapter 13

OPINION ARTICLES

Opinion articles can be found in various types of publications—newspapers, magazines, and blogs. For example, in its opinion section, *The New York Times* runs columns, editorials, letters, and op-eds. The amount of opinion in magazines varies: Some have little or none; some have editor's notes, letters to the editor, and so forth, which run near the front matter ("front matter" is publisher jargon for the first few pages of a book or magazine); some, such as the *The New Republic* and the *National Review,* are chock-full of opinion. (Both *The New Republic* and *National Review* are political rags. *The New Republic* is liberal, and the *National Review* is conservative. Politics is intrinsically opinionated.) Finally, in addition to aggregating news content and acting as a superblog, The Huffington Post, an online publication, has many contributors post opinion pieces every day.

Before moving forward, it's important to explain some of the differences between editorials, op-eds, and columns. Editorials represent the views of a publication, and their content is dictated by the publisher or an editorial board. Editorials can either be "signed" and attributed to an author representative of the publication or be "unsigned" and, by default, attributed to the publication. Ostensibly, the editorial board works to represent the principles and convictions of the publisher.

Op-eds run opposite the editorials and, as is the case with *The New York Times*, which arguably runs some of the most popular op-eds in the publishing world, represent opinions of authors neither associated with the editorial board nor the publication itself. Columns are commentaries written by experts who are educated and experienced with respect to a topic. These columns can take various forms, and columnists often use news pegs (journalism jargon for some story in the news that makes the article timely), questions from readers, and essay format to expound on their opinions and views. Examples of columns include George F. Will's syndicated political column at *The Washington Post* and Dan Savage's syndicated sex column *Savage Love.*

As their name implies, opinion articles explain an author's or, in the case of an editorial, a publication's, opinion or point of view. An opinion is a judgment or appraisal of a subject or issue and is not fact. But opinions should be argued with fact in order for the audience to be affected and persuaded by them.

(In an effort to distinguish any subjectivity expressed from the publisher's stance, some publications are hesitant to use the word *opinion* for anything other than editorials and prefer "point of view" instead. For the purposes of this book, however, "point of view" and opinion can be used synonymously.)

Although opinion articles can share some of the same characteristics with news and feature articles, they are intrinsically different because they serve a different purpose. An opinion article is explicit in its intention to change a person's thinking and benefit the audience—and society—as the author or publication see fit.

Editorializing

When a news or feature article injects author opinion, the writer is *editorializing*. Editorializing is poor journalistic practice. Other examples of editorializing include the assumption that audience members "know" what the writer is referring to. For example, if a writer were to use the medical jargon *laparotomy* in a feature or news article without explaining that the term refers to abdominal surgery, the author would be editorializing.

The opinion article has a long history in journalism—especially newspaper journalism. In the years before the American Revolution and up until the beginning of the twentieth century, opinion articles dominated American journalism. Opinion articles played an important role in establishing American independence. But by the twentieth century, journalism—especially newspaper journalism—became increasingly dispassionate. This sentiment affected editorials, and by the 1950s, newspaper editorials were less authoritative and fairly muted in their sentiments.

By the 1980s, the pendulum had swung the other way. Better editorials became shorter and more interpretive. They were also presenting opinion in their ledes and had moved away from dispassionate summary ledes. Furthermore, better editorials were calling their audience to action. These changes were reflected in the selection criteria for Pulitzer Prize winners for editorial writing. The committee started looking for "clearness of style, moral purpose, sound reasoning, and power to influence public opinion in what the writer conceives to be the right direction, using any available journalistic tool."

As we approached the new millennium, the *actual* opinion or point of view expressed by the best editorials, columns, and other opinion articles became less important than their ability to express a strong and informed viewpoint that engaged the public. A good opinion-article writer wears many hats: thinker, storyteller, and provocateur. In an article titled "The Case of the Vanishing Columnist," published in the *Columbia Journalism Review,* author Steve Twomey writes: "In short, people like to have their buttons pushed. There's a much greater chance they'll bail out of a column from boredom than because of an irritating opinion."

With the increasing popularity of blogs and resultant self-exposure and self-actualization through electronic means, bleeding out opinions has become en vogue. Everywhere we look, we're hit by various iterations of opinion articles, some of them good and many of them bad. But even when they're bad, many still seem to catch our attention and imaginations.

Opinions are important—they help us comprehend the world in which we live. Without opinions, we would have trouble functioning and making decisions. Our opinions affect every decision we make and color our perception. Without opinions, we would vote however, marry whomever, have whichever number of children, and eat whatever. We'd live lives of apathy. The best opinion writers help us understand ourselves and articulate our own opinions. But it's important that journalists learn how to better structure opinion articles and lay a logical foundation for their arguments.

The key to a good opinion article is the strength of the arguments. A writer must support opinions with logic and fact, or nobody is going to care about them, consider them seriously, or be persuaded by them. Three Aristotelian *appeals,* or principles, are useful when characterizing arguments: *logos, ethos,* and *pathos.* The term *logos* refers to the clarity, logic, and consistency of an argument, that is, whether an argument is supported by fact and makes sense. *Ethos* refers to the credibility of the writer or speaker. For example, a rocket scientist writing about space travel is probably more credible than a kindergarten teacher writing about the same subject. The term *pathos* refers to an argument's appeal to the audience's sensibilities and emotions. An argument with the proper pathos can identify with audience morality and sense of good; it can encourage audience members to change, not only to help themselves but also others. For example, a persuasive editorial on the value of making charitable contributions during the holidays may inspire audience members to make donations and spread the wealth. Ideally a good editorial will incorporate elements of logos, pathos, and ethos.

ARGUING OPINION

There are several good—and some bad—ways to construct your arguments. Below you'll find some principles to consider. Keep in mind that this information can not only be used to help structure your own arguments but also poke holes in the arguments of others.

Deductive Reasoning

When used properly, deductive reasoning can be one of the strongest methods of persuading your audience. Deductive reasoning refers to applying general principles to a specific situation. For example, physicians engage in deductive reasoning whenever evaluating a patient. If an older patient comes in with severe chest pain that radiates to the arm, based on more general knowledge, a good physician will consider the diagnosis of a heart attack.

When structuring a deductive argument, it's important to articulate the major, or general, premise of your argument; the minor, or specific, premise of your argument; and the conclusion that can be drawn from these premises.

During the presidential election of 2012, opinion writers attempted to use deductive reasoning to argue the legitimacy of Mitt Romney's proposed dedication to the needs of the middle class.

> **MAJOR PREMISE:** Rich people don't understand what it's like to be a middle-class citizen because they make too much money.

> **MINOR PREMISE:** Mitt Romney grew up privileged, and, as an adult, made a lot of money after he co-founded Bain Capital, a very successful asset-management firm.

> **CONCLUSION:** Mitt Romney doesn't understand what it's like to be middle class.

Writers of opinion articles and liberal politicians alike have used this conclusion to question Mitt Romney's sympathy for and ability to understand the middle class. In fact, President Obama himself often brought up his own humble beginnings—his mother was a single woman who struggled financially—to juxtapose Romney and identify with the middle class.

This argument, however, isn't perfect; you can poke holes in it. For example, while Mitt Romney was governor of Massachusetts, he represented many middle-class citizens and understood their situation by closely observing and working with them. Nevertheless, the argument has been strong enough for many smart people to cite and serves as an example of the power of deductive reasoning.

Inductive Reasoning

The process of inductive reasoning is the opposite of the process of deductive reasoning. With inductive reasoning, a series of examples is used to form a conclusion. Inductive arguments are leaky and wide open to criticism. In order to debunk an argument made by inductive reasoning, all you have to do is find one exception. Stereotypes are examples of inductive reasoning, and most rational people are quick to dismiss stereotyped thinking.

Going back to the 2012 presidential campaign, the American Society for Federation, State, and Municipal Employees ran a series of advertisements in which they interviewed the garbage collectors who pick up Mitt Romney's trash outside his $12-million-dollar residence in La Jolla, California. These people claimed to be "invisible" to Mitt Romney and said they felt unappreciated because he didn't acknowledge them with smiles, hugs, or bottles of water. In their advertisements, the American Society of Federation, State, and

Municipal Employees used these examples to conclude that Mitt Romney doesn't care about working-class people. But a closer examination of the issue proves that Mitt Romney does in fact know what it's like to be a garbage man. In fact, as pointed out by Charles C.W. Cooke at the National Review Online, while governor of Massachusetts, Romney worked as a garbage man for a day.

Examples

Examples can make for great arguments, especially when they're based on fact. For example, if you were trying to persuade somebody that rich politicians exist, you could point to Mitt Romney as an example. Even though Romney's tax records haven't been released, everybody knows that Mitt Romney is rich.

The problem with using examples presents itself when you use one example to create another one.

Consider the following example:

> Matt Damon and Ben Affleck are friends who share political views.

Therefore:

> President Barack Obama and the Reverend Jeremiah Wright are friends who share political views.

Although it's true that Obama and Wright are (or at least were) friends at one point—Wright provided spiritual counsel to Obama—Wright has a history of making divisive and inflammatory statements. The President ended up censuring these remarks and stopped going to Wright's church. In fact, both John McCain and Mitt Romney, Republican candidates in the 2008 and 2012 elections respectively, have dismissed the claims of some conservative commentators, such as Tucker Carlson, that Obama and Wright share similar ideologies.

Correlation and Causation

Two variables or factors can be correlated or related without having a cause-and-effect relationship. For example, all American presidents speak English, but speaking English doesn't cause somebody to become President of the United States. You have to be careful to avoid arguing that two characteristics are in a causal relationship when they may merely be associated. Journalists can fall into this trap when trying to interpret (scientific) journal articles on their own. Keep in mind that determining association or causation is a statistical endeavor, and if you want to argue causation in order to bolster an opinion but are unsure of how to interpret statistical results, you may want to contact an expert source, such as a statistician.

A well-known example of correlation being confused with causation involved hormone-replacement therapy and coronary heart disease. At first, researchers concluded from observational studies that hormone-replacement therapy protected postmenopausal women from heart disease. Undoubtedly, this conclusion makes for good copy, which may influence a postmenopausal reader to consider hormone-replacement therapy. But on closer examination and further testing, researchers determined that this association was untrue and cited confounding factors, including socioeconomic status and the fact that gynecologists were probably prescribing hormone-replacement therapy to postmenopausal women who were at less risk for heart disease. In reality, hormone-replacement therapy either had no effect on heart disease or slightly increased the chances of coronary heart disease in research study participants.

ANALOGY

So how rich is Mitt Romney? Mitt Romney is so rich that he could buy a new Nissan Versa every day for the rest of his life and still live comfortably.

If somebody were to dispute Romney's wealth, the preceding analogy would go a long way to convince this person otherwise. With opinion writing, analogies can drive home a point and persuade members of your audience.

Absurd Arguments

Absurd arguments are entertaining in humor pieces but should never be used in any serious opinion piece.

Here's an example of an absurd argument taken from a commentary in *The Onion*, a satire publication. The piece is titled "Would A Man Who Doesn't Support Women Let His Wife Pick Out Any Oven She Wants For Her Birthday?" In the article, a writer from *The Onion* pretends to be Mitt Romney and posits the argument that if Romney didn't care about women's rights and issues, then he wouldn't let his wife choose the appliances, decorate the kitchen, and perform other unsupervised domestic duties.

> Who was it that let her decide where we went on vacation this year, and the year before that? Who was it that let her pick out almost all of my dress shirts? Who was it that said, "Sure, you can have your book club meeting at our house," even though it meant ceding the living room to ten of her chattering friends for an entire night? That's right: me. Mitt Romney. So no one on this earth, neither the president nor his increasingly belligerent league of supporters, can accuse Mitt Romney of undermining the progress of women.

In addition to being an intentionally flawed example of an inductive argument—using specific examples of Romney's behavior to argue his support of women—it's also absurd.

WRITING AN OPINION ARTICLE

How do you write an opinion article? As with many other types of articles, the default answer to this question is "in whatever way engages your readers." That being said, you'll find plenty of additional advice on structuring an opinion article in this section.

An opinion article is often written as an essay. It starts with a clear-cut introduction that sets the scene for the rest of the article. In part, the introduction clarifies the importance of the essay and compels the reader to read on. The introduction also includes a thesis statement. Keep in mind that with an opinion piece, the thesis statement should be argumentative and not descriptive—there must be two sides to the thesis.

The body paragraphs of the essay support the author's thesis and are grouped logically. Usually, the first part of an essay's body provides support for a thesis. This support is followed by explanation and refutation of significant counterarguments. The arguments you present should be grounded in logic and appropriately use facts to back them up.

The conclusion of the essay reiterates the thesis or point of the piece and, like the conclusion of a feature article, can provide perspective or expound on the significance of the issues raised, make a call for action, or look toward the future. It's important that the introduction and conclusion be especially engaging.

In many ways, the structure of the essay is reminiscent of the structure of a feature: The introduction is similar to the lede and may be referred to as an opinion lede, the theme paragraph is similar to the nut graph, and both essays and feature articles use conclusions that provide closure.

As with features, opinion articles incorporate narrative elements in their structure and prose. For example, some opinion articles benefit from interviews and interfacing with the public. Steve Lopez, a metro columnist for the *Los Angeles Times*, is well known for hitting the streets and eliciting public opinion. Similar to any news or feature writer, Lopez incorporates quotation support into his columns. Lopez also does a good job of including descriptive and narrative elements more typical of feature writing into his columns, including the use of anecdotes and imagery. For example, in an October 2012 article titled "Poor Go Unheard in Presidential Race," Lopez examines how 2012 presidential and vice-presidential candidates barely addressed the topic of poverty. He then hit the streets of Los Angeles and spoke with people who considered themselves poor, such as a dog walker who was on Social Security and a home health-care worker who made $700 a month. In another article titled "Mayoral Candidates Step into Sidewalk Debate," Lopez uses anecdotes to describe injuries sustained by Los Angelinos on account of more than 5,000 miles of unmaintained sidewalk. These injuries range from scratches and bruises to fractures.

As with any other article, one should consider the audience, scope, and purpose when writing an opinion piece. For example, some experts complain that local newspapers waste space by publishing editorials and columns that deal solely with national issues. They argue that national issues only have a place in local publications in as much as they influence the community and specific audience members of the publications.

Magazines also carefully consider scope, purpose, and audience when publishing their opinion pieces. For example, the Fall 2012 of *High Times Medical Marijuana*, which has a long history of advocating for the legalization of marijuana, published an editorial criticizing President Obama. Here's how the opinion lede read.

> With just a few months left before the election, I thought you might be interested to know how the more than 70 percent of Americans who support 'states rights' when it comes to medical marijuana feel about the way your administration has handled the issue. The answer, to be, well, *blunt*, is that we tend to fall in a continuum somewhere between deeply disappointed and extremely pissed off.

TIPS ON OPINION WRITING FROM A PULITZER PRIZE WINNER

In 2009, Mark Mahoney, an editorial writer at *The Post-Star* in Glens Falls, New York, won the Pulitzer Prize for editorial writing. As written on the Pulitzer website, Mahoney won the award "for his relentless, down-to-earth editorials on the perils of local government secrecy, effectively admonishing citizens to uphold their right to know." In an interview for this book, Mahoney provides plenty of great tips on the writing of editorials and, more generally, opinion articles.

TIP 1. "You have to build an editorial. The first thing you need is a strong foundation for your argument. You have to have a strong argument or you don't have an editorial. You have to do a lot of research and make sure that you have your facts straight so that when somebody comes back to argue with you, you can defend your arguments with either anecdotes or straight fact."

Mahoney then gave me an example of how, in one editorial, he was describing chemicals used in the process of hydraulic fracturing (a method to extract petroleum and natural gas), and he decided to list the chemicals used. When the American Petroleum Institute complained about the list, he referred them back to the source of his information, the website for the Environmental Protection Agency.

TIP 2. "Make sure you consider the other side. If you write an editorial that [describes only] your position, and if you don't acknowledge that there's another view that people might hold, your argument is actually weaker. Always make sure to include the other side. There's always another side, or you wouldn't have a need to write the editorial."

Mahoney recalls how, with one of his first editorial pieces, he supported Americans' right to burn flags. His editor was quick to point out that this position may offend many veterans who fought for this country; consequently, in the article, Mahoney acknowledged the sacrifices that veterans made to defend the United States.

TIP 3. "Make sure that you give them [the readers] something to do with the editorial other than just saying, 'Here is what I think … isn't this wonderful?' Let them take action or the public officials take action. It doesn't have to be your idea that they actually take, but maybe it will get their wheels turning and they'll come with something else."

Mahoney gave me an example of how he once wrote an editorial calling for the construction of a guard fence to protect cyclists and pedestrians. This call for action worked; his kids now call the fence "Daddy's fence."

In order to facilitate such action, Mahoney recommends referencing telephone numbers, websites, e-mail addresses, and street addresses.

TIP 4. "If it's boring and you don't connect with people on the subject … get something in their heads that they can relate to. … Tell them a story."

In one of his Pulitzer Prize-winning editorials, Mahoney compared a seemingly ho-hum closed-door meeting among town board representatives to a "clandestine affair at a sleazy roadside motel." The analogy worked and stirred readers.

TIP 5. "You can use [emotion] in concert with the factual argument. … A lot of times I try to get people pissed off. … That's the way to get people to act. … Sometimes you want to stir people up … sometimes you want to stir emotions … sometimes you want to stir anger … sometimes you want to inspire people. … Appeal to their emotions with the language."

Mahoney tells me that one easy way for him to relate to readers is to reference his kids. Everybody either has kids or has been a kid.

TIP 6. "Everybody disses the English language for having too many words [and] misspellings and [for] all [its] influences. I think the English language is phenomenal for writing editorials because you can find words that will capture even the subtlest emotion or feeling. You can string sentences together that put images in [readers'] heads. Use the patterns of sentence structure, alliteration, onomatopoeia, [and so forth] … anything you can to put images and thoughts in peoples' heads so they can really relate to what you're doing. You really have to work hard when you're writing an editorial to find that word or phrase to drive home your point."

TIP 7. Finally, Mahoney suggests that the editorial writer engage the community and create an interactive discussion through electronic means—blogs and social media.

"I would interact with people, and that's why the blog was successful. It wasn't just taking my editorials and putting them on the Internet or commenting further. It was a chance for people to interact. And that's where online and print can complement each other … where you can use the blog and even Twitter and Facebook to generate discussion about topics and get people involved. People like commenting on stuff."

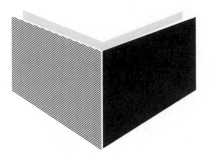

chapter 14

BLOGS

According to the *Encyclopaedia Britannica*, a blog is defined as an "online journal where an individual, group, or corporation presents a record of activities, thoughts, or beliefs." The emergence of blogs has given great power to the citizen journalist. Now anyone with access to the Internet can create a blog.

Although I realize that some bloggers don't consider themselves "journalists," others, such as Kevin Sites, known for his war reporting, and Rebecca MacKinnon, who co-founded Global Voices, a citizen media initiative, are definitely journalists. I consider blogs to be a form of journalism and blog postings a type of article intended for the public. Countless people are undeniably influenced by the work of bloggers, many of whom herald a new age of citizen journalism. Moreover, blog postings can benefit from the style, structure, and narrative elements that characterize other types of articles.

BLOGS: A BRIEF HISTORY

Jorn Barger, an early blogger and proprietor of the website RobotWisdom.com, introduced the term "Web log" into the English lexicon in December 1997. By 1999, Peter Merholz, another early blogger, started using the portmanteau *blog*. By October 2005, there were approximately 19.6 million blogs in existence, with that number doubling every five months. Every second, at least one new blog is being started somewhere in the world. Although many of the earliest blogs dealt with current events, today several different types of blogs exist: "filter" or topical blogs that deal with news and political stories; "knowledge" blogs, where people share expertise; travel blogs; blogs for support groups; blogs that serve as personal journals or diaries; notebook blogs, which contain external or internal content written as long-form essays; and open blogs.

The history of the blog is fundamentally tied to the advent of the Internet. In 1992, Tim Berners-Lee, widely credited for inventing the Internet, documented the development of the Web in what can be considered the first online blog. In 1995, Carolyn Burke started publishing Carolyn's Diary. By 1997, Slashdot aggregated "news for nerds" and linked to sites that became so overwhelmed with traffic that they became known as *slashdotted*.

From the very beginning, blogs were community oriented and focused on the bloggers and the readers. Blogging software such as Blogger or WordPress had not yet been invented, and bloggers used HTML code to post their blogs on their own websites. These early blogs served to aggregate interesting news and information.

Some of the earliest news and "filter" blogs proved to be highly influential. For example, in 1998, after *Newsweek* killed a story about President Bill Clinton and how he had "sexual relations" with Monica Lewinsky, Matt Drudge of the The Drudge Report jumped on the news. Other victories notched by early bloggers include exposing U.S. Senator Trent Lott's bigoted support of Strom Thurmond's 1948 presidential platform in 2002. And in December 2004, thousands of citizen bloggers helped report the Indian Ocean tsunami.

Many citizens used early blogs to criticize media coverage of the news and politicians. In a 2005 article titled "Journalism's Backseat Drivers," Barb Palser writes that "bloggers' charges against journalism begin with gross negligence: omission, laziness, herd-think."

By the 2004 presidential election, bloggers became a force to be reckoned with. Bloggers famously questioned CBS News's coverage of President George Bush's service in the National Guard and called out presidential candidate John Kerry's military record, too. Furthermore, presidential candidate Howard Dean developed a strong blogger following and enlisted the help of his grassroots campaign to oppose the second Persian Gulf War. Finally, Dan Rather was nudged into retirement by right-wing bloggers who questioned his coverage of the 2004 presidential campaign and aired their concerns on the blog RatherBiased.com.

Soon the blogosphere encompassed more than just citizen watchdogs, war bloggers, political pundits, partisans, and people sharing information and news. More people started blogging about their own feelings, and self-disclosure became popular. A study in the Winter 2005 *Journalism and Mass Communication Quarterly* found that nearly 80 percent of A-list bloggers wrote about their day and their feelings. Additionally, 53.6 percent of A-list bloggers used the work of experts to support their own writing, and 74.2 percent addressed their audience directly. Ultimately, many A-list blogs hosted "mixed" blogs that incorporated both news and external information combined with personal perspectives.

In this study, A-list blogs were defined as web pages that were authored by one person with entries listed in reverse chronological order. A-list blogs also had high readership and were "linked to" by at least one hundred other blogs. Interestingly, many of these A-list blogs had readerships that rivaled small publications and were even more trusted than mainstream media outlets. Although the study doesn't give great examples of which A-list blogs it sampled, blogs that would probably meet these criteria include PerezHilton.com, written by gossip columnist Perez Hilton, and KevinMD.com, authored by Dr. Kevin Pho, who proclaims to be "social media's leading physician voice."

According to the study, A-list bloggers put much thought into managing their online identities and strived to present their "real" selves. Interestingly, this premeditated self-presentation is similar to acting. An actor stages a performance and projects an imaginary identity. Similarly, when blogging, a blogger can stress certain aspects of her personality and minimize others, thus projecting an engineered identity of sorts. These A-list bloggers engaged readers by providing continuous content that reflected their thoughts and feelings. Of note, 83.26 percent of these bloggers used their real names.

Big concerns among A-list bloggers were likeability and competence. Few preferred to show off and would rather "ingratiate" themselves to the public. These A-list bloggers were quick to respond to reader comments and concerns and were highly cognizant that their A-list status was dependent on their readers, including the large proportion of online readers who "lurked" and didn't comment on blog postings.

In a 2008 article titled "Blogonomics," published in the *Columbia Journalism Review*, writer Chris Mooney characterized most bloggers who write for websites such as Daily Kos, The Huffington Post, and ScienceBlogs as "political activists or college students or professors or celebrities, or simply opinionated and informed citizens. In many cases, they have day jobs (or are retired) and blog for 'fun' or out of devotion to a cause. They don't expect to be paid well, if at all—or they don't know that they *should* expect it."

Initially, mainstream-media journalists and bloggers were wary of one another. Mainstream-media reporters disregarded blogging for its perceived bias and lack of credibility and dismissed bloggers for their lack of journalism training. Conversely, bloggers argued that mainstream journalists were elitists who had no desire to include the public in deciding what is newsworthy. But it soon became apparent that blogs and mainstream media could synergize. Consider the following excerpt from a journal article titled "Uses and Perceptions of Blogs: A Report on Professional Journalists and Journalism Educators" by Deborah S. Chung and colleagues:

> Pundits, however, point out that blogging can benefit traditional journalism by providing different perspectives, by helping to regain trust traditional news organizations have lost, and by increasing interactivity in journalism. …
>
> Bloggers also recognize that they need to learn traditional news values, the benefits of editing, and the importance of original reporting from traditional journalists in order to be perceived as credible sources of news information.

By the late 2000s, blogs had made a transition from media fringe to media foreground, and it seemed as if nearly every news organization hosted blogs: *The New York Times, The Wall Street Journal, Wired, Discover Magazine, The New Yorker, ESPN, The Atlantic,* and many more. Entire news organizations that were built around blogs—for example, Gawker and The Huffington Post—became known as "superblogs." In a *Columbia Journalism Review* story titled "The State of the Blog," blogger Felix Salmon of Reuters writes, "There's convergence going on—news organizations are becoming bloggier, and blogs are becoming newsier—and that process works to the benefit of both."

In more philosophical terms, in addition to converging with news, blogs disseminated by everyday citizens (nonjournalists) have converged with and contributed to a collective intelligence and participatory culture. Traditional or mass media doesn't have a monopoly on this participatory culture. Creation and consumption of media has become a collective process that involves mass media when necessary but is not dependent on it. The threat to traditional media is rooted in capitalism: When newspapers, magazines, cable television, and so forth no longer provide the only entertainment at the party, what happens to the bottom line?

Recently, there has been concern—voiced by bloggers including Salmon and others—that various media organizations that have devoted several members of their staff and whole newsrooms to their team blogging efforts pose a threat to first-person blogging. Obviously, these blogging outfits are better prepared to break news and present new ideas and can engage readers with new information. In all reality, however, if a first-person blog is interesting enough, its readers will likely continue to follow it even with the proliferation of blog sites with more resources and manpower.

Many bloggers have found it extremely difficult to use their blogs to consistently come up with breaking news and original ideas. These bloggers have come to the realization that it's easier to comment on the news, post their own opinions, and so forth. A cautionary tale may be that of writer and journalist Jonah Lehrer. In 2012, Lehrer was caught self-plagiarizing on his blog at *The New Yorker*. In this blog, Lehrer reused content from material he wrote for *The Wall Street Journal*. Lehrer, a prolific writer and lecturer with much on his plate, gave the impression that his material was original, but it wasn't. Interestingly, Lehrer was later found guilty of fabricating quotations from Bob Dylan in his bestselling book *Imagine: How Creativity Works* and other unethical acts.

One of the most exciting recent developments in blogging involves science writing. Many researchers, scientists, and physicians use their knowledge to comment on media coverage of research. Examples of such blogs can be found on ScienceBlogs and the Discover Magazine website. Another exciting development in blogging is the *niche* blog. Many people are finding their own (small) audiences in the increasingly fragmented blogosphere by writing about avocations such as quilting and home-brewed beer.

STRUCTURING A BLOG POSTING

Short

In the early days of the Internet, many writers followed the 50 percent rule, which was proposed by web-usability expert Jakob Nielsen in 1997. Nielsen advised that in light of "refresh" rates and limited screen resolution, people read web content about 25 percent slower than the printed word. Consequently, web content should be about half as long as a printed counterpart. Although screen resolutions have improved immensely, many experts still recommend that Internet content—including blogs—should be concise.

"It isn't just a question of word count," says Jonathan Price, a web writer, consultant, and journalist. "It's a question of shorter words, shorter sentences, and shorter paragraphs."

With the majority of blog postings, "short and simple" seems to best suit most audiences. Most of the communication that takes place via the Internet is short, whether it takes the form of e-mail messages or bursts of information transmitted over social-media sites. But it should be acknowledged that short formats might not always be best.

Some people may like long and more structurally complex blog postings for three reasons. First, during the past several years, people have become both smarter and accustomed to increasingly complex media that has taken the form of television shows, video games, and hypertext. Second, interest in online long-form journalism has increased—a trend that the Pew Research Center has acknowledged: "Tablets allow readers to 'pause, linger, read, and process very important ideas,' Chris Hughes explained after buying *The New Republic*, adding, 'The demand for long-form, quality journalism is strong in our country.'" (Chris Hughes is a Facebook co-founder who, in a prime example of Old Media merging with New Media, purchased *The New Republic* magazine in 2012.) This increased interest in reading longer and more complex articles online may bode well for longer blog postings. Third, people may be willing to reread a longer, more complex posting as many times as they have to in order to fully appreciate its message.

Because many blogs are inherently serialized, a reader may be willing to refer back to previous blog postings for clarity, further augmenting a blog's ability to incorporate more complexity. In recent years, this willingness for audience members to repeat and re-view has been apparent to executives in Hollywood who have zealously green-lit television shows with complex narratives—such as *The Sopranos* and *The Wire*. These more complex television shows have proven popular with both critics and audiences.

Lean-Forward vs. Lean Back Experiences

It's important to distinguish what Sara Quinn, director of the EyeTrack Studies at the Poynter Institute, refers to as lean-forward and lean-back experiences. (The original use of this terminology is likely attributable to Jakob Nielsen, an early web-usability expert.) With lean-forward experiences, a reader is intently focused on the information at hand—maybe she's sitting in a chair and reading from a desktop computer, laptop computer, or mobile phone screen. With lean-back experiences, a reader will relax with the content and be ready for an immersive experience; a reader reclining on a La-Z-Boy using a tablet to read long-form journalism is engaging in a lean-back experience.

Links

One main advantage of blogs is that they can link to other sources of information. Short, declarative statements can be used to introduce a scientific paper, article, or video clip without having to go into long explanations. By linking out, a blogger can rely on the work of others to provide more detailed, factual information. A blogger who links out also limits liability and avoids the possibility of copyright infringement. Remember, however, to describe the relevance of the information to which you're linking. The declarative sentence that introduces the link should also be robust enough to facilitate understanding of your article without necessitating that the reader click a link.

As Dr. Tom Linden says, "If you're describing something and you have access to visuals and audio that give you a fuller picture, you can link to them and they make [the blog posting] that much richer."

In addition to linking to more-detailed factual information, good links can also boost a blogger's credibility. "A blog has the ability to link to really cogent thoughts," says Sara Quinn. "In a book or in print you can write references, but the ability to aggregate really strong links helps bloggers' credibility. Additionally, if the reader clicks on a link and they find it worthwhile and satisfying, that reflects on you. … You're actually like a curator of good content, and you're helping guide people to that content. Everything that you can do that gives people what [they] need and want adds to your own credibility."

Photos

When choosing photos for a blog posting, try to include photos that are specific and relevant to the posting. Furthermore, check the terms in the copyright information. Many people who download images from Google or Wikimedia Commons assume that the images are open source and free to use. Sometimes, however, the images belong to somebody. Other times the owner will allow use of the picture as long as the work is attributed.

The New York Public Library's website houses a large collection of free images. If you need to buy royalty-free photos for a good price, you may want to check out the "value collection" at iStockphoto (Getty Images owns iStockphoto). You can also purchase cheap photos at Dreamstime.

EyeTrack Studies

The EyeTrack Studies done by the Poynter Institute have provided excellent research on reader interaction with digital media. By tracking reader interaction with print and online media, researchers were able to infer various insights that can be applied to online publications, including blogs.

One of the most interesting findings from the Poynter study involved how much of an online article a reader will finish. Online readers on average completed 77 percent of any story they chose to read—more than print readers. Additionally, 63 percent of story text read by online readers was read to completion, which was also more than print readers.

The EyeTrack Studies found that online readers were just as likely to be methodical readers or scanners whereas print readers were more likely to be methodical readers. "A scanner, in our definition," says Quinn, "is somebody who might read some text … go to a photograph or headline … without necessarily going back to that same spot in that text … where a methodical [reader] always went back to where they began."

Whereas print readers who scanned were less likely to return to text and complete it, online readers were likely to return to text they found interesting and more thoroughly read it.

"When people scan," says Price, "they try to get a coherent and consistent picture of what the blog posting is about and whether it's relevant to their interests. … Most writers make the false assumption that people will read what they write. It's just not that way on the Web."

Scanners may engage in a four-part cycle of probing, hypothesizing, reprobing, and thinking—a process originally postulated by games and education scholar James Paul Gee and called the Probing Principle. If engaged in this cycle, scanners are constantly appraising content and hypothesizing about it before deciding on what to read. Consequently, content may be best laid out to appeal to such readers by using design and textual elements that make this process more effective. For example, and as discussed later in this chapter, headers could be made more specific and use proper nouns.

Figure 14.1

PROBING PRINCIPLE

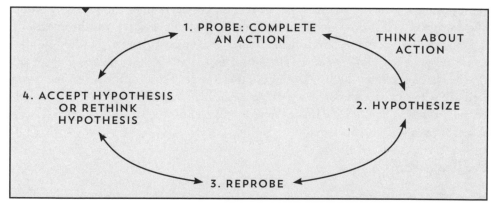

Results from the EyeTrack Studies have design implications for blogs and other forms of online media, too. One possible consideration is that online media must be designed with both types of readers in mind: lists for methodical readers and intuitive design for scanners.

Finally, based on my interpretation of the Poynter EyeTrack Studies, if a blog posting were long, it may be best to base its structure on a lead piece in a newspaper with a prominent headline, big color photos, intriguing captions, and alternative story forms such as infographics, Q&As, time lines, and so forth.

Tone

Many experts recommend that, when appropriate, the general tone of a blog should be conversational and personal. "The key difference between print and Web is [that online writing] has to be more conversational," says Price. "Particularly with blogs and social media, you have to be more personal. It's sometimes difficult for writers to decide their boundaries. … How far am I going to go in revealing my personal life, my tastes, my friends? … The question is to what extent can you write in a personal style, not a corporate style and not the neutral, bland *New York Times* style that was the ideal for many years. … Are you revealing something emotional in your attitude and in the details that you provide that gives people a little sense of who you are? … [There should] be emotion in the text and details that suggests your attitude or your life. … For some people it's too uncomfortable, and for others it comes naturally."

Blogs: Synthesis

Based on research and input from various experts, a typical blog posting can be presented in the following way. First, the sentences and paragraphs should be short, written in a fashion similar to newspaper articles and broadcast scripts, with the emphasis on the backend of the sentence. For example, the dependent clause would follow the independent clause. (This idea is very Strunk & White-esque, and I discuss it in Chapter 1.) Second, a good blog posting could incorporate intriguing textual sidebars, pictures, teasers (decks), headers (subheads), and so forth that capture the reader's attention and serve as points of entry. Third, natural points of entry, including captions, pictures, introductions, and decks or teasers, should be intriguing and hook the reader much like the lede of a typical print or online article. Fourth, headlines, teasers, and headers should use proper nouns and be specific when engaging the reader's attention—not only because readers tend to scan rather randomly and could benefit from specificity—but also because search engines tend to post blog headlines without any contextual information. Finally, it's a good idea to avoid disjointing blog postings with pictures, sidebars, and other elements or overburdening your text with too much "extra" information. Breaking the continuity of text could try the reader's patience. For example, if you want to incorporate several pictures into a blog posting, it may be smart to put the pictures in a gallery with clear, relevant, and engaging captions.

Figure 14.2

BLOGS BORROW FROM NEWS, FEATURE, AND OPINION ARTICLES

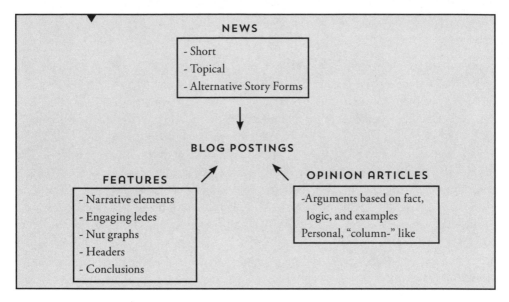

Ultimately a good blog posting may in many ways draw on characteristics of news, features, and opinion pieces. First, the content of most blogs is timely—much like a news article. And like many news articles, which use the inverted-pyramid structure, the paragraphs in a blog are often shorter, with quotations that may also be broken off into different paragraphs. Additionally, sidebars may use alternative story forms that draw the reader in: Q&As, mini-profiles, time lines, and more. Second, a blog posting could make use of some of the more engaging and narrative aspects of feature writing—strong ledes and nut graphs that read like stories; headers or subheads to break up text; and conclusions that provide perspective, look to the future, or tie back to the introduction. Third, much like an opinion piece, bloggers can decide to inject themselves into the posting and make their own arguments based on fact, logic, examples, and secondary sources. Thus a blog posting may in many ways resemble a column. In fact, National Magazine Award-winner Priscilla Long considers her blog, Science Frictions, more of a column.

"I write a weekly column, Science Frictions, on science and how it rubs up against the rest of life, for *The American Scholar*," writes Long in an e-mail interview. "Because it appears online, it is called a 'blog,' but I in fact call it a column. I work very hard on them, sometimes spending as much as thirty or forty hours on a 900-word piece. So I do not call it a blog. Each one has a core of science and often a personal story and sometimes poetry or mythology. I am a poet and in prose remain very aware of the sound of the language, of words as notes.

"Most blogs are a bunch of blathering. I want substance. How many writers are blathering out their writing existence on blogs? Having said that, there are some superb blogs. To me, a good blog posting has information that I want in it by someone who is following a subject of interest that I do not have time to personally follow."

A BLOGGER'S AUDIENCE

It's important to remember that blogs started as public communication with readers, and many of the best blogs are still interactive. By tuning out your audience, you lose the essence of what blogging is all about. Furthermore, your audience can provide valuable insight or perspective that can help clarify your own thinking or be used as fuel for further blog postings. Of note, EyeTrack researchers found that readers were drawn to reader feedback and comments. Keep in mind that the blogger who is interested in establishing a strong platform, web presence, and following should be wary of dismissing thoughtful comments, even if he disagrees with a reader's position.

According to Jonathan Price, readers notice when there are no reader comments beneath a blog posting or comments have been selectively expunged. "Being able to see the pros and cons ultimately reassures the reader that this is the straight stuff and that you're willing to have this conversation." Superblogs such as Gawker enjoy controversy and conversation generated by comments, and replies to comments drive up traffic.

I write a blog for *Psychology Today* titled the "Red-Light District." I once blogged about handshakes and made the observation that many people are starting to forego handshakes in lieu of waves and "pounds." For a news peg, I used a study that suggested that a firm and friendly handshake makes for a positive first impression. My lede was personal and anecdotal; I discussed how I went to a picnic and somebody refused to shake my hand while they were eating lunch. It peeved me.

One of my readers commented that it's acceptable for a person to refuse an extended hand while they're eating and that it's best that I not take personal offense. What he said made good sense to me and was cathartic. I no longer felt bad about having my extended hand turned away.

On a similar note, I've found that the instant feedback provided by readers who comment on blog postings has improved my writing. Under no other circumstance is my writing subject to instant feedback that I can act on—it could take days, weeks, or months before I receive feedback from an editor. If I were to write something that made little sense in a blog posting, however, a reader's comment served up in short order will help clarify my writing. For example, in a blog posting on medical jargon, I thoughtlessly confused sensitivity, specificity, positive predictive value, and negative predictive value (these are all epidemiology terms). Within hours, an astute reader caught my mistake and corrected me. I thanked the reader by online rejoinder in the comments section of my blog and corrected the posting.

Under certain circumstances, it's understandable to delete a comment. If a comment is solicitous spam; is bigoted, sexist, or racist; uses foul language; or has co-opted copyrighted information without proper attribution or permission, it's a good idea to delete it. If hosting your own blog, consider drafting a "Terms of Use" that bars any comments that can be considered disrespectful, unethical, litigious, or illegal.

On a positive note, many interactions in the blogosphere are resoundingly supportive, and bloggers do their best to elicit such interactions and drive up their traffic. Many bloggers generate memes that link back to their blogs in order to drive traffic to it. Inevitably, the success of these memes is dependent on relations with other bloggers and audience members. Bloggers often belong to supportive local, national, and international communities. These bloggers not only respond to each other's postings but sometimes meet up in person and form friendships.

Ultimately, it takes a lot of work to cultivate a blog, and bloggers must be vigilant in maintaining a balance between comments that add to their blog and those that detract from their site. According to Rebecca Blood, an early blogger and author of *The Weblog Handbook*, "… You can't have a thriving comment community without moderation since an unmoderated comment thread, once found, will instantly be filled with spam—which will tell anyone who ventures there that the blogger isn't paying attention to their own site.

"Trolls are a different matter. They are individuals whose sole purpose is to provoke a fight, either with you or with another commenter. They are not the same as someone who disagrees with you; they are someone who is deliberately disagreeable in order to provoke a response, and they will adopt (and pursue) any position in order to do that.

"The presence of either spam or trolls says to people who might be interested in making a thoughtful comment, 'No one cares about this place,' and most commenters will move on to other blogs where they can have the conversations they crave.

"Many bloggers have turned comments off on their sites since it takes time to comb through all submitted comments every day, 99 percent of which are guaranteed to be spam. Those who are committed to cultivating communities on their own sites must be willing to set aside time every day in order to ensure that genuine comments are posted when they are received. It is a big-time commitment, especially since, ideally, this should happen in real time so that those who are reading the post soon after it goes up can see that a conversation has started. Readers are unlikely to revisit an empty commenting thread the day after they've read the original post in order to see if any comments were released overnight."

On a final note, if you're fortunate enough to blog with a major publication, much of the spam is expunged by the publication's web specialists. Trolls, however, are less readily recognizable.

BLOGGING: VENIAL AND MORTAL SINS

Many writers blog regularly, and this regularity can breed mistakes. It's okay to make an unintentional mistake when blogging. Maybe you misinterpreted a journal article or attributed an idea to the wrong person. Oftentimes your readers will point out your mistakes in the comment section. If you do make a mistake, it's best to correct the mistake while retaining the text of your original posting, thus retaining your blog's transparency. You may also want to link to correct information. Most likely, your readers—and, if you're blogging for a publication, your editor—will accept this act of contrition and forgive this venial sin.

Some transgressions, however, are more serious—they are the mortal sins of blogging. Taking money or gifts for doing a blog post and not apprising your readers of this conflict of interest is one big mistake. (Even if you apprise your readers of taking money to do a blog posting, it's still most likely an ethical problem.) The mere whiff of financial impropriety can taint a blog's (and blogger's) reputation. For example, in 2010, many expert bloggers, including chronobiologist and blog guru Bora Zivkovic, left ScienceBlogs after it became known that the well-respected blog site had taken money to host a nutrition blog for PepsiCo.

Another mortal sin is using your blog to insult, intimidate, or harass others. Racism, sexism, ageism, religious intolerance, homophobia, and so forth should not be promoted in your blog or anywhere else for that matter. In 2007, Tim O'Reilly came up with the "Blogger's Code of Conduct," wherein he suggested that "we won't say anything online that we wouldn't say in person."

In conclusion, blogs are a form of journalism that offers numerous benefits to writers and readers. Many blogs enable readers to interact with writers—asking questions and making contrary points. They also provide an easy way for readers to access useful information. For instance, the Pew Research Center has found that 61 percent of all people look for health information online, and 42 percent of all people say that they or someone they knew had found useful health information on the Internet. Additionally, the information provided by expert bloggers can inspire other journalists and find its way into other publications. Fifty-one percent of journalists read blogs, and 53 percent get story ideas or sources from blogs. These findings suggest the importance of blogs in disseminating newsworthy information. According to an article in the *American Journalism Review* titled "Journalism's Backseat Drivers," blogs also act "as conduits between mainstream media and the online zeitgeist." Journalists, activists, political decision makers, and others use blogs as a barometer to evaluate public sentiment on the Internet at any given moment.

Considering that the information provided in blogs has the potential to affect the thinking of countless others, it's important that the blogger engage in principled journalism and ensure that, when feasible, blog postings be coherent, verifiable, and transparent.

Tips for Bloggers

- Blog about your interests.
- Prefer short to long (short sentences, short paragraphs, and short postings).
- Keep the weight of the sentences on the back end (independent clause followed by the dependent clause).
- Keep tone conversational and personal.
- Support opinion with logic, facts, and examples.
- Use specific headlines, teasers, and headers (when possible use proper nouns).
- Point to detailed facts with links.
- Describe your links.
- Use relevant photos.
- Leave text continuous (don't break up text with photos, sidebars, and so forth).
- Engage your audience (respond to comments).

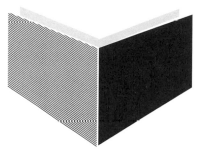

chapter 15

PUBLICATION & PLATFORM

While the rest of this book is devoted to style, theory, structure, and mechanics, this section is more utilitarian: It deals with getting published. For the new writer, nothing is as exciting as having that first article green-lighted for publication and then eventually seeing your name on a byline. The reality, however, is that getting published is difficult, and few people enter the world of publishing at the upper echelons. Securing those first few clips requires persistence, skill, and luck. Fortunately, you can control the necessary persistence and skill.

MARKETS AND PUBLICATION

For most writers, the brass ring of article publishing is the national consumer magazine, including publications such as *Men's Health*, *Wired*, *GQ*, *Pregnancy*, and *O, The Oprah Magazine*. Many of these publications also have online counterparts that accept pitches, while some large publications, such as Slate, are online only. In fact, whereas the market for newspapers and print magazines is contracting, the market for Internet publications is growing rapidly.

For most writers, it takes years of diligent effort to secure work in such national consumer magazines. Fortunately, other types of publications provide valuable exposure and experience working with editors. Here's a partial list:

- association magazines
- trade journals
- hobbyist magazines
- spiritual and faith-based magazines

- children's magazines
- in-flight magazines
- business publications (for example, company newsletters, company magazines, and annual reports)
- blogs
- consumer newsletters
- university publications
- newspapers (freelancers can sometimes land features, travel articles, and articles in special sections)

Plenty of great resources provide excellent information about freelance writing opportunities. Arguably the most robust source from which to learn about publications and freelance writing opportunities is Writer's Market (www.writersmarket.com). If you're interested in consumer magazines, Mediabistro (www.mediabistro.com) provides tips on how to pitch as well as providing editorial calendars, mastheads, job listings, courses, and much more. Other helpful e-zines, newsletters, and websites include Journalism Jobs (www.journalismjobs.com), Writers Weekly (www.writersweekly.com), and Writing for DOLLARS! (www.writingfordollars.com). If you're interested in writing for company publications, you may want to check out American Business Media (www.americanbusinessmedia.com). Finally, for an exhaustive list of publications, check out the *Gale Directory of Publication and Broadcast Media* at your local library.

Recently, media companies, brands, and nonprofits have been employing writers to produce "journalistic" content. One start-up that aims to commercialize this process in a novel way is Contently. At Contently, a writer submits a portfolio and is accepted to the network. Once accepted, the writer's talents are offered to Contently's partners, which include Mashable, Buzzfeed, and Coca-Cola. In addition to scoring freelancing gigs, members of the Contently community are provided access to online publications such as *The Content Strategist* and *The Freelance Strategist,* which offer tips for writers and information on trends.

"We basically realized that this was an opportunity to use the Internet to filter and connect people who were looking for opportunities on both sides of the equation," says technology journalist and Contently co-founder Shane Snow. "Freelancers are a huge trend. ... Brands becoming publishers is a huge trend which is reliant on freelancers. ... So we built a lot of new technology to support those things.

"[On our platform], we're trying in a way to emulate the newsroom model. ... If publishers want pitches or if an editor is looking for pitches, they say so. ... If they're not looking for pitches, you can't pitch them. ..." Furthermore, Contently clients must currently select the writers whom they want to receive pitches from.

The founders of Contently have big plans, many of which are inspired by their own personal experiences. "When I'm freelancing," says Snow, "it's either finding work on Contently or it's talking to editors whom I know personally. The alternative to our system is going out and networking and trying to get face time with the editors or e-mailing them like crazy until somebody finally gives you a shot. I'm hoping that our system will one day get every magazine and newspaper editor to organize their queries on Contently and people [to] submit their portfolio through Contently [where they] can organize their freelance life. That, I think, is the ideal world if we could sort of digitize that process that's happening manually. That's a big undertaking that's coming together piece by piece."

Contently hints at exciting opportunities in the future for freelance writers hoping to get published. The company itself brought in about $1 million in revenue during 2011, its first year of operation. Although less than the price per word of many print publications, the pay at Contently is decent, and it is based on rough word count, difficulty, and number of sources used. Snow estimates that a freelancer may receive $150 to $200 for a 700-word article that uses one source.

Contently, however, is still in its early stages of growth and apparently can't support an extensive pool of freelancers. Nevertheless, other websites offer freelancers some lower-paying opportunities to get their work out to the public. Although the experienced freelancer will likely balk at the prospect of writing for such websites and publications, the newbie may want to consider these opportunities, if only to gather some clips and a bit of experience. A word of caution: Make sure you know your publication rights when putting out content for some publications and clients. You may not be entitled to republish any of the content that you submit. Here's a short list of websites and publications that the new writer may want to consider:

- **EHOW:** A website that publishes service and how-to articles on a variety of topics. The publisher, Demand Media, pays about $15 to $30 an article.
- **HELIUM:** An Internet content provider where writers can make a couple bucks an article
- **CONSTANT-CONTENT.COM:** This website pays for articles that are used for search-engine optimization (SEO).
- **SMASHWORDS, SCRIBD, APPLE STORE, NOOK, KINDLE STORE, AND OTHER SELF-PUBLISHING SITES:** You can try your hand at publishing and selling your own content.
- **CRAIGSLIST, ELANCE, WWW.FREELANCER.COM, WWW.FREELANCEDAILY.NET, GURU.COM, AND ODESK:** These sites offer mostly lower-paying freelance writing opportunities.
- **SOCIETY OF PROFESSIONAL JOURNALISTS WEBSITE:** In addition to providing plenty of great resources and learning tools, this website has a job bank.
- **ABOUT.COM:** This site pays guide and topic writers who have some specialized expertise.
- **PATCH:** Offers opportunities for writers and editors to cover local and "hyper-local" news, including news on government, crime, schools, and pastimes. Opportunities at Patch, however, are likely limited (see sidebar on the next page).

Looks Like AOL Will Set a Match to Patch

In recent years, AOL has done its best to transform from a superannuated dial-up service to a contemporary web publisher; it spent nearly $600 million on The Huffington Post, TechCrunch, and Patch. Despite parent company AOL's $300-million-dollar investment in Patch, however, in 2012 the collection of local and "hyper-local" news brought in about $35 million dollars in revenue on operating costs of $126 to $162 million. Experts have stated that the 2013 fiscal year will be crucial to Patch's survival.

Seemingly undaunted, AOL CEO Tim Armstrong promised profitability by the end of 2013. But with rolling reductions to staff and continued difficulty as 2013 wore on, the promise of profitability seemed remote. By mid-2013, it was apparent that the death knell for Patch had probably rung.

The day before an August 9, 2013, Patch conference call, Armstrong announced that Patch was cutting the number of local news sites from nine hundred to six hundred. In a surprising turn of events, during the conference call, a seemingly frustrated Armstrong fired Abel Lenz, creative director at Patch, in front of one thousand of his co-workers. (Lenz's wasn't the only executive head to roll. Recently appointed Patch CEO Steve Kalin and Chief Content Officer Rachel Feddersen were fired, too—but, lucky for them, behind closed doors.)

In the days following the conference call, Patch's financial picture became a little clearer. We learned that AOL was closing or consolidating about 150 of its nine hundred sites and looking to partner its other sites. AOL was also going to lay off as many as five hundred of its one thousand Patch employees. Sadly, some of these employees had been hired by Patch after being laid off recently by newspapers. Ultimately, Patch learned what newspapers have known for some time: It's both costly and difficult to report the local news.

In February 2013, EveryBlock, NBC's crack at hyper-local news, folded. A farewell posting on its blog most likely forebodes Patch's future:

> We're sorry to report that EveryBlock has closed its doors. It's no secret that the news industry is in the midst of a massive change. Within the world of neighborhood news, there's an exciting pace of innovation yet increasing challenges to building a profitable business. Though EveryBlock has been able to build an engaged community over the years, we're faced with the decision to wrap things up.

PLATFORM

It's never too early for the budding journalist to begin building a platform. A platform is an online presence that showcases your skills and accomplishments. It helps create a "personal brand" that convinces editors and potential employers that you're a suitable choice to write an article or do a job.

Ted Spiker has worked hard to establish his online presence, and the result is definitely worth a look: www.tedspiker.com. "I think the smart journalist—smart writer—creates a central hub for his or her work," says Spiker. "We're moving into a media environment where young people especially are going to have new kinds of jobs. They're not going to be working for a newspaper and then moving up to another newspaper and then working for their dream newspaper for thirty years. They're going to be entrepreneurs, and they might be doing some web design for one client, writing stories for another, creating a social-media platform for another. I feel that students today need that hub to showcase their work. There should be examples of their work no matter what their specialty, a blog element to show their writing ability or visual ability—if it's a visual blog, you want it to be clean and easy to navigate. When potential clients and employers are approaching you, you want a place to direct them that's beyond your resume-cover-letter package. This is today's 'resume-cover-letter' package: … Your cover letter is your blog because it shows your writing style. … Your resume is your bio page, and your clips are exactly that—it may be links, PDFs, slide shows, or videos. I don't think it's ever too early to start [creating a platform]. We encourage our students as soon as they get into our program to create an online presence. That's your business card. … It's moving, evolving, changing, and constantly updating. … The smart student has that right from the start. … A strong Twitter account that's professional but [has] some personality to it is [also] a really good thing."

Here are some vital platform components that you should consider establishing:

- **PERSONAL WEBSITE:** Don't worry if you don't know much about web design. You can establish a website at WordPress and Blogger or a portfolio page with about.me. Make sure that your website has a short bio page, a link to your resume or Curriculum Vitae (CV), a link to your writing samples, your contact information, and a link to your blogs—your Twitter account (microblog) and your regular blog.

- **SOCIAL-MEDIA PRESENCE:** Get a Twitter handle and start tweeting. You may also consider creating a LinkedIn and Facebook account. Make sure you don't post anything embarrassing on your Facebook page that could discourage somebody from working with you—no drunk pics! Do your best to pull in any contacts you've met along the way. For example, if you meet an editor at a conference, reach out to that person.

  You'll want to cultivate and groom your social-media presence over time. Do your best to engage your audience with interesting and relevant messages and tweets that foster conversations. (When tweeting, don't use the entire allotted 140-character count. Limit your tweets to about 120 characters so they can be retweeted.) Respond to comments and make friends with every reasonable contact—especially with Twitter, where you can only "direct message" followers. Remember that your professional platform serves a different purpose than a personal one—you don't have to "vet" friends based on likeability for your professional platform. You may want to engage your audience in dialogue, conversation, or chatter about 60 to 70 percent of the time and promote your work the rest of the time. Finally, no matter how narcissistic this advice may sound, you may want to Google yourself in order to gauge your web presence.

- **BLOG:** Blogs are easy to create, and you can tailor them to your desires. You can design your own blog or use a hosting service such as WordPress or Blogger. Blogs showcase your visual and writing skills and interests. Go ahead and set up a blog, and write entries a few times a week.

  If you're crunched for time, you can always stockpile blog postings and release them in a pulsed fashion. Make sure, however, that these posting have evergreen content. (The stockpiling of blog postings is reminiscent of the economic concept of consumption smoothing. In other words, by stockpiling posts, you're saving up for a rainy day.)

  One free way of advertising your blog involves cultivating relationships with other bloggers and cross-linking content. (You link to another blogger's post, and in return, the blogger links to yours.) Other free ways of gathering more limelight for your blog include bouncing content off social media. For example, when you write a new blog posting, you can tweet about it or promote it on Facebook. You can also repost specific blog content on your Tumblr account or link users to your content using StumbleUpon or Reddit. Consider joining the Yahoo! Contributor Network, which provides potential access to Yahoo! publications, including Yahoo! Sports, omg!, Yahoo! Movies, and Shine. When used effectively, your platform and social-media presence can catch audience members.

  Don't underestimate the value of starting your own blog. Screenwriter Diablo Cody—who won an Academy Award for her screenplay for the movie *Juno*—rose to prominence in part thanks to her blog The Pussy Ranch, which dealt with the sex industry in Minneapolis-St.Paul. Brian Stelter, a reporter with *The New York Times*, also started his career as a blogger.

  A personal blog also offers much creative freedom. You can use your blog to write articles that may never see the light of day at any mainstream publication. When posting articles to your own blog, you won't have to worry about a query letter or pitch getting passed over.

One definite disadvantage to blogging is that unless your blog posting goes viral and you get a cut of the advertising revenue, blogging rarely pays well. Even at the best publications, many bloggers are paid a percentage of digital-advertising revenue generated by their postings. At some publications like The Huffington Post, most bloggers post for free. Although you may not be able to milk any serious money from your blog, remember that blogging helps establish your platform, which will pay indirectly by generating recognition and writing opportunities. For example, Jessica Valenti, who founded Feministing, a feminist blog, has landed book deals, consulting work, and other choice opportunities.

- **BELLS AND WHISTLES:** Think broadly about what else you can offer, and link to it on your website as part of your online presence. For example, many writers incorporate video, PDF documents, and e-books into their platform. Posting a PowerPoint presentation on SlideShare is a good idea. Remember that even if you only want to write articles, showcasing your other talents and interests may help you get work. If you know CSS, XHTML, JavaScript, or how to use parts of the Adobe Creative Suite such as Dreamweaver, InDesign, Photoshop, or Illustrator, let people know that. (If you want to learn how to develop these skills, consider taking classes at your college or university or continuing your education through extension programs at paid websites such as Lynda.com.)

  Video can make for a particularly exciting component of your platform. If you've been able to put out some good pieces of "smartphone journalism"—check out the Society of Professional Journalists' websites for detailed videos on the subject—link to them on websites such as YouTube, Vimeo, Viddler, Livestream, or Flickr (which posts video in addition to pictures).

  Assuming that you have access to your website's source code, it's really easy to link video content from a site such as YouTube to your website. YouTube automatically generates the XHTML code that you need, which you can then cut and paste into your own website's code.

- **BUSINESS CARDS:** Just in case you run into somebody who may be able to help you score an article or freelance job, have professional business cards made. Websites such as Vistaprint.com will print up nice business cards for little money.

HootSuite and FriendFeed

If you're finding it difficult to manage all the different facets of your social-media platform, consider employing organizational tools offered by websites including HootSuite and FriendFeed.

HootSuite boosts productivity by offering a dashboard on a single interface to manage all of your social-media networks. It can also analyze your traffic on these social-media networks and schedule your outgoing messages. Although commercial clients can pay for premium service, the basic version of HootSuite is free.

Google and Your Platform

Google provides services that can help beef up your platform. First, if you have access to your website or blog's source code, you can track your website's traffic using Google Analytics. The basic version of Google Analytics is free and should be sufficient. Second, although this tactic may get expensive, you can pay to promote your website or blog using Google Adwords. Third, if you find that you want to devote a separate phone number to your article-writing and freelance projects, consider using Google Voice. Among its many services, Google Voice offers Google users a free phone number that can be forwarded to a cell phone or landline as well as free voicemail that can be checked online.

Generalist or Specialist?

While establishing a platform, consider whether you want to write articles or engage in projects that are general or specialized—in other words, determine whether you want to be a "generalist" or a "specialist." There are pros and cons to being a specialist or generalist. For example, although a generalist can take on a variety of interesting projects, such projects often don't pay as well and tend to be less challenging. The specialist, however, can take on very well-paid projects that are challenging and lead to further work opportunities such as white papers (authoritative, bureaucratic, or governmental reports and documents), conference proceedings, newsletters, and ghostwriting. Nevertheless, such projects can limit your audience and exposure. Furthermore, if you don't have specialized training and background, it's difficult to create a specialized portfolio. Most writers start out as generalists and, depending on their opportunities and interests, evolve into specialists.

Holly G. Miller, a veteran journalist who has written more than three thousand articles, makes an interesting argument for remaining a generalist and writing for a variety of publications. She says, "You don't have to be a member of the audience that you're writing for … if you're a writer, you're a hired pen."

Whatever you do, make sure that your platform accurately reflects your skills and interests—don't promise too much (or too little). In a video produced by the Society of Professional Journalists titled "Personal Branding: What Is your Personal Brand?" Lara Salahi recommends, "Especially for freelancers, the risk is always promising more than you can deliver or pretending your expertise covers too wide an area. Being consistent and coherent on- and offline is the best approach to ensure your success."

On a final note, in some ways the initial toil to establish your own platform is comparable to the "T-shirt phase" that developing countries must face in order to become rich and economically diverse. No country starts out making computers and airplanes; rather, they start by making textiles and simple garments with the hope of eventually producing goods that carry financial cachet. The United States, Britain, Japan, Korea, Taiwan, and China all went through a T-shirt phase—and so will you.

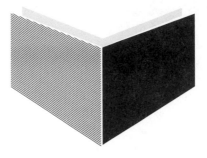

chapter 16

STORY IDEAS & QUERY LETTERS

QUERY LETTERS

Getting published begins with a query letter or pitch. If you've never worked with an editor before and have an idea for an article, no matter how long or short the piece, you must query for it.

A query letter is a specialized form of cover letter. It's a solicitation or sales letter sent to a publication. But instead of selling something tangible (like bananas), it sells a story idea.

Before you send a query letter or pitch to any publication, first become acquainted with the publication. For example, if you're interested in getting published in *Men's Health*, you'll want to read *Men's Health* before you query the publication. If you were to send *Men's Health* an idea on pap smears, no matter how good the idea is, it will likely get passed over.

The more time you spend studying a publication, the better prepared you will be to write a query that's structured in a way that appeals to an editor at that publication. Robert Irion has had much success with helping his students land assignments at a number of large consumer publications. Here's his advice:

"We look at several sample articles from a given publication in detail and look at the style points within those articles … so that when a young writer approaches a new publication for the first time with a story proposal, if they write that proposal in the style of that publication, they are much more likely to get an assignment, and if they submit the first assignment—the first draft—in the desired style, the editor will come back to them.

"Some of the style points that we look for [in the publication] are story structure; [the number of] paragraphs a typical story contains; the length of those paragraphs; [if] they have a short, sharp lede or ever use first person; [if] they use one source, two sources, three sources; the relationship between story length and source expectations; dispassionate, personal, playful puns; [whether the stories are] snarky; what units [of measurement] they use; [and] British spelling. We typically go back six to twelve months." (In other words, Irion and his students typically review six to twelve months of back issues.)

The Snarky Voice

With respect to journalism, snarky can mean "playfully irreverent." For countless examples of snarky voices, check out *The Onion*, a satire news publication. For example, consider the following lede that deals with the very simple premise of a dog being walked by his owner on a leash:

> According to neighbors living near local French bulldog Ruggles, the humiliation-loving canine apparently derives intense pleasure from being stark naked, clipped to a movement-constricting leash, and paraded around in public.
> Witnesses say that Ruggles, who is reportedly totally shameless about his demented, anything-goes lifestyle, seemingly takes some sort of twisted glee in wearing a thick harness and walking around on all fours while being fully subdued by his owner, 34-year-old Brian Paulson.

Editors at many publications, including *Esquire*, *Entertainment Weekly* and *GQ*, love a snarky voice. Here's an example of the snarky voice from *GQ*. It's the lede from a tongue-in-cheek service article titled "You Named Me ... *What?*"

> Congratulations, your wife/girlfriend/au pair is pregnant! A little bundle of colicky delight awaits you mere months from now. And one of the great joys of this period of anticipation is brainstorming all kinds of kick-ass names for your offspring.

Keep in mind that when you write a query letter, it's a formal letter (typically an e-mail) that begins with a formal salutation, and, if possible, should be addressed to the appropriate editor. (If two or more editors could accept your query letter, target the editor who is lowest in the editorial hierarchy. For example, choose an associate editor over an editor or editor-in-chief.) If you're having trouble tracking down the appropriate editor, look at the masthead: a list found on the publication's editorial page. Alternatively, you could turn to the Writer's Market or a site like Mediabistro (www.mediabistro.com).

Today most query letters are sent as e-mails. When sending a query letter via e-mail, make sure to include a copy of the query letter in the body of your e-mail. Most editors are wary of opening attachments from unknown senders. Additionally, make the title of the e-mail informative, relevant, and catchy—as if it were a headline. In order to avoid the appearance of spam, you might want to specify "pitch" in parentheses and designate the department you're querying. Of note, some publications allow you to submit a pitch through their websites.

Begin your query letter with an attention grabber: an interesting tidbit, a question, a humorous observation—whatever you feel grabs the reader's attention. Many writers write the entire first paragraph of a query letter as if it were a potential lede, especially if they're querying for a longer piece.

Margaret Guroff, features editor at *AARP The Magazine*, has had years of experience fielding query letters and has a reputation for being particularly attentive and responsive. Guroff states, "What you're trying to do with a magazine query is give the editor a sense of what the story will look like. Beginning with an anecdotal lede that draws the editor into the story … you want to suck the reader into the query enough to get them tantalized, and then you can say a little more about what the story will actually be and why you're the right person for the story."

Holly G. Miller, a senior editor at *The Saturday Evening Post*, recommends that a query letter exhibit personality. "A query letter," says Miller, "has to ooze personality. … It's not good enough to be correct or even flawless. If it doesn't have personality and color, it's no good."

The body of the query letter should expound on the idea you're pitching. If possible, briefly provide factual information on the subject—you can even do so using a bulleted list. Explain the *hook* or why the story is newsworthy to a particular publication's audience. Make sure the angle of the query letter is similar to the angle of other stories in the magazine itself. If you have potential sources, including people to interview and relevant journal articles, go ahead and list them. Furthermore, explain why you are the right choice for this story. In light of decreasing financial budgets at many publications, it may also be a good idea to offer to provide professional-quality pictures with the article. Securing pictures for your piece may not require that you actually take any pictures—simply contacting a media-relations specialist with a request for pictures may do the trick.

If an editor has never worked with you before, be sure to explain who you are and cite previous work. Refer a potential editor to your website and platform (see Chapter 15) for more information. You want to convince the editor she can trust you to do this piece based on your professional history. Finally, you should give the editor an idea of the planned length of the piece and how long it will take you to complete it. Editors have strict *budgets,* or space allotments, within a magazine and must be careful when making decisions about which articles to run.

Try to keep your query letter to 500 words (about one page double-spaced in Microsoft Word). Most editors receive several pitches a day, and an editor doesn't want a query letter that's several pages long. An editor wants to see that you can concisely explain your idea in an engaging manner. Don't send a pitch that's longer than the piece you plan to write! Some writers suggest that a pitch be no longer than 300 words, while other online publications have gone so far as limiting pitches to a mere 100 words!

When writing a query letter, be as specific as possible. Incorporate information and statistics from sources like journal articles, archival research, magazine articles, newspaper articles, census data, data from public polling (Gallup polls), and more. Oftentimes such work requires the writer to search through library databases and databases like LexisNexis and Google Scholar. In other words, a cursory Google search won't suffice.

The tone of your query letter shouldn't be cocky, sketchy, wordy, egotistical, intrusive, inappropriate, or careless. Don't make promises that you can't keep or otherwise mislead an editor. For example, if you know that you can't interview a celebrity because his publicist declined you access, don't promise the interview.

On Spec

If you think there's no way your story will be accepted until an editor sees it in its entirety, consider offering your query *on spec*. The term *on spec* is journalism jargon for a story that's accepted by an editor only after it's written in its entirety. In other words, if you were to offer a story on spec you would have to do all the work up front, tender a completed article, and hope that the editor accepts it for publication and thus pays you for it. More than likely, if the article is good and an editor has agreed to take it on spec, you have a good shot at getting it published. Nevertheless, you could end up doing a lot of work for neither recognition nor pay. Of note, pieces that are written as memoirs or first-person narratives are often so idiosyncratic that they must be offered on spec.

Sometimes you can establish a relationship with a publication without sending an initial query letter at all. For example, if you look through Mediabistro, you may notice that many reputable publications actually solicit freelance writers when they're in need. Editors at these publications (blogs, magazines, and newspapers) will request a cover letter, resume, and writing samples, and if they like you, they'll set up a phone interview. During this phone interview, they'll explain their publication and the type of article they want, thus giving you an excellent understanding of their editorial needs. After explaining their needs, these editors will often ask you to send along a few query letters. Because these editors are requesting query letters, if your query letter meets their needs, there's a very good chance you will land an assignment.

In many ways, when editors come looking for freelancers to house their stables, it's like they're offering you a job. Treat the opportunity with the requisite respect. Learn about the publication before you get on the phone with your potential suitor, and read through whatever articles are available. (Editors may send along clips to demonstrate what type of work they desire.) And don't forget to ask good questions that will help you assess a publication's editorial needs.

Mistakes and Missteps

A big mistake some authors make is writing a query letter that's better than the final product. This practice annoys editors to no end—sometimes enough for the editor to issue a *kill fee* and pay you a small amount of money to discontinue the assignment. In order to avoid this disheartening repercussion, strive to send in a completed article that's *at least as good or even better* than your query letter!

Resist the temptation to concurrently query several publications with the same pitch using a "gang" query. Doing so can place you in an awkward and unethical situation: What happens if more than one publication accepts your query letter? Writing the same article for two places will result in self-plagiarism and possible legal wrangling. One way to avoid this dilemma is to query the same topic using different angles. For example, when pitching a piece on for-profit education, maybe one query letter could deal with the income generated by these institutions and another query letter could deal with attrition rates. Another way around this dilemma is to put an expiration date on the query. Write something like, "If I don't hear back in two weeks, I'll assume that your publication has passed on this story idea."

Many new writers fear that an editor or publication will steal a pitch. Although it's possible that an editor will steal your story idea or pitch, it's highly unlikely. Even if a publication were to run an idea that you had queried about, it's likely that either somebody at the magazine or another freelancer thought of the idea, too.

It's tempting to think that getting a pitch accepted is based more on luck and connections than merit. The truth is that a strong query letter that's on target always stands a good chance of getting accepted. When creating a pitch, it's important to take your time and carefully consider the publication. Do your homework! Remember that pitching is not a numbers game. Taking a couple of weeks to create one or two good pitches is infinitely more productive than sending out a ton of subpar pitches. Remember that editors know a garbage pitch when they see one.

Another reason you don't want to send out garbage pitches is because the rejection can wear you down and discourage you. This discouragement will likely cause you to quit sending out queries altogether—to stop trying. Avoid the despair of repeated rejection by doing your homework and sending out quality pitches every time.

When submitting a pitch, it's important to be patient. It can take days, weeks, or months before an editor accepts your pitch and contracts you for a story. In addition, the lead time between when your pitch is accepted and when your piece is published may be several months. Don't pester an editor about your pitch—doing so is an instant turnoff.

STORY IDEAS

When possible, it's a good idea to pitch a story rather than an idea. A story has a time line, conflict, main characters, story arc, and so forth. Make the pitch exciting, especially if it deals with people who are dynamic.

Keep in mind that it's almost impossible for a newbie to land a full-length feature in a national consumer or major association magazine. Sometimes the best way to break in is to query for a short piece in a specific department. For ideas on which departments may be willing to entertain pitches, check out the "How to Pitch" features on Mediabistro.

Inspiration for story ideas can come from anywhere. For example, I sometimes write about medicine; consequently, I like to flip through the pages of recent issues of peer-reviewed journals like *The New England Journal of Medicine, JAMA, Annals of Internal Medicine,* and *American Family Physician.* Occasionally, I find newspaper or magazine articles that serve as a strong news peg or basis of a story. I also like to check out EurekAlert! for press releases that could serve as news pegs.

But the inspiration for a piece may be more mundane than the literature. For example, I once spoke with an editor who picked up a piece on middle-aged men who dye their hair. Apparently, the writer who queried had been inspired by rumors that President Obama may have dyed his hair. The editor picked up the piece because she liked the potential "shock" factor of the story.

Editorial Calendars

Editorial calendars are remarkably useful when trying to successfully pitch a story idea to a prospective publication. An editorial calendar outlines the themes or topics that a publication plans to cover in coming issues. You can use an editorial calendar to figure out what types of story ideas to pitch or whether your story idea will match any publication's future needs. Keep in mind that when sending a pitch to a publication, lead times vary. An online or weekly publication may accept query letters weeks in advance of publication whereas a monthly or quarterly publication may need several months.

There are several ways to get your hands on an editorial calendar. First, Mediabistro offers its members an Editorial Calendar Guide. The Guide covers about fifty publications, including *Seventeen, Ebony, Shape, W,* and *Woman's Day.* Second, you may be able to find the editorial calendar for a specific publication online. Pull up the publication's website, and try looking in the advertiser's section. Alternatively, you could look in a publication's media kit, which also contains advertising rates and demographic information. This demographic information can also prove valuable when trying to understand a publication's audience. Third, you can always e-mail or call the publication's media or advertising department and request a media kit.

A smart approach to querying involves pitching stories about holidays. Magazines have a long history of running holiday-related fare. Be sure to approach holidays in a novel way. For example, many companies dole out Christmas bonuses, but what would happen if, instead of a gift card or money, one company decided to give away golden retrievers? When querying for a holiday piece, be sure to send your pitch several months before publication. The lead time or time between green-lighting a query and publication is typically six months for larger publications, so if you want to write a Christmas feature, query for it in July.

Another smart approach to querying involves anniversaries. A good query letter can revisit a newsworthy topic on its anniversary—one year, ten years, fifty years, or even one hundred years after it occurred. Search the Web for reference materials to figure out when an anniversary will occur. For example, 2013 marks the tenth anniversary of the Iraq war. An enterprising journalist may query a piece related to the Iraq war—maybe on how Iraqis are faring ten years after the United States and Great Britain invaded.

According to the *Writer's Digest Handbook of Magazine Article Writing*, "To snag an anniversary assignment, you'll need three things: an interesting occasion, a unique angle, and pitch-perfect timing." It also recommends two resources that are useful when researching anniversaries: the "On this Day" archive at *The New York Times* and a quirky book titled *The Optimist's Guide to History*. Wikipedia also has a section titled "On this Day ..." (Make sure to verify anything you pull off Wikipedia!)

One of the best ways to develop story ideas is to keep abreast of news, trends, press releases, and social media. Spend an hour each day surfing the Internet, and then read through a general-interest publication such as *The New York Times*. Doing so not only gives you a greater foundation of knowledge from which to develop story ideas but also introduces you to the writing of other authors. Remember, a good article writer is a voracious reader of books, magazines, blogs, and more.

Movies—especially documentaries—can provide fodder for a query letter. For example, in the documentary titled *Something Ventured*, which dealt with the history of venture capitalism, one of the final frames of the movie lists trends and state-of-the-art technology that could serve as bait for venture capitalists. The list includes holography, implantable electronics, quantum computing, gesture technology, eco-manipulation, cyber drugs, location-specific computing, smart buildings, robotic surgery, organ replacement, intelligent fabrics, and wireless energy. This simple list hints at dozens of story ideas for the tech or business writer.

You can also stumble on story ideas after reviewing quotations, maxims, idioms, aphorisms, memes, and so forth. These pithy statements often hint at more global, newsworthy, and interesting ideas. For example, the media had a field day with the song "One Pound Fish," which was written by a Pakistani fishmonger intent on enticing people to buy his fish. After the song went viral, this lede from a syndicated article written by Sebastian Abbot played on the old adage "Give a man a fish … ": "Muhammad Shahid Nazir is a testament to the age-old adage that if you give a man a fish, he will eat for a day, but if you teach a man to sing about fish, his song will shoot up the British pop chart."

When considering ideas for a story, it may be helpful to assume a contrarian perspective. Warren Buffett, a multibillionaire, made his fortune as a contrarian. He consistently invests in stocks that other people undervalue. For example, in 2011, Buffett invested $5 billion into the beleaguered Bank of America, and by 2013, the stock nearly doubled its value.

A contrarian will look at a story in a way that others would find counterintuitive or perverse; it's the classic "man bit dog" story scenario. For example, stories about sexual abuse and clergy always make for media fodder because, although not as shocking as it once probably was, the basic premise is contrarian. No one expects that a religious figure—who is supposed to protect and advise the community—would abuse others.

In the wake of the financial crises of 2007 and 2008, Bitcoin, a form of digital or virtual currency, was introduced. The currency is neither backed by assets (gold) nor a central government (fiat currency), and Bitcoins are virtually untraceable and anonymous (which apparently makes them a perfect currency for dealing illegal drugs on the Internet). It may seem strange that anybody would take their greenbacks and turn them in for a potentially unstable virtual coin; nevertheless, many speculators who support the idea of currency that is immune to economic turmoil brought about by government and banking institutions bought into the Bitcoin craze, and in 2013 a bubble developed. This contrarian mindset—that people spend real money to purchase virtual money—made for great copy.

Here's an idea for a story inspired by contrarian thinking. When most people think of 7-Eleven, they think "iconic American institution." Lots of people associate 7-Elevens with the Slurpee, their flagship product, and—at least where I came from—many young people regularly spend hours loitering in the parking lots smoking cigarettes. But, however surprising this fact may sound, 7-Eleven is a Japanese company. It would be interesting to examine whether the idiosyncratic Japanese corporate culture has influenced employment practices at 7-Eleven.

Here's a list of contrarian story ideas that made for entertaining copy:

- A lottery winner in Detroit remained on food stamps after winning one million dollars.
- A pit bull thwarted the kidnapping of an infant.
- A West Virginia teenager gets arrested and suspended for wearing a National Rifle Association T-shirt to school. On his first day back in school, he once again wears the same T-shirt.

- A nonagenarian graduates from college.
- A washerwoman donates her life savings—$150,000—to set up a scholarship fund for the University of Southern Mississippi.

Finally, remember that no matter how good you think a story idea is or how much time you put into it, some story ideas will never see the light of day. In other words, the story idea is unsuited for the audience of any prospective publication. Sometimes you need to cut your losses and move on. In business, there's the idea of sunk costs—costs that can never be recouped no matter what the effort. Chasing sunk costs results in wasted time and wasted resources. Don't waste your time with a pitch that can't find a home—chalk the pitch up to a sunk cost, and move on. Alternatively, you could do the story and post it to your own blog or self-publish it.

PAYMENT AND CONTRACTS

Currently publications pay anywhere from about 50¢ to more than $2 per word. And although the practice is becoming increasingly rare thanks to financial constraints, larger publications may provide a budget for travel and incidentals. When starting out as a freelancer, don't quibble about payment. Whatever a publication is willing to pay you is probably adequate. If you appear petty and ask for a few more cents per word, you may leave a bad taste in an editor's mouth. Honestly, when starting out, your goal should be to get your foot in the door. That said, unless you are working on spec, make sure you get paid for your work, and never accept a paid assignment without a contract. Additionally, never send an editor a final piece without having signed a contract and an agreed price.

Savvy writers are sure to specify what rights they sell to an online or print publication if these things are not explicitly stated in a contract. When a writer sells *first rights* to an article, he retains the right to sell the article to other publications once it's published. In other words, there can be a secondary market for the article. In fact, many writers have made considerable cash reselling stories. Publications that are likely to reprint an article and thus purchase *reprint rights* have audiences and circulations separate from the original publication. When a writer sells *all rights* to a publication, the writer can't sell reprint rights. Syndicated columnists will sell their work using *simultaneous rights,* which allow various publications to publish the content at the same time. Other considerations to examine when selling rights are whether and what type of *electronic rights* you're selling to an article and whether such rights cover a North American or international distribution. (Electronic rights refer to the publication of material in online form.)

Ultimately, pitching is difficult—no doubt about it. But there's a silver lining to the process. Once you establish a rapport with an editor, the process of pitching a story idea becomes simpler and streamlined. An editor will come to trust your judgment and insights. But the seed for such a relationship is planted with a strong initial query letter.

ADVICE OF OTHERS

To some extent, query letters are idiosyncratic and depend on the experiences of the writer. While researching for this book, I stumbled on advice from two different journalists that may connect with the reader.

Pitching Magazines

At the Future of Freelancing Conference held at Stanford University in 2010, journalism professor and freelance magazine writer Jennifer Kahn shared her thoughts on query letters. Kahn's been published in several magazines, including *Sports Illustrated*, *The New Yorker*, and *Wired*.

Here's a summary of some of her advice:

- Do a lot of research before you query. Kahn estimates that she places about ten one-hour phone calls before she pitches a piece and has about 25 percent of the research done before a pitch is accepted. Furthermore, only a fraction of the query letters that she researches prove "pitchable."
- "Pre-pitch" the appropriate editor. Kahn suggests that when pitching an editor cold (pitching an editor for the first time), send along a short e-mail that introduces yourself and contains a two-sentence summary of your story idea. Ask the editor if it's okay to send along a full pitch.
- Kahn proposes a five-paragraph pitch that takes up a page or page and a half. (This length is longer than what I and others suggest. Most likely, as evidenced by her background, Kahn is probably referring to pitches for very long features.):
    - **PARAGRAPH 1:** This paragraph is an engaging summary lede or engaging excerpt that showcases your voice.
    - **PARAGRAPH 2:** This paragraph is a nut graph ("why we care about this story").
    - **PARAGRAPH 3:** This paragraph features further support for the story. Explain how this story affects and impacts other people.
    - **PARAGRAPH 4:** Logistics. This paragraph details specific sources and travel plans (if any).
    - **PARAGRAPH 5:** The kicker. This paragraph reiterates the idea for your story and explains why the story will appeal to the publication's core audience.
    - Optional "biography" paragraph
- Be able to explain the main characters in your story and as much of the story's arc or storyline as possible. If the resolution is unfolding, explain why any possible outcome will still remain newsworthy.
- Keep in mind that most magazines have a three-month lead time.
- If possible (and prudent), consider name-dropping a contact.

- Remind an editor every couple of weeks that you have a pitch outstanding. When doing so, be brief and courteous. If you eventually want to take the pitch elsewhere, inform the editor in an e-mail.
- Repurpose rejected query letters for different publications.
- Don't lie and say that another magazine is interested in the pitch—editors know that this is a desperate and bullshit move.

Pitching Newspapers

Some newspapers won't entertain cold pitches. Nevertheless, understanding how to pitch a newspaper article can help any writer. Tom Huang, an editor at the *Dallas Morning News*, suggests that the writer consider the following list of questions:

- Why are you interested in the story?
- What research have you done?
- What's new with respect to the story, and why is now a good time to write it?
- Where does the story lie on a time line?
- Why does this story interest the reader?
- Does the story concern money, health, safety, or education?
- How can this story be told digitally? Is there an online package for the story? Is the story tablet friendly? Can we use video to tell the story? Does the story lend itself well to interactive design?
- What questions need to be asked? What do you want to find out? What's the central question? Who will you need to speak with?
- How much time is needed to write the story? How much space will you need budgeted?

SAMPLE QUERY LETTERS

Before I introduce two sample query letters, I want to present you with the assurance that I've done my homework and assumed the mentality of a true freelancer. Let's imagine that I've researched and learned the style and intended views of a particular magazine's audience. I've disengaged from all bias and preconception and completely abdicated myself to the voice, resources, and needs of the publication's audience. I've taken veteran magazine writer Holly Miller's advice to write for any audience.

Here is a query letter for a hypothetical magazine titled *Alternative Healer*.

The year was 1978. In the throes of an existential crisis, Roger La Borde walked away from all that he knew: his lucrative job as a recruiter at a prestigious oil firm, the comforts of the single-bedroom apartment that he rented in the wake of an unwelcome divorce, and his son whom he saw only on the weekends. La Borde made his way to Montana where he was adopted and educated by Gerald Red Elk, a Sioux medicine man and shaman. He spent the next three-and-a-half years of his life, which were Red Elk's last, immersed in study. Shortly before Red Elk's death, the medicine man bequeathed La Borde with a shaman's pipe and moccasins beaded with their own unique design. La Borde would later learn that the beaded pattern on the moccasins symbolized what Red Elk knew all along: La Borde was destined to reenter the world as a shaman and healer.

Today La Borde lives in the mountains of Colorado and extensively travels the world (South Africa, Taiwan, Israel, France, and more), "facilitating" the healing process in others. In the process, he's befriended Rabbi Rami Shapiro, Father Thomas Keating, and Swami Budhananda. La Borde is also a member of the Snowmass Interreligious Council, one of the world's longest running interfaith dialogues, whose proceedings are chronicled in the book *The Common Heart*.

La Borde is probably best recognized for his ability to help coma patients. According to information found on La Borde's website (www.shamansdoor.com), EEG researcher Dr. Edgar S. Wilson attributes La Borde's ability to help people in comas to this unusual brain-wave activity. La Borde is often called on as a measure of last resort by family members desperate to see any improvement in a loved one. According to media reports and testaments from physicians, La Borde has helped several coma patients, including Australian musician Hans Poulson and internationally renowned helicopter pilot Peter Peelgrane. La Borde's work with coma patients has been profiled by *That's Incredible*, *BBC Television*, and others.

La Borde has lectured on healing at a variety of American hospitals and universities, including the University of California San Diego School of Medicine and the University of Wyoming. Furthermore, he has both allopathic and osteopathic admirers from across the country. In fact, should this pitch be accepted, I plan to speak with Dr. E. Lee Rice, a San Diego family-medicine physician and the CEO and medical director of the Life Wellness Institute. In the past, Dr. Rice has enlisted La Borde's help as his own family healer after witnessing La Borde help one of his patients who was in a coma.

I'm interested in digging into this story further. Most of my information on La Borde is based on a preliminary interview with him and research I've done using his website as a resource, and I'd like to flesh out this story. (I drop-referenced a few facts but need to spend more time …) I plan to write a 2,000-word article on La Borde and his work. I hope to speak with physicians, psychologists, spiritual leaders, people who La Borde has worked with, and more. I also want to consider La Borde's work within the greater context of alternative medicine.

My name is Naveed Saleh, and I'm a freelance writer and editor. Please feel free to link to several samples of my work at www.naveedsaleh.com.

Sincerely,

Naveed Saleh

03/25/2013

Here is a second sample query letter for a hypothetical magazine titled *Education and Community.*

In 1994, Dr. Larry Johnson, a Texas A&M University reproductive-biology faculty member and veterinary-school researcher, was invited to give lectures to schoolchildren. One of his early lessons was on the "Health of the Respiratory System"; he used age-appropriate anatomical models as visual aids. His efforts were well received and soon flourished; thus, the Partnership for Environmental Health and Rural Health (PEER) was born.

Today PEER is funded by the National Science Foundation and the National Institutes of Health. Members of PEER include Texas A&M professors and graduate students. They expose rural Texas schoolchildren to science, technology, engineering, and mathematics using various resources. They also train schoolteachers to promote learning in the classroom and engage in a variety of outreach efforts intended to inspire the scientists of tomorrow. PEER serves as an educational model that integrates the best of what Texas A&M has to offer with the mentoring and guidance needs of thousands of rural Texas schoolchildren, kindergarten through twelfth grade: a population that has fallen by the educational wayside in recent years.

I propose a 1,000-word feature on PEER that in part focuses on the interaction between university scientists and schoolchildren. I plan to interview Johnson and other members of PEER: Texas A&M faculty, Texas A&M students, and schoolteachers. I also want to speak with education experts and administrators to figure out whether PEER can be used as a blueprint for similar educational programs among other universities and school districts.

Please feel free to link to my resume and some samples of my recent work at www.naveedsaleh.com.

Sincerely,

Naveed Saleh

02/03/2011

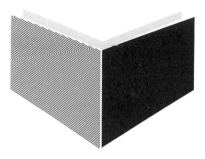

chapter 17

THE AUTHOR-EDITOR RELATIONSHIP & MORE

It's funny—many times you'll only hear from an editor when receiving a rejection. For whatever reason, your e-mailed query letter and their e-mailed rejection is the only interaction you will ever establish. But sometimes things click: An editor connects with your query letter, and an author-editor relationship is born.

Although courting an editor with a query letter and then having it accepted may seem romantic—almost as if an editor has agreed to go out on a date with you—be careful to remain professional. Remember that when dealing with an editor, a friendly relationship is mandatory. But keep in mind that an editor is your boss—at least while she is assigning you pieces—and you should treat her with the same respect (and professional distance) that you would any boss.

It should be noted, however, that during the span of several years, editors and writers often become friends—it's the nature of the business. Furthermore, in journalism, unlike between journalist and source, no strict professional boundary exists between editor and writer. In the world of freelancing, editors and writers switch professional roles, and often someone who is an editor one day will be a freelancer another. In the beginning, however, it's best to maintain a friendly and professional distance from your editor.

COMMUNICATION

If an editor has expressed interest in your query letter and offered you an assignment, don't hesitate to e-mail her with relevant questions. Remember to keep your e-mails well written, concise, and professional. There's no reason to send your editor a five-paragraph missive every time you want to check in with a quick question. Also, with new topics, be sure to use an explanatory title in the subject line instead of responding to a previous e-mail, and always be sure that your e-mail clearly outlines a call to action. In other words, make the reason for your e-mail apparent. With well-written e-mails, you can establish a strong virtual presence in the minds of your editor and others. (An editor once offered me a job because I was always meticulous with my e-mails to her.)

When responding to e-mail, make sure to acknowledge any incoming e-mail within the first twenty-four hours. This is common business practice. If you plan to be away from your e-mail account for several days, it's a good idea to compose an auto-reply message with a quick explanation.

Before you begin writing any article, you should clarify by e-mail or phone whether your editor wants you to summarize events or information, speak with one or numerous sources, speak with specific sources, examine opposing viewpoints, create sidebars, and so forth. You may want to be proactive and anticipate a publication's needs; doing so can be a good way to please an editor. For example, you may want to ask your editor whether you can help take or track down high-quality photos.

Nowadays, many editors prefer to use Dropbox when communicating with a writer. Dropbox is a free data repository service that works on a virtual cloud. Documents, pictures, and so forth are dropped into a folder in Dropbox and shared with other parties. The basic version of Dropbox is free and comes with 2 gigabytes (GB) of online space. Although this amount of space is usually sufficient, if you want more space, you can pay for it.

AFTER THE PIECE IS WRITTEN

Try to submit your piece a few days before the deadline. Everybody likes wiggle room, especially a busy editor. By getting your piece in a few days early, you will save yourself the frustration of typing up something last minute and will impress your editor with your timeliness.

When it comes time to send sources copies of a published piece, you sometimes need to send your editor an e-mail request for these copies. (I always try to send my sources a copy of the final publication along with a thank-you note as a courtesy. If I'm dealing with a digital publication, I send the published piece as a PDF attachment or link and thank the source via e-mail.) With a smaller publication like an association magazine, often the only way to secure a copy of the final piece is to request it from the editor or editorial staff.

(Sometimes smaller publications are gracious enough to send copies to sources on your behalf. If this were to happen, I still suggest sending along your own thank-you note. Remember that a good source is a lifetime resource.)

Editors are busy people, and many months can pass between the time you turn in a final piece and when it's published. By the time you request copies, your request may seem less important than more pressing editorial concerns. Furthermore, editors are not required to send writers a copy of the final piece but often do (or have their assistants do so) as a courtesy. Don't be shy when requesting a few copies of a piece—one for each source and a couple of hard copies for your portfolio. Just be careful not to request too many—I once heard about an author who wanted twenty-five copies of a magazine for one source!

Obviously, if you are writing for a national consumer magazine, which are sold at newsstands, there is no need to request copies. After all, you can go to your local bookstore or newsstand and purchase as many copies as you want. Sometimes an editor won't even tell you when to expect a piece, so you must hit up a bookstore, Walmart, or Target a few times a month so as not to miss it.

When submitting a final piece to an editor, make sure to title the document and include a word count and source list. Typically, the word count for any final piece should be within 10 percent of what was initially agreed on. After you complete your assignment, you may also need to submit an invoice. Invoice templates are available through Microsoft or can be generated using bookkeeping programs such as QuickBooks.

Most writers do their own bookkeeping using programs such as QuickBooks; thus, it's important to keep copies of invoices and any tax documents (1099s) sent to you by the publisher. Unless you're pulling in a large salary from freelancing and need to incorporate, most writers file taxes as sole proprietors and submit records to an accountant who files taxes. If you do your own taxes, be careful when claiming deductions. For example, don't deduct the rent of your entire apartment as a business expense if you only use one room to write. Instead deduct a fraction of the rent.

DEALING WITH EDITOR ISSUES

Occasionally, you'll make a mistake and anger or offend an editor. If this were to happen, apologize and don't make the mistake again. For example, I once missed a phone appointment with an editor. It was embarrassing, and the editor was miffed. I apologized and never made the mistake again. We still have a good working relationship.

While working with an editor, remember that her job is to edit even if that means changing your article around and possibly deleting parts that you like. When you receive edits, do your best to work with your editor. Accept the edits that you think improve the piece, and politely voice your concerns about the edits that you feel compromise the meaning or the message of a piece. Just as you would never unilaterally accept all edits made to a piece, be careful not to spurn edits that improve a piece.

Nowadays, most editors use track changes in Microsoft Word when providing edits. (A minority send edits in a PDF document, which requires that you own Adobe Professional to make changes to the document directly.) When raising concerns about a specific edit, reply using track changes in Microsoft Word. If you don't understand how to use the track changes or editing functions in Microsoft Word, you can find some quick instructional videos on YouTube. When responding to an edit, try to frame your concerns in terms of the five Cs: conciseness, comprehensibility, cohesiveness, clarity, and correctness. By doing so, you are able to think like an editor and better make a case for your argument. When arguing a point, feel free to clue your editor in on any extra information that you may have learned about the subject or source.

Remember to always respond to edits in a timely fashion and always be courteous. Sometimes an editor will "hack a piece to death." Your first temptation may be to fight back and make the situation adversarial. Whatever you do, don't fight back! Respond to the edits in a courteous manner. Remember that the vast majority of edits are done to improve the piece and publication. And remember that ultimately, the publication commissioning the piece owns, at the very least, first rights to your article and, in the end, has the right to merely proofread it, edit it, or completely rewrite it.

If you feel completely justified in debating a change that your editor has made, try to be tactful. First, acknowledge the validity of the concern. Second, make your point clear and don't oversell it with extraneous information—one or two good reasons are usually enough. Third, if possible, consider compromise.

Keep in mind that good editors change only what they have to; consequently, nearly all edits are made for a reason. "I do what I have to do for a story," says Margaret Guroff, features editor at *AARP The Magazine*. "Even a piece that I truly love might need changes to work for my reader. And if it doesn't need changes, I won't lift a finger."

Sometimes an editor or publication will edit a story without contacting you, or the editor may even rewrite the story completely. Although you may be displeased by this practice, there is little that you can do. If a publication were to warp your story without your input, your only recourse may be to express concern that the final piece (with your name on the byline) is off base and never work with the editor or publication again.

The topic of money sometimes comes up when dealing with an editor. When first trying to establish a relationship with an editor, it's best not to quibble over a few cents per word. But sometimes, if you've been writing for an editor and publication for a while, you may be tempted to ask for more money, which may be justified. Editors are often sympathetic to the financial needs of freelancers because they were once (or still are) freelancers themselves. If an editor has no way to pay you because her resources are tapped—as is often the case in a time of dwindling advertising revenues and diminished circulation—there may be different ways you can receive payment. You may want to request a credit as a *contributing editor* in the masthead. (A contributing editor is a fancy name for somebody who contributes to the magazine often.) Getting credited in such a way could look good

258

on your resume and secure you future work. Keep in mind, though, that sometimes editors will not only reject your requests for more money but also your request to be designated a contributing writer or editor.

Although your editor and the staff at the publication for which you're writing can be of great help and support, in case of a lawsuit, you may be on your own. Consequently, you must make sure to avoid libel or the unjust defamation of another person in print. (Some people confuse libel and slander. Although similar, slander is verbal defamation.) If you're practicing good journalism—journalism of coherence, verification, and transparency—the likelihood that you will engage in libel is low. Additionally, in the United States at least, it's very difficult to prove libel in court. Nevertheless, if you are engaged in high-risk (investigative) reporting, you may want to consider covering yourself with media liability insurance, which is available through organizations such as Mediabistro and the Author's Guild.

On a final note, one of the great things about journalism in the United States is that, to some extent, journalists enjoy certain freedoms that improve the quality of published work. For example, although there is no federal shield law, in almost every state there are shield laws in place to protect journalists. Furthermore, thanks to the pioneering work of colonial publisher John Peter Zenger and his lawyer Andrew Hamilton, truth is a defense against libel—a major win for freedom of the press. If what you write is true, then there's no reason to fear libel.

EPILOGUE

It's been a long read, but I hope it was worth it. I was fortunate to have enough time to speak with many people and really comb through the literature and research. It was enlightening and taught me much about the field of journalism. In many ways, journalism is an old field, but it's also a very new one.

With this book I drew together a verifiable work that was coherent and, when needed, transparent. Everything in this book can be traced back to an expert or the literature, and I did my best to present options and variations in pedagogy. Moreover, I balanced the information that I found and worked hard to explain the middles and the extremes. Finally, I paid much attention to the bibliography. (To learn more, I encourage you to turn to the bibliography.)

Although many journalists are smart people who are grounded in a firm understanding of the world, there is little solid ground in journalism. Ethics, style, roles, structure, craft, and so forth hold different definitions for different people. Even the word *journalist* doesn't have a definite meaning.

This text is not meant to be dogma. It's a coherent work meant to inspire your writing. Take what you want from it. I truly believe that anybody who appreciates this work in its entirety will be able to write strong articles. I also believe that this book will help improve the writing of anybody interested.

Remember that in many ways it's helpful to be obsessive when you write. You need to pay attention to the details. But don't let the details cloud the larger picture. You'll never be able to write the "perfect" article, but you will be able to write a very good one that entertains and informs others.

I'm very grateful to all the people who helped me and to all the great sources who devoted their time when interviewing with me. I'm also grateful that I live in the digital age and was able to pull together a mini meta-analysis of sorts using the Internet. I am awed by technology.

If anybody is interested in contacting me, my e-mail is writer@naveedsaleh.com.

BIBLIOGRAPHY

"95-Year-Old Woman Graduates from College." *ABC News.* May 12, 2007. http://abcnews. go.com/GMA/LifeStages/story?id=3167970 (accessed August 17, 2013).

A General Summary of Aristotle's Appeals ... http://courses.durhamtech.edu/perkins/aris.html (accessed February 4, 2013).

Abbot, Sebastian. "Pakistani Fishmonger Now Pop Star with 'One Pound Fish.'" *Detroit Free Press.* December 29, 2012. http://www.freep.com/article/20121229/ENT04/121229006/ Pakistani-fishmonger-pop-star-Muhammad-Shahid-Nazir-One-Pound-Fish (accessed January 21, 2013).

About Reddit. *Reddit:* http://www.reddit.com/about (accessed July 9, 2013).

Abramson, Alana. "Inscription on Martin Luther King Memorial Removed." *ABC News.* August 2, 2013. http://abcnews.go.com/blogs/headlines/2013/08/inscription-on-martin-luther-king-memorial-removed/ (accessed August 13, 2013).

Jad Abumrad and Robert Krulwich. "The Trouble with Everything" (podcast). June 13, 2013. *Radiolab:* http://www.radiolab.org/blogs/radiolab-blog/2013/jun/13/trouble-everything (accessed July 9, 2013).

Jad Abumrad and Robert Krulwich (hosts), Various episodes. *Radiolab.* NPR.

Adler, Ben. "Piecemeal Existence." *Columbia Journalism Review.* July 31, 2012. http://www. cjr.org/feature/piecemeal_existence.php?page=all (accessed February 17, 2013).

Michael Agnes, editor-in-chief. *Webster's New World College Dictionary.* Cleveland: Wiley Publishing Inc., 2004.

George A. Akerlof. *Encyclopaedia Britannica:* http://www.britannica.com/EBchecked/topic/764254/George-A-Akerlof (accessed July 9, 2013).

Sonny Albarado and the editors of the *Encyclopaedia Britannica.* "Citizen Journalism." *Encyclopaedia Britannica.* http://www.britannica.com/EBchecked/topic/1271506/citizen-journalism (accessed January 22, 2013).

Amanda Clayton, Michigan Lottery Winner Who Used Food Stamps, Charged with Welfare Fraud. April 17, 2012. The Huffington Post: http://www.huffingtonpost.com/2012/04/17/ amanda-clayton-michigan-lottery-winner-food-stamps_n_1431777.html (accessed July 8, 2013).

American Diabetes Association. http://www.diabetes.org/diabetes-basics/diabetes-statistics/ (accessed February 6, 2013).

Angier, Natalie. "True Blue Stands Out in an Earthy Crowd." *The New York Times*. October 22, 2012. http://www.nytimes.com/2012/10/23/science/with-new-findings-scientists-are-captivated-by-the-color-blue.html?pagewanted=all&_r=0 (accessed February 20, 2013).

Appalachian Trail Conservancy. http://www.appalachiantrail.org/about-the-trail (accessed February 6, 2013).

Appalachian Mountain Club. http://www.outdoors.org/conservation/trails/at/at-faq.cfm (accessed January 22, 2013).

Armstrong, Tim. "AOL CEO Tim Armstrong (8/9/2013) Transcript at jimromenesko.com (digital recording)." *SoundCloud*. August 9, 2013. https://soundcloud.com/jim-romenesko/aol-ceo-tim-armstrong-8-9-2013 (accessed August 13, 2013).

Associated Press. "Disputed 'Drum Major' quote to be removed from Martin Luther King memorial by carving grooves over the lettering." *Mail Online*. July 22, 2013. http://www.dailymail.co.uk/news/article-2373139/Disputed-Drum-Major-quote-removed-Martin-Luther-King-memorial-carving-grooves-lettering.html (accessed August 13, 2013).

David Auburn et al. *Oxford American Writer's Thesaurus*. New York: Oxford University Press, 2008.

Ballotpedia. http://www.ballotpedia.org (accessed January 14, 2013).

Banco, Erin. "Sculptor Removes Phrase From Memorial to King." *The New York Times*. August 1, 2013. http://www.nytimes.com/2013/08/02/us/sculptor-removes-phrase-from-memorial-to-Martin-Luther-King-Jr.html (accessed August 13, 2013).

Barbaro, Michael. "The Candidate Next Door." *The New York Times*. June 6, 2012. http://www.nytimes.com/2012/06/07/garden/mitt-romney-the-candidate-next-door.html?pagewanted=all (accessed August 13, 2013).

Martha Barnette and Grant Barrett. Chiasmus and Antimetabole. December 29, 2012. *A Way with Words*: http://www.waywordradio.org/chiasmus-antimetabole/ (accessed July 9, 2013).

Baron, Naomi S. *Always On*. Oxford: Oxford University Press, 2010.

Barry, Dave, interview by Naveed Saleh. (November 8, 2012).

Barry, Ellen. "Protests in Moldova Explode, With Help of Twitter." *The New York Times*. April 7, 2009. http://www.nytimes.com/2009/04/08/world/europe/08moldova.html?pagewanted=all (accessed February 4, 2013).

Bartlett, John. *Bartlett's Familiar Quotations 17th edition*. New York: Little, Brown and Company (Inc.).

Becker, David. "Using Serial Commas." April 7, 2011. American Psychological Association APA Style: http://blog.apastyle.org/apastyle/2011/04/using-serial-commas.html (accessed July 9, 2013).

Beil, Laura. "The Dirty Truth About Hospitals." *Men's Health*, October 2012: 124–130.

Berger, Judson. "Plagiarism Detection Tools." *American Journalism Review*. June/July 2004. http://www.ajr.org/article.asp?id=3671 (accessed February 23, 2013).

Bernstein, Theodore M. *The Careful Writer*. New York: Atheneum, 1973.

Bevins, Vincent. "Dengue, Where is Thy Sting?" *Los Angeles Times*. November 1, 2012. http://articles.latimes.com/2012/nov/01/world/la-fg-brazil-mutant-mosquitoes-20121102 (accessed January 24, 2013).

Bezos, Jeff. *10,000 Year Clock*. http://www.10000yearclock.net/learnmore.html (accessed August 13, 2013).

Bienenstock, David. "Dear President Obama." *High Times Medical Marijuana*, Fall 2012: 4.

"Big Spending Fails to Drive Attendance." *Chicago Tribune*. March 8, 2013.

Blood, Rebecca, interview by Naveed Saleh. (November 21, 2012).

Blood, Rebecca, e-mail communication (February 14, 2013).

Deborah Blum, Mary Knudson and Robin Marantz Henig (editors). *A Field Guide for Science Writers*. New York: Oxford University Press, 2006.

Blundell, William E. *The Art and Craft of Feature Writing*. New York: Penguin Group, 1988.

"Bob Woodward." *Encyclopaedia Britannica*. http://www.britannica.com/EBchecked/topic/1016587/Bob-Woodward (accessed August 15, 2013).

Bonner, Staci. "Hard Facts on Fact Checking." *Writer's Digest*, August 1995: 37–39.

Bowden, Mark. "The Case of the Vanishing Blond." *Vanity Fair*. December 2010. http://www.vanityfair.com/culture/features/2010/12/vanishing-blonde-201012 (accessed January 25, 2013).

Boylan, James. "A History of American Literary Journalism: The Emergence of a Modern Narrative Form" (book review). *Columbia Journalism Review*, November/December 2000: 82.

Brady, John Joseph. *The Craft of Interviewing*. Cincinnati: Writer's Digest Books, 1978.

Bragg, Rick. "All She Has, $150,000, Is Going to a University." August 13, 1995. *The New York Times*: http://www.nytimes.com/1995/08/13/us/all-she-has-150000-is-going-to-a-university.html (accessed July 9, 2013).

Bragg, Rick. "Where Alabama Inmates Fade into Old Age." *The New York Times*. November 1, 1995. http://www.nytimes.com/1995/11/01/us/where-alabama-inmates-fade-into-old-age.html?pagewanted=all&src=pm (accessed January 24, 2013).

Brainard, Curtis. "Columbia Journalism Review." *Gladwell Makes Excuses for Lehrer.* June 21, 2012. http://www.cjr.org/the_kicker/malcolm_gladwell_jonah_lehrer.php (accessed February 17, 2013).

Brandt, David. "Think 'Necessary Skills,' Not 'Print Journalism.'" *Quill*, November-December 2012: 31.

Brewster, Emily. Drive Safe: In Praise of Flat Adverbs - Merriam-Webster Ask the Editor. August 5, 2011. YouTube: http://www.youtube.com/watch?v=7epnfcHy5SA (accessed July 9, 2013).

Brians, Paul. *Common Errors in English Usage.* Sherwood: William, James & Co., 2009.

Brink, Susan. "One Thing We Know About Autism: Vaccines Aren't to Blame." *National Geographic.* July 16, 2013. http://news.nationalgeographic.com/news/2013/07/130716-autism-vaccines-mccarthy-view-medicine-science/ (accessed August 13, 2013).

Brookshire, Bethany. "Dopamine is [blank]." *Slate*, July 13, 2013. http://www.slate.com/articles/health_and_science/science/2013/07/what_is_dopamine_love_lust_sex_addiction_gambling_motivation_reward.html (accessed July 11, 2013).

Bryant Jr., Robert L. "Skip the Salad, Pass the Meat." *Columbia Journalism Review*, May 1993: 72.

Bugeja, Michael J. *Guide to Writing Magazine Nonfiction.* Needham Heights: Allyn & Bacon, 1997.

Burchfield, R.W. *Fowler's Modern English Usage.* Oxford: Oxford University Press, 2004.

Bureau of Labor Statistics. http://data.bls.gov/timeseries/LNS14000000 (accessed January 27, 2013).

Burgard, Stephen D. "More Than a Mouthpiece." *Columbia Journalism Review*, March/April 2003: 61.

Burstein, David Kline and Dan. *Blog!: How the Newest Media Revolution Is Changing Politics, Business, and Culture.* Durham: CDS Books, 2005.

Campbell, John. "Numbers Can Make or Break Your Copy." *Folio*, September 1989: 108–110, 113–115.

Campbell, Titchener B. *Reviewing the Arts.* Mahwah, New Jersey: Lawrence Erlbaum Associates, 1998.

Capper, Andy. "The Vice Guide to Liberia." *CNN World.* January 27, 2010. http://www.cnn.com/2010/WORLD/africa/01/18/vbs.liberia/index.html (accessed March 9, 2013).

Carlson, Nicholas. "AOL CEO Tim Armstrong Fired Patch's Creative Director In Front Of 1,000 Coworkers (AOL)." *SFGate.* August 9, 2013. http://www.sfgate.com/technology/

businessinsider/article/AOL-CEO-Tim-Armstrong-Fired-Patch-s-Creative-4720914.php (accessed August 13, 2013).

Carlson, Nicholas. "AOL CEO Tim Armstrong Fired This Man In Front Of 1,000 Coworkers." *Business Insider.* August 9, 2013. http://www.businessinsider.com/aol-ceo-tim-armstrong-appeared-to-fire-this-man-in-front-of-1000-coworkers-2013-8 (accessed August 17, 2013).

Carlson, Nicholas. "AOL Won't Deny The Rumor That Patch's CEO Is Out After Just Two Months On The Job." *Business Insider.* August 8, 2013. http://www.businessinsider.com/aol-wont-deny-the-rumor-that-patchs-ceo-is-out-after-just-2-months-on-the-job-2013-8 (accessed August 17, 2013).

Carlson, Nicholas. "Listen to AOL CEO Tim Armstrong Fire a Patch Employee in Front of 1,000 Coworkers." *Yahoo! Finance (Business Insider).* August 12, 2013. http://finance.yahoo.com/news/listen-to-aol-ceo-tim-armstrong-fire-a-patch-employee-in-front-of-1-000-coworkers-140600015.html (accessed August 13, 2013).

Carmichael, Mary. "The Pepsi Challenge." *The Daily Beast.* July 26, 2010. http://www.thedailybeast.com/newsweek/2010/07/26/the-pepsi-challenge.html (accessed January 31, 2013).

Carr, David. "Left Alone by Its Owner, Reddit Soars." September 2, 2012. *The New York Times*: http://www.nytimes.com/2012/09/03/business/media/reddit-thrives-after-advance-publications-let-it-sink-or-swim.html (accessed July 9, 2013).

Carr, David. "Newspaper Monopoly That Lost Its Grip." *The New York Times.* May 12, 2013. http://www.nytimes.com/2013/05/13/business/media/in-new-orleans-times-picayunes-monopoly-crumbles.html?pagewanted=all&_r=0 (accessed August 13, 2013).

Carr, David. "The Washington Post Reaches the End of the Graham Era." *The New York Times.* August 5, 2013. http://www.nytimes.com/2013/08/06/business/media/the-washington-post-reaches-the-end-of-the-graham-era.html (accessed August 13, 2013).

Carl J. Caspersen, PhD, MPH, Kenneth E. Powell, MD, MPH, and Gregory M. Christenson, PhD. "Physical Activity, Exercise, and Physical Fitness: Definitions and Distinctions for Health-Related Research." *Public Health Reports*, March-April 1985: 126-131.

Jessica Chasmar and David Eldridge. "West Virginia teen returns to school with NRA shirt, classmates' support." April 22, 2013, *The Washington Times*: http://www.washingtontimes.com/news/2013/apr/22/west-virginia-teen-returns-to-school-with-nra-shir/ (accessed July 9, 2013).

Chicago Tribune staff and *South Bend Tribune*. "South Bend Plane Crash: Ex-Oklahoma QB Among Dead." *Chicago Tribune.* March 18, 2013. http://www.chicagotribune.com/ (accessed March 18, 2013).

Dan Childs and Lauren Cox. "Lancet Retracts Controversial Autism Paper." *ABC News.* February 3, 2010. http://abcnews.go.com/Health/AutismNews/autism-vaccines-lancet-retracts-controversial-autism-paper/story?id=9730805 (accessed August 13, 2013).

Edited by Darrell Christian, Sally Jacobsen, and David Minthorn. *The Associated Press Stylebook.* New York: Basic Books, 2011.

Deborah S. Chung, Eunseong Kim, Kaye D. Trammel, and Lance V. Porter. "Uses and Perceptions of Blogs: A Report on Professional Journalists and Journalism Educators." *Journalism & Mass Communication Educator,* 2007: 305–322.

Clark, Brian E. "Pick Your Own Pumpkins, and Apples, too." *JSOnline.* October 17, 2012. http://www.jsonline.com/entertainment/holidays/pick-your-own-pumpkins-and-apples-too-0377e2c-174585811.html (accessed January 26, 2013).

Clark, Roy Peter. "Beware Loaded Language in Islamic Center Debate." CNN Opinion. September 10, 2010. http://www.cnn.com/2010/OPINION/09/10/clark.islamic.center.language/index.html (accessed January 26, 2013).

Clark, Roy Peter, e-mail interview by Naveed Saleh. (November 6, 2012).

Clark, Roy Peter, *The Glamour of Grammar,* New York: Little, Brown and Company, 2010.

Clark, Roy Peter. "Joe Paterno and the Stained Soul of Penn State." CNN Opinion. November 11, 2011. http://articles.cnn.com/2011-11-11/opinion/opinion_clark-penn-paterno_1_joe-paterno-father-holy-family?_s=PM:OPINION (accessed January 26, 2013).

Clark, Roy Peter. "Stephen Colbert's Got Sway." CNN Opinion. September 24, 2010. http://www.cnn.com/2010/OPINION/09/23/clark.colbert/index.html (accessed January 26, 2013).

Clark, Roy Peter. "We Owe It to King to Revise Inscription on His Monument." March 30, 2013. http://www.cnn.com/2011/10/11/opinion/clark-king-monument-inscription (accessed April 1, 2013).

Clark, Roy Peter. *Writing Tools.* New York: Little, Brown and Company, 2008.

Clark, Taylor. "The Most Dangerous Gamer." *The Atlantic.* May 2012. http://www.theatlantic.com/magazine/archive/2012/05/the-most-dangerous-gamer/308928/ (accessed January 24, 2013).

CNN Wire Staff. "Onion: We just fooled the Chinese government!" November 28, 2012. http://www.cnn.com/2012/11/27/world/asia/north-korea-china-onion (accessed March 30, 2013).

"Code of Ethics." *Society of Professional Journalists.* http://www.spj.org/pdf/ethicscode.pdf (accessed January 20, 2013).

Cohen, Rachel. "AP Makes 'Illegals' Illegal." *The Baltimore Sun.* April 5, 2013. http://articles.baltimoresun.com/2013-04-05/news/bs-ed-ap-style-20130405_1_ap-stylebook-term-language (accessed April 6, 2013).

Cohen, Rich. "They Taught America How to Watch Football." *The Atlantic.* October 2012. http://www.theatlantic.com/magazine/archive/2012/10/they-taught-america-to-watch-football/309083/# (accessed February 20, 2013).

Congressional Diabetes Caucus. http://www.house.gov/degette/diabetes/facts.shtml (accessed February 6, 2013).

Cooke, Charles C.W. "Mitt Romney Worked as a Garbage Man." *National Review Online.* October 2, 2012. http://www.nationalreview.com/corner/329098/mitt-romney-worked-garbage-man-charles-c-w-cooke (accessed February 4, 2013).

Cooper, Marc, interview by Naveed Saleh. (November 21, 2012).

Cope, Victor Cohn and Lewis. *News & Numbers.* Ames: Iowa State Press, 2001.

"Core Purpose & Values." *The New York Times Company.* http://www.nytco.com/careers/mission.html (accessed January 20, 2013).

Corry, Carl. *Smartphone Journalism.* http://www.spj.org/trainingondemand.asp (accessed February 6, 2013).

Coyle, Jim. "'Argo': Former Ambassador Ken Taylor Sets the Record Straight." *thestar.com.* October 7, 2012. http://www.thestar.com/news/canada/article/1267937--argo-film-gives-former-canadian-ambassador-ken-taylor-chance-to-set-the-record-straight (accessed January 28, 2013).

"Crime in Chicago." *Chicago Tribune.* http://crime.chicagotribune.com/chicago/ (accessed March 14, 2013).

"Cullinan Diamond." *Encyclopaedia Britannica.* http://www.britannica.com/EBchecked/topic/146080/Cullinan-diamond (accessed April 10, 2013).

Cutler, Jeff. *Connect, Communicate and Follow the Noise.* http://www.spj.org/trainingondemand.asp (accessed February 6, 2013).

Davidson, Adam. Economic Recovery, Made in Bangladesh? May 14, 2013. *The New York Times Magazine*: http://www.nytimes.com/2013/05/19/magazine/economic-recovery-made-in-bangladesh.html?pagewanted=all&_r=0 (accessed July 9, 2013).

"Debates (Episode 119)." *Mansome.* http://screen.yahoo.com/mansome-episode-119-debates-130000987.html.

Dennis, Michael Aaron. "Blog." *Encyclopaedia Britannica.* http://www.britannica.com/EBchecked/topic/869092/blog (accessed November 30, 2013).

DePice, Dylan. "The Scientific Method for Reaching a Wider Audience." *Columbia Journalism Review*. February 11, 2011. http://www.cjr.org/the_observatory/the_scientific_method_for_reac.php?page=all (accessed February 17, 2013).

Dominick, Roger D. Wimmer and Joseph R. *Mass Media Research: An Introduction*. Boston: Wadsworth Publishing, 2011.

Martin, Douglas. "Yvonne Brill, a Pioneering Rocket Scientist, Dies at 88." *The New York Times*. March 30, 2013. http://www.nytimes.com/2013/03/31/science/space/yvonne-brill-rocket-scientist-dies-at-88.html?pagewanted=all&_r=0 (accessed April 1, 2013).

Dubinsky, Donna. *A Lesson on Sunk Costs* (video). Harvard Business School Institutional Memory: http://institutionalmemory.hbs.edu/leadership/a_lesson_on_sunk_costs.html (accessed July 8, 2013).

"Editorial Calendar Guide." *Mediabistro*: http://www.mediabistro.com/editorialcalendar-guide.html (accessed August 13, 2013).

The Editors at the *Columbia Journalism Review*. "Twitter Turns Five." *Columbia Journalism Review*. March 22, 2011. http://www.cjr.org/news_meeting/twitter_turns_five.php (accessed February 4, 2013).

Einsohn, Amy. *The Copyeditor's Handbook*. Berkeley and Los Angeles: University of California Press, 2006.

Encyclopaedia Britannica. http://www.britannica.com/ (accessed August 13, 2013).

The EveryBlock Team. "Farewell, neighbors." *EveryBlock Blog*. February 7, 2013. http://blog.everyblock.com/2013/feb/07/goodbye/ (accessed August 17, 2013).

Marcus Errico, John April, Andrew Asch, Lynnette Khalfani, Miriam A. Smith, and Xochiti R. Ybarra. *The Evolution of the Summary News Lead*. http://www.scripps.ohiou.edu/media-history/mhmjour1-1.htm.

Eyetracking the News: A Study of Print and Online Reading. http://www.poynter.org/extra/Eyetrack/keys_01.html (accessed January 31, 2013).

Fineman, Howard. "HuffPost Launches OffTheBus Citizen Journalism Project Ahead of 2012 Elections." *The Huffington Post*. July 7, 2011. http://www.huffingtonpost.com/howard-fineman/offthebus-huffington-post_b_891921.html (accessed January 19, 2013).

Fogarty, Mignon. "Capitalizing Titles." *Quick and Dirty Tips*. June 9, 2011. http://www.quick-anddirtytips.com/education/grammar/capitalizing-titles?page=all (accessed August 13, 2013).

Fogarty, Mignon. *Grammar Girl's Quick and Dirty Tips for Better Writing*. New York: Holt Paperbacks, 2008.

Franklin, Jon. *Writing for Story*. New York: Penguin Group, 1994.

Fredette, Jean M. (editor). *Writer's Digest Handbook of Magazine Writing.* Cincinnatti: Writer's Digest Books, 1988.

Fry, Erika. "Obama's Twitter Townhall." *Columbia Journalism Review.* July 6, 2011. http://www.cjr.org/campaign_desk/obamas_twitter_townhall.php (accessed February 23, 2013).

Fryxell, David A. "Editor's Standard Time." *Writer's Digest,* June 1999: 56, 58.

Fryxell, David A. "Go Back in Time." *Writer's Digest,* July 2003: 20–22.

Fryxell, David A. "If Your Mother Says She Loves You ..." *Writer's Digest,* September 1999: 24, 26.

Fuller, Jack. (1996). *News Values: Ideas for an Information Age.* Chicago: University of Chicago Press.

Funt, Peter. "So Much Media, So Little News." *The Wall Street Journal.* October 12, 2011. http://online.wsj.com/article/SB10001424052970203499704576623022643257778.html (accessed March 7, 2013).

Gahran, Amy. "ePublishing: Why Web Writing Must Get to the Point." *Writer's Digest,* December 2002: 42.46.

Gaines, William G. *Investigative Journalism: Proven Strategies for Reporting the Story.* Washington, DC: CQ Press, 2007.

Gardner, Susannah and Shane Birley. *Blogging for Dummies.* Hoboken: John Wiley & Sons, Inc., 2012.

Bob Garfield and Brooke Gladstone (hosts). "The Future of Egyptian Media, the Bitcoin Bubble, and More." *On the Media.* NPR, April 4, 2013.

Bob Garfield and Brooke Gladstone (hosts). Various episodes. *On the Media.* NPR.

Garner, Bryan A. *A Dictionary of Modern American Usage.* Oxford: Oxford University Press, 1998.

Barbara Gastel, various communications.

Gastel, MD, MPH, Barbara. "A Strategy for Reviewing Books for Journals." *BioScience,* 1991: 635–637.

Gastel, MD, MPH, Barbara. *Health Writer's Handbook.* Ames: Blackwell Publishing, 2005.

Gee, James Paul. *George Mason University.* http://mason.gmu.edu/~lsmithg/jamespaulgee2 (accessed January 27, 2013).

Tia Ghose and LiveScience. "'Just a Theory': 7 Misused Science Words." *Scientific American.* http://www.scientificamerican.com/article.cfm?id=just-a-theory-7-misused-science-words&page=3 (accessed April 5, 2013).

Heather Gillers and Jason Grotto. "Dinosaur-Size Debt." *Chicago Tribune.* March 8, 2013. http://articles.chicagotribune.com/2013-03-08/news/ct-met-field-museum-debt-20130308_1_field-museum-public-museum-capital-projects (accessed March 31, 2013).

"How a Startup Went From Zero Revenue to $1 Million in a Year [VIDEO]." *Mashable.* December 6, 2011. http://mashable.com/2011/12/06/contently-video/ (accessed August 16, 2013).

Gordon, Joye C. "Transformative Explanations: Writing to Overcome Counterintuitive Ideas." *Journal of Extension*, 2003: http://www.joe.org/joe/2003october/tt1.php.

Gotye featuring Kimbra. "Somebody That I Used to Know" (song). *Making Mirrors* (album). 2011.

Nathan Groepper and Jon Benedict. "Time-Saving Story Forms." http://www.slideshare.net/chrissnider/alternative-story-forms.

Jacques Duchesne-Guillemin and the editors of *Encyclopaedia Britannica.* "Zoroastrianism." *Encyclopaedia Britannica.* http://www.britannica.com/topic/658081/contributors (accessed August 13, 2013).

Guroff, Margaret, interview by Naveed Saleh. (October 10, 2012).

Guroff, Margaret. "Diagnosis: Love." *AARP The Magazine*, December 2011/January 2012 December/January: 40–44 and 60–63.

Guzmán, Mónica. "After Boston, Still Learning." June 6, 2013. *Quill*: http://www.spj.org/quill_issue.asp?ref=2008 (accessed July 9, 2013).

"H.W. Fowler." *Encyclopaedia Britannica.* http://www.britannica.com/EBchecked/topic/215317/HW-Fowler (accessed August 14, 2013).

Haik, Cory Tolbert. "@seattletimes and the Social Media Wave During Lakewood Cop Shooting." *The Seattle Times.* December 1, 2009. http://seattletimes.com/html/localnews/2010398753_webwave.html (accessed February 6, 2013).

"hamartia." *Encyclopaedia Britannica.* http://www.britannica.com/EBchecked/topic/253196/hamartia (accessed August 13, 2013).

Robert J. Hamper and L. Baugh. (2011). *Handbook for Writing Proposals, Second Edition.* New York: McGraw-Hill.

Hancock, Elise. *Ideas into Words.* Baltimore: The Johns Hopkins University Press, 2003.

"Handout #6: American Society of Newspaper Editors Code of Ethics." *ASNE (American Society of Newspaper Editors).* http://www.pbs.org/newshour/extra/teachers/lessonplans/media/mediaethics_handout6.pdf (accessed January 22, 2013).

Hargrove, Dorian. "Mitt Romney moves forward on massive renovation of La Jolla home." *San Diego Reader.* February 4, 2013. http://www.sandiegoreader.com/wcblogs/news-ticker/2013/feb/04/mitt-romney-removes-hold-on-major-renovation-of-la/ (accessed August 13, 2013).

Haughney, Christine. "Bezos, Amazon's Founder, to Buy The Washington Post." *The New York Times.* August 5, 2013. http://www.nytimes.com/2013/08/06/business/media/amazon-com-founder-to-buy-the-washington-post.html?pagewanted=all (accessed August 13, 2013).

High Times Medical Marijuana. "The Emerald City Goes Green." Fall 2012: 33.

HootSuite. https://hootsuite.com/ (accessed August 13, 2013).

Houston, Brant. *The Investigative Reporter's Handbook.* Boston: Investigative Reporters and Editors, Inc., 2009.

Howard, Alexander. "Top 15 Twitter Acronyms." *Pistachio.* January 12, 2009. http://pistachioconsulting.com/top-15-twitter-acronyms/ (accessed February 6, 2013).

Howe, DK. "Yoga Teacher Sues Bikram Choudhury for Sexual Harassment." *examiner.com.* March 29, 2013. http://www.examiner.com/article/yoga-teacher-sues-bikram-choudhury-for-sexual-harassment (accessed March 29, 2013).

Howerton, Michael, interview by Naveed Saleh. (October 3, 2012).

Huang, Tom. "6 Questions Journalists Should Be Able to Answer Before Pitching a Story." *Poynter Institute.* August 22, 2012. http://www.poynter.org/how-tos/newsgathering-storytelling/185746/6-questions-journalists-should-be-able-to-answer-before-pitching-a-story/ (accessed February 23, 2013).

"hubris." *Encyclopaedia Britannica.* http://www.britannica.com/EBchecked/topic/274625/hubris (accessed August 15, 2013).

Huetteman, Emmarie. "In Response to Criticism, Officials to Remove Quote From Memorial to King." *The New York Times.* December 12, 2012. http://www.nytimes.com/2012/12/13/us/officials-removing-quote-from-king-memorial.html?_r=0 (accessed August 13, 2013).

Hynds, Ernest C. "Changes in Editorials: A Study of Three Newspapers, 1955–1985." *Journalism Quarterly,* Summer 1990: 302–312.

IMDB. http://www.imdb.com/ (accessed August 17, 2013).

"Income, Poverty and Health Insurance Coverage in the United States: 2011" (press release). *United States Census Bureau.* September 12, 2012. http://www.census.gov/newsroom/releases/archives/income_wealth/cb12-172.html#tablea (accessed February 6, 2013).

Information Point: Prevalence and incidence. http://www.blackwellpublishing.com/specialarticles/jcn_9_188.pdf (accessed February 5, 2013).

Information provided by Sandra G. Smith, EdD, LCSW.

Informational handouts provided by the University Writing Center at Texas A&M University.

Ipsos. http://www.ipsos.com (accessed December 26, 2012).

Irion, Robert, interview by Naveed Saleh. (October 19, 2012).

Irion, Robert. "Homing in on Black Holes." *Smithsonian.com.* April 2008. http://www.smithsonianmag.com/science-nature/black-holes.html (accessed January 25, 2013).

"Israeli Ambassador Deletes Tweet After Saying That They Would Be Willing to Sit Down with Hamas over Missile Attacks." *Mail Online.* November 18, 2012. http://www.dailymail.co.uk/news/article-2234979/Israeli-ambassador-Michael-Oren-deletes-tweet-saying-willing-sit-Hamas-missile-attacks.html#axzz2JtOwgOAl (accessed February 4, 2013).

Cheryl Iverson et al. *AMA Manual of Style A Guide for Authors and Editors* 10th edition. New York: Oxford University Press, Inc., 2007.

Jacob, Dianne. "Food Writing With Flavor." *Writer's Digest*, May/June 2013: 20–23.

Jaggard, Victoria. "James Cameron on Earth's Deepest Spot: Desolate, Lunar-Like." *National Geographic News.* March 27, 2012. http://news.nationalgeographic.com/news/2012/03/120326-james-cameron-mariana-trench-challenger-deepest-lunar-sub-science/ (accessed January 24, 2013).

Jargon, Julie. "How Do You Spell Hipster? It Could Be B-I-N-G-O." *The Wall Street Journal.* April 9, 2013. http://online.wsj.com/article/SB1000142412788732488360457839897368246 0716.html (accessed April 11, 2013).

"Jeri Ryan: Biography." *TV Guide.* http://www.tvguide.com/celebrities/jeri-ryan/bio/156757 (accessed August 13, 2013).

"John Peter Zenger." *Encyclopaedia Britannica.* http://www.britannica.com/EBchecked/topic/656490/John-Peter-Zenger (accessed April 6, 2013).

Johnson, Bradley. "Internet-Media Employment Fuels Digital Job Growth." *Ad Age.* October 1, 2012. http://adage.com/article/media/internet-media-employment-fuels-digital-job-growth/237440/ (accessed January 23, 2013).

Johnson, Larry. E-mail communication, June 4, 2013.

Johnson, Steven. *Everything Bad Is Good for You: How Today's Popular Culture Is Actually Making Us Smarter.* New York: Riverhead Books, 2005.

Johnson, Steven. *Where Good Ideas Come From.* New York: Riverhead Books, 2010.

Harold I. Kaplan M.D. and Benjamin J. Sadock M.D. *Kaplan & Sadock's Synopsis of Psychiatry.* Philadelphia: Lippincott Williams & Wilkins, 1998.

Karl, Jonathan. "A Romney-Biden Administration? It Could Happen." *ABC News*. October 23, 2012. http://abcnews.go.com/blogs/politics/2012/10/a-romney-biden-administration-it-could-happen/ (accessed January 26, 2013).

Kaufman, Leslie. "Bombings Trip Up Reddit in Its Turn in Spotlight." April 28, 2013. *The New York Times*: http://www.nytimes.com/2013/04/29/business/media/bombings-trip-up-reddit-in-its-turn-in-spotlight.html?pagewanted=all&_r=0 (accessed July 8, 2013).

Keeler, Robert. "Eight Steps to Writing Articles on Unfamiliar Topics." *Writer's Digest*, July 1991: 52.

George Kennedy, Daryl R. Moen, Don Ranly. *Beyond the Inverted Pyramid: Effective Writing for Newspapers, Magazines and Specialized Publications*. New York: St. Martin's, Inc., 1992.

Keshelashvili, Kaye D. Trammell and Ana. "Examining the New Influencers: A Self-Presentation Study of A-List Blogs." *Journalism and Mass Communication Quarterly*, Winter 2005: 968–982.

Klein, Julia M. "If You Build It ..." *Columbia Journalism Review*, November/December 2007: 40–45.

Knox, Olivier. "Energy Secretary Chu steps down, blasts climate-change skeptics." *Yahoo! News*. February 1, 2013. http://news.yahoo.com/blogs/ticket/energy-secretary-chu-steps-down-blasts-climate-change-170625879--politics.html (accessed February 1, 2013).

Komando, Kim. "Sites Make It Simple to Sell Your Writing Online." *USA Today*. June 25, 2009. http://usatoday30.usatoday.com/tech/columnist/kimkomando/2009-06-25-writing-online_N.htm (accessed February 7, 2013).

Kovach, Steve. "TIM ARMSTRONG: I Made An Emotional Mistake Firing That Guy." *Yahoo! Finance*. August 13, 2013. http://finance.yahoo.com/news/tim-armstrong-made-emotional-mistake-204926034.html (accessed August 13, 2013).

La Borde, Roger, interview by Naveed Saleh. (March 25, 2011).

La Borde, Roger. *Shaman's Door LLC*. http://www.shamansdoor.com/ (accessed April 2, 2013).

Lang, Thomas A. *How to Write, Publish and Present in the Health Sciences*. Philadelphia: American College of Physicians, 2010.

Lang, Tom. "What YOU Need to Know about Communication, Writing, & Science." (PowerPoint presentation). AuthorAID: http://www.authoraid.info/resource-library/Lang%20Aug%202008%20Slides.ppt/view?searchterm=tom%20lang (accessed July 12, 2013).

Jeff Latzke and Tom Coyne. "Ex-Oklahoma QB killed in plane crash in Indiana." *Yahoo! (Associated Press)*. March 18, 2013. http://sports.yahoo.com/news/ex-oklahoma-qb-killed-plane-155316645--ncaaf.html (accessed March 18, 2013).

Laureys, Steven. "Eyes Open, Brain Shut." *Scientific American*, May 2007: 84-89.

Debbie A. Lawlor, George Davey Smith and Shah Ebrahim. "Commentary: The Hormone Replacement–Coronary Heart Disease Conundrum: Is This the Death of Observational Epidemiology?" *International Journal of Epidemiology*, 2004: 464-467.

"Lee Boyd Malvo Fast Facts." *CNN*. April 3, 2013. http://www.cnn.com/2013/04/03/us/lee-boyd-malvo-fast-facts (accessed August 15, 2013).

Lee, Edmund. "AOL's Patch Limps Toward Profitability." June 18, 2013. http://www.bloomberg.com/news/2013-06-18/aol-s-patch-limps-toward-profitability.html (accessed August 17, 2013).

Lee, Edmund. "AOL Said to be Closing or Finding Partners for 400 Patches (1)." *Bloomberg Businessweek*. August 9, 2013. http://www.businessweek.com/news/2013-08-09/aol-said-to-be-closing-or-finding-partners-for-400-patch-sites (accessed August 17, 2013).

Leibovich, Lori. "'The Kids Aren't Safe With Me.'" *The Huffington Post*. October 26, 2012. http://www.huffingtonpost.com/lori-leibovich/nanny-psychotic-break_b_2024822.html (accessed January 26, 2013).

Leydon, Joe, interview by Naveed Saleh. (October 5, 2012).

"Library Instruction: Finding Articles in Databases." *Sacramento State*. http://library.csus.edu/services/inst/ASP-4-2012.pdf (accessed February 7, 2013).

Linden, Tom, interview by Naveed Saleh. (October 17, 2012).

Tom Linden, M.D., and the writers of *The New York Times*. *The New York Times Reader: Health and Medicine*. Washington, DC: CQ Press, 2011.

Liu, Ziming. "Reading behavior in the digital environment." *Journal of Documentation*, 2005: 700–712.

Long, Priscilla, e-mail interview by Naveed Saleh. (October 4, 2012).

Lopez, Steve. "Mayoral Candidates Step into Sidewalk Debate." *Los Angeles Times*. September 30, 2012. http://articles.latimes.com/2012/sep/30/local/la-me-0930-lopez-pavement-20120930 (accessed February 4, 2013).

Lopez, Steve. "Poor Go Unheard in Presidential Race." *Los Angeles Times*. October 16, 2012. http://articles.latimes.com/2012/oct/16/local/la-me-1017-lopez-debates-20121016 (accessed February 4, 2013).

Lulofs, Neal. "The Top 25 U.S. Consumer Magazines for June 2013." *Alliance for Audited Media*. August 6, 2013. http://www.auditedmedia.com/news/blog/2013/august/the-top-25-us-consumer-magazines-for-june-2013.aspx (accessed August 14, 2013).

Regina E. Lundgren and Andrea H. McMakin. *Risk Communication: A Handbook for Communicating Environmental, Safety and Health Risks.* Hoboken: John Wiley & Sons, Inc. 2009.

Mackey, Robert. "With Rodman Stunt, American Reality TV and North Korean Propaganda Fuse." *The New York Times.* March 1, 2013. http://thelede.blogs.nytimes.com/2013/03/01/with-rodman-stunt-american-reality-tv-and-north-korean-propaganda-fuse/ (accessed March 9, 2013).

Macur, Juliet. "Details of Doping Scheme Paint Armstrong as Leader." *The New York Times.* October 10, 2012. http://www.nytimes.com/2012/10/11/sports/cycling/agency-details-doping-case-against-lance-armstrong.html?pagewanted=all (accessed February 20, 2013).

Mahoney, Mark, interview by Naveed Saleh. (September 8, 2012).

Marche, Stephen. "Is Facebook Making Us Lonely?" *The Atlantic.* May 2012. http://www.theatlantic.com/magazine/archive/2012/05/is-facebook-making-us-lonely/308930/ (accessed January 25, 2013).

Martin, Clancy. "The Overheated, Oversexed Cult of Bikram Choudhury." *Details.* February 2011. (accessed March 29, 2013).

Maxim. "How To" (department). November 2012: 25–34.

"Maya Angelou." *Encyclopaedia Britannica.* http://www.britannica.com/EBchecked/topic/24569/Maya-Angelou (accessed August 13, 2013).

McCarthy, Andrew, interview by Naveed Saleh. (November 8, 2012).

McCarthy, Andrew. "In Search of the Black Pearl." *National Geographic Traveler.* October 2010. http://www.andrewmccarthy.com/overlays/writing_ngt_blackpearl.html (accessed January 26, 2013).

Greg McCune (Reuters). "Sour End to 2012 Masks Positive Trends in America." *Yahoo! News.* December 31, 2012. http://news.yahoo.com/sour-end-2012-masks-positive-trends-america-015300137.html (accessed January 27, 2013).

Magary, Drew. "You Named Me ... *What?*" *GQ.* July 2013. http://www.gq.com/entertainment/humor/201307/nine-baby-naming-rules-2013 (accessed August 13, 2013).

"Masochist Dog Enjoys Being Walked Around On Leash While Naked." *The Onion.* August 7, 2013. http://www.theonion.com/articles/masochist-dog-enjoys-being-walked-around-on-leash,33399/ (accessed August 13, 2013).

McGaughey, Steve. "Science Reveals the Power of a Handshake." *Beckman Institute.* October 19, 2012. http://beckman.illinois.edu/news/2012/10/dolcoshandshake (accessed August 16, 2013).

McGrath, Ben. "Head Start." *The New Yorker,* October 15, 2012: 38–44.

McLaughlin, Neil. "100 Years in the Making." *Medical Economics*, March 29, 2010: 24.

"Meet Brian Stelter." *Towson University*. http://www.towson.edu/main/discovertowson/brianstelter.asp (accessed August 17, 2013).

Merriam-Webster Online Dictionary. http://www.merriam-webster.com/

Meyer, Philip. "Learning to Love Lower Profits." *American Journalism Review*, December 1995: 40–44.

Meyer, Philip. *Precision Journalism: A Reporter's Introduction to Social Science Methods.* Lanham: Rowman & Littlefield Publishers, 2002.

Miller, Holly G., interview by Naveed Saleh. (October 15, 2012).

Minneapolis/St. Paul City Pages. http://blogs.citypages.com/dcody/authors.php?author=dcody (accessed February 7, 2013).

Mitchell, Bill. "Ethics Guidelines for Poynter Publishing." *Poynter.* July 6, 2012. http://www.poynter.org/archived/about-poynter/20209/ethics-guidelines-for-poynter-publishing/ (accessed January 22, 2012).

"Mixed America's Family Trees." *The New York Times.* http://www.nytimes.com/interactive/us/family-trees.html#index.

Mogelson, Luke. "The Scariest Little Corner of the World." *The New York Times Magazine.* October 18, 2012. http://www.nytimes.com/2012/10/21/magazine/the-corner-where-afghanistan-iran-and-pakistan-meet.html?pagewanted=all&_r=0 (accessed January 25, 2013).

Montagnes, Ian. *Editing and Publication: a training manual.* Manila: International Rice Research Institute, 1991.

Mooney, Chris. "Blogonomics." *Columbia Journalism Review*, January/February 2008: 18–19.

Moretti, Anthony. "Watching the Watchdog: Bloggers as the Fifth Estate/Blogging, Citizenship and the Future of Media (book review)." *Journalism & Mass Communication Educator*, Autumn 2007: 324–326.

Morris, Roger, interview by Naveed Saleh. (November 26, 2012).

Morris, Roger. "The Best of Both Worlds." *Writer's Digest*, May/June 2012: 32-37.

Moynthan, Michael. "Nicholas Lemann: Journalism Is Doing Just Fine." *The Daily Beast.* October 14, 2012. http://www.thedailybeast.com/articles/2012/10/14/nicholas-lemann-journalism-is-doing-just-fine.html (accessed February 20, 2013).

"Muckraker." *Encyclopaedia Britannica.* http://www.britannica.com/EBchecked/topic/395831/muckraker (accessed December 24, 2012).

Mundy, Alicia. "Is the Press Any Match for Powerhouse P.R.?" *Columbia Journalism Review*, September 1992: 27–34.

Murray, Donald M. *Writing to Deadline: The Journalist at Work*. Portsmouth: Heinemann, 2000.

Myers, Steve. "Jonah Lehrer resigns from New Yorker after fabricating Bob Dylan quotes in 'Imagine.'" July 30, 2012. Poynter: http://www.poynter.org/latest-news/mediawire/183298/jonah-lehrer-accused-of-fabricating-bob-dylan-quotes-in-imagine/ (accessed July 9, 2013).

Sylvia Nasar (editor). *The Best American Science Writing 2008*. New York: Harper Perennial, 2008.

National Diabetes Fact Sheet, 2011. http://www.cdc.gov/diabetes/pubs/pdf/ndfs_2011.pdf (accessed February 6, 2013).

"#numbers." March 14, 2011. The Official Twitter Blog: https://blog.twitter.com/2011/numbers (accessed July 8, 2013).

Victor Navasky with Evan Lerner. "Magazines and Their Websites." *Columbia Journalism Review*. March 2010. http://www.cjr.org/resources/magazines_and_their_websites/index.php (accessed March 7, 2013).

Neal, Robert Wilson. *Editorials and Editorial-Writing*. Forgotten Books, 2012.

Neuts, Dana. *Freelancing*. http://www.spj.org/trainingondemand.asp (accessed February 6, 2013).

Newcott, Bill. "Everybody Loves Tony ... and the feeling is mutual." *AARP The Magazine*, September/October 2011: 70.

Nielsen, Jakob. Writing Style for Print vs. Web. June 9, 2008. NN/g Nielsen Norman Group: http://www.nngroup.com/articles/writing-style-for-print-vs-web/ (accessed June 9, 2008).

Nieva, Richard. "Washington Post just one of many wacky Bezos buys." *CNNMoney*. August 6, 2013. http://money.cnn.com/2013/08/06/technology/bezos-investments/index.html (accessed August 13, 2013).

O'Neil, L. Peat. "Wish You Were Here." *Writer's Digest*, May/June 2012: 24–27.

Ogintz, Eileen. "Your Ticket to Travel Writing." *Writer's Digest*, August 2003: 47–49.

Ohlsen, Becky. "Avoid Common Grammar Pitfalls." *Writer's Digest*, August 2002: 19–20, 53.

Olen, Helaine. "Rich Dad, Poor Dad, Bankrupt Dad?" *Forbes*. October 10, 2012. http://www.forbes.com/sites/helaineolen/2012/10/10/rich-dad-poor-dad-bankrupt-dad/ (accessed January 23, 2013).

OneLook Dictionary Search. http://www.onelook.com/.

Ortutay, Barbara. "AOL's Patch local news site to lay off up to 500." *Yahoo! Finance* (Associated Press). August 16, 2013. http://finance.yahoo.com/news/aols-patch-local-news-lay-161212222. html;_ylt=A2KJjb0cMA9SKk0AAxqTmYlQ (accessed August 17, 2013).

"Outcry after NOLA's daily paper cuts back." *60 Minutes.* January 6, 2013. http://www.cbsnews.com/video/watch/?id=50138326n (accessed August 13, 2013).

Palmer, Alex. "Freelance Writing: 10 Tips to Better Interviews." *Writer's Digest.* April 3, 2012. http://www.writersdigest.com/whats-new/freelance-writing-10-tips-to-better-interviews (accessed February 2, 2013).

Palser, Barb. "Journalism's Backseat Drivers." *American Journalism Review.* August/September 2005. http://www.ajr.org/article.asp?id=3931 (accessed January 30, 2013).

Patch. http://www.patch.com/ (accessed August 13, 2013).

PEER. http://peer.tamu.edu/.

"PEER Perspectives 2006." https://dst.sp.maricopa.edu/DWG/STPG/JuniorACE/Shared%20 Documents/STEM/PEER_perspectives%20Broadening%20the%20Reach%20of%20University%20Resourc.pdf.

"PEER Perspectives, Volume II." http://www.gk12.org/files/2010/04/PEER_Perspectives_ Vol_II.pdf (accessed March 19, 2013).

Perrine, Jennifer Wolff. "The New Fatherhood." *Best Life*, Fall/Winter 2012: 82–87.

Piskorski, Bill Heil and Mikolaj. "New Twitter Research: Men Follow Men and Nobody Tweets." *Harvard Business Review.* June 1, 2009. http://blogs.hbr.org/cs/2009/06/new_twitter_research_men_follo.html (accessed February 3, 2013).

"Pit Bull Saves Nayeli Garzon-Jimenez's Baby from Kidnappers During Indiana Burglary." November 24, 2012. The Huffington Post: http://www.huffingtonpost.com/2012/11/24/pit-bull-saves-nayeli-gar_n_2176158.html (accessed July 9, 2013).

Planet Money. Various episodes. NPR.

Pogue, David. "Pogue-o-Matic Product Finder." *The New York Times.* November 18, 2008. http://www.nytimes.com/interactive/2008/11/18/technology/personaltechspecial/20081118-pogue-o-matic.html (accessed February 3, 2013).

Polson, Kelli. "Eyetracking the News: Voice of the Reader." *Poynter Institute.* March 3, 2011. http://www.poynter.org/archived/poynter-high/poynter-high-reporting-writing-editing/84462/eyetracking-the-news-voice-of-the-reader/ (accessed January 31, 2013).

Ponder, Stephanie E. "Online, and Beyond." *The Costco Connection*, November 2012: 37–39.

Porsolt RD, Bertin A and Jalfre M. "Behavioral Despair in Mice: A Primary Screening Test for Antidepressants." *Archive of International Pharmacodynamics and Therapeutics*, 1977: 327–336.

Potter, Deborah. *Handbook of Independent Journalism.* United States Air Force Public Affairs Center of Excellence. http://www.au.af.mil/pace/handbooks.htm (accessed January 24, 2013).

Pratt, Timothy. "What Happens in Brooklyn Moves to Vegas." *The New York Times Magazine.* October 19, 2012. http://www.nytimes.com/2012/10/21/magazine/what-happens-in-brooklyn-moves-to-vegas.html?pagewanted=all (accessed January 25, 2013).

Price, Jonathan, interview by Naveed Saleh. (October 10, 2012).

Prohibition. Directed by Ken Burns and Lynn Novick. 2011.

"Prohibition: A Film by Ken Burns & Lynn Novick (Lois Long)." *PBS.* http://www.pbs.org/kenburns/prohibition/media_detail/2082501823-long/ (accessed August 13, 2013).

ProPublica. http://www.propublica.org (accessed February 25, 2013).

Prues, Don. "Query Letter Clinic." *1998 Writer's Market,* by Kirsten C. Holm and Don Prues, 25–35. Cincinatti: Writer's Digest Books, 1997.

"Public relations." *Encyclopaedia Britannica.* http://www.britannica.com/EBchecked/topic/482470/public-relations (accessed February 1, 2013).

Quart, Alissa. "Lost Media, Found Media." *Columbia Journalism Review.* May/June 2008: 30–34.

Quick and Dirty Tips. http://www.quickanddirtytips.com/ (accessed August 13, 2013).

Quinn, Sara, interview by Naveed Saleh. (November 19, 2012).

Quinn, Sara Dickenson. "Alternative Story Forms Are Effective." *Poynter Institute.* March 3, 2011. http://www.poynter.org/how-tos/newsgathering-storytelling/visual-voice/84368/alternative-story-forms-are-effective/ (accessed February 3, 2013).

Jennifer Rauch, K.D. Trager and Eunseong Kim. "Clinging to Tradition, Welcoming Civic Solutions: A Survey of College Students' Attitudes Toward Civic Journalism." *Journalism & Mass Communication Educator.* Summer 2003: 175–186.

Reddy, Sanhita. "Talking Shop: Karyn Ravn." *Columbia Journalism Review.* June 15, 2009. http://www.cjr.org/the_observatory/talking_shop_karen_ravn.php?page=all (accessed February 17, 2013).

Reeves, Hope. "Is There Mood Lighting, Too?" *The New York Times Magazine.* October 19, 2012. http://www.nytimes.com/2012/10/21/magazine/the-cow-jumped-over-a-water-bed.html/?_r=0 (accessed January 26, 2013).

Ries, Brian. "The Story Behind the Photo." *The Daily Beast (Yahoo! News).* November 20, 2012. http://news.yahoo.com/story-behind-photo-094500527--politics.html (accessed February 3, 2013).

Michael Roberts (The Arizona Republic). "Alternative Story Forms." http://www.slideshare.net/michael.roberts/alternative-story-forms-2116272.

Roethel, Kathryn. "The Science (Not Art) of the Magazine Pitch." *The Future of Freelancing.* http://freelance.stanford.edu/reports/pitch/ (accessed April 11, 2013).

Rosentiel, Amy Mitchell and Tom. *The Pew Research Center's Project for Excellence in Journalism: The State of the News Media 2012.* 2012. http://stateofthemedia.org/2012/overview-4/ (accessed January 31, 2013).

Rosentiel, Bill Kovack & Tom. *The Elements of Journalism.* New York: Three Rivers Press, 2007.

Page One: Inside The New York Times. Directed by Andrew Rossi. 2011.

Rovi: http://www.rovicorp.com/ (accessed July 10, 2013).

Royal, Cindy. "Convergence Culture: Where Old and New Media Collide/Information Please: Culture and Politics in the Age of Digital Machines" (book reviews). *Journalism & Mass Communication Educator,* 2008: 411–416.

"RT this: OUP Dictionary Team Monitors Twitterer's tweets." *OUP Blog.* June 4, 2009. http://blog.oup.com/2009/06/oxford-twitter/ (accessed February 3, 2013).

Edited by Michelle Ruberg and introduction by Ben Yagoda. *Writer's Digest Handbook of Magazine Article Writing.* Cincinnati: Writer's Digest Books, 2005.

Russell, Cristine. "The Hottest Thing in Science Blogging." *Columbia Journalism Review.* January 18, 2011. http://www.cjr.org/the_observatory/the_hottest_thing_in_science_b.php?page=all (accessed February 17, 2013).

Benjamin J. Sadock and Virginia A. Sadock. *Kaplan and Sadock's Synopsis of Psychiatry.* Philadelphia: Lippincott, Williams & Wilkins, 2007.

Salahi, Lara. *Personal Branding.* http://www.spj.org/trainingondemand.asp (accessed February 6, 2013).

Saleh, Naveed. "Copyediting Confusion." *Science Editor,* 2010: 65–66.

Saleh, Navced. "Diet Soda Double Whammy." *Psychology Today.* July 31, 2011. http://www.psychologytoday.com/blog/the-red-light-district/201107/diet-soda-double-whammy (accessed January 24, 2013).

Saleh, Naveed. "Cell Phones and Brain Cancer: Should You Be Worried." *Johns Hopkins Medicine Medical Letter: Health After 50,* October 2011: 1–2.

Saleh, Naveed. "Myths and Pregnancy." *Psychology Today.* May 29, 2011. http://www.psychologytoday.com/blog/the-red-light-district/201105/myths-and-pregnancy (accessed January 24, 2013).

Saleh, Naveed. "Shake my Hand!" *Psychology Today.* October 29, 2012. http://www.psychologytoday.com/blog/the-red-light-district/201210/shake-my-hand (accessed January 31, 2013).

Saleh, Naveed. "Do Dollars Make Educational Sense?" *The New Physician*, September 2010: 14–19.

Saleh, Naveed. "Don't Mess with TCOM." *The New Physician*, January–February 2010: 12–15.

Saleh, Naveed. "If We Build Them, Who Will Come?" *The New Physician*, January–February 2011: 12–16.

Saleh, Naveed. "Monitor" (department). *The New Physician*, December 2010: 4–5.

Saleh, Naveed. "Other Trades' Tricks." *The New Physician*, April 2010: 16–18.

Saleh, Naveed. "Rethinking Disability." *The New Physician*, April 2010: 22–26.

Saleh, Naveed. "The Global Draw." *The New Physician*, December 2010: 18–22.

Saleh, Naveed. *The Red-Light District* (blog at Psychology Today). http://www.psychologytoday.com/blog/the-red-light-district.

Saleh, Naveed. "The Superhero Within." *Psychology Today.* May 9, 2011. http://www.psychologytoday.com/blog/the-red light-district/201105/the-superhero-within (accessed March 29, 2013).

Salmon, Felix. "How Jonah Lehrer Should Blog." *Reuters.* June 20, 2012. http://blogs.reuters.com/felix-salmon/2012/06/20/how-jonah-lehrer-should-blog/ (accessed February 20, 2013).

Salmon, Felix. "The Bitcoin Bubble and the Future of Currency." *Medium.* April 3, 2013. https://medium.com/money-banking/2b5ef79482cb (accessed April 6, 2013).

Salmon, Felix. "The State of the Blog." *Columbia Journalism Review.* July 1, 2011. http://www.cjr.org/the_audit/the_state_of_the_blog.php (accessed February 20, 2013).

Salmon, Felix. "Why Twitter Will Get More Annoying." *Reuters.* March 22, 2012. http://blogs.reuters.com/felix-salmon/2012/03/22/why-twitter-will-get-more-annoying/ (accessed February 23, 2013).

Sass, Erik. "Magazine Employment Shrinks 29% in 10 years." *Mediapost News.* September 28, 2012. http://www.mediapost.com/publications/article/184075/magazine-employment-shrinks-29-in-10-years.html (accessed January 24, 2013).

Saying farewell to the extraordinary Mike Wallace. July 8, 2012. *60 Minutes*: http://www.cbsnews.com/video/watch/?id=7414222n (accessed July 9, 2013).

Scanlan, Chip. "Birth of the Inverted Pyramid: A Child of Technology, Commerce and History." *Poynter Institute.* February 16, 2011. http://www.poynter.org/how-tos/newsgathering-storytelling/chip-on-your-shoulder/12755/birth-of-the-inverted-pyramid-a-child-of-technology-commerce-and-history/ (accessed February 3, 2013).

Scanlan, Chip. "Five Boxes Story: Deconstructing a Rick Bragg Story." *Poynter News University*. http://www.newsu.org/angel/content/nwsu_wawapa06/factoids/five_boxes_deconstruction.php (accessed January 24, 2013).

Scanlan, Chip. "The Hourglass: Serving the News, Serving the Reader." *Poynter*. March 2, 2011. http://www.poynter.org/how-tos/newsgathering-storytelling/chip-on-your-shoulder/12624/the-hourglass-serving-the-news-serving-the-reader/ (accessed January 24, 2013).

Scanlan, Chip. "The Nut Graf and Breaking News." *Poynter*. March 2, 2011. http://www.poynter.org/how-tos/newsgathering-storytelling/chip-on-your-shoulder/11472/the-nut-graf-and-breaking-news/ (accessed January 24, 2013).

Scanlan, Chip. "The Nut Graf, Part 1." *Poynter*. March 2, 2011. http://www.poynter.org/how-tos/newsgathering-storytelling/chip-on-your-shoulder/11371/the-nut-graf-part-i/ (accessed January 24, 2013).

Scanlan, Chip. "Too Young to Diet." *Poynter*. March 2, 2011. http://www.poynter.org/how-tos/newsgathering-storytelling/chip-on-your-shoulder/11380/too-young-to-diet/ (accessed January 24, 2013).

Scanlan, Chip. "Write Tight!" *Poynter Institute*. August 13, 2002. http://www.poynter.org/uncategorized/1786/write-tight/ (accessed February 23, 2013).

Scanlan, Chip. "Writing from the Top Down: Pros and Cons of the Inverted Pyramid." *Poynter Institute*. March 2, 2011. http://www.poynter.org/how-tos/newsgathering-storytelling/chip-on-your-shoulder/12754/writing-from-the-top-down-pros-and-cons-of-the-inverted-pyramid/ (accessed February 3, 2013).

Schafer, Jack. "Doubting Twitter." *Slate*. June 17, 2009. http://www.slate.com/articles/news_and_politics/press_box/2009/06/doubting_twitter.html (accessed February 23, 2013).

Schaffer, Amanda. "What's That Doing in My Head?" *Newsweek*, October 15, 2012: 11–12.

Scherer, Michael. "Does Size Matter?" *Columbia Journalism Review*, November/December 2002: 32-35.

Schultz, Connie. "A Neighborly Gesture Is a Reminder of the Kindness Hiding Inside of Us." *cleveland.com*. September 15, 2011. http://www.cleveland.com/schultz/index.ssf/2011/09/returning_the_favor_of_unearne.html (accessed January 26, 2013).

Schultz, Richard C. Overbaugh and Lynn. *Bloom's Taxonomy*. http://ww2.odu.edu/educ/roverbau/Bloom/blooms_taxonomy.htm (accessed January 29, 2013).

Science News Stylebook.

"Senate Race Sex Scandal." *The Smoking Gun*. June 22, 2004. http://www.thesmokinggun.com/documents/crime/senate-race-sex-scandal (accessed August 15, 2013).

Sherman, Scott. "'New' Journalism." *Columbia Journalism Review*, November/December 2001: 59.

Shirky, Clay. *Here Comes Everybody*. New York: The Penguin Press, 2008.

Sidley, Emily. "Editorial Calendars for Press Pitching: What They Are & How To Use Them." *Three Girls Media, Inc.* March 31, 2013. http://www.threegirlsmedia.com/2011/03/31/editorial-calendars-for-press-pitching-what-they-are-how-to-use-them/ (accessed August 13, 2013).

Siegel, Matt. "Swamped!" *The Atlantic*, October 2012: 22.

Silverman, Craig. "Is This the World's Best Twitter Account?" *Columbia Journalism Review*. April 8, 2011. http://www.cjr.org/behind_the_news/is_this_the_worlds_best_twitter_account.php?page=all (accessed February 4, 2013).

Silverman, Jacob. Jonah Lehrer's 'Self-Plagiarism' Scandal Rocks *The New Yorker*. June 20, 2012. *The Daily Beast*: http://www.thedailybeast.com/articles/2012/06/20/jonah-lehrer-s-self-plagiarism-scandal-rocks-the-new-yorker.html (accessed July 9, 2013).

Silverman, Stephen M. "Jeri Ryan's Sex Claims Dog Ex-Husband." *People*. June 22, 2004. http://www.people.com/people/article/0,,656517,00.html (accessed August 15, 2013).

Simurda, Stephen J. "Trying to Make Editorials Sing." *Columbia Journalism Review*, September/October 1997: 46–50.

Marjorie E. Skillin and Robert M. Gay. *Words Into Type*. Englewood Cliffs: Prentice-Hall, Inc., 1974.

Smolkin, Rachel. "USA Tomorrow." *American Journalism Review*. August-September 2005. http://www.ajr.org/article.asp?id=3914 (accessed February 17, 2013).

Snow, Shane, interview by Naveed Saleh. (October 27, 2012).

Sorkin, Andrew Ross. "Newspapers Are Billionaires' Latest Trophies." *Dealbook The New York Times*. August 5, 2013. http://dealbook.nytimes.com/2013/08/05/billionaires-latest-trophies-are-newspapers/ (accessed August 13, 2013).

Something Ventured. Directed by Daniel Geller and Dayna Goldfine. 2011.

Sonderman, Jeff. "NBC closes hyperlocal, data-driven publishing pioneer EveryBlock." *Poynter*. February 8, 2013. http://www.poynter.org/latest-news/top-stories/203437/nbc-closes-hyperlocal-pioneer-everyblock/ (accessed August 17, 2013).

Sony Pictures Classics. "A Dangerous Method (press kit)." http://www.sonyclassics.com/adangerousmethod/adangerousmethod_presskit.pdf.

"Speaking Bad." *Wired* (digital edition). January 2013.

Spiker, Ted, interview by Naveed Saleh. (October 16, 2012).

Spikol, Art. "Eating Your Words." *Writer's Digest*, May/June 2012: 28–31.

Stableford, Dylan. "Beef over female rocket scientist's obit prompts Times to change it." *Yahoo! News*. March 31, 2013. http://news.yahoo.com/blogs/lookout/yvonne-brill-obit-nyt-rocket-scientist-beef-184815745.html (accessed April 1, 2013).

M.L. Stein, Susan F. Paterno, and R. Christopher Burnett. *Newswriter's Handbook*. Ames: Blackwell Publishing Professional, 2006.

Stelter, Brian. "Daredevil Media Outlet Behind Rodman's Trip." *The New York Times*. March 3, 2013. http://www.nytimes.com/2013/03/04/business/media/dennis-rodman-in-north-korea-with-vice-media-as-ringleader.html?_r=0 (accessed March 9, 2013).

Stepp, Carl Sessions. "A Valentine to the Art of Writing." *American Journalism Review*. June 2000. http://www.ajr.org/article_printable.asp?id=2962 (accessed January 25, 2013).

Stepp, Carl Sessions. "Center Stage." *American Journalism Review*. April/May 2006. http://www.ajr.org/article.asp?id=4075 (accessed February 20, 2013).

Stepp, Carl Sessions. "I'll Be Brief." *American Journalism Review*. August/September 2005. http://ajr.org/Article.asp?id=3927 (accessed January 25, 2013).

Stepp, Carl Sessions. "Offering Options." *American Journalism Review*. August/September 2005. http://www.ajr.org/article.asp?id=3950 (accessed January 25, 2013).

Stepp, Carl Sessions. "Reader Friendly." *American Journalism Review*. July/August 2000. http://www.ajr.org/article.asp?id=227 (accessed February 23, 2013).

Stepp, Carl Sessions. "The Blog Revolution" (book review). *American Journalism Review*. February/March 2006. http://www.ajr.org/article.asp?id=4045 (accessed January 30, 2013).

Bruce Sterling and the editors of *Encyclopaedia Britannica*. "Science Fiction." *Encyclopaedia Britannica*: http://www.britannica.com/EBchecked/topic/528857/science-fiction (accessed July 9, 2013).

William Strunk Jr. and E. B. White. *The Elements of Style*. New York: Longman, 1999.

Sumner, David E., interview by Naveed Saleh. (October 2, 2012).

Sumner, David E., interview by Naveed Saleh. (October 5, 2012).

Sumner, David E., e-mail communication. (October 5, 2012).

David E. Sumner and Holly G. Miller. *Feature and Magazine Writing: Action, Angle and Anecdotes*. Ames: Blackwell Publishing Professional, 2005.

"Talk to the Newsroom: Interactive News Collaborative." *The New York Times*. http://www.nytimes.com/2009/01/19/business/media/19askthetimes.html?pagewanted=all (accessed February 3, 2013).

Tapply, William G. "Invisible Writing." *Writer's Digest*, January 1994: 79–80.

"The 2009 Pulitzer Prize Winners." *The Washington Times*. April 20, 2009. http://www.washingtontimes.com/news/2009/apr/20/the-2009-pulitzer-prize-winners-1/?page=all (accessed February 4, 2013).

The Chicago Manual of Style 15th Edition. Chicago: The University of Chicago Press, 2003.

The Economist. "Looking for a Google." October 6–12, 2012: 78.

"The New York Times Company Policy on Ethics in Journalism." *The New York Times Company.* http://www.nytco.com/press/ethics.html (accessed August 22, 2013).

The Pulitzer Prizes. http://www.pulitzer.org.

The Simpsons Movie. Directed by David Silverman. 2007.

Thomas, Ken. "Obama Accuses Romney of Suffering from 'Romnesia'" *Associated Press via Yahoo! News.* October 19, 2012. http://news.yahoo.com/obama-accuses-romney-suffering-romnesia-163023522--election.html (accessed January 26, 2013).

Thompson, Matt. "10 Questions to Help You Write Better Headlines." *Poynter.* August 1, 2011. http://www.poynter.org/how-tos/newsgathering-storytelling/140675/10-questions-to-help-you-write-better-headlines/ (accessed January 2012, 2013).

Thompson, Robert J., interview by Naveed Saleh. (November 8, 2012).

Thompson, Robert J. *Television's Second Golden Age.* Syracuse: Syracuse University Press, 1997.

Titchener, Campbell B. *A Method for Reviewing the Arts.* Mahwah: Lawrence Erlbaum Associates, 1998.

"Top 25 U.S. Newspapers for March 2013." *Alliance for Audited Media.* http://www.auditedmedia.com/news/research-and-data/top-25-us-newspapers-for-march-2013.aspx (accessed August 14, 2013).

"Twitter." *Encyclopaedia Britannica.* http://www.britannica.com/EBchecked/topic/1370976/Twitter (accessed February 3, 2013).

Twomey, Steve. "The Case of the Vanishing Columnist." *Columbia Journalism Review*, September/October 2005: 25–29.

United States Air Force Public Affairs Center of Excellence. http://www.au.af.mil/pace/ (accessed August 13, 2013).

United States Census Bureau. http://factfinder2.census.gov/faces/tableservices/jsf/pages/productview.xhtml?pid=ACS_11_1YR_B25010&prodType=table (accessed February 6, 2013).

George Unwin, Philip Soundy Unwin, David H. Tucker, and the editors of the *Encyclopaedia Britannica*. "History of Publishing." *Encyclopaedia Britannica*. http://www.britannica.com/ EBchecked/topic/482597/history-of-publishing (accessed November 15, 2011).

Urban Dictionary: http://www.urbandictionary.com (accessed July 8, 2013).

Vaughn, Stephen L., ed. *Encyclopedia of American Journalism*. New York: Routledge, 2008.

Wang, Linda. "Barely Hanging On." *Chemical & Engineering News*. November 5, 2012. https://cen.acs.org/articles/90/i45/Barely-Hanging.html (accessed March 30, 2013).

Wang, Linda, interview by Naveed Saleh. (November 19, 2012).

Carlton Ward Jr. "Florida's Last Frontier" (Department: "Living West"). *Cowboys & Indians*, December 2012: 196–203.

Weaver, Caity. "OMG Did Taylor Swift Cheat on Conor Kennedy with His Cousin? Text Me Back When U Get This." *Gawker*. October 10, 2012. http://gawker.com/5950564/omg-did-taylor-swift-cheat-on-conor-kennedy-with-his-cousin-text-me-back-when-u-get-this (accessed January 26, 2013).

Weiner, Rachel. "Obama's Grassroots Operation Will Live On." *The Washington Post*. November 20, 2012. http://www.washingtonpost.com/blogs/post-politics/wp/2012/11/20/obamas-grassroots-operation-will-live-on/ (accessed February 4, 2013).

Weiner, Richard. *Webster's New World Dictionary of Media and Communications*. New York: Macmillan General Reference, 1996.

Weinger, Mackenzie. "Politico." *A Year in Prison, Rod Blagojevich in Good Spirits*. March 15, 2013. http://www.politico.com/story/2013/03/rod-blagojevich-jail-88904.html (accessed March 25, 2013).

Wells, Pete. "As Not Seen on TV." *The New York Times*. November 13, 2012. http://www.nytimes.com/2012/11/14/dining/reviews/restaurant-review-guys-american-kitchen-bar-in-times-square.html?_r=0 (accessed January 27, 2013).

Richard S. Westfall and the editors of *Encyclopaedia Britannica*. Sir Isaac Newton. *Encyclopaedia Britannica*: http://www.britannica.com/EBchecked/topic/413189/Sir-Isaac-Newton (accessed July 9, 2013).

Robert S. Westman and the editors of the *Encyclopaedia Britannica*. Johannes Kepler. *Encyclopaedia Britannica*: http://www.britannica.com/EBchecked/topic/315225/Johannes-Kepler (accessed July 9, 2013).

"What is the difference between jails and prisons?" *Bureau of Justice Statistics*. http://www.bjs.gov/index.cfm?ty=qa&iid=322 (accessed August 13, 2013).

"What Makes a Winning Editorial." *Columbia Journalism Review*, 1997: 50–51.

White, Kate. "Know it All." *Women's Health*, November 2012: 114–118.

Wikipedia. http://www.wikipedia.org.

Willis, Judy. "Neuroscience Insights from Video Game & Drug Addiction." *Psychology Today.* October 29, 2011. http://www.psychologytoday.com/blog/radical-teaching/201110/neuroscience-insights-video-game-drug-addiction (accessed July 11, 2013).

Winship, Scott. "What 'Lost Decade'?" *National Review*, October 1, 2012: 38–40.

Woods, Geraldine. *English Grammar for Dummies.* Hoboken: Wiley Publishing, Inc., 2001.

Worstall, Tim. "Why AOL Should Not Have Bought Huffington Post And Patch." *Forbes.* May 9, 2013. http://www.forbes.com/sites/timworstall/2013/05/09/why-aol-should-not-have-bought-huffington-post-and-patch/ (accessed August 13, 2013).

Jenna Wortham and Amy O'Leary. "Bezos Brings Promise of Innovation to Washington Post." *The New York Times.* August 6, 2013. http://www.nytimes.com/2013/08/07/business/bezos-brings-promise-of-innovation-to-washington-post.html?pagewanted=all (accessed August 13, 2013).

"Would a Man Who Doesn't Support Women Let His Wife Pick Out Any Oven She Wants for Her Birthday?" *The Onion.* October 17, 2012. http://www.theonion.com/articles/would-a-man-who-doesnt-support-women-let-his-wife,29966/ (accessed February 4, 2013).

Writer's Digest Books House Style Guidelines. March 3, 2012.

"Yellow Journalism." *Encyclopaedia Britannica.* http://www.britannica.com/EBchecked/topic/652632/yellow-journalism (accessed November 14, 2011).

Zinsser, William. *On Writing Well.* New York: Collins, 2006.

Zongker, Brett. "Martin Luther King Jr. Memorial In D.C. Has Controversial 'Drum Major' Inscription Removed." *The Huffington Post.* August 1, 2013. http://www.huffingtonpost.com/2013/08/01/martin-luther-king-jr-memorial-inscription-removed-_n_3690744.html (accessed August 13, 2013).

Zongker, Brett. "MLK Memorial 'Drum Major.'" *Huffington Post.* December 11, 2012. http://www.huffingtonpost.com/2012/12/11/mlk-memorial-drum-major-quote_n_2279440.html (accessed January 26, 2013).

INDEX

WD WRITER'S DIGEST